Islam and Anarchism

"This is one of the fiercest books I've ever read. It is a call to action. It is conceptually rich and gives us new methodological tools for thinking theory and politics together. It is unrelenting in its critique of liberal assimilationist tendencies in diasporic and BIPOC knowledge production and movement organizing. Abdou is a truth-teller of the highest order. Drawing together disparate geographies and thought into a dazzling web of interconnectedness and dialogue, *Islam and Anarchism* proffers a kaleidoscopic vision of what could be otherwise."

—Jasbir Puar, author of *Terrorist Assemblages* and *The Right to Maim*

"A passionate plea for a spiritual decolonial movement. Mohamed Abdou advances a vision of Islam that is abolitionist at its core, reminding us that Islam has been and can still be a religion of the oppressed, one that is anti-capitalist, egalitarian, anti-ableist, anti-patriarchal, queer feminist and for Muslims and non-Muslims alike."

—Sherene H. Razack, Distinguished Professor and Penny Kanner Endowed Chair, Gender Studies, UCLA

"An uncompromising queer-feminist vision of decolonial, abolitionist, and anti-capitalist praxis that is keyed to the pluralistic traditions of Islamic spirituality and anarchic thought."

—Iyko Day, Elizabeth C. Small Associate Professor of English and Critical Social Thought, Mount Holyoke College, Massachusetts

Islam and Anarchism

Relationships and Resonances

Mohamed Abdou

PLUTO PRESS

First published 2022 by Pluto Press
New Wing, Somerset House, Strand, London WC2R 1LA

www.plutobooks.com

British Library Cataloguing in Publication Data
A catalogue record for this book is available from the British Library

ISBN 978 0 7453 4191 0 Hardback
ISBN 978 0 7453 4192 7 Paperback
ISBN 978 1 786807 14 4 PDF eBook
ISBN 978 1 786807 15 1 EPUB eBook

This book is printed on paper suitable for recycling and made from fully managed and sustained forest sources. Logging, pulping and manufacturing processes are expected to conform to the environmental standards of the country of origin.

Typeset by Stanford DTP Services, Northampton, England

Simultaneously printed in the United Kingdom and United States of America

Contents

Preface vii
Acknowledgments xi
A Note on Transliteration and Translation xiv

1. Introduction: Panegyric Desert of the Present 1
The Destructive Legacy of (Neo)Liberalism and Colonial Modernity in the Production of Neo-Orientalist and Neo-Fundamentalist Muslim Subjectivities 2
A Match to a Powder Keg 14
Islām and Anarchism Are Dead: Muslim Anarchists in Turtle Island's Newest Social Movements 18
Positionality: Who Is Speaking? 32
A Sum Exceeding the Whole, Everything Divided: The Argument Condensed 33

2. Authoritarianism, Capitalism, and Capitalist Nation-States: Anarcha-Islām's Playground and Ethical-Political Consciousness 40
On Decolonization and Reindigenization, and the Crises of Fleeting Tahrir Moments 41
Thus Spoke God: The Method of Anarchic Ijtihād 46
Deleuze and Guattari's Oedipal Triad: The Nation-State (Daddy) – Capitalism (Mommy) – and Me/Us 56

3. Anarcha-Islām: An Anti- and Non-Authoritarian Islām 72
Anarcha-Islām's Osteological Left-Side 72
Arise: An Anti- and Non-Authoritarian Islām 83
Modern Uses of Waṭaniyyah, Qawmiyyah, and Dawla, and Decolonized Vestiges of the Umma and Īmāmah in Arab and Muslim Lexicons 112

Muslim and Non-Muslim Glossaries of Indigeneity Towards a Resurgent Umma: Anti-Blackness and Anti-Indigenous Politics 128

4. Anarcha-Islām: An Anti- and Non-Capitalist Islām 147
Anarcha-Islām's Osteological Right-Side 147
Awaken: An Anti- and Non-Capitalist Islām: Micro- and Macro-Economics 149
As Patients We Come to Each Other's Aid 175

5. Uprisings: On (Im)Possibilities and Militant Resistance 178
The Delusional Myth of Nonviolence 179
Violence, *Jihād*, and *Qitāl* in Islām: A Single Blunder Can Fuel a Great Fire 191
From the Deception of "Nonviolence" to Red, Black, and Brown Power 211
Liberatory Victory 220

6. Conclusion: There Are Only Middles, No Beginnings and No Ends. Between BLM, NoDaPL-INM, and Tahrir 222

Notes 241
Index 324

Preface

How did it become a universal truth that electoral democracy is the sole democracy model that most are willing to participate in? When did it become acceptable that governing politicians could truly represent the governed – you, me, and us? When have enshrined laws ever compelled "self-made men" and capitalist-corporations to act ethically or in any people's interests, particularly in a contemporary neoliberal age in which there is no separation between capitalism and nation-states, or politics and economics? This book attends to these questions. Although the histories of individual Muslim anarchists or *anarchistic* Muslims, from early twentieth century figures such as Gustave-Henri Jossot, Isabelle Eberhardt, Shibili Shumayyil, and Leda Bruna Rafanelli to more contemporary thinkers such as Peter Lamborn Wilson, Michael Muhammad Knight, Abdennur Prado, and Yakub Islam, are well known, little has been written or *imagined* about how the Holy Qur'ān and the *Sunnah* through the *aḥādīth* – the Prophetic practice and oral tradition – could be used to flesh out the theology, politics, and philosophy of an Islamic anarchism. Starting from the position that Islām is not a monolithic, unified belief system, but a heterogeneous and pluralistic series of traditions, perspectives, and practices, *Islam and Anarchism* constructs an anarchistic interpretation of Islām and an Islamic interpretation of anarchism, which I call Anarcha-Islām. It offers a decolonial, social justice framework that elides the prevalent Orientalist and Fundamentalist tropes of Muslims and Islām and seeks to interweave Indigenous, Black, and People of Colors' lives and narratives together.

As a participant in the Orientalized "Arab Spring/Islamist Winter" uprisings and as an anarchist and a Muslim settler in Turtle Island, I have witnessed troubled times as a result of extreme divisions that exist between these two identities and communities. In response, I offer an Anarcha-Islām that disrupts two commonly held beliefs: one, that Islām is necessarily authoritarian and capitalist; two, that anarchism is necessarily anti-religious and anti-spiritual. Anarcha-Islām is a basis for exploring a new transnational politics and an ethics of friendship and disagreement between these traditions in the context of both the Tahrir uprisings in Egypt and what Richard J.F. Day has called the "newest" social movements in settler-colonial societies of the U.S./Canada.

The book operates from the premise that colonialism never ended in settler-colonial societies such as the U.S./Canada or in franchise "post-colonial" societies such as Egypt that inherited the capitalist-State model. Since modernity, Muslims have been globally struggling with an exponentially growing identity crisis, which has led to two reactionary responses. The first response is that we seek to become neo-Fundamentalist terrorists re-enacting our colonially internalized traumas by adopting wanton-impotent violence as a sole holistic strategy. This is exhibited in non-statist movements such as al-Qaeda and proto-statist movements such as ISIS that have embraced warped notions of non-Qur'ānic concepts as the *Caliphate* as well as Qur'ānic concepts as *Umma* (i.e., a global community of Muslims that historically and traditionally included non-Muslims). The second response is one in which we, as Muslims, re-enact projects of self-Orientalization. An example of this is how diasporic Arabs, Muslims, South West Asians, and North Africans in the U.S./Canada strive to become good law-abiding citizens, who reify and mimic anti-Blackness and participate in the U.S./Canadian states' settler-colonization of Indigenous peoples. Furthermore, self-Orientialization does not only occur in the context of assimilation: it was visible in the initial 18 days of the 2011 Tahrir Uprisings. During Tahrir, Egyptians were united under the false banner of patriotic nationalism and abstract chants of "freedom, bread, social justice" that camouflaged ethical-political, ethnic, gendered, and spiritual factional differences between them.

Anarcha-Islām can help diasporic Muslims under Euro-American assimilation as well as Muslims in predominantly conservative societies such as Egypt to begin again the transnational radical recreation and re-imagination of their subjectivities and social justice orientations in a way that is conducive to Islām's post-9/11's confrontations with a Euro-American "Age of Terror."

Anarcha-Islām is vital in light of the Euro-American perception that Muslims are incapable of assimilation as well as the global perception of Muslims as unable to incept suitable social justice alternatives to Euro-American capitalist nation-state paradigms. The absence of Anarcha-Islām from social movement horizons leads Muslims, Arabs, South West Asians, and North Africans in non-Euro-American and Euro-American societies to engage in false (neo)liberal-reactionary choices in the form of Orientalism and Fundamentalism. This is stated while noting that an underlying premise of this book is that the so-called "East" and "West" are not in a binary relationship, but rather represent a discursive formation that in fact obscures dialectics that cross-cut identities, migrating bodies, and movements. No one is completely oppressed or an oppressor, a victim or victimizer, and in the absence of decolonization all we learn from our internalized violence, trauma, and victimization is its reproductive radiation upon others. That does not deny the subjects of violence agency. It merely affirms that fascism is a mass psychology that has already won, given how we all embody micro-fascistic tendencies in light of our positionalities and the distinct penalties and privileges structurally and symbolically afforded us across race, gender, sexual practices, abilities, age, class, and so forth. Revolutionary social change is not a narcissistic affair embodied in individualistic notions of "self-care" but rather one that represents a collective responsibility that is also conditioned by land as the existential-spiritual-environment that animates, if not creates, us as subjects.

Anarcha-Islām offers infinite possibilities and opportunities for Muslim resistance to the horrors and neuroses of our daily lives while contending with Empire. Muslims supported by Anarcha-Islām's vernaculars can be bodies that are not frozen in their current catatonic socio-political state of coma and naiveté. Anarchism and anarchists, in the newest social movements also stand to learn from interacting with Muslims and from Anarcha-Islām. For instance, anarchists could benefit by learning how to better offer hospitality to each other as well as disagree ethically as a community as opposed to tearing each other apart over ideological and personal differences. Albeit not followed by contemporary Muslims, Islamic interpretations developed these types of ethics early on, in what is referred to as *Uṣūl al-Ḍiyāfa* (an ethics of hospitality) and *Uṣūl al-Ikhtilāf* (an ethics of disagreements), as a compassionate and forgiving form of etiquette for Muslims to address disagreements.

More widely, this book aims to engage academic and activist literatures on radical and revolutionary social action. Drawing on radical Indigenous, Black, Islamic anarchistic, transnational queer-feminist of color, and new social movement discourses, Anarcha-Islām seeks to transcend not only statist pan-Arab and pan-Islamist trajectories and conservative Islamist movements such as ISIS and al-Qaeda, but also strives to transcend Euro-American liberal-leftist social movements like that of Bernie Sanders and the Women's March. After all, the latter movements rely on a strategy that is anchored in a patriotic-national assimilationist politics of rights and an insistence on an unapologetic congruency of "hyphenated-American" citizen-identity. Both further the ongoing settler-colonialism on stolen Indigenous lands, as well as global imperialism, neoliberalism, and Orientalism elsewhere. Decolonization operates from the premise that these liberal-leftist movements are ultimately anchored in capitalist nation-state structures that represent a neocolonial product of modernity. As radical Indigenous movements and scholarships have argued, decolonization is not only concerned with constructing anti-statist and anti-capitalist rhetorical stances relative to land and (non) human life, but also non-statist and non-capitalist spiritual alternatives as well.

To summarize, first, this book arms transnational decolonial Muslim and non-Muslim social justice activists with an alternative to the dichotomous Orientalist vs. Fundamentalist representations of Islām and Muslims. Second, the book counters two misconceptions of Islām and Muslims amongst social movement participants in non-Euro-American and Euro-American societies: the incompatibility of anarchism and Islām and the impossibility of the co-existence of Muslim and anarchist identities in a single subjectivity. Third, this book carves a space where Muslim anarchists and transnational social movement activists in non-Euro-American and Euro-American societies can collaborate.

Acknowledgments

بسم الله الرحمن الرحيم

How can one speak of acknowledgments and summarize the innumerable lives that have challenged, supported, shared, and breathed life into this book and me, and without which neither would see daylight? How am I to deliver a eulogy honoring those whose bodies fell in Tahrir Square, were dumped in the desert, and fished out of the waters of the great River Nile after the uprisings? How am I to do justice to those who have been forcibly disappeared and are languishing in punitive carceral prisons dedicated to missionizing human misery and sadistic suffering? How do I reconcile and pay back what was entrusted to me to relay while contending with the infinite debt I owe others? There is infinite debt and responsibility at work here.

My love and gratitude to my Creator, Allāh, my mother, my father, distant relatives, and ministering angel of a sister, Marwa. All of you sacrifice yourselves every day to breathe life into me. I pray your hearts and that of others forgive my shortcomings towards you, as I stand guilty of being indebted to you all for eternity. Thank you for your grace, love, and benison.

In what was an overwhelmingly difficult decade for me, I am particularly indebted to my Doctoral supervisor Adnan Husain, and committee members Scott Lauria Morgensen and Dana Olwan for their counsel, relayed and transmitted knowledge, for challenging and emboldening my spine, tongue, and standing up for me on countless occasions, as well as their faith in me, which, my doctorate aside, has given me much to reflect on regarding myself and my relationships with others so far into my life. I am indebted as well to those taking the time to read, engage, and listen patiently to what I have to say and what this book aims to contribute within and across a multiplicity of interdisciplinary discourses and fields of knowledge.

To my teachers, elders, friends, communities, students, allies, and those who have stood in love and solidarity, I would not be standing here without you. Bring your ears closer to my lips. To you all, I say: "I love you," was never meant to be written, only syllabically uttered. I am humbled knowing you and am eternally grateful for what you continue to trust with me of your stories, words, and lives that give further meaning and purpose to mine. I pray I convey but a partial measure of your radiance, thank you: Robert Lovelace, Sarita Sarivstava, Frank Pearce, Richard J.F. Day, Villia Jefremovas, Joaquim and Larysa Voss, Katherine McKittrick, Trish Salah, Eleanor Macdonald, Wilson Chacko Jacob, Linda Jessup, Karen Dubinsky, Susan Lorde, Bonita Lawrence, Glen Coulthard, Uri Gordon, Alexandre Christoyannapoulos, Eve Tuck, Stevphen Shukaitis, Melissa Houghtaling, Taiaiake Alfred, Ashanti Alston, Viviane Salah-Hanna, Biko and Yasmine, Steven Salaita, Gustavo Esteva, Jacqueline, Laith Marouf, Yafa-Zein, Saja Marouf, Gretchen King, Sabine, Chadi, Fehr, Tarafa, Breanne, Krista, Corey, Ko-Ko, Wahtha, Ahanu, Susan Delisle, Susan T., Leen, Gill, Mohga, Maysam, Deepa, Tiane, Mathieu, Rawan and Wael, Alaa, Salah, Abeer, Michelle Hartman, Rosalind Hampton, Dahlia, Fatima and Milad, Mubeenah, Hameed, Farah, Doaa Abdelaal, Dina Wahba, Urooj Arshad, El-Farouk Khaki, Troy Jackson, Yasir S. Abdullah, Tamer Mowafy, Mai, Sally, Fatma Emam, Azza Sultan, Sarah Mangle, Sayyida and Scott, Monica, David, Perick, Pancho, Chivis, Kris, Noor, and my brothers and sisters in Chiapas and Oaxaca, the Fahmy, Bayoumi as well as the Hafiz-Al-Rahman families, the entire Queen's Students for Palestinian Human Rights (SPHR) cohort of 2015–18, the Queen's University Muslim Student Association (QUMSA), the Queen's Gender, Sociology, and Development Studies departments, as well as the faculty and first Queen's Cultural Studies unit of 2010–11, AKA, EPIC, OPIRG, volunteers and staff at CFRC, members and non-members of the Sleepless Goat and workers at Sipps cafes, and doubtless many others. To the unwavering and dedicated Sheelagh Frame, Angela Pietrobon, and Nancy Wills, Editorial Assistants, as well as Elaine Ross and Robert Webb for their behemoth labor on the copy-edits. To my new mentors, Rachel Beatty Riedl and

Karim-Aly Kassam, as well as faculty, staff, and the Grad Fellows at Cornell University's Einaudi Center. To Harsha Walia, Jasbir Puar, Jodi Byrd, and Juliana Hu Pegues for the friendships ahead. To my colleagues at the American University of Cairo's Sociology, Anthropology and Egyptology department. To C. Marouf for the book cover and Pluto and David Shulman for the gamble.

Dedicated to the children, to womyn, to the elderly, to queers, to People of Color, to the poor, to the differently abled, and the wretched who are always the first to endure, grieve, and be martyred. If this collective struggle to see through this earth's rebellious rebirth denotes our fall then it is an honor to undergo it while by your side.

Thank you Allāh for the countless blessings I have been afforded. Whatever shortcomings exist in this text are my own which I take full responsibility for, and whatever goodness exists is by Your will and those who have guided and taught me. *Rabī Ishraḥ Lī Ṣadry, Wayasir Lī Amry, Wa'ḥlul 'Uqdatan Min Lisānī, Yafqahu Qawlī* (Moses' prayer in the Qur'ān: My Lord! Expand for me my breast! Make my affair easy for me, and untie a knot from my tongue, that they may understand my speech) (20: 25-28). La Fe no se vende (Faith is not for sale).

A Note on Transliteration and Translation

In general, I have used a modified version of the *International Journal of Middle Eastern Studies*' (IJMES) system to transliterate Arab and Muslim terms and expressions in a way that reflects their spoken pronunciation. However, for consistency, when reporting important concepts and terms that are also well established in Modern Standard or Classical Arabic (particularly terms that are part of Islamic traditions), I have (mostly) rendered these according to the IJMES system. I maintain diacritical marks, although I have not altered transliterations of direct quotations from published material. All of the translations from Arabic, whether from colloquial dialects or Modern Standard/Classical Arabic, are my own, unless otherwise indicated. This includes written materials (e.g., newspaper articles, Islamic and Arabic texts). The only exceptions are Qur'ānic citations, all of which, unless stated otherwise, are from Seyyed Hossein Nasr, *The Study Quran: A New Translation and Commentary* (New York, NY; HarperOne, an imprint of HarperCollins Publishers, 2017).

1

Introduction: Panegyric Desert of the Present

When we talk about waking people up from complicity, is to say that we can't be only upset with Trump because he's not a politician who sells us his policies in the most perfect way. His policies are bad. But many of the people who came before him also had really bad policies. They just were more polished than he was. And that's not what we should be looking for anymore. We don't want anybody to get away with murder because they are polished. We want to recognize the actual policies that are behind the pretty face and the smile.

Ilhan Omar, *Politico Interview* (March 8, 2019)

The notion of reform is so stupid and hypocritical. Either reforms are designed by people who claim to be representative, who make a profession of speaking for others, and they lead to a division of power, to a distribution of this new power which is consequently increased by a double repression; or they arise from the complaints and demands of those concerned. This latter instance is no longer a reform but revolutionary action that questions (expressing the full force of its partiality) the totality of power and the hierarchy that maintains it.

Gilles Deleuze (1972)[1]

Much of the liberal controversy about Islam and democracy has really been about the West's *own* antidemocratic imperial and domestic commitments (which denied, and in many cases still deny, rights to Native Americans, to blacks, to Catholics, to Mormons, to Jews, to Muslims, to women, to communists et al.), *its* "hatred of democracy", its checkered history in relation to

> this much touted political system and its fantastical deployment as the very essence of Western culture which allegedly emerged from the very bosom of [Euro-American] Christianity. The liberal project is in effect a missionary project to convert Islam to the highest stage of Christian reigning in the West, even if this is carried out under the banner of a "reformed Islam".
>
> Joseph A. Massad (2015, 106)[2]

The Destructive Legacy of (Neo)Liberalism and Colonial Modernity in the Production of Neo-Orientalist and Neo-Fundamentalist Muslim Subjectivities

On March 9, 2019, 37-year old Somali-American Ilhan Abdullahi Omar, the first hijābi-Muslim congresswoman, tweeted that news media outlet Politico had distorted her statements, given above, critiquing Barack Hussein Obama. Over the next 48 hours, both neoliberal news outlets, such as CNN, MSNBC, and CBC, and right-wing media outlets, such as Fox News, the Drudge Report, and Breitbart fixated on her comments that President Obama was a "pretty-face" responsible for "droning … countries around the world" and the concentration camp practice of "caging … kids." Following the outcry, the former refugee Omar, who never shies away from retelling her hallmark success story as an affirmation of the "American Dream," deleted her so-called controversial tweet. Omar – an institutionalized politician who has praised the mother of neoliberalism Margaret Thatcher as a role model as well as warmonger Madeleine Albright as an exemplary immigrant – then proceeded to insist she had become a victim of "fake news." She proceeded to tweet, "[No] I'm an Obama fan! I was [just] saying how [President] Trump is different from Obama, and why we should focus on policy not politics." Omar hardly stopped there. She continued to openly profess and affirm her "unwavering love for America" and proclaimed that as a country it "was founded on the ideas of justice, of liberty, of the pursuit of happiness." Insisting on her unquestionable allegiance to America she decried the hypocrisy (*nifāq*) of how, "We export American exceptionalism … The Great America. The Land of liberty and Justice … But we don't live those values here." Then, on May 1, 2019, flanked by abolitionist Angela Davis, during one of many rallies in her defense, Omar asserted in typical contradictory fashion that settler-colonial America, or in other words, occupied Turtle Island (U.S./Canada), "was founded on the history of Native American genocide, on the backs of black slaves, [that] this is not going to be the country of white people."

But which is it, "genocide" or "justice, liberty and the pursuit of happiness"?

Congresswoman Omar's contradictory statements and their undergirding conceptions of positionality, history, and solidarity continue to simultaneously inspire and deeply trouble me. Her settler-colonial politics, as for many diasporic Muslims who exhibit these stances, speak to the struggles, irreconcilable loyalties, and identity crises that Muslims face globally. The identity crisis is a consequence of diasporic exile and displacement. Indeed, it is born out of having to contend with rediscovering a new homeland and meanings relative to the notion of "home" and "belonging," while also engaging in the resettlement of Indigenous peoples who continue to struggle against their ongoing genocide, the theft of their land and calls for its repatriation and rematriation. The crisis is anchored in having to prove one's loyalty to a nation that fetishizes and romanticizes its imperialist veterans that participate in expansionist adventurism elsewhere, while also assimilating and constructing a Euro-American identity and cultural formation 'based on the territorial dispersal and political fragmentation' of Muslims.[3] This book argues that this identity crisis has pre-modern roots that have been heightened by modernity's advent.

Liberalism's effect on a majority of diasporic Muslims in North America is to seek to achieve a multicultural-progressive humanitarian utopian vision of an "American/Canadian" belonging premised on interracial, gender, sexual, and class social solidarities and political justice pluralisms. However, in adopting liberal-progressive stances, at the expense of more decolonial/radical social justice trajectories, diasporic Muslims reinforce the problematic notion that there is a "moderate" Islām and that there is congruence between, on the one hand, patriotic allegiance to nation-states that structure gender, racial, and sexual power, and on the other hand, ethico-political Muslim and Qur'ānic ontological/epistemological commitments. The irony is that innumerable progressives like Rashida Tlaib, Omar Suleiman, Dahlia Mogahed, and Linda Sarsour, as well as more conservative Muslims like Hamza Yusuf and Sherman Jackson, and others in between such as Zaid Shakir, market themselves as supporters of Malcolm X and Muhammad Ali's radical Black legacies, while neglecting the fact that Malcolm X, in particular, explicitly adopted an anti-American stance.

Assimilation's seductive lure, even when seemingly progressive, reifies the hollow mantra that diverse citizenship is an American/Canadian value; an individualist slogan that ignores the fact that the very political institution of citizenship in settler-colonial North America is constructed upon continuing anti-Black foundations and Indigenous genocide and dispossession. This identitarian formation undermines core existential struggles involved in what W.E.B. Du Bois referred to as a "double-consciousness," as in possessing "two souls, two thoughts, two unreconciled strivings; two warring ideals in one dark body."[4] Unlike much liberal-Muslim scholarship and its idealization of individualist choices, representative democracy, and a politics of rights, this book engages with Islamic anarchistic and radical Indigenous, Black and People of Color (BIPOC) social movement literatures and movements that argue for a politics of responsibility anchored in direct and horizontal forms of democracy that are more egalitarian and socially just, with regards to both our species and its relationships to nonhuman life.[5] It argues that the civil rights project of reform of the nation-state and associated assimilationist agendas disregard the asymmetrical hierarchies between and within various segments of domestic populations and thus "perpetuate the dangerous illusion that liberal politics are a refuge from right-wing racism," when the truth is that the former are "constructed of many of the same components and hence occlude continuities and similarities with the Islamophobia of liberal governments like Obama's or Trudeau's."[6] These reform-based political approaches ignore Indigenous and non-Indigenous critiques of settler-colonization and the need for decolonization in addressing what Jodi Byrd refers to as the geostrategic "cacophony of struggles," which argue that the quest for inclusion normalizes the colonization of Indigenous nations and emboldens neocolonial/neoimperial assemblages acted upon predominantly Muslim societies elsewhere.[7] In other words, the preoccupation with assimilation and civic rights in the U.S./Canada, and the insistence on the unapologetic congruency of American/Canadian identities, actively promotes the colonization and dispossession of Indigenous and Black peoples within and elsewhere upon people of color beyond white supremacist Empire.

In contrast to these white-civilizational assimilationist strivings, liberalism's reactive effect on orthodox Muslims is their infantilization such that they are driven towards impotent-violent strivings in the name of ushering in a totalitarian and exclusive puritanical "Muslim world." This orthodox worldview informed by "conversion or death" narratives is one that we can see in Omar Mir Seddique Mateen's case in which the Euro-American concept of sexuality is thrown into the mix. On June 12, 2016, in one of the deadliest "terror" attacks since 9/11, Mateen, a "closeted" Afghani-American and an employee of G4S – one of the world's largest global security and paramilitary corporations – murdered 49 people and injured 58 in Florida's Orlando Pulse nightclub, an LGBTIQ refuge that attracts a mostly Latinx crowd. Evidence suggests that on account of being unable to reconcile his sexual *practices* with his Muslim identity as well as the tension between the hyper-masculine expectations of his militarized occupation and queer tendencies that drove him to frequent Pulse, Mateen, in a 911 call from Pulse's bloodied scene, pledged allegiance to Abu Bakr al-Baghdadi, the now dead leader of the Islamic State in Iraq and Syria (ISIS).[8] From a grander Orientalist/Fundamentalist political standpoint both visions represent diametrical opposite reactionary responses along the same continuum.

Settler-colonialism and liberal politics impact both conservative and progressive Muslims. Conservative Muslims denounce critical race theories, feminism, and queerness during Friday prayer (*ṣalāt al-jumuʿah*) and sermons (*khuṭbahs*) as Euro-American frameworks that are antithetical to Islām. On the other hand, liberal-progressive Muslims engage in the wholesale adoption of

Eurocentric LGBTIQ categories, corporate pride, Euro-American and modern humanitarian-militarized sexual politics. This occurs despite transnational queer Indigenous, queer of color, and queer diasporic critiques of how strivings for assimilation erase complicity in the continued genocidal and white-supremacist erasure of Indigenous peoples.[9]

Ironically, if either the progressive or conservative Muslims critically studied or engaged with queer of color critiques that distinguish between queer-feminist identities and practices, they would comprehend that since modernity's advent we have all been queered by the sexual civilizationism of Euro-America whether we like it or not, given the intimate geopolitical relationship between racialized perceptions of gender and sexuality in settler and post-colonial societies, particularly in light of how the persistent condition and project of imperialism violently disfigures gendered conceptualizations of the Other relative to land and nonhuman life. The forced queering of Muslims can be witnessed in the hyper-racist, gendered, and sexualized depiction in New York's subways of Osama Bin Laden anally penetrated by the Empire State Building, post-9/11, with the words "Empire Strikes Back." This resonates with the Fundamentalist/Orientalist representation of 9/11's main hijacker Muhammad Atta, as well as Omar Mateen, as racially queered monstrous terrorist "fags" who debase themselves to roles supposedly assigned to women.[10] The colonial intention of these simulacric images is to not only associate Muslim militancy with barbaric, savage, and inferior acts, but also to indicate that in the absence of women on whom they may enact their heteropatriarchal masculinity, Muslim militants repress their latent effeminate, homosexual rage and shame.

In this sense, Pulse shooter-Mateen, as other arrivant newcomers, is not only differentially racialized, but also cast and projected upon the hyper-visibilized and invisibilized gendered and sexualized anti-Indigenous and anti-Black landscapes that inform Empire. Reactionary Orientalist/Fundamentalist responses are schizophrenic products of the simultaneous construct of Muslims as victims and perpetrators of oppression. Both conservative and progressive Muslims replicate problematic colonial statist-assumptions and neoliberal frameworks regarding the (in)compatibility between Muslim values and modern Euro-American national and sexual-identitarian aspirations and the competing sets of loyalties they performatively engender. Conservative Muslims are ambivalent to, erase, and sanitize medieval erotic Muslim literature that offers fluid understandings of gender, sex, love, and sexual practices, as well as expressions of intimacies and vulnerabilities in *hammam* (bathhouse) cultures. Examples of this literature include the twelfth century *Farīd al-Dīn 'Aṭṭār*'s *Conference of the Birds*, the fifteenth century 'Umar ibn Muḥammad al-Nafzāwī's *The Perfumed Garden* (an Arabic sex manual), the writings of Abbasid scholar Abū 'Uthman 'Amr ibn Baḥr al-Kinānī al-Baṣrī's (Al-Jāḥiẓ) (800 AD) on the ways of young men and women, 'Ali ibn Naṣr Al-Kātib's tenth century *Encyclopedia of Pleasure*, the Seljuk Empire's *Assemblies of al-Hariri* about same-sex attractions, the thirteenth century polymath Naṣīr al-Dīn al-Ṭūsī's *The Sultan's Sex Potions* on sexual stimulants and erotic sex positions.[11] These demonstrate the openness of medieval Muslims and jurists on subject matters currently regarded as shameful taboos. In turn, more radical Islamic anarchic trajectories that center on colonialism/imperialism and emphasize anti-statism, gender egalitarianism, and sexual ethics are also ignored.[12]

It is critical to note the distinction here between whiteness (as a phenotypical racial/ethnic category) and liberal "cultures of whiteness," which refers to ontological white values, conceptualizations of civility and progress, as well as epistemological practices and paradigms. The practice of whiteness has consistently (de) humanized, infantilized, sweetened, feminized, exaggerated, and flattened the psychic life of diverse BIPOC and is associated with hegemonic Eurocentric ideas and notions of civilizational hierarchies (or what Lisa Lowe refers to as "colonial divisions of humanity") that continue to be internalized and exercised by whites and non-whites alike.[13] After all, "post"-colonial subjects have adopted cultures of whiteness in relationship to spirituality land and nonhuman life as individualist property. Vandalizing territory and land precedes if not coincides with the disfiguration of a native people's non-heteronormative conceptualizations of spirituality, gender/sexual ontologies/epistemologies, kinship structures, sovereignty, polygamy, marriage, intimacy, family, (il)licit sexual practices, desire and vitally their non-anthropocentric relationship to land and communal meanings of what constitutes property.[14]

The (neo)liberal internalization of "cultures of whiteness" incepts within BIPOC and Muslims' inferiority complexes and shame (*ʿār*), as well as drives them to embrace reductionist misconceptualizations relating to the merits of atheism (*ilhād*) and uncritical Euro-American Christian exegetical perceptions regarding Euro-American secularism (*ʿalmāniyya*), democracy and human rights, which in turn they strive to emulate (*taqlīd*). By a similar token, it is this same assaultive impact of *al-haymana al-thaqāfiyyah al-gharbiyyah* (Euro-American hegemonic cultural influence) and *al-ʿawlama al-neo-liberaliyya al-gharbiyyah* (Euro-American neoliberal globalization) that drives both (neo)conservative state and non-state Muslims, who actually rely on the state, to denounce Euro-American foreign interventionism while also harkening for the prowess of its military, economic, scientific, medicinal, capitalist laws, and civilizational theories of development that cast rural territories as undeveloped, underdeveloped, and primitive towards political expansionist metropolitan superiority. Despite these (neo)conservative sterile longings, they equally also reject music, the arts, humanities, social sciences, as well as mannerisms/attitudes and, most importantly, ethical-political social justice horizons, based on perceived Islamic moralistic grounds, that include anti-queerphobia, anti-blackness, anti-feminism, classism, anti-ageism, and anti-ableism that ought to be Muslim causes. (Neo)conservatives embark on this agenda despite anti-liberal, anti-racist, decolonial, and intersectional narratives by BIPOC as well as Muslim women of color. In this sense, Euro-America has not only managed to capture and capitalize on cultivating an internalized sense of Islamophobia within Muslims but rather also incepted within BIPOC a sense of resentment regarding our own mother tongues, color of skins, languages, spiritualities, cosmologies, and oral traditions. Ex-Muslims are not only content with leaving Islām (which they have every right to) but rather have made it their mission to viciously critique Islām as if it bears no redeemable qualities unlike other spiritual traditions, and do so in exchange for "rationalist" and new atheist, secularized, racist, and misogynist positions, such as those propagated by Sam Harris, Richard Dawkins, and Christopher Hitchens, that instead anthropologically pay homage to the purported superiority of Eurocentric scientific knowledge systems.[15]

The irony, as Talal Asad notes, is that these self-styled atheists are not rejecting "transcendent forces," but rather are in fact (re)making themselves subject to different transcendent forces whether that of "the market," or Euro-American nation-state citizen discourses, or even a "non-religious" exalted appeal to abstract (neo)liberal humanitarian subjectivity. As Carl Schmitt's asserts in *Political Theology*: "All significant concepts in the modern theory of the state are secularized religious concepts."[16] For this reason, the decolonial question of spirituality and the need for distinguishing between the interrelated, yet distinct, Islamic concepts of spirituality (*rūḥāniyya*), faith (*īmān*), as well as organized and unorganized religion (*dīn*), is fundamental to this book's concerns. Spirituality is a central pillar of decolonization.

M. Jacqui Alexander and others have made similar arguments regarding the necessity for decolonial spiritualities and that scholar-activists step out of the "spiritual closet."[17] We can find a similar call by Michel Foucault who states,

> What meaning is there for the men inhabiting this little corner of earth, whose ground and underground are stakes in world strategies, when they seek, even at the price of their own lives, something that we have forgotten, even as a possibility, since the Renaissance and the great crises of Christianity: a political spirituality. I can already hear the French laughing. But I know they are wrong.[18]

Zahir Kazmi writes in *The Limits of Muslim Liberalism* that the discourses of both (neo)liberal and (neo)conservative Islamists invest in political liberalism and collectively contribute to the (neo)colonized ground on which the meanings and names of Islām are contested.[19] He also notes that this is another binary discourse of Muslim militancy versus Muslim liberalism, which in fact suppresses "more radical and creative departures in Islamic thought, departures that might fuel a more genuine" decolonial resurgence.[20] As a consequence of this destructive legacy of liberalism that infiltrates mainstream and Muslim circles as well as both left- and right-wing politics, what is often sidelined in terms of the interlocking grids is the dismissal of social justice conditioned by gendered coloniality and persisting neoimperial conditions in Euro-American and non-Euro-American societies.[21] Privatizing religion and segregating it from politics goes against this book's argument, because Islām, as arguably any idea that requisites belief (including Marxism and anarchism), inherently entails spiritual and ethical-political dimensions within it, including atheism.

Furthering the geopolitical disorientation, whether in the context of diasporic Muslims in settler-colonial societies or in or so-called "post"-colonial Egypt, is that Muslims are theologically bound by the critical Islamic anti-authoritarian concept/practice of *Tawḥīd*. Modern Muslim scholars continue to tirelessly debate the possibility of being a Muslim nationalist in light of the idea of *Tawḥīd*, which stresses that the paramount duty of Muslims is to recognize and pledge allegiance to the absolute authority of Allāh and not a nation, leader, tribe, or state.[22] From an Islamic perspective, *Tawḥīd* is a fundamental *ʿaqīdah* (creed). Tawḥīd relies on the conceptualization of God as the sole sovereign and protector of rights and accompanying responsibilities associated with them to all beings, land, and nonhuman life. Tawḥīd is the acknowledgment that the only authority is that of Allāh's, with the association or deification of any other referred to as *širk* (polytheism), contrary to what occurs nowadays in the rampant worship (*ʿibādah*) of materialism, power, prestige, celebrity-influencer status, and cultural capital. The deification of any other (be it through pledging allegiance to an authority figure, a nation-state, one's tribal allegiances, or even deification of one's family and children) is in fact *širk*. Tawḥīd is a fundamental premise and pillar for *Anarcha-Islām*, the non-ideological interpretation of Islām and Islamic interpretation of anarchism that this book Qurʾānically constructs using a methodology I refer to as *Anarchic Ijtihād*. In this book, Tawḥīd condemns fidelity to anyone but a Creator, including one's place of birth or residence, and even whether the so-called "authority figure" or "ruler," under the guise of blind "leadership," is referred to as *Īmāms*, *sheikhs*, *Khulafā*, *mullahs*, *muftīs*, *mutakallimūn* (scholastic theologians), *'ulamā* (religious scholars), *fuqahā* (jurists), *qāḍīs* (judges that are regarded as deified "experts"), or any other entity for that matter.

This book builds on the work of scholars such as Wael Hallaq, who argues in *The Impossible State* that the Prophet Muḥammad himself yearned for and created an unbound community of Muslims and non-Muslims alike, indeed that included monotheistic People of the Book (*Ahl al-Kitāb*), Zoroastrians, Sabeans, and even atheists, known as an *Umma* in Medina, all who were bound by the Medina Charter. The Umma (often mistranslated in the contemporary as "nation") was to be founded upon shared ethical-political commitments that arguably all spiritualities and purported "ideologies" are or ought to be premised upon. In this way, even the faithless possess faith.

In North America, progressive as well as so-called radical leftists continue to be informed by state-centric notions of "culture," "renaissance," "progress," "liberation," "human rights," "freedom," "secularism," "democracy," "civilization," "nonviolence," "urbanization," "the private/the public," "sexuality," "development," and "progress." These notions tend to animate what are often anti-spiritual and state-centered (post-)leftist social movements, theories, stances, and practices. This is the case, even when progressive liberals and leftists critique (neo)liberalism and condemn imperialism, global Orientalism, anti-blackness, Indigenous genocide, sexism, class-reductionism, ableism, and queerphobia. Often enough, the former fail to recognize (neo)liberalism's insidious effects not only through their adherence to Enlightenment assumptions but also a "culture of whiteness" that whitewashes notions of feminism and, queer rights.[23] Another example of this is "Green New Deals" which have been criticized from Indigenous perspectives that instead advocate for a "Red Deal," arguing that the GNDs fails to undermine settler-colonialism..[24]

Since colonial modernity, Muslims in non-Euro-American societies have adopted capitalist nation-state structures and paradigms, despite the fact that these structures represent colonial frameworks. In the specific case of the Middle East and Northern African region (MENA), this "colonial redefinition," as Tamim al-Barghouti writes, echoing Edward Said, means that the "Arabs and Muslims had two contradictory foci of loyalty, two mutually exclusive images to serve, one was the colonially imposed focus of loyalty, the nation-state: Egypt, Jordan, Palestine, Qatar, Syria, Lebanon, and the other was the Umma."[25] In fact, this colonial project is part of the Crusading project that Salman Sayyid and other scholars have given the birth day of 1492 – "year zero of the contemporary world."[26] That year – as opposed to the year 1619 that *New York Times* journalist Nikole Hannah-Jones proposed as marking the Middle Passage's commencement as the start of America's history – was the beginning of the decline of Muslim global power, even prior to the commencement of the decline of the Ottoman Empire in 1798, and ironically, falls in serendipitous tandem to the Columbian conquistador invasion of the Americas that heralded an imperialist settler-colonial project.[27] I build on the historical, spiritual, as well as socio-political and economic significance of 1492, one that a minority of transnational feminist, religious studies, and critical race scholars such as Ella Shohat and Sylvia Chan-Malik are addressing relative to the fact that it is impossible "to *do* religion without race" or "race without religion."[28] We can discern congruences between the pre-modern "phantasmatic imagery" that prefigures "colonialist racism" and that cast upon pre-modern Muslims and Jews who were Orientally considered as "enemies" and inferior "heathens" and "savages" prior to Indigenous and Black peoples who were also "imaged to various degrees as 'blood drinkers', 'cannibals', 'sorcerers', 'devils'."[29]

As a component of its religious and cultural war on Muslims, European Enlightenment aimed to disfigure Islām's reputation through a dual-pronged approach that racialized Islām to foment an "African Islām," an "Asian Islām," an "Arab Islām" etc., as well as inciting a neo-sectarian war, in which multiplicitous racial and sectarian denominations are pitted against one another.[30]

The Euro-American Orientalist/Fundamentalist binary schema by which Muslims are assaulted is facilitated through oppositional constructs like good/bad, hero/villain, victim/perpetrator, innocent/evil, enemy/ally, nature/culture, mind/body, proper/improper, normative/abject, Black/white, truth/rhetoric, speech/writing, natural/unnatural, male/female, and with us/against us.

In turn, and as a consequence of exposure to these colonial domestications, Muslims have internalized shame that leaves the native feeling inferior and naked, and solicits violent, "psycho-affective" and reactionary Fundamentalist and inverted Orientalist assimilationist responses.[31] Shame instigates a longing for integrationist identities and narratives of belonging on the colonizer's terms, while also provoking repressive hyper-masculine Muslim statist and neo-orthodox reactions in non-Euro-American societies. Viewed through the lens of shame and the traumatic distortion of concepts of masculinities and femininities, as well as their schizophrenic geopolitical disorientation, Muslims are both fundamentally sexually conservative, and yet hedonistic and animalistic hoards who are unable to control their urges. Shame prevents Muslims from achieving a deeper level of decolonial positional introspection (*muḥāsabah*) and blocks possibilities for transcendental ethical-political practices beyond the reactionary positions adopted in actualizing a borderless Umma.

My argument is that decolonizing Islām is not only fundamental to the repositioning of settler-diasporic Muslims, but to the liberation of all peoples, not only because of the geopolitical context of Islamophobia and Islām as a quintessential Other relative to a Euro-American (secularized) Christianity, but also arguably because of Islām's founding upon, and relationship to, social justice. Aligned appropriately, and as a quintessential signifier in whose global Orientalist shadow others are cast (as with Indigenous water protectors who are compared by U.S. mercenary firms like TigerSwan to "Jihadi movements" and Black Lives Matter activists who are designated by the FBI as "Black Identity Extremists"), Islām is ideally positioned to geopolitically demystify the intimate intersections between queerphobia, sexism, ethnocentrism, spirituality, settler and franchise colonialism, imperialism, and anti-Black and anti-Indigenous racism, as well as Arab supremacy festering within Muslim communities.[32] Decolonizing Islām, through the Anarcha-Islām that is advocated for here, means resurrecting a Qur'ān of the oppressed. In tandem to this, decolonizing Islām requires resurgent Muslims to embody this socially just Qur'ān and to address our multiple and intersecting oppressions. These injustices and sicknesses fester within our own communities and demonstrate the costly trade-offs between our Muslim responsibilities and the "American Dream."

A Match to a Powder Keg

While the notion of a uniform Muslim identity never existed, the idea of a monolithic Islām died the instant Prophet Muḥammad rose to be with the Creator, Allāh. In addition to the crucial concept of *Tawḥīd*, this book argues that following the Prophet's departure, only the universal Qur'ān, the Sunnah (Prophetic practice), and the *aḥādīth* (Oral Tradition) ought to act as the *Īmām* (the spiritual guide); there is no necessity for a human leader or guide, especially if Muslims chose to abide by Islām's revolutionary macro- and micro-anti-authoritarian commitments. Most Muslims concede that the notion of a central church, hierarchy or hereditary rule are all rejected in Islām. Islām seldom offers concrete guidance, in either the Qur'ān or the Sunnah, regarding macro-politics, whose mode of enacting is left open to choose as long as it is consistent with micro-anti-authoritarian commitments relative to the Qur'ānic concepts of *Umma* and *Dawla*.[33] Islām and Prophet Muḥammad's example is of pragmatic and Qur'ānically foundational micro-political and micro-economic, social justice concepts and practices that were embodied by the initial polity in private and public. Islām develops these political and economic concepts and practices to teach and limit all Muslims, individually and as a community, from derision and egoism. Allāh created us knowing our insatiable appetites and strivings towards the accumulation of power and coveting of authority which constantly threaten the possibility of our egalitarian co-existence as a species. These concepts and practices inform the cornerstone of Islām's anti-authoritarian stance, besides its anti-materialist commitments. As Wael Hallaq notes in *The Impossible State*, there is no such thing as an "Islamic state" in pre-modern times, only varying confederate, decentralized forms of Muslim governance. Instead, Hallaq rightfully argues that the Prophet Muḥammad himself created a borderless wide-reaching community embodying a collectivist Umma. In Islām, religion (*dīn*), faith (*īmān*), and spirituality (*rūḥāniyya*) are three interrelated non-individualist and communitarian concepts. Islām acknowledges that at least 124,000 prophets have been sent to different tribes and nations since creation so that we may, as the Qur'ānic Verse 49:13 states, "get to know one another" and vie with one another. Separately and collectively, all three concepts have been historically deployed across space and time by all peoples and societies to uphold liberation and social justice, but also to suppress them.

The crises amongst contemporary Muslim and non-Muslim scholarship in terms of what constitutes legitimate Muslim governance can be roughly divided into two areas. First, most Muslim movements tend to neglect Islām's anti-authoritarian commitments and how they must act as "building blocks" or binding principles for an egalitarian social justice and horizontalist framework of Muslim governance through the Qur'ānic concepts of *Umma* and *Dawla*. Instead, most scholars and Islamic movements begin from the historically emergent albeit non-Qur'ānic framework of governance that arose as a political reference following the Prophet Muḥammad's death and referred to as the "Caliphate." During Islām's early pre-modern period there were a multiplicity of Dawlas within one Dawla, loosely resembling a decentralized confederacy and Qur'ānically referred to as an Umma. Within pre-colonial Muslim usage, sovereignty lay with the Umma and not the Dawla, because a "Dawla, by definition, cannot form an Umma seeing that the Umma, as an idea, is the purpose beyond the Dawla, not in defining matters of worship, but in defining matters of political identity and relation with the other."[34] Furthermore, as Tamim al-Barghouti writes, the legitimacy of a Dawla, in pre-modernity, was not gauged "by the welfare the Dawla provides to its own inhabitants regardless of the Muslims or regardless of the ideal image of the Umma, rather it is measured by both, the welfare of its inhabitants as the welfare of other Muslims and the service of that ideal image."[35]

Anarcha-Islām is then, in part, founded on the premise that in the wake of post-colonial independence movements Muslims (and in particular, Arabs) altered the meanings of their own language to correspond with European definitions, ontologies, and terminologies associated with "the nation" and capitalist-states.[36] The history and consequences of these alterations are discussed in detail in Chapter 2.

The second problem with the belief in a singular Khalīfa or "Caliph," often interpreted as "political successor," as the proper form of Muslim governance is the fact that the concept is not in fact a fundamental part of Islām. Rather, both the terms "Caliph" and its associated framework of "Caliphate" that organically emerged after the Prophet's death are derived from the pluralistic Qur'ānic term *Khulafā* or *Khulafāh* as in Verses 2:30 and 6:165. As a pluralistic term, the Qur'ān regards all of our species as *Khulafā*, which can be translated as Caretakers or Viceregents who are locked in dynamic and temporary symbiotic liaisons with the Creator. The ramifications of this definition are also discussed in Chapter 2.

Moreover, my argument distinguishes itself in terms of the understanding of the concept of the Īmām (spiritual successor). After all, the same pre-modern and modern scholars who argue for the need of a single human Īmām also argue that the "Umma is independent of the human ruler Īmām."[37] Most scholarships on Muslim governance also always affirm that human leaders must "be subordinate, in one sense or another, to those supreme textual Īmāms," the Qur'ān and aḥādīth (the Oral Tradition).[38] Modern Muslims have internalized the misleading and unnecessary puritan goal of emulating the non-Qur'ānic, organic, pre-modern governance model that immediately followed the Prophet, without reflecting on the revolutionary commitments that informed Muslim mannerisms during what is often referred to as "Golden Era of Islām." What led to the successive accumulation of tyranny and decadence particularly following this era is the collective Muslim abandonment of the revolutionary anti-authoritarian spirit of mutual consultation (*Shūrā*), consensus (*Ijmāʿ*) and collective welfare (*Maṣlaḥa*) that informed the early period. It is ironic that most scholars are not attuned to the fact that the gradual authoritarianism that came after this era is also limited because socio-political-economic territorial power was more diffuse during the pre-modern period. This facilitated successive horizontalist resurgences against absolutist acts and authoritarian rulers, very much unlike the delineated capacity for resistance in a modern world informed by high-tech-surveillance Counter-Intelligence Program (COINTELPRO) disciplinary and control societies facilitated by capitalist-states and "border imperialism."[39] Moreover, in pre-modern societies, unlike now, the ability of any Muslim to engage in *Ijtihād* (independent reasoning and critical exegesis or the *tafsīr* of unsettled issues in the Qur'ān, the Sunnah, and *aḥādīth*, as well as within Islamic texts and legal sources) permitted and encouraged dissent in the face of injustice and embodied the noted micro-anti-authoritarian practices.[40] Thus, there can be no doubt that an alternative radical understanding of horizontalist and anarchistic Muslim governance can be posited, given the non-binding nature of the ideas of a singular Īmām or Khalīfa, especially given the fact that the Caliphate undermines and runs counter to Islām's micro-anti-authoritarian commitments, as well as the reality that none of even the pre-modern classical criteria (assuming one accepts them) for "electing" or "assigning" a leader can be fulfilled in a world of capitalist-states, as will be later discussed.

For this reason, as Patricia Crone writes in *Ninth-Century Muslim Anarchists*, we can see that Muslim anarchists are not a contemporary phenomenon, but rather existed in pre-modernity, namely, a subsect of the *Khārijites* (whose name means "rebels") were referred to as the *Najadat* or Najdiyya as well as Mu'tazilites (*suffiyat al-mu'tazila*) who contested the notion of a central authority figure.[41] Amongst the Mu'tazilites were "Ja'far ibn Harb (d. 850), Al-Asamm (d. 816 or 817), al-Naẓẓām (d. between 835 and 845), Hishām al-Fuwaṭī (d. 840) and his pupil Abbad ibn Slayman (d. 870)."[42] These "Muslim anarchists" lived near Basra between the seventh and tenth centuries and held "that Muslim society could function without what we would call the state."[43] Unfortunately, as al-Barghouti argues, Kharijism, in general, "has lost most of its revolutionary zeal."[44] Nowadays, most Muslim scholars and governments in predominantly Muslim societies would hasten to condemn every revolutionary movement as Khārijite.

Islām dictates that anyone striving to at once become a scholar-pupil-teacher and who is capable of bearing the responsibilities of interpreting the Qur'ān through the methodology of Ijtihād, upon study and in a manner exceptional to them, should embark on doing so. Indeed, anyone who does so and can convince others of their interpretations, symbolically acts as an *intermediary*, and temporary knowledge keeping servant of the Creator, while realizing that all political-cultural-economic and spiritual power will always reside in an Īmāmah encapsulated in the Qur'ān, Sunnah, and aḥadīth.[45] The wisdom behind this right to Ijtihād, that all Muslims can and should partake in, is to delimit spiritual hegemony, sustain the fluidity of power and minimize its crystallization in the hands of an individual or a few. Ijtihād, in matters that the Qur'ān has purposefully left open, is a means of engendering debate amongst Muslims, and between them and non-Muslims.

The question then of whether or not Islām is compatible with democracy is a misguided and misleading one, as democratic models are numerous, including the often dismissed anarchism. In the contemporary, the former inquiry, in fact, camouflages the more vital concern of whether or not Islamic political frameworks are congruent with modern nation-states that claim to be democratic, and not in principle whether Islām itself is so.

Islām and Anarchism Are Dead: Muslim Anarchists in Turtle Island's Newest Social Movements

Anarchism is dead. Anarchism means "communitarian rule without rulers" despite its common misunderstanding as "chaos," "disorder," and "lack of rule." In turn, Arabic scholars and speakers often mistranslate anarchism as *fawḍāwiya* to signify "disorganization" and "mayhem," as opposed to the more correct term *la sulṭāwiya* (literally meaning "without authority and authoritarian rule"). As an anti-authoritarian tradition that promotes *thaqāfa tahruriya* (or libertarian critical cultural consciousness and intellect), anarchism is only alive in so far as it manifests itself in its classical and contemporary texts, and as embodied by anarchists.[46] Anarchism is ever reinterpreted by its adherents but is bound by faith to an "anarchist tradition" and as a "spiritual" ethical and political modality of living. Indeed, it represents a chimeric way of evolutionary becoming with the universe. Anarchism denotes a morphing ideal to strive for in an unjust world. Those who sincerely embrace it bear the ever explosive responsibility of becoming further anarchistic towards creating a just communitarian environment for themselves and others. Anarchism writes itself on anarchist bodies, no less than Islām writes itself on Muslims, ad infinitum. Anarchism, as Islām, bears fruit to a multiplicity of different interpretative traditions. As Jason Adams writes: "anarchists from all kinds of backgrounds with all kinds of ideas have sought to make contemporary anarchisms relevant to them in their own unique situations."[47] The consequence of time immemorial, unique situations are numerous-variant elucidations of anarchism. These arrive not only through revaluations of it, as it is classically understood as a Euro-American tradition.[48] Rather, they arrive too through explications of it as possessing non-Euro-American roots, despite the fact that these connotations of anarchism are not as well recognized and publicized.[49]

Still, despite this ingrained Euro-centrism, in need of interminable vigilant decolonization, anarchism is to be acknowledged as a pluralistic tradition, with vibrant, rich, contemporary variant renditions imbued within it like: anarcha-feminism, anarcho-Indigenism, anarcho-syndicalism, green-anarchism, queer-anarchism, post-structuralist anarchism (or post-anarchism), anarcho-primitivism, African-anarchism, Arab-anarchism, Cuban-anarchism, Black-anarchism, Buddhist anarchism, Christian anarchism, Jewish anarchism, Islamic anarchism, and so forth. All the former are renderings that arrive from a multitude of cultures and land-based practices that anarchism has encountered.[50] If anything, the arrival of these variances is a testament to anarchism's appeal and seductive ability, as Islām's, not to reform, but rather to be reinvented anew.[51] The possibilities for anarchism to be fomented in the image of individuals and communities and for it to address the particular struggles individuals and communities encounter is then, as for Islām, boundless, provided its central ethical-political tenets are preserved.

It follows that Anarcha-Islām is an Islamic reinterpretation of anarchism, and more particularly post-anarchism. Using Anarchic Ijtihād that I discuss in Chapter 2, I locate, extract, and interrogate post-anarchic commitments, concepts, and practices in Islamic sources and Muslim traditions, but particularly as they exist in the Qur'ān, aḥādīth, and Sunnah, such that the concepts and practices that organically exist in the former resonate with the post-anarchic interpretative tradition of Islām I seek. Seeing that Anarcha-Islām is a post-anarchic (re)interpretation of Islām, and given post-anarchism's critique of engrained Euro, logo, and phallo-centric tendencies in classical Euro-American anarchism, Anarcha-Islām is anti-Euro-logo-phallo-centric. In this vein, it is Anarcha-Islām's resistance to Euro, logo, and phallocentricity that leads me to adopt for Anarcha-Islām the queer-feminine "Anarcha" as opposed to "Anarcho-Islām." "Anarcha" is moreover adopted to dispel the general Euro-American false image that all interpretative traditions of Islām are naturally anti-feminist. For now, and in relation to Islām, Anarcha-Islām is grounded in anti-authoritarian and anti-capitalist commitments, concepts, and practices I find and that foundationally inform the primordial Medinian Charter socially just Umma and a Qur'ān of the oppressed that Prophet Muḥammad found. Anarcha-Islām therefore operates on the promise of identifying and coordinating shared ethico-political commitments between Islām(s) and anarchism(s) using reconcilable concepts and practices.

For pragmatic reasons, and for this book's purposes, these affinities adopt the form of ethico-political commitments confined to anti-authoritarian and anti-capitalist concepts and practices due to the fact that it is these two commitments that materially, politically, and symbolically represent the commitments upon which classical anarchism was founded and continues to predominantly operate; that is, they symbiotically present themselves historically as the most significant to anarchism's histories. Anarcha-Islām nevertheless is not imprisoned within the former two commitments. Nor are the two commitments regarded as less or more critical than inherently intersectional "new" commitments established in forthcoming works that more explicitly address gender and sexuality which have been mobilized by Euro-America as a means of imperialist and colonial conquest.[52] Instead, I am drawn towards the continual search for what I regard as vital Islamic socio-political and economic principles, commitments, and frameworks resonating with post-anarchism's dedications and within a decolonial anti-statist and anti-imperialist framework.[53]

Islām is dead. Like anarchism, Islām is only alive in so far as it manifests itself in a bequeathed Muslim *thaqāfa* (critical cultural consciousness and intellect) and *turāth* ("living compendiums of the past in the present"), as well as the aḥādīth, Sunnah, and more critically the ethical-political ideals of the Qur'ān which all Muslims irrespective of denomination share, and in which absolute authority is vested, since Islām does not subscribe to a centralized institution and rejects hereditary rule, given the creed of Tawḥīd.[54] Every Muslim is ever striving to *become* Muslim, as in thoughtfully following Prophet Muḥammad's example and teachings. In so doing the individual and communitarian metamorphoses of Muslims dynamically mutate both the composition of the Umma as well as non-Muslims alike. Particularly, that is, when one Islamically expands the definition of who and what is a spiritual believer to depend on the ethical-political commitments and practices we all follow despite our diverse traditions and paths to the same Creator and in relation to (non)human life. In this sense, in a modernity fraught with identity crises, it is irrelevant from a Qur'ānic perspective and, as I argued elsewhere, whether or not individuals and communities explicitly identify as Muslim per se or not.[55] Besides the Qur'ānic injunction that there "is no compulsion in religion," in numerous verses such as 2:251, 7:56, 7:74, 8:73, 11:116, 12:73, 13:25, 26:152, 27:48, 47:22, etc., the Qur'ān explicitly describes disbelievers, amongst many other facets, as those who are "arrogant" and neglectful of the rights of the "meek," the "poor," "orphans," "women," as well as those who dabble in "hypocrisy (*nifāq*)," "gossip," "excess," and uphold "injustice," spread "mischief" and "corrupt the earth." These attributes associated with the corrupt and disbelieving soul (*nafs*) exist in Muslims and non-Muslims alike.

Islām is not a monolith. The variant interpretations, or what could be referred to as the *names of Islām*, arrive as a consequence of the divine concept and practice of Ijtihād, granted to all Muslims by the Creator. Ijtihād serves as divine mechanism embedded within Islām in resistance to a conception of Islām as monolithic. For instance, as a consequence of Ijtihād's practice during the Iranian revolution of 1979, Shi'ism, a traditional branch of Islām, bore the fruit of the "Islamic-Leftist Mujahedeen al'Khalq," "the Marxist-Leninist Fedayeen i-Khalq," and "Ali Shariati's synthesis of Marxism, existentialism, Heideggerianism [with] ... a militant form of 'traditional' Shi'ism."[56] These interpretations of Shi'ism are just three examples that bear witness to the power of Ijtihād. In the absence of spiritual and cultural spatial-temporal context, it is blasphemous to pronounce or write a word with respect to Islām as a whole. As Aziz Al-Azmeh writes in *Islams and Modernities*, "there are as many Islams as there are situations that sustain it," particularly after Prophet Muḥammad's passing.[57]

As a consequence of this, in modernity, we find (neo)liberal and (neo)conservative and even "moderate Muslims." Indeed, we find all types of subjectivities and formations from so-called culturally patriotic Muslims (in Saudi-Arabia, Turkey, and Iran) to anti-patriotic zealot Islamic proto-state Muslims (ISIS) and not hardline enough Salafi-Jihadist Muslims (al-Qaeda). We find Arab supremacist Muslims to Black nationalist Muslims to ex-Muslims to atheist Muslims to queer Muslims to feminist Muslims, and from double Muslims to self-styled Muslims. The emergence of these endless Muslim currents is hardly due to the emergence of what Asef Bayat and Olivier Roy refer to as "post-Islamism" such that, in the wake of the so-called "failure of Political Islam," Islamists are instead now "rationally" and "individualistically" attempting to "resecularize religion" towards establishing "a pious society within a democratic state" in a desire to "combine the concerns for national dignity with social justice and democracy."[58] After all, this Orientalist view of Bayat and Roy not only constructs religion, faith, and spirituality as irrational and anti-scientific but also reifies colonial concepts as "political Islām," while upholding the supremacy of a "politics of rights" over responsibility relative to the nation-state that these authors adhere to as a historical marker of civilizational progress.

The long-standing identity crisis spawns from the fact that most Muslims neither fundamentally understand political concepts in Islām like Dawla or Caliphate or Umma, nor do they comprehend the historical relationship between capitalism and the nation-state and how they individually and jointly function. This misunderstanding led and continues to drive innumerable prominent so-called Islamists to attempt to seize the nation-state in order to establish an Umma or alternatively become reactionary militants. The position of anti- and post-Islamist liberal scholars such as Roy and Bayat derives from their further assumption that colonialism/imperialism have ended and that, at least according to Olivier Roy, "the key question is not what the Quran says, but what Muslims say it says."[59] But the Qur'ān is essential as it is what Allāh vowed to protect, besides a Muslim's ability to provisionally contextualize, historicize the present and speak in the name of Islām, through an interpretative Ijtihād and God's *ilhām* (inspiration). Fundamentally, Roy ignores that in Islām, it is the Creator, Allāh, who is the conclusive abettor and attendant of the Qur'ān, the source from which Islām and Muslims derive unparalleled force, when God affirms: "Absolutely, we have revealed the reminder, and, absolutely, we will preserve it."[60] What Bayat and Roy perceive as a new post-Islamist phase is in fact a continuation of an identity crisis and a poverty of imagination that Muslims are contending with. What is shared by most Muslim movements is they have all come to neutralize decolonial possibilities of resistance given their lack of engagement or understanding of what decolonization exactly entails.

This crisis can be seen in the Muslim thinkers from the late 1800s like Muhammad Abduh and early 1930s, 1940s, and 1950s, such as non-conformist militant conservatives like Sayyid Qutb (1954) and Abul Alā Al-Mawdūdī (1967) as well as liberal reformists like Muhammad Iqbal (2000) and Fazlur Rahman Malik (1982). Though some of these non-conformist orthodox Muslims like Qutb laid the foundation for non-statist Islamist movements ranging from Hamas, Hezbollah, to al-Qaeda, and ISIS, other Islamists like Iqbal and Rahman ultimately propagated views that subjugated Islām to political platformism relative to the liberal-state when they saw no other path in which an Umma can be achieved.

Al-Mawdūdī regarded customs as a "'diabolical conspiracy' of nationalism," given that the Qur'ānic emphasis in Islām is on the concept and practice, indeed the doctrine of Tawḥīd (the paramount duty of a Muslim to solely affirm loyalty to the oneness, and thus, the Absolute Authority of Allāh).[61] To Al-Mawdūdī, to love the nation was to divert love away from the Creator. Al-Mawdūdī's thoughts continue to exert a profound influence on al-Qaeda and Muslim movements of similar character, who overcame this contradiction by adhering to his theme of nationalism as "an extreme ideology and [as] unacceptable," while simultaneously justifying state seizure by arguing that "nationality, by contrast, is simply an administrative classification, a matter of exercising privileges and meeting the obligations of citizenship, and is acceptable."[62]

However, this state-national vs. nationality division posited its own problems, as noted by the anti-secularist reformer Fazular Rahman:

> Secularism is not the answer – quite the opposite … instead of settling themselves [Muslims] to genuinely interpret Islamic goals to be realized through political and government channels – which would subjugate politics to interpreted Islamic values … – what happens most of the time is ruthless exploitation of Islam for party politics and group interests that subjects Islam not only to politics but to day-to-day politics; Islam thus becomes demagoguery.[63]

I argue that one may love the Divine through variant non-statist conceptualizations of "nationhood" embodied in horizontalist expressions of community that are anchored in and founded upon non-identitarian ethical-political social justice commitments relative to spirituality. Or, once more, alternatively, to whatever it is that one humbles oneself to, as symbol(s) for sacred principles that one is willing to sacrifice-die for.

Nonetheless, these variant ethical-political enumerations of Islām, Muslim subjectivities, and social movements affirm two central facts that most theses on Islām and Muslim governance contradicts. First, the instability of our identities, irrespective of what they are, in our ever-lasting engagements with conditions and ethical-political projects of our own *becoming*, are strategically distinct from Enlightenment identity politics that structuralist-Euro-American (neo)liberal thought seeks to impose. Second, the hegemonic notion of "Western" is in fact limited, given that global culture has been interconnectedly forged through polyvalent encounters, across pre-modern and modern history. The vivacity of this perspective exists in the work of scholars like Guy Burak, Rudolph Peters, Khaled Fahmy, and Liat Kozma, who situate contested, contingent, and changing fields of legal practice in progressive ways that are amenable to the objective of envisioning more radical decolonial possibilities, as, for instance, in the overturning of colonial racial hierarchies that impacted domains of law and international politics.[64] This agentive capacity of the Other to defy resonates with José Esteban Muñoz's concept of "disidentification" in which the Other as a subject neither seeks to assimilate into Euro-American queerness nor entirely reject it.[65] Instead, they engage in disidentifying political acts as they negotiate the historical traumas, systematic, epistemic, and systemic violences and identity crises wrought through (neo)colonialism.

I therefore take seriously Gayatri Chakravorty Spivak's notion of "translation *as* assimilation and *as* violation."[66] Spivak's work exposes the cataclysmic ethico-political crises associated with the European and non-European assumption that there can or must be a forced and direct hegemonic linguistic search for equivalence and correspondence between European and non-European paradigms, terminologies of reference, and corporeal practices and experiences. Spivak states:

> The word "culture" belongs to the history of Western European languages. If we want to move into the elusive phenomenon in

> other places, below the shifting internal line of cultural difference, we will not look for translations and approximations of the word. Such synonyms carry on their back the impulse to translate from the European, which is a characteristic of the colonized intelligentsia under imperialism, and thus is the condition as well as the effect of that differentiating internal line. They will not let us go below it. We must rather learn a non-European language well enough to be able to enter it without ready [sic?] reference to a European one. We may encounter creole versions of the word "culture" which will complicate our argument. But they are neither the same word nor its translation.[67]

Similar to Spivak, but writing in the context of Muslim and Egyptian women in Egypt's piety movements, the late Saba Mahmood (building on the work of Janice Boddy and Lila Abu-Lughod) issued a cautionary tale against the Euro-American feminist impulse to interpret the experiences of others, noting that one should "not assume that in the process of culturally translating other lifeworlds, one's own certainty about how the world should proceed can remain stable."[68] This process of translation has essentialized a non-monolithic Islām and a non-existent "Arab and Muslim identity world" that upholds the myth of authentic stable identities and subjectivities. In fact, Saba Mahmood's ethnographic research in the *Politics of Piety*, conducted between 1995 and 1997, exposes the false binaries in liberal secular/religious as well as Islamist/feminist identity politics which scholars such as Roy and Bayat uphold.

Building on such critical feminist scholarships I argue that Muslim anarchist and anarchist Muslim subjectivities and ethical-political subjectivities are in fact transcending Euro-American – both liberal-statist as well as militant Jihadist – narratives and Fundamentalist/Orientalist representations of Muslims. Identity politics – as a product of modern (neo)liberalism – are tactically useful because of the ongoing, real, symbolic, structural, and material violences suffered by the multiple "Other" every instant of every day. However, identity politics are also strategically limited, as they are themselves informed by white-supremacist Enlightenment and (neo)liberal structural and symbolic ontologies/epistemologies. I therefore build and reread the concept of *indigeneity* in non-racial/non-ethnic terms as the compass that ought be sought through the fulfillment of our ethical-political-spiritual commitments derived from and contingent on each of our positionalities.

This position is rooted in Islām's anti-identitarian and universalist message that inherently advocates for spiritual, anarchistic, feminist, and queer ethical-political commitments as a solemn pledge (*mīthāq*) to be shared with others. These ethico-political commitments in Islām challenge Euro-American compartmentalized perceptions of queer/feminist/anarchist/Islamist as spiritually contradictory, unrelated, and mutually exclusive labels. The strategic limits to identity politics have been constantly demonstrated in endless insurrectionary moments such as that of 2011's Tahrir's Uprising. The theoretical and social movement analysis that inform Anarcha-Islām arise from observations of xenophobia, anti-blackness, queerphobia, sexism, and misogyny in mosques as well as anarchistic communities and circles, as well as familiarity with the cultural norms in modern Egypt, my place of birth, as well as Arabic, Islām, and the Qur'ān. In constructing an anti-authoritarian, anti-capitalist, egalitarian, anti-ablest, anti-patriarchal, and queer-feminist Qur'ānic anarchistic interpretation of Islām, I draw on anti-racist feminist and transnational queer diasporic literatures. I am also inspired by the decolonization theories that have emerged from Indigenous discourses and queer Indigenous and Two-Spirit studies in Turtle Island that not only engage in immanent critiques of neoliberal capitalism, but also do not take post-colonialism and the Eurocentric framework of the nation-state for granted. Indigenous discourses are particularly critical of Eurocentric understandings of what constitutes revolutionary praxis, agency, and resistance. For instance, they insist that the struggle against capitalism cannot be separated from that against the nation-state given nation-states' politics of assimilation and recognition. In a similar vein, radical Indigenous, Black, queer and feminist scholars and activists argue that the struggle against cisheteropatriarchy cannot be separated from the struggle against settler-colonialism, which, in this case, transnational queer theories tend to elide given how gender and queerness is snarled in the relationship between settler-and-franchise colonial societies that are symbolically and materially related.[69] Radical Indigenous scholars argue against reform or multicultural neoliberalism, which play to the cisheteropatriarchal capitalist nation-state politics of integration and recognition.[70] Although varying in their decolonial visions, radical Indigenous scholars often emphasize engagement with non-statist frameworks of decolonization; they privilege land-based struggles, recognizing the way that land itself structures relationships to and with space, time, autonomy, access to political-economic power, spiritual notions of kinship and understandings of polygamy, as well as gender and sexual relationship practices. Though not all Muslim scholarship does, I distinguish between Islamic principles and Muslim cultural practices. I engage both religious and cultural approaches to reflect Muslims' struggles, within Muslim communities, liberal, feminist and leftist circles, and broader societies, to theologically justify and reconcile the criticality of fusing anarchist *and* Muslim commitments towards furthering radical, decolonial, social action. Although I do consider theological and spiritual debates that anarchists and leftist social movements tend to elide, my objective is not simply to just extend Islamic studies' discussions on whether or not nationalism, states, and capitalism are licit or forbidden in Islām, at the expense of dismissing and keeping in focus broader colonial/imperial conditions that animate and frame the former debate. Engaging in the theological debates is necessary, because since modernity South West Asian and North African (SWANA) Muslims have failed to conceptualize genuine revolutionary change that has not subscribed to colonial Euro-American frameworks that capitulate to the nation-state as the organizing order as in the case of Pan-Arabism, Pan-Africanism, and Third-Worldism.

In this sense, while the modern rendezvous between so-called non-Euro-American and Euro-American societies undeniably impose generalized reproductions of colonial/imperial Eurocentric, capitalistic, statist, and androcentric practices and thought, this does not eliminate a constant, violent process of the negotiation of a difference of subjectivity on behalf of the Other or native either. Nevertheless, the underlying premise stands, despite countless Muslim responses that demonstrate our agency, we, yet, mimic ethical-political dimensions of internalized "cultures of whiteness" in our reactionary response on a geopolitical and meta-historical level that limits the animus of our liberation as well as that of others. Neoliberal globalization has simultaneously scattered our fragmented nations, exposing our fractured repressive and repressed realities and identities as many Others, and yet also paradoxically ushered in new, lived, and re-envisioned encounters of how we can become together. Always subsequently, assimilation demands submissive encounters that also creatively inspire resistive power in the shape of the Other's political views.

Under such circumstances, it would seem that Muslims in general, and diasporic Muslims in particular, have one of two options: we must either use (neo)liberal mainstream media and politics in reactionary stances in the continual proving of our "Americanness/Canadianess" against those who represent us, or continue to silently accept our lot and truly live in hell. This book shows that franchise post-colonial and settler modes of colonization are materially and symbolically interrelated.[71] In other words, diasporic POC residing in Canada/U.S. and insisting on the unapologetic congruency of American/Canadian identities are not only actively participating in the relentless colonization and dispossession of Indigenous peoples, but they are also assisting in a contrived War on Terror when they support the Clash of Civilizations worldview, in which Islām and socialism are presented as in conflict with crusading Euro-American societies. Thus, the modus operandi and object of one category of colonialism in Euro-American societies *can be* (if not in fact is) the intersectional agent of another colonialism in non-Euro-American societies. The multiple racial and gendered colonialisms are as entwined as grape vines. Their interconnections are mitigated through the normalized transnational authoritarian and macro-fascistic emigrational adoption of capitalist nation-states as the means through which populations ought be socio-politically, spiritually, culturally, and economically organized.

Many Muslims globally have chosen one of these options. Some, however, are resisting this false choice, by recreating alternatives to it, by *becoming* Muslim anarchists. Muslims are taking it upon themselves to open desiring processes by reconstructing a new understanding of what it "is" to identify and to be identified as a Muslim transnationally. In their revolutionary force, anarchistic politics truly mark for Muslims a radical move politically. A move that permits them to cast off their shame of being Muslim, of being able to respond, tactfully, tactically, and strategically, to what is intolerable, the dichotomous representations, and what gendered, sexualized and racialized worlds, they, and indeed, we face. Muslim anarchists are taking it upon themselves to pierce open compartmentalized identitarian silos by reconstructing new understandings, indeed horizons, of what it "is" to identify and be identified as Muslim in (non-)Euro-American spatiality and temporalities, if not the world all over. And it is because of anarchism's anti-authoritarian and anti-capitalist orientations that Muslims are particularly drawn to it. Anarchism offers Muslims new political avenues for their identity's reformulation. Modern examples of these Muslim anarchistic leanings, if not identification, include Abdennur Prado, Yakub Islam, Isabelle Eberhardt, Shibili Shumayyil, Gustave Henri Jossot, Leda Bruna Rafanelli, Michael Muhammad Knight, and influential anarchist theorist, Peter Lamborn Wilson, or "Hakim Bey."[72] Not to mention the burgeoning critical mass, alongside other anarchists, in groups like No One Is Illegal (NOII), Solidarity Across Borders (SAB) as well as within the San Francisco Bay area and disparately, but widely, within the SWANA region.[73]

In an age of resurgent nationalisms and globalized liberal-state-multiculturalism, Islamic anarchism is beginning to germinate as discourse, even if its parameters, through its variant models are still being identified and defined.[74] This embracing of anarchism by a minority of Muslims as a response to the "problem of Muslims and Islam," and this presentation of Muslims as a socio-political-economic force, allows us to see Islamic anarchism as an example of what Richard J.F. Day calls the *newest social movements*.[75] What particularly distinguishes Day's newest social movements from other anti-imperialist and anti-colonial social movements is their practice of a *logic of affinity*; a logic whose practice includes the construction of communities founded on "non-universalizing, non-hierarchical, non-coercive relationships based on mutual aid, and shared ethical commitments."[76] It is in this context, and because of the critical role it has to play, by acting as a safe space for Muslims' (further) resistance, that in the newest social movements I see liberatory hope, not only for Muslim anarchists, but also for a majority Muslims of the diasporas (if not the world all over). It is in this critical space carved out by the newest social movements that I see a place for Muslims and Muslim anarchists to begin again and again the radical recreation of their socio-political identities in a way conducive to Islām's present confrontations with(in) contemporary Euro-American societies, and their imperialist hegemonic logics and settler-colonial individualist orders. Muslims, whether across the Atlantic or the Pacific, supported with time by a passage through anarchism's vernaculars can become bodies no longer frozen in their catatonic socio-political-economic state.

Equally important, it is in the newest social movements in particular that anarchism and anarchists also stand to learn from interacting with Muslims. For instance, anarchists could benefit by learning how to better disagree ethically as a community as opposed to tearing each other apart over ideological and personal differences. Islām developed this type of ethics early on, in what is referred to *Uṣūl al-Ikhtilāf*, or the ethics of disagreement/conflict resolutions, as a compassionate and forgiving form of etiquette for Muslims to address disagreements amongst themselves, which I discuss in detail in Chapter 3.[77] Anarchists in the newest social movements, as much as Muslims, indeed stand to gain, culturally, aesthetically, politically, and ethically, should they learn to accept that others who are not exactly like them ought to be able to join them in their anti-authoritarian and anti-capitalist revolt.

Although the newest social movements can potentially act as a safe space, Muslims and Muslim anarchists still have a long way to journey in terms of being made to feel welcome and comfortable by anarchists. This necessitates the opening of a *panegyric desert of the present*, a metaphor that stands for a more hospitable space carved out for Muslims and Muslim anarchists in the newest social movements. That is, a space where they can interact with anarchists and anarchism, and similarly for anarchism and anarchists to interact with Islām and Muslims. This panegyric desert is exceptionally pertinent given that critical interpretative misconceptions exist between Muslims and anarchists, which hinder collaborations and relationships between the two. These miscalculations have an especially adverse effect on Muslim anarchists. They leave Muslim anarchists facing difficulties because of their ostracization by anarchists on top of what is already their ostracization by Muslim communities. There is no way to eradicate misunderstandings completely, making the ethics of disagreement necessary in the mitigation of any community's social affairs (in Islām, *mu'āmalāt*), be it composed of Muslims, non-Muslims, or, ideally, both. This is particularly urgent as capitalist nation-states continue to plant and sow division between BIPOC via brainwashing campaigns and disinformation apparatuses of state and corporate media control that as Edward S. Herman and Noam Chomsky noted in their seminal *Manufacturing Consent*, "are effective and powerful ideological institutions that carry out a system-supportive propaganda function by reliance on market forces, internalized assumptions, and self-censorship, and without overt coercion."[78]

Positionality: Who Is Speaking?

In developing Anarcha Islām, I draw on non-ideological and tenuous non-Euro-American trajectories in the Qur'ān and their affinity with post-anarchism's anti-authoritarian and anti-capitalist ethico-political commitments and decentralized conceptualization of power. I also draw on my positionality and transnational social movement experiences following the Seattle 1999 anti-Globalization mobilizations, including the Anti-Afghanistan and Iraq War protests to more contemporary contexts as the Tahrir Uprisings of 2011–13, the Indigenous Zapatista movement in Chiapas, and the Mohawks of Tyendinaga and community members from the sister territories of Kahnawake, Akwesasne, and Kanehsatake, during their standoff with the Canadian federal government over the Culbertson Tract, as well as close to 20 years of scholarly-activist research and organizing experience towards Palestinian, Indigenous, Black, and people of color liberation. I am a North African and Arab Egyptian Muslim anarchist activist-scholar and first generation immigrant turned self-identifying diasporic settler of color, currently living on Gayogo̱hó:nǫ', Anishinaabe and Haudenosaunee territory, straddling work at two neoliberal institutions, namely, Cornell University and the American University of Cairo in Egypt. I am an unsettling non-ideological Muslim anarchist or Anarcha-Islamist, as Orientally problematic as the term Islamism is, as noted. With others, I know the impossible becomes possible. I am an able person of color with a desire that is heteronormalized, yet gendered and queered, as arguably all others, by Euro-American sexual civilizationism and my exposure to both matriarchal and patriarchal practices, in part shaped by a cosmopolitan upbringing as a consequence of middle-class privilege; a luxury that afforded me the ability to look out the window seeing joy, but also exploitation that I am complicit in.

A Sum Exceeding the Whole, Everything Divided: The Argument Condensed

Anarcha-Islām transcends the false narrative of Muslim, Arab, North African, and POC aspirations to emulate the secularized Christian Euro-American state, emergent from Rome and centralized Frankish Kingdoms. It also rises above the so-called neo-Islamist paradigms that advocate for traditionalist nation-state party politics in the form of an "Islamic State," even when, unlike post-Islamists, they are animated by *daʿwa* or a collective moralistic call to the so-called "shariatisation of the state and society" in a way that nonetheless reifies liberal-democratization and human rights charades. Both projects fail to grapple with decolonization, as they both reflect inferiority complexes and the desire to accommodate Euro-Americanist paradigms of "human rights" and "democracy," while completely displacing these terms from both history and geopolitics.

The stakes have never been higher, especially given what former Al-Jazeera journalist, now independent filmmaker, Ali al-Arian referred to as the "Ice Cream Politics of Muslim Americans" that "promotes moral relativism and political apathy by presenting important political choices as morally inconsequential personal preferences," a condition which extends globally due to colonized mindsets.[79] This can be seen in the participation of Hamza Yusuf, founder of the (neo)conservative Zaytuna Institute, in Trump's Human Rights Commission and Yusuf's collaboration with the UAE and Saudi Arabia, who are keen on normalizing ties with Israel and have long exported and logistically supported *takfiri*-Wahhabi movements all over SWANA region. Not unrelatedly, we find professional politicians like "The Squad" and many activists who elide addressing their own settler-of-color complicity in settler-colonialism, and consistently advocate for an unapologetic progressive "American-Islām" strictly focused on civic engagement and performative allegiance to the American dream and flag while lacking roots in decolonization.

Islām has become foreign to Muslims and non-Muslims alike, as Muslims are unable to identify what are core tenets to apply in a present which they fail to grasp. The only vision of an Umma that most Muslims see is exemplified in movements such as Daesh or al-Qaeda, which are reactionary products of the past. In all these cases, Anarchic Ijtihād offers a genuine opportunity for their liberation as Muslims as well as allies responsible for the liberation of others and to whose fate they are tied.

The potential to make a difference does not lie in Anarcha-Islām itself, which is simply a product of many encounters, but in the contentions and terrains upon which Anarcha-Islām is premised. Amongst these contentions is the fact that figures valorized by the contemporary Left such as Alexandra Ocasio-Cortez, Bernie Sanders, as well as movements such as the Women's March are not decolonial.[80] Their strategies – voting, reforming laws, protests for equality, and a national assimilationist politics of citizen rights – evoke two central pillars of representative democracy: (neo) liberal humanism and multicultural identity politics. However, as numerous radical BIPOC knowledge keepers and movement organizers have argued, these paradigms and identitarian reference points structurally and symbolically humanize white bodies while dehumanizing BIPOC. Relying on approaches based on investments in as opposed to divestments from these (neo)colonial/imperial ideals ultimately, although perhaps not intentionally, re-entrenches white ascendance and individualism. Adopting an unapologetic "hyphenated-American" citizen-identity is adopting a (neo)colonial identity that allows settler-colonialism, imperialism, neoliberalism, and global Orientalism to thrive. In our own settler-colonial U.S./Canadian landscape, our integration as diasporic SWANA Muslims arrives at the expense of Indigenous and Black peoples. The adamant refusal by diasporic SWANA Muslims to critically interrogate their settler-colonial positioning and to decolonize their colonized identities and interpretations of Islām makes us no different from Zionist settlers in Palestine.

In contrast, decolonization operates from the premise that representative democracy, which is ultimately anchored in capitalist-state structures, is a neocolonial product of modernity. It is an extension of an ongoing Euro-American neoimperialist project that we ceaselessly subordinate ourselves to in non-Euro-American and Euro-American societies. Thus, decolonial strategies are not focused on the seizure of the nation-state, with the aim of enacting change from within. Decolonial approaches do not strategically invest in the reform of Euro-American nation-state laws that evict BIPOC. Rather, decolonization recognizes that in a neoliberal age, there is no separation between capitalism and nation-states and that there is a direct correlative relationship between settler-colonial societies (such as the U.S./Canada) and franchise or so-called post-colonial societies such as Egypt, neither of which have undergone decolonization.

In Chapter 2, I illuminate Anarchic Ijtihād, the method I use to construct Anarcha-Islām in Chapters 3 and 4. This method is derived from its classical form Ijtihād, which is the Islamic practice of using independent and rigorous reasoning while interpreting and re-interpreting Islamic principles in the Sunnah and the Qur'ān. After introducing Anarchic Ijtihād, I defend its use against possible objections, such as those of some orthodox Muslim scholars as well as progressive Muslims. I argue for Anarchic Ijtihād given the general absence within Muslim communities of local *thaqāfa* (critical cultural consciousness and intellect), *al-intāg al-maʿrify* (knowledge production), and Ijtihād (independent reasoning and critical exegesis or *tafsīr* of unsettled issues in the Qur'ān, the Sunnah (the prophetic practice), and the aḥādīth (the prophetic Oral Tradition), as well as within Islamic texts and legal sources). I conclude this chapter with a discussion of what transnational decolonization is. Specifically, I argue that social movements in Egypt and Turtle Island need to engage in struggles that emphasize gender egalitarianism, the feminization of our politics, and the critique of cisheteropatriarchy embedded within the capitalist-state through an alternative focus on land-based struggles.

I then discuss, from a macro-political perspective, and in line with Saul Newman (2001), Rolando Perez (1990), Gilles Deleuze, and Félix Guattari (1980), the relationship between Anarcha-Islām and the capitalist-state. I do this by defining a triadic relationship that consists of: *Daddy*, symbolizing authoritarian practices of the types macro and micro, *Mommy*, symbolizing capitalist practices, and *Me*, as an Oedipal subject. After defining the Oedipal relationship according to these parameters, I discuss the particular role of the modern-state and capitalism.[81] Anarcha-Islām's relation to the capitalist-state is that it resembles a clinic that I, an Oedipal subject, recurrently visit to become relatively de-Oedipalized. In other words, I construct Anarcha-Islām as an act of resistance to the capitalist-state. I do this while recognizing the impossibility of ever constructing a space of resistance "free" of capitalist and authoritarian practices and the representations ascribed to me by the capitalist-state.

In Chapter 3, I construct, using Anarchic Ijtihād, Anarcha-Islām's anti-authoritarian commitments with respect to micro and macro forms of authority. First, I introduce three micro-anti-authoritarian concepts and practices I extract from Islām: *Shūrā* (mutual consultation), *Ijmāʿ* (community consensus), and *Maṣlaḥa* (public interest). I read *Shūrā*, *Ijmāʿ*, and *Maṣlaḥa* as micro-anti-authoritarian concepts and practices that inform Anarcha-Islām's commitment to minimizing micro-authoritarian practices amongst individuals and communities. From there, given that "the State is not a point taking all the other [authoritarian practices] upon itself, but a resonance chamber for them all," I construct Anarcha-

Islām's anti-authoritarian commitment at the macro-level.[82] Anarcha-Islām's anti-authoritarian commitment at the macro-level involves an anti-institutional and anti-statist critique.

After constructing Anarcha-Islām's anti-statist commitments, I address the "authority" of Prophet Muḥammad and God. I argue, using the Qur'ān, that the Prophet Muḥammad is nothing beyond a *Rasūl*, a messenger, for a religious call, working purely for the sake of the call on behalf of Islām. With respect to the "authority" of God, I first argue that in Anarcha-Islām "there is no compulsion in religion."[83] That is, according to Anarcha-Islām and in line with the Qur'ānic verse cited, anarchists are not required to accept Anarcha-Islām's God, only to recognize the right of a Muslim to believe in God. Second, I argue, in line with Newman, that "God has not been completely usurped ... as has always been claimed [in anarchism] ... only reinvented in the form of essence."[84] According to this analysis, anarchists ought to acknowledge the difference between resisting God and resisting institutionalized religion. When anarchists resist God, God is not truly the object of resistance. Rather anarchists are resisting institutionalized religion. There is a difference between the two and therefore the two must not be conflated. Having addressed the authority of Prophet Muḥammad and God, Anarcha-Islām's resistance to micro- and macro-authoritarian practices will be constructed. In concluding Chapter 3, I discuss concepts such as the Nation, Waṭaniyyah, Qawmiyyah, the Dawla and the Umma in Arab and Muslim lexicons. Tamim al-Barghouti argues that in the wake of post-colonial independence movements Arabs and Muslims altered the meanings of their own language to correspond with European definitions, ontologies, and terminologies associated with "the nation" and capitalist-states.[85] I examine the history and consequences of these "translations" and conclude the chapter by reclaiming these terms and constructing an alternative Muslim and non-Muslim vision for a resurgent Umma based on Prophet Muḥammad's Medina Charter (*Mīthāq al-Madīnah*) and the Treaty of *Al-Ḥudaybiyah* (*Ṣulh al-Ḥudaybiyah*).

In Chapter 4, I construct, using Anarchic Ijtihād, Anarcha-Islām's resistance to capitalism through concepts and practices extracted from Islām. These concepts include: *Property*, *Communal* and *Individual Caretakers*, *Muḍārabah/Mushārakah*, *Ribā*, *Zakāt*, *Ramaḍān* or *Ṣawm*, *Ṣadaqat Al-Fiṭr* and *Islamic banking*. I interrogate each of these concepts to demonstrate Anarcha-Islām's anti-capitalist commitments. Having established Anarcha-Islām's anti-authoritarian and anti-capitalist commitments, I make two claims. First, that I am no longer Oedipalized but becoming relatively de-Oedipalized. Second, that Anarcha-Islām's construction is the symbolic act of delineating the two misconceptions of Islām and Muslims amongst anarchists.

In Chapter 5, I discuss the myth of nonviolence while engaging in social action and change. To do so I draw on radical Indigenous, Black, anarchistic, and Muslim social movement scholarship. I also distinguish between the concepts of *Qitāl* ("to battle") and *Jihād* ("to struggle") in Islām. Revolutions and decolonization inherently entail violence in the recomposition of society's forces. This goes against the Euro-American ostensible belief in the moral superiority of nonviolence, given that scholars and activists have long argued how violence is not a monolithic category and that "nonviolence protects the nation-state," and how revolutionary violence is a tactic and composes but a mere parcel of a grander strategy of resistance. Scholarship has long identified violence is non-monolithic and possesses distinct forms (symbolic, systemic, objective, subjective, revolutionary, violence that conserves laws, violence that founds laws).[86] In fact, as Frantz Fanon states, "violence is a cleansing force" because it fractures righteous, ideological and puritanical notions of self-identity and bears with it the potential to "free the native from" their "inferiority complex," "despair and inaction," through the instigation of "fearlessness" and restoration of "self-respect."[87]

In the final chapter, I re-emphasize the book's argument to facilitate the stalemated mainstream Arab, North African, and Muslim dialogue/mobilization on decolonization and social movements. This chapter re-emphasizes the book's arguments from a social movement perspective and transnationally connecting radical Indigenous, Black, and Muslim struggles to each other. I reassert the importance of decolonization given that the global entanglements of Muslims in Orientalist/Fundamentalist narratives is one of the factors in the reproduction of internalized discriminations, cisheteropatriarchy, queerphobia, biphobia, transphobia, racism/ethnocentrism, and classism, as well as internalized shame and Islamophobia in non-Euro-American and Euro-American societies.

2
Authoritarianism, Capitalism, and Capitalist Nation-States: Anarcha-Islām's Playground and Ethical-Political Consciousness

I have been thinking about the notion of perfect love as being without fear, and what that means for us in a world that's becoming increasingly xenophobic, tortured by fundamentalism and nationalism.

bell hooks[1]

Breaking the settler colonial triad, in direct terms means repatriating land to sovereign Native tribes and nations, abolition of slavery in its contemporary forms, and the dismantling of the imperial metropole. Decolonization "here" is intimately connected to anti-imperialism elsewhere. However, decolonial struggles here/there are not parallel, not shared equally, nor do they bring neat closure to the concerns of all involved – particularly not for settlers. Decolonization is not equivocal to other anti-colonial struggles. It is incommensurable. There is so much that is incommensurable, so many overlaps that can't be figured, that cannot be resolved. Settler colonialism fuels imperialism all around the globe. Oil is the motor and motive for war and so was salt, so will be water. Settler sovereignty over the very pieces of earth, air, and water is what makes possible these imperialisms. The same yellow pollen in the water of the Laguna Pueblo reservation in New Mexico, Leslie Marmon Silko reminds us, is the same uranium that annihilated over 200,000 strangers in 2 flashes. The same yellow pollen that poisons the land from where it came. Used in the same war that took a generation

> of young Pueblo men. "Indian Country" was/is the term used in Vietnam, Afghanistan, Iraq by the U.S. military for "enemy territory".
>
> Eve Tuck & K. Wayne Wang (2012, 31–2)[2]

> Fascism is a mass psychology … It's too easy to be antifascist on the molar level, and not even see the fascist inside you, the fascist you yourself sustain and nourish and cherish with molecules both personal and collective. Desire is never an undifferentiated instinctual energy, but itself results from a highly developed, engineered setup rich in interactions: a whole supple segmentarity that processes molecular energies and potentially gives desire a fascist determination.
>
> Gilles Deleuze and Félix Guattari[3]

On Decolonization and Reindigenization, and the Crises of Fleeting Tahrir Moments

Fascism and totalitarianism are interrelated. However, Gilles Deleuze and Félix Guattari argue that unlike totalitarianism, fascism is a mass psychology: "The former [totalitarianism] impose[s] order and oppression from above through force (maybe through legislative power, police action, or military regimes), the latter [fascism] produces repression and order on the 'molecular' levels of family, neighborhoods, schools, etc."[4] In connecting the macro-political with the micro-political they add that it is easy to protest against the state and corporations, but more difficult to recognize that we tend to affirm the same repressive powers of racial capitalism and the state in our intimate relationships and communities, in our languages, in our habits, and in the infinitesimal casual horizontal and vertical negotiations of power that accompany them in our re-enacted micro-politics every day. Examples of internalized micro-fascistic practices are the diasporic settler of Indigenous dispossession and theft of land, participation in sexism, anti-blackness, ableist practices, even the advocating and promotion of the homonationalist and colonial/imperial enforcement of queer rights (marriage, pride) elsewhere vis-à-vis neoliberal social movements, as well as militarized development and human rights paradigms.

As I noted elsewhere, "when recent social movements claim they fear that Donald J. Trump has ushered-in fascism, they are naively mistaking fascism for totalitarianism."[5] Totalitarians impose draconian order from above through force, be it via police repression, legislative and judicial power, or even national emergencies, imposed curfews, and military regimes.[6] Fascism is promulgated at the "horizontal levels of the family, neighborhoods, schools, factories, hospitals," etc., and its goal is to transform us all into egoistic little Mussolinis and mini-gods in our public and private behaviors.[7] Fascism is facilitated through the dissemination of cultural and spiritual stereotypes that we all reproduce. Countering fascism requires the individual and collective struggle against our internalized authoritarian, utilitarian-materialist, and patriarchal micro-fascisms through *al-jihād al-akbar* (otherwise understood as the "greater jihād" in Islām). Fascism spirals from the top down, but is reinforced from the bottom up and is re-enacted horizontally in our daily lives. Fascism is the "cancer" we must fight and our liberation depends on its defeat.[8] What makes fascism more dangerous than totalitarianism is its insidiousness: fascism is mobilized on a mass scale, operating in all vectors and spiraling directions. In particular, "fascism is encoded within and reinforced by the capitalist-States" and we express our internalized micro-fascisms relative to the symbolic and structural privileges that we each enjoy and reproduce at the grassroots during our social encounters.[9] Struggling against fascism means struggling against our own selves.

Richard J.F. Day notes that there is a monumental distinction, as per the example of the Tahrir Uprisings of 2011–13, between an anti-statist "politics of the act" and "politics of demand."[10] The latter relies on reformist assimilation and the seizure of state power to enact social change from above and within and hence "assumes the existence of a dominant nation attached to a monopolistic state, which must be persuaded to give the gifts of recognition and integration to subordinate identities and communities."[11] Islamic anarchism and Anarcha-Islām is constructed on the recognition of the limits of the politics of demand for civic rights, whether through the reformist reshuffling of state power or appeals to Euro-American humanist international development organizations. Historically, efforts to alter state laws have often been hijacked by regional forces, nationalist elites, and imperialist agendas that hinder post-colonial capitalist nation-states, even at the height of 1955 Bandung conferences, pan-Arab, pan-African, pan-Asiatic, as well as Third-World and non-aligned movements. This commandeering prevents changes that transcend the (neo)colonial state frameworks and genuine reconciliation and decolonization. In contrast, a logic of affinity is premised on the realization that "as individuals and members of communities, [we] must free ourselves, in an effort that cannot be expected to terminate in a final event of revolution."[12] This entails not only an active refusal of state control, but also the radical recreation of native and Indigenous systems of spiritual and ethico-political governance, as per the example of the Zapatista movement in Chiapas, Mexico, since 1994. Decolonization recognizes that our spiritual evolution as a species has been hindered by tyranny, poverty, and mass ignorance. Historically, it is striving towards the accumulation of wealth, power, prestige, and authority, that has acted as an insatiable motivating force and justification to inflict and re-enact cycles of racial and gendered violence while also scapegoating religion as the source of war and violence.

Decolonization through an engagement with affinity-based politics implies channeling our ache for liberation towards a collective means of production, in which we are all contributing producers and not mere individualist consumers. Decolonization means being free to love and possess collective access to food, clothing, homes, and medicine, indeed being free to cultivate rhizomatic networks of hospitality, caring, an ethics of sharing, and disagreeing. It also denotes the legitimate freedom to determine the spiritual-political education of our children in communal responsibilities and self-governance, traditional ecological knowledges and ethical technologies, non-Euro-American civilizational architectures, non-intrusive healing practices, as well as what constitutes healthy active communication skills relative to our entwined histories, knowledge systems and literatures, including the arts, all that are grounded in land upon which our families and communities are nourished, can thrive, and flourish.[13] Contrary to progressive-statist agendas imaginatively caged by liberalism's blinding spell, decolonization demands the construction of diffuse and decentralized political power. It also requires the determination of cooperative and cumulative meanings to truth, falsehood, and dissent, to make sense and possible broad and multiple interpretations of our ethico-political principles, spiritualities, and philosophies as a foundation for all our relations to nonhuman life. Decolonization warrants exposing the biopolitical/necropolitical collaborations of dehumanized bodies that differentiate between white subjects, who are optimized and folded (back) into life and productivity (i.e., marriage and reproductive kinship) and racialized-gendered-queered subjects that are endlessly reinscribed into death as dehumanized figures to conjunctively fuel "the oscillation between the disciplining of subjects and control of populations."[14] The theme of land and how it defines desire relative to settler-futurities to simultaneously evict Indigenous peoples "out of time" (in an effort to construct them as past signpost ghosts to history) and POC as "out of space" (in an effort to cast them as displaced subjects and unbelonging diasporas and migrants) is a key theme in decolonization discourses that seek to understand how restructuring land transforms practices and perceptions of spirituality, gender, and sexuality in settler and post-colonial nations such as the U.S./Canada as well as Egypt.[15] At once, diasporic SWANA settlers to Turtle Island are violently exploited and, yet, complicit in Indigenous disappearance. Explored in Chapter 3 is that one cannot be *Indigenous*, or more precisely engage in *indigeneity*, *decolonization*, and *reindigenization*, if one acquiesces to the authoritarian and materialist logics of racial and gendered (neo)colonialism. To do so is to actively partake in self-dispossession and immolation from land-based relationships that make us human and secure our *humanity* in the first place. To "become indigenous" dictates us to think of expansive authoritarian statist and individualist racial-materialist exorcism as the gendered removal of our bodies, hearts, minds and dirt-ridden fingers from the intimacies of earthen yellow, green, black, red, and brown soils.[16]

Decolonization also (further) presupposes a violent unsettling of everything internalized that "cultures of whiteness" and their "civilizational progressive" values ushered in. This, in fact, constitutes most of the presuppositions you and I know of our entwined (neo) colonially fractured histories and present identity crises. Decolonization implies unavoidable violence in the unmaking of our own (neo)liberal-constructed identities and the dismantling of the "Oppression Olympics" or the competition between entwined struggles that endlessly pit us against one another, when as colonized BIPOC communities and marginalized groups we ought to be natural allies. In turn, decolonization is an active (not a reactive neocolonial) act. Decolonization calls for the recognition of our species' creative and unfathomable feats, yet also our disposability, finiteness, and insignificance.

An ethic of healing must be conceived and embraced, but this cannot happen either without acknowledging and being accountable for the ways that we, as BIPOC, and all that is in between, collectively hurt and wound each other. White supremacy must be recognized as a "key pillar of the settler colonial state" and this knowledge can be "mobilized as common ground for solidarity among [colonized] people."[17] Clearly, it is neither the responsibility nor place for white settlers, even those engaged as radical allies with Indigenous peoples, to ascribe or school POC, "even if in the [latter's] capacity to oppress Indigenous people."[18] In other words, white allies possess their own settler-culpabilities and imperialist complicities, and it is their responsibility to allow and permit us the space and time – as BIPOC communities – to order and rearrange our own house. It is ours to strategize, and theirs to engage, participate in, and support, even if that entails placing their bodies on the line for us, as ours have been all along and continue to be.

It is also the case that even when Euro-American allies polemically espouse more radical non-statist and non-capitalist social movement trajectories, beyond the reformist liberal-progressive agendas described above, they delimit their activism, teaching, and scholarly citation trails to European literatures that suit their philosophical debates, fragile egos, guilt, and comfort. Euro-American allies cannot continue to ornamentally deploy intersectionality without understanding that in the absence of a decolonial/anti-colonial/and anti-imperial framework in their analyses, their narrative is, in fact, toothless. Euro-American allies cannot conveniently continue to teach gender and queer theories without engaging Indigenous and radical Black feminisms as well as Two-Spirit, queer Indigenous, queer Black, and queer of color critiques, particularly when the former discourses center settler-colonialism. Empire's settler-colonialism informs the very context in which all theories must be applied and the trajectory in which radical social movements are mobilized relative to both local struggles and similar resistances worldwide.

Therefore we cannot predetermine or predict what a decolonized and reindigenized world will look like but we can and must prepare for it. Decolonization entails what I refer to as a *biodiverse strategy of resistance*. Decolonization is filled with anxieties because it relies on the understanding that land, its clay from which we are made, and nonhuman life have much to teach us spiritually and materially regarding our species' purpose and existence as well as the transcending of mind/land and mind/body dichotomies. In other words, we must understand that all "the answers are not fully in view and will not emerge from friendly understanding either" as what is required is a "dangerous understanding of uncommonality that un-coalesces coalition politics – [and hence involves] moves that may feel very unfriendly."[19]

Thus Spoke God: The Method of Anarchic Ijtihād

True liberation exists outside of the neocolonial/neoimperial framework of capitalist nation-states that geopolitically (re)produce racialized, gendered, sexualized, Orientalized, and dehumanized non-Euro-American unfortunates who must be saved or overcome. This framing shapes debates on Islām that all too often begin with predetermined assumptions about Islām's compatibility with Euro-American democracy, feminism, queerness and much more, obscuring how these discursive interjections are constructions of settler-and-franchise colonial societies.[20] This leaves both (neo) conservative and (neo)liberal-progressive Muslims the choice of identifying with either a so-called assimilationist superior Euro-American identitarian belonging or an intolerant and savage Islām and non-Euro-American existence. To liberate ourselves, we must rediscover what it is to dream dangerously again – to reimagine ourselves and reclaim our own decolonial, non-authoritarian, SWANA, Indigenous and Black models of governance, non-materialist ethical-political values, and spiritual knowledge systems.[21]

To liberate our colonized minds and free our hearts and souls from the false binary choices, decolonized knowledge production and education are indispensable. As Audre Lorde states, "the master's tools will never dismantle the master's house."[22] This boundless disassembling and rebuilding has less to do with engaging in high-theory, itself a culturally specific and privileged way of knowing, than with teaching ourselves how to symbiotically fuse liberatory theory and praxis. This is done to enable critical thought and acceptance of criticism such that we can strategically determine and contextualize what we are fighting against and for. Thus, liberatory theory arrives from and is grounded in frontline social movement experience and praxis.[23]

To build such a liberatory theory, I draw on theoretical frameworks such as transnational queer of color and queer diaspora critiques, SWANA and Muslim feminisms, and post-colonial and critical race, settler-colonial, and decolonization theories. I also draw on schizo/psychoanalytic and post-anarchist social movement discourses in light of Tahrir Square and recent impetuses such as Idle No More, NoDAPL, Black Lives Matter, and historical revolutionary Red and Black Power trajectories as well as contemporary movements like La Vía Campesina and the Zapatistas. The result is a decolonial, anti-racist, and queer-feminist methodology I call *Anarchic Ijtihād*.

Using Anarchic Ijtihād as a method of interpretation, I carry out a critical exegesis of the Qur'ān, as well as other Islamic and anarchistic texts. Some orthodox Muslim scholars, known in Arabic as *muftīs*, *sheikhs*, or *Īmāms*, will doubtless regard this method as heresy, whereas liberal-secularist Muslims and non-Muslims such as Asef Bayat and Oliver Roy will regard it as useless and irrelevant. The accusation of heresy will be levied under the guise of safeguarding Islām from an impure and tainted Euro-American reading, when, truthfully, the issue relates to discursive power, specifically its hegemonic concentration within institutions versus its dissemination amongst the Muslim populace at large. On the other side, (neo)liberal Muslims such as Bayat, while not exactly anti-Islamic, argue that the political role of religion should be strictly limited, given his consistent assumption that the burden of responsibility is always on Islām and Muslims to make the case for their compatibility with Euro-American civilizational values.[24] In his critique of Bayat's post-Islamism, Milad Dokhanchi argues this secularist viewpoint not only fails to recognize how Islām can inform political consciousness, but also fails to recognize the antipathy of early Islamist movements to statism and more recent cultural and political movements that "resist identifying with Islam as an ideology of state domination."[25]

In defense of Anarchic Ijtihād, I argue that Islām grants the right to conduct a critical exegesis of the Qur'ān. This right, whose classical form is referred to as Ijtihād, literally implies striving. Ijtihād denotes not only an Islamic right, but an obligatory duty, entrusted by God to Muslims involved in scholarly-activist study, to rigorously (re)interpret Islamic ethico-political principles and thereby engage in "independent reasoning."[26] Anarchic Ijtihād is so-named to highlight that it is an anarchistic type of Ijtihād. Anarchic Ijtihād is the "deconstructive" logic and force I use to reread conceptual and pragmatic practices in the Qur'ān and the Prophetic Oral Tradition(s) and practice(s) that inherently resonate with anarchism.

As a method, Anarchic Ijtihād is derived from its classical form Ijtihād. Ijtihād is the Islamic utility of deploying independent and rigorous reasoning while (re)interpreting Islamic principles in the Sunnah (Prophetic practice), *aḥādīth* (Prophetic Oral Tradition), and the Qur'ān. This expounded act of re-interpreting is referred to as "*tafsīr*."[27] The interpretation or study of aḥādīth is its own scientific discipline (*'lm al-aḥādīth*). Though there might be overlaps, each use of sacred scripture and practical/oral tradition needs to be understood in the context of their use and their interrelated discourses, conventions, and so forth. It is the very pragmatism of the aḥādīth, the Sunnah – complexities of critical exegesis of the Qur'ān aside – that allows those employing the concept and practice of Ijtihād (independent judgment) to reach varying jurisprudential positions.[28] When engaging in Ijtihād, scholars give differing degrees of consideration to *naskh al-naṣ* (abrogation of a Qur'ānic injunction by the Sunnah or vice versa), *akhbār* (traditions of "Īmams"), *asbāb al-nuzūl* (reasons for revelation), *taqwā* (the degree to which one's "piety" demonstrates attentive care relative to knowledge inspired by God), *taqiyya* (the degree to which caution is exercised), *Ijmāʿ* (degree to which consensus is exercised), *istiṣlāḥ* (the degree to which consideration of what is inconsistent with *maṣlaḥa*, or social justice and public interest is illustrated), *istiḥsān* (the degree to which there is preference for interpretations or rules in other schools of law that seem more in line with considerations of equity), *taqlīd* (the idea that precedent must be faithfully followed or "imitated"), *qudrah* (creative power), and even the extent to which there is *ʿaql* (reasoning by syllogism).[29] Ijtihād also requires attentiveness towards social justice (*al-ʿadala al-ijtimāʿiya*), *qamʿ* (suppression), *ẓulm* (oppression), the Qur'ānic demand for proper intuition (*yatadhakarūn*), wisdom (*hikma*), mystical gnosis (*ʿirfān*), the science of words or speech-acts (*ʿIlm al-kalām*), balanced rational-thinking (*afalā yaʿqilūn* or *Yatafakarūn*), as well as due consideration to the ephemerality of judgments (*ahkām*). All these traversing dimensions in turn impact *al-Qawāʿid al-Fiqhiyyah* (Islamic legal jurisprudential maxims) as well as *al-Uṣūl al-ʿAmaliyyah* (procedural principles), which cannot be ignored in discerning and interpreting dimensions of a non-monolithic and non-totalizing moralistic and ethical-political *Sharīʿa* and its accompanying *al-ʿaqāed al-akhlākiya* (corpus of Islamic ways and laws).[30]

The aforementioned procedures allow Muslims to distinguish not only between morals and ethics, but also between practical Islamic laws (*ḥukm wāqʿy*) and the derived meanings and lessons (*maqāṣid*) which are contingent on the former. Maqāṣid are contingent on situational ethico-political realms (*uṣūl* and *al-siyāsāt*) and depend on the spatial-temporal existence of social justice within a society.[31] *Ḥukm wāqʿy* is dependent on *ḥukm ẓāheri* (apparent Islamic law) and allows Muslims to determine what is indeed *wājib* (obligatory) and what constitutes *fiqh* (jurisprudential ethics) in relation to maqāṣid.

Anarchic Ijtihād this way distinguishes intersections and distinctions between non-holistic moralistic corpuses (*Sharīa*) always open to interpretation relative to ethics (*uṣūl*). Sharīa or "morality asks what people *should* do, while ethics [through *uṣūl al-fiqh*] asks what people *can* do."[32] With this distinction, this Islamic interpretation centralizes ethics as a license (*rukhṣah*) that grants exceptions under cautionary circumstances (*iḥtiyāṭ*) from abstract ideal-moralistic generalized standards, as when the Qur'ān states, "God has forbidden you only carrion, blood, the flesh of swine, and what has been offered to other than God. *But whosoever is compelled by necessity – neither coveting nor transgressing – no sin shall be upon them.* Truly God is Forgiving, Merciful."[33] Hence, in exceptional circumstances something that is otherwise forbidden (carrion, blood, and swine) *may be* granted an epistemically valid rukhṣah as a form of alleviation, based on the legitimized basis of the divine values of compassion and mercy that encompasses all. As the Qur'ān states, "God tasks no soul beyond its capacity. It shall have what it has earned and be subject to what it has perpetrated."[34]

By ignoring distinctions between ethics and morals, (neo)conservative scholars elide the Muslim scholar's (*mujtahid/ah*) quest for intellectual self-reflexivity, and the interdisciplinary necessity of engaging broader Muslim discourses. Khaled Abou El Fadl notes in "The Epistemology of the Truth in Modern Islam," the realities of different historical and cultural contexts in which Islām exists means that the constant, objective truth (*ḥaq*), which is the "reality of an ever creative and creating God," can only be comprehended through the never-ending quest for all knowledge (*ʿilm*) and wisdom (*ḥikma*) of a given era to attain an adequate balance (*mizān*) that honors every historical moment's circumstances with all its ethical-political contingencies. Furthermore each era must find the epistemologies (*maʿrifa*) that are suitable for this process while addressing the *ẓāhir* (exoteric surface) and *bāṭin* (esoteric depth) particularly as they relate to Qur'ānic verses.[35] After all "Godliness means an ever-present Creator and an ever-present inventor

… in partnership with human beings."[36] The role of the Muslim scholar, according to Abou El Fadl, is to "unveil the esoteric depths of revelation through spiritual interpretation [*tawīl*]."[37]

Unfortunately most contemporary *muftīs* (Muslim jurists) in predominantly Muslim societies, extending the nation-state institutions, seek to confirm their own predetermined convictions through the manipulation of aḥādīth, the Sunnah, and the Qur'ān with the aim of strictly maintaining authoritarian, cisheteropatriarchal and racial-materialist social norms and orders. In my own work on queer-feminist Egyptian Muslims, for instance, relating to the conflation of modern gender and sexuality, Grand muftīs of pre-eminent institutions such as al-Azhar University make strict and selective use of legalistic and archival pre-modern sources to support their settled conclusions. In contrast, a hardly insignificant number of medieval Muslim jurists recognized that their Ijtihād and adjudications (*fatwā*) ought to embody the Islamic ethic of *raḥma* (mercy and compassion) and that the Creator is the sole authority and arbiter of intents (*niyya*). Instead, most muftīs today exacerbate injustices and tend to demonstrate a lack of consideration for social justice (*'adāla ijtimā'iya*), *qahr* (repression), *qam'* (suppression), *ẓulm* (oppression), and gender egalitarianism. In so doing they do not heed the ḥadīth that states: "Beware of the supplication of the oppressed for there is no barrier between it and Allāh."[38]

Anarchic Ijtihād is committed to identifying and re-interpreting, if necessary, anti-capitalist and anti-authoritarian principles in the Sunnah, aḥādīth, and the Qur'ān. Anarchic Ijtihād is positioned to identify these anarchic commitments in Islām, such that the interpretation I am advocating for, Anarcha-Islām, reveals its resonances with anarchism. Similarly, Anarchic Ijtihād is used to reread Islamic anti-capitalist and anti-authoritarian commitments in anarchism such that they may divulge Anarcha-Islām. Because Anarchic Ijtihād is an anarchically oriented Ijtihād, it is not only a form of critical or discursive form of analysis. Anarchic Ijtihād, by virtue of the very definition of Ijtihād, is a method I use to confer judgments in favour of Anarcha-Islām, an ethical and political Islām I believe in. Furthermore it affords me the capacity to critique interpretations of Islām that do not uphold Anarcha-Islām's anti-authoritarian and anti-capitalist commitments. I regard these commitments as Islamic commitments, just as I regard them as anarchist commitments. Anarcha-Ijtihād too is the method I use to coalesce the individual anti-authoritarian and anti-capitalist concepts and practices from Islām for Anarcha-Islām. As a mujtahid/ah, I prefer to "deconstruct," or genealogically work through, challenging the historical revelatory contexts of the Qur'ānic *ayāt* (verses), and if necessary within ethical and political contexts re-envision them to provide the Islamic justification(s) for the verse's re-interpretation using Anarchic Ijtihād. I do this not to demonstrate weak alternatives for the verse, but rather to construct a stronghold around a rightful position from it in Anarcha-Islām, as "derived" from Islām. This is the case even when it comes to so-called "ugly" verses in the Qur'ān that specifically pertain to issues of gender and sexuality, even slavery, the subject of my forthcoming work and which Muslim feminist scholars have already addressed, and on whose analyses respectively I build on and further to, in my doctorate on *Islam and Queer Muslims: Identity and Sexuality in the Contemporary World* (2019) through what I refer to as *queer Muslim critique* as an extension of Anarchic Ijtihād when discussing SWANA Muslim gender and sexualities.[39]

This analysis recognizes that the language of the Qur'ān is, at different times, (a) explicit and precise, describing matters and events or offering reminders, clear lessons, codes, or meticulous principles and ethical-political grounded "guidelines" to Muslims, (b) fraught with metaphors, allegories and parables that call upon its readers to contemplate or reflect, as they are verses explicit in their narration of scripture that could be easily taken as informed by and informing ethical-political trajectories and historiographies, or (c) charged by the use of Divine phrases that are sacredly "secret" and to which *al-ghayb* (the divine unforeseen) is applicable.[40]

One example of such (*al-ghayb*) verses resides in the second chapter of the Qur'ān. The chapter is titled "The Cow," inaugurated with the verse "Alif Lām Mīm." The verse is comprised of three Arabic letters "Alif," "Lām" and "Mīm," which do not articulate an Arabic word. The particularities of this verse, of which there exist ample similar Qur'ānic examples, are "beyond the reach of human perception included in the term al-ghayb."[41] In this light, no mujtahid/a possesses the ability to delve into interpretation of al-ghayb verses (otherwise referred to as *ḥurūf mutaqāṭ'a*) as "Alif Lām Mīm." While a mujtahid/ah is permitted commentary upon these types of verses, their interpretative comments are bound to and cannot contradict or nullify what has been generally stated in other verses in the Qur'ān. That is, "Alif Lām Mīm" cannot contravene enshrined principles of faith as the divinity of God. Allāh, states in Verse 3:7 of the Qur'ān of these types of ambiguous verses:

> It is They who has sent down to you, [O Muḥammad], the Book; in it are verses [that are] precise – they are the foundation of the Book – and others unspecific. As for those in whose hearts is deviation [from truth], they will follow that of it, which is unspecific, seeking discord and seeking an interpretation [suitable to them]. And no one knows its [true] interpretation except Allāh. But those firm in knowledge say, "We believe in it. All [of it] is from our Lord". And no one will be reminded except those of understanding.

Creator therefore strictly demands in the antecedent verse from a mujtahid/ah that when a verse as "Alif Lām Mīm" appears that the mujtahid/a simply accepts its ambiguity, not that they should not engage it. In a sense, a mujtahid/a's responsibility here is one that exceeds that of conducting a discursive analysis of the text. That is what *faith* is. This means a mujtahid/ah's duty exceeds that of Ijtihād, as in incessantly analyzing, rationalizing, and comprehending the circumstances responsible for the revelation of a verse as "Alif Lām Mīm" or the linguistic boundaries of the verse itself. The mujtahid/ah ultimately accepts the verse as God's verse, as "is." The verse is not to be interrogated excessively, understood or misunderstood, but above all appreciated as it exceeds, indeed lies beyond a mujtahid/a's grasp and comprehension, belonging to the realm of the invisible spirit which will, at least in this life, evade truth. For this reason, I defer to no such types of verses to construct Anarcha-Islām. These types of verses are noted because they exist to humble in particular Arabs as to their own language as well as their ability to reason rationally – all that rationality ultimately represents is a region carved out of that which is irrational; one individual may rationalize Creator, while another does not. As the Qur'ān states in Verse 9:101, "The wandering Arabs are more hard in disbelief and hypocrisy, and more likely to be ignorant of the limits which Allāh hath revealed unto Them." In Verse 2:62 the Qur'ān also notes, "And among those around you of the wandering Arabs there are hypocrites, and among the townspeople of Al-Madinah (there are some who) persist in hypocrisy whom thou (O Muḥammad) knowest not. We, We know them, and We shall chastise them twice; then they will be." It is clear that the Qur'ān is a complicated text that necessitates a reader comprehend its exceptional abilities composed of lyrical pauses, ebbs, flows, each verse subject to the tidal sails of its reader and journeyer's soul, mind, and heart, as one becomes a nomad mariner amongst 114 chapters composing an ever-grandest ocean. The Arabic word *ʿayn* in the Qur'ān may shift from meaning "an organ of sight" to "running water," from "pure gold" to a "spy."[42] Through Ijtihād the Qur'ānic "word qar' (plural: quroo') can either mean menstruation" or the exact opposite, "purity following menstruation."[43] Moreover, the Qur'ān is laced with descriptive accounts of tales of past prophets, calling upon its Muslim and non-Muslim listeners and readers to contemplate the very truth of words divine, their multiplicitous signification(s), and consequences, to derive and draw reason(s), substance, from the roots of former histories, and of what in essence is an Oral Tradition whose emphasis and purpose is the dissemination of knowledge and the sharing of egalitarian practices. Peter Lamborn Wilson (aka Hakim Bey) is respectively merited when he claims, "the Qur'ān is to be listened to first" besides triangulating between various translations and exercising one's judgment, in comprehending, contextualizing, and applying what one learns.[44] It is with this intent, purpose, and in action that Ijtihād is guided and anchored in *musāwāh* (equality) and *ʿadāla* (justice) as its compass while distinguishing between what are mutually obligated responsibilities (*al-masuliyyāt al-jamāʿi-*

yyah) among members of the same polity (*jamāʿat al-mūmineen*) and what pertains to particularities of an individual (*khuṣuṣiyāt*) to both preserve communal responsibilities while maintaining the autonomy of an individual subject.[45]

As an Arab and Arabic reader keen on *Fiqh al-lughah*, a pre-modern field of study that includes "literary theory, linguistic theories, literary criticism, grammar, and philology," I find the Qur'ān a formidable text for this type of analysis.[46] For there can be little doubt that the Qurʾān can speak a thousand untold secrets, truths, and "falsehoods," to modern readers, especially those unfamiliar with the distinct grammatical context and syntax, creating volatile uncertainty. There are always more blank spaces in a text than what is written in black. Moreover, as much as the Qur'ān consistently calls for unwavering faith, to root out hypocrisy (*nifāq*), it also designates non-compulsive and reflexive expectations to that faith, calling on all believers and readers to reflect (*al-tafakur*), to contemplate (*i'tibār*), to deliberate (*tadabur*), to ponder (*istibṣār*), to remember (*tadhakur*), to examine (*nathr*), and to meditate (*taʿāmul*), while respecting the universe and al-ghayb, as is clear in innumerable verses (such as 2:219, 2:266, 3:191, 6:50, 7:176, 7:184, 10:24, 13:3, 16:69, 16:43, 16:44, 16:69, 30:8, 30:21, 34: 46, 39: 42, 45: 13, and 59:21). The Qurʾān creates this variability while also disabling the degree to which heresy can be committed against it. This is because the Qur'ān prides itself on being a text of moderation, that is, lucid yet considerate to the understanding and comprehension of readers; particularly, those engaging its untranslated and unmitigated words in Arabic. As a text, it is the Qurʾān that haunts, binds, and sustains Islām, amongst whose meanings is "the middle path," and without which Islām does not exist. It is God that protects the Qur'ān, Muslims, and Islām, when God claims in two verses: "Absolutely, we have revealed the reminder, and, absolutely, we will preserve it"[47] and "This is an honorable Qurʾān in a protected book. None can grasp it except the sincere. A revelation from the Lord of the universe."[48] It is in light of these complexities of interpreting Islām that anarchists should not feed into its stereotyping Islām, because the East and Islām "don't have the same regimes of truth" as the West.[49]

Deleuze and Guattari's Oedipal Triad: The Nation-State (Daddy) – Capitalism (Mommy) – and Me/Us

Nation(alism), Patriotism, and the Modern-State (Daddy)

Although nations are products of the human imagination, they nonetheless evoke real, even zealous, sentiments, because they speak to our innate communal longing. But it is clear that modern nationalism is philosophically bankrupt when even its most avid and sympathetic of students, Tom Nairn, acknowledges that nationalism is a

> pathology of modern development history, as inescapable as "neurosis" in the individual, with much the same essential ambiguity attaching to it, a similar built-in capacity for descent into dementia, rooted in the dilemmas of helplessness thrust upon most of the world (the equivalent of infantilism for societies) and largely incurable.[50]

Nationalism is the product of colonialism and an imperial product of modernity. Nations are inventions, which is not to say that nations are false, but rather that they are created.[51] The identities that a people imagine for themselves in this context, and the concurrent nationalist binding, aspirations, and artificial forms of solidarities they evoke are informed and defined by ongoing experiences of (neo)colonial/imperial joys, pains, and traumas. Furthermore, national narratives are constantly recreated and re-envisioned through continual back and forth attempts at reifying but also resisting the encroaching penetrations of colonialism.[52] Nations construct realities of and for themselves as a unified, monolithic, community, defined in relation to a white-supremacist world and the "cultures of whiteness" that depict colonized peoples as purportedly inferior savages.

Modern nationalism's power is that it invests in cisheteropatriarchal statist politics of citizenship. The contemporary architectural framework of the state is what binds both the communitarian idea of nation together and exposes its fragmented constituents as disparate minorities who are subsequently exposed to xenophobic patriotic sentiments that imagine the nation-state's identity as eternal and pure. For instance, modern Egyptians are xenophobically and discriminately socialized to think of themselves as white and Pharaonic, denying their North African roots.[53] The perception persists even though Egyptian racial/ethnic identity is, like any other, contrived. The Egyptian population reflects the conquest and colonization by the Hyksos, Persians, Greeks, Romans, Arabs, Ottomans, French, and British, and a more recent influx of Sudanese, Ethiopian, Somali, Iraqi, and Palestinian refugees.

Contemporary Arab literature generally recognizes "nationalism," the "nation," the "state," and "patriotism" as four distinct but interrelated concepts whose significations and meanings have also been repositioned in modernity because of the conflation between their pre-modern Islamic native roots and contemporary Arabization, as will be discussed in Chapter 3.[54] Nevertheless, for many colonized peoples, modern nationalism is nothing more than an apparition, and is a consequence of ethno-racial-cultural and spiritual interactions among colonized peoples who have (re) settled, and are residing temporally within the same territories, particularly along the metropolitan-peripheral boundaries that (neo)colonialism/imperialism structured and that are constantly being redefined by political and corporate elites.

Indigenous critiques, decolonial and anti-racist feminist scholarship have long argued that decolonial land struggles must challenge nationalist narratives, which are entwined with colonizers' exploitative feminization and sexualization of native and indigenous places.[55] Patrick Wolfe states, "Whatever settlers may say – and they generally have a lot to say – the primary motive [of settler colonialism] is not race (or religion, ethnicity, grade of civilization, etc.) but access to a nation's territory. Territoriality is settler colonialism's specific, irreducible element."[56] Though Wolfe is speaking of settler-colonialism, his statement is also applicable to what he and Lorenzo Veracini refer to as "franchise-colonial" societies, given how post-colonial subjects have adopted cultures of whiteness in relationship to land and nonhuman life as Lockean private property.[57] Vandalizing territory as a colonial/imperial project precedes or coincides with the disfiguration of a native people's non-heteronormative conceptualizations of gender/sexual epistemologies and practices, kinship structures, sovereignty, their composition as a nation and desire.[58] In addition to the overconsumption of natural resources that results in the forced displacement of men and women of color in favor of resource extraction and the Euro-American construction of neo-development resorts and accommodation, colonialism facilitates the prostitution of its native subjects. Similarly, sex tourism by white men/women to societies such as Egypt's involved the hyper-sexualization and eroticization of Egyptian men/women or the depiction of them as sexless. Sex tourism not only projected cis-heteropatriarchal practices but also eroticized the natives of the Global South.[59]

Narratives of the nation are individualized, feminized, and queered as queer diasporic and POC critiques have identified, even in how most queer scholarship is written in English, which in effect reifies already "uneven exchanges [that] replicate in uncomfortable ways the rise and consolidation of U.S. empire, as well as the consistent positing of a U.S. nationalist identity and political agenda globally."[60] These discourses note that the restriction of sexuality to an individual's sexual behaviors ultimately hinders queerness' political potential by disregarding its conjunction with race/ethnicity, gender, ability, nation, class, religion, capitalism, the state, and continuing imperialist/colonialist projects in non-Euro-American societies. In contrast, queer diasporic studies focus on expanding the interrogation of sexuality's relationship to citizenship, nationalism, race, and gender politics while undermining the triumph of individualist neoliberal marketplaces that obscure conflicts between global capital, labor, and the biopolitics and necropolitics of gendered, racialized, and sexualized bodies in a 9/11 era.[61] For example, in *Aberrations in Black: Towards a Queer of Color Critique*, Ferguson interrogates the ways in which Black scholarship and African American activism subvert their racialization through non-heteronormative nationalist practices while also reproducing heteronormative nightmares that consciously and unconsciously reproduce cisheteronormativity, American exceptionalism, and imperialism.[62]

Other queer of color critiques, like those of David Eng, have exposed the depoliticizing effects of queer liberalism's construction of gayness as the new blackness, which assumes the teleological disappearance of (inter)national racism, in a supposed post-racial, multicultural, colorblind age.[63] Extending this insight, South Asian queer of color critics like Gopinath have argued for "making the study of sexuality central to an anti-imperialist, antiracist project."[64] Drawing on the critical works of Paul Gilroy and Stuart Hall, as well as cultural literary genres, musicals, and Bollywood film representations of family, home, the nation, and diaspora, Gopinath challenges the construction of queer diasporic female/male South Asian subjectivities as either transnational, homonormative, and eroticized model minority neoliberal citizen-subjects seeking multicultural assimilation or alternatively terrorists who are perverse and homophobic.

Similarly, the work of José Esteban Muñoz builds on Michel Pêcheux's conceptualization of "disidentification," in the context of minority queer POC who have been erased by colonialism, white nationalism, and heteronormativity.[65] Muñoz examines how the former not only subvert and resist their mainstream nationalist assimilation into dominant white queer figurations, but also engage in disidentifying political actions as a deliberate response to the historical trauma and systemic violence to which they have been exposed.[66] In these disidentifying anti-national instances, queer POC do not necessarily seek to assimilate into "Gay Internationalist" narratives nor do they entirely reject them or engage in constructing a radical decolonial counter-identity to challenge the former's hegemony. Rather, they partake in a third self-actualized survivalist strategy that seeks to rework hegemonic cultural-national identities in order to alter their own futurities, as part of a queer counterpublic.[67] In this instance, as Hiram Perez notes, queer diasporic works are a call for queer theory to re-examine its collusions with nationalism and, in particular, Euro-American imperialism/colonialism and embrace the rich vocabularies that non-Euro-American discourses have to offer.[68]

Nationalism is one of the many reasons that modern identity politics are tactical necessities for alliance and solidarity, in light of the differential and hierarchical racialized, sexualized, and gendered realities that BIPOC face. However, they are also strategically limited given how they represent what George Lipsitz refers to as "possessive investments in whiteness."[69] Our investment in identity politics occurs at the expense of our focus on radical decolonial ethico-political commitments and a politics of collective responsibility and accountability centered around what Richard J.F. Day refers to as a "politics of affinity," which would usurp the nation-state as an arbiter of our rights and responsibilities.[70]

For the same reason, Marxism is insufficient as a revolutionary trajectory. Euro-American Marxism remains committed to the (settler) state-form and phantasies of its seizure for liberation by new elites anchored in the logic of "hegemony of hegemony" that implies the need for an authoritarian vanguard that leads, saves, and ameliorates society as a whole while contributing to Black fugitivity and fungibility.[71] While Black and Third-World Marxist traditions exist, they equally strive towards state capture for revolutionary ends, failing to contend with the problem of "hegemony of hegemony," hierarchy, as well as Nietzschean/Foucaultian post-structuralist, post-anarchist, and Black anarchistic conceptualizations of power that identify how power does not originate but rather conglomerates around not one, but multiple and different sites.[72] Only then, upon its conglomeration, power interplays "among these different sites in the creation of the social world."[73] The interplay implies that oppression does not start nor end with the modern-state and capitalism. As Todd May argues, this is "not to deny that there are points where various (and perhaps bolder) lines intersect" but rather that "power does originate at those points."[74] Unlike Marxisms, according to post-anarchism and Black-anarchistic traditions, power thus operates everywhere and in its operation everywhere offers individuals the means for oppressing and repressing others at the micro or myopic level. In this sense, revolutionary power and oppression are irreducible to the modern-state and capitalism. Generally speaking, Marxist traditions are disinterested in decolonial governance models and analyzing "mutually intersecting lines of power" to contextualize how an oppression visibly peaks one moment, but then "disappears" only for another oppression to peak in its stead.[75] Marxism represents a (neo)colonial/imperial product of liberal modernity as much as it strives to contest it. While Marxist theories are useful, Marxism's emphasis on state control to enact social change is what leads Tuck and Yang to aptly note how "socialist and communist empires have also been settler empires (e.g. Chinese colonialism in Tibet)."[76] Leftists like the Egyptian Revolutionary Socialists often elide the Eurocentric liberal-state assumptions imbued within their frameworks. The revolutionary socialist implementation of a strict class-based analysis where "labor" or "workers" act as an agential political class fails to activate a more thorough decolonizing project because it fails to adopt a decolonial intersectional approach to the racialization, gendering, and sexualizing of labor and sustains the myth of the existence of and need for a democratic state. For example, as progressive as movements as Occupy Wall street in the U.S. may seem, the colonial overtone in the very term "occupy" itself serves as "another settler re-occupation on stolen land [and hence] relies upon problematic assumptions about social justice and is a prime example of the incommensurability between 're/occupy' and 'decolonize' as political agendas."[77] Therefore, as Tuck and Yang note, though the strict "pursuit of worker rights (and rights to work)" by Marxist-Leninist movements in franchise-colonial societies and "minoritized people's rights in a settler colonial context can appear to be anti-capitalist," "this pursuit is nonetheless largely pro-colonial" as both approaches and their respective movements are still anchored in the anthropocentric idea that "land is property; land is/belongs to the U.S.; land should be distributed democratically."[78]

Islām, on the other hand, seeks to transcend all forms of identity politics and defines community through ethical-political, spiritual belongings and social justice commitments. After all, a central component of decolonization is the determination of forms of native governance that are not colonial, through the construction of decolonized spiritual, political, and economic land-based practices that offer alternatives in re-envisioning a people's relationship to geographic terrains and coming communities.[79]

Capitalism (Mommy)

As I noted in the Introduction and elsewhere, May'68 scholars like Michel Foucault, Gilles Deleuze, and Félix Guattari as well as historians like Fernand Braudel argue that "it is a historical fact that capitalism and the nation-state evolved symbiotically."[80] Although "they can become disjointed over the short-term, creating ruptures with local and even regional implications, the relationship between capitalism and nation-states over the long-term is rooted in their undeniable, mutual interests."[81] Neoliberalism, in particular, "is deeply anchored in the idea that the relationship between the nation-state and capitalism is irreversible, and both are codependent on the dissemination of repressive racializing, gendering, sexualizing, classist, debilitating and ableist logics that we have internalized and replicate at the horizontal level, beyond their systematic and systemic reifications."[82] Capitalist-states are "not just administrative structures; they shape our understanding of the world, including our own identities and selves."[83] They structure our thoughts, and fine-tune our behavioral patterns, and our emotions. In other words, "they are founded upon structural inequities and enable subjects that reproduce the violent inequalities of institutions given that subjectivities are also formed, defined, and regulated by these structures."[84] In this sense, "[capitalist] nation-states are a central component of the problem because they are assumed to be a neutral entity that can be instrumentally mobilized as a tool to usher in revolutionary social-change."[85]

In their seminal *Anti-Oedipus: Capitalism and Schizophrenia*, Deleuze and Guattari adopt a schizo-analytic approach to argue that each capitalist nation-state family is constructed as a triadic heteronormative relationship modeled on the Freudian Oedipal structure of *Daddy-Mommy-Me.*[86] Within this macro-Oedipal structure, "Capital[ism]" acts as a symbolic materialist mother, signifying materialist and individualist practices, and the "Holy State," represents the symbolic paternalistic, disciplinarian father, embodying macro-authoritarian practices. Each of us is weaned on them as the Oedipalized subjects.[87] The macro and micro are interconnected in a extractive cyclical relationship. As our "real father," the nation-state teaches us how to become authoritarian, to hierarchize and covet and hoard political power, to categorize, discipline, and control others and ourselves. Capitalism, our "representative mother," teaches us how to commoditize, individualize, and commercialize as well as materialize not only space and time, but also love, friendships, solidarity, ally ship and land. We even commercialize symbols of anti-capitalist resistance on our t-shirts and MacBook stickers.

This internalized Oedipal structure inscribed by both parties and parents into each individual's psyche has the destructive purpose of delimiting our individual and collective capacity for self-directed action.[88] Each individual becomes their own legislator, subjugated to both parents and the fascistic repression of ourselves and others as a result of having internalized disciplinary and hierarchical practices encoded by capitalist-states. Our subduing is due to our collective unwillingness to creatively imagine new socio-political-economic governing alternatives to the dominating authoritarian and capitalist practices internalized by each of us as a consequence of the Oedipal relationship. Of course, the uneducated assumption is that in the absence of capitalist-states, there would be violence and "anarchy" would prevail, as in the case of Libya, in the aftermath of an ongoing Arab Spring/Islamist Winter. This lie persists, despite the fact that anthropologists and decolonial social movements have long argued that life without governments (and institutionalized hierarchy more generally) was possible – and indeed, common – for human beings in the past, and is within reach again in the present-future.[89]

In discussing the distinctive roles of modern nation-states and capitalism in the lives of individuals, while maintaining a non-reductionist approach to the role of either, Day argues that "States hope 'to capture flows of all kinds', to make order where is chaos, convert outside into inside … whatever is outside and not part of the plan is to be brought in, reduced to a the known, and thereby rendered manageable."[90] Similarly, Deleuze and Guattari argue that modern nation-states function as an "apparatus of capture [which] has a *power of appropriation*."[91] Modern nation-states form maps that establish imperialist borders and walls to cordon and conquer landscapes and social expanses. Unlike God who appreciates and creates differences amongst individuals and peoples so that, as the Qur'ān states, "they may get to know and relate to each other," the objective behind the modern nation-state's construction of maps is to identify each individual so that they can be assigned, categorized, labeled and made to belong to a stereotype to assure their recognition and insertion within matrices of hierarchies. Modern nation-states operate through their establishment of institutions that apply authoritative practices to individuals under regimes of *normalization*. For instance, "racism operates: by the determination of degrees of deviance in relation to the White-Man face."[92] As not only institutions, but networked relations of powers embodied in individuals, modern-states depend on isolating and normalizing each of us singularly, given their inability to ameliorate the suffering of the collective.[93] Their premise is vertical hierarchies and derived power from lateral disorganization through which they assume hegemony over violence and exercise brute top-down force as original incipients of terror.

To understand capacities for resistance, and how power and authority relate to the nation-state, one must understand the cardinal rule and principle that Michel Foucault teaches: "relations of power are ubiquitous," as power is present in all relationships.[94] Power always begins horizontally; as Scott Uzelman writes, it is the freedom that subjects have to "to resist limitations and constraints that gives power its relational quality."[95] However, due to the ubiquitous asymmetry of relations of power, not all subjects have equal freedom to adopt or promote certain behaviors.[96] As Uzelman notes, "it is only in these agonistic situations, where power flows, as 'reversible' and unstable" that "the potential exists for subjects to resist, to alter their situations, direct the behavior of others and have theirs directed via 'strategic games between liberties'."[97] When the potential for the less powerful to alter the behavior of the more powerful disappears the "relation of power tends toward becoming a state of domination."[98] Foucault sees domination as distinct from oppression. Those dominated are "at the complete mercy of others" as per victims of "torture" and/or slavery, whereas those oppressed retain some ability to enact their own tactical interests, strategically constrained as they may be.[99]

In essence then, "power is both relational and immanent – it is not something that is possessed, once and for all, by powerful subjects; rather it exists only when it is put into action."[100] The failure to recognize this has led to the collapse of many insurrectionary moments, as per the example of the initial 18 days of the January 2011 Tahrir Uprisings. Given Egypt's complicity in the Zionist occupation of Palestine, dethroning of a former, now dead, pharaoh, Muhammad Hosni El Sayed Mubarak was not the real struggle. After all, Mubarak, who spent a short stint in prison, was since replaced by a then incarcerated, but now also dead, Mohamed Morsi, in exchange for the ever more ruthless military-junta of dictator Abdel-Fattah El-Sisi whose current regime makes Mubarak's 30-year reign seem like utopia. Rather, the real struggle has always been how Egyptians (and perhaps others all over the world) can permanently invest in and sustain decolonial, horizontalist momentum of non-authoritarian and non-materialist, as well as anti-colonial and anti-imperial, organizing by divesting from and making capitalist-states totally irrelevant, regionally and transnationally. Although during the initial Tahrir Uprisings, Egyptians were united under the false patriotic banner of nationalism that camouflaged their ethical-political, ethnic, gendered, and spiritual differences, the Tahrir moment also offered a hopeful glimpse of an alternative world manifested in the innovative initiatives it incepted. Examples of these include *al-lijān al-shaʿbiyah* (or "popular assemblies"), neighborhood councils, security checks points (given, that over 99 police stations were burnt to the ground), and the sharing of necessary food and shelter (while sleeping and living on what are and should have always been a people's public streets and squares). What was always missing was the active creation of land-based social justice, spiritual alternatives, and the genuine internalization of this revolutionary understanding of power and spirit that ought to have been enacted in the way we reconceive and act practically within our households, communities, neighborhoods, schools, and factories etc.

Expanding on this notion of power, Day distinguishes between "live power," which characterizes situations in which most of the actors have some ability to change the circumstances they are in, and "dead power," which is the "condition in which power relations have ossified such that some actors, most of the time, find themselves unable to alter their situation."[101] To construct decolonial alternatives, we must develop strategies and tactics that keep "power 'live' and ward … off dead power."[102] Uzelman identifies multiple tactics for challenging established relations of power: "democratic organization; participatory production processes; facilitating horizontal and dialogic flows of communication; encouraging new representational forms; building and maintaining working environments that are relatively free of dead forms of power (e.g. racism, sexism, classism, ableism, etc.)."[103] In this sense it is pertinent to always be vigilant to prevent live power from congealing into dead power given that revolutions must deal with practical questions of managing everyday life, such as waste disposal, in addition to their more abolitionist transformative-justice dimensions.[104]

Me/Us

As noted, modern-states can function not only to discipline but also to control.[105] According to Foucault, a disciplinary society subjects people to progressive stages of training to shape them into docility.[106] In Egypt's case, this means that entire generations of civilian populations were indoctrinated to submit to orders, whether in schools, hospitals, factories or the barracks, cultivating the desire for their own mass fascistic servitude and repression. Disciplinary societies adopt binary logic, where everything becomes divisible by two: male/female, black/white, and hetero/homo.

In contrast, control societies are far more insidious, given the way surveillance capitalist-states through militarized technologies and artificial intelligence data-harvest and mine us as data sets that go beyond our spatial-disciplinary confinement, with the express purpose of anticipating our thoughts while indoctrinating us to become self-disciplinarian and micro-fascistic subjects. In so doing, modern-states transform each one of us into "'little command centres' proliferat[ing] everywhere, making coaches, teachers and cops, all little Mussolinis," who exert authoritarianism and domination over our surroundings as a way to reactively overcompensate for our inability to reassert control over our own lives.[107] In turn, "free subjects in open environments" like school students and factory workers become indistinguishable from prison inmates. Deleuze and Guattari refer to these reinscribed coded, codifying, and codified behaviors as *micro-fascisms*, which provide the necessary breeding ground, impetus, and war-like conditions for the germination of thinking that resonates with and (re) affirms the existence of and need for capitalist-states, making a *macro-fascism* possible.[108] In this way, capital-states are not external to us, to be resisted and fought outside us, but rather are internally engrained, necessitating a battle within us. Both *fascisms* resonate with the other, *micro* to *macro* and *macro* to *micro.* Fascism's embodiment within the micro-Oedipal family is after all facilitated and contingent on the macro-Oedipal formations disseminated by capitalist-state's uninhibited dominions and logics, such that the masses are made to desire their own humiliation, repression, subjugation, and enslavement.[109]

Our fundamental adversary is the fascism that rests within all of us, in our hearts and behaviors, and that feeds off our insecurities, wounds, traumas, vulnerabilities, hesitancies, anxiety-ridden inhibitions and that we resort and appeal to in order to attain a false sense of welfare, protection, survivability, while we strive to exploit and dominate all that surrounds us. Fascism operates through the particular set of penalties and privileges each of us enjoys in relation to others and hence transforms each individual into "micro-Oedipuses, microformations of power, micro-fascisms."[110] In turn, we become the capitalist-state's handymen, where in each iterative interaction we exercise power that affects and is affected by others, having internalized dynamic assemblages of hierarchies built upon Eurocentric conceptualizations of ethnicity/race, gender, sexuality, ability, and class dynamics.

Although capitalism's role is also disciplinarian and coercive, its particular role in the Oedipal relationship is that of seducing each individual's desire such that nothing is sacred.[111] Capitalism's primary objective first and foremost is the material exploitation of a social field. In other words, capitalism breeds in individuals the (un)conscious ability to materialize their relationships with a friend, community, or lover, towards utilitarian ends, such that the sole intent of an individual's pursuits of friendship or love is one's egoistic interest. It is capitalism's ability to seductively free, yet when necessary seize and channel an individual's insatiable desire towards markets that permits capitalism to thrive. Capitalist practices are authoritarian in so far as they are intent on transforming everything in a social space into a commodity for the forceful extraction of "surplus value."[112]

Capitalism constitutes all production funneled into "one centered world market, the capitalist one, in which even the so-called socialist countries participate."[113] Capitalism thrives on interest that eventually leads to infamous short-term fickle investment opportunities in the rapid (re)creation of exponential wealth and subsequently a steep downfall of bubbles like the Dutch Tulip mania of the early 1600s, the Wall Street crash of 1929, the Japanese property bubble in the 1980s, the dot-com financial collapse between 2000 and 2001, including the 2008 deflated housing crisis in the U.S. in which financial liquidity reached its strained extremities. Capitalism is not only driven by profit, interest, and debt, but rather the unrestricted proliferation of regimes of enterprise and accounting domains spanning genetic screening and risk calculation, the bio-materialization of life and death be it through crime prevention or promotional self-help strategies, including developmentalist "Green New Deals" that annex discussions of an ongoing genocidal settler-colonialism, all while transferring responsibility for crises onto the shoulders of individuals. In so doing, capitalist-states naturalize and therefore neutralize our collective capacities for resistance.

This is not to deny or claim that tactically vying for the attainment of particular demands such as higher wages, hate-crime legislations, equal rights, universal healthcare, student debt cancellations, housing and immigrant rights, racial and environmental justice, dismantlement initiatives and worker protections, or even a judicial end to draconian policing does not represent resistance or is useless.[114] Rather, the disaster predicament arises when this reformist approach to decolonization becomes the sole strategy. These piecemeal scrambles for social justice causes can be useful when they severely disrupt and explicitly expose the limits of capitalist-state rehabilitations, and incite strain and pressure upon the former. However, recurrently investing in them leaves minimal room for the necessary creation of alternatives that can replace the dominant order; especially given the exhausting emotional, physical, mental, psychological toll, as well as labor and resources these cathartic "hit or miss" solutions entail, including the diminished morale and activist fatigue that accompanies an overreliance on direct action protest. As I noted above, "enacting change from within" through voting, reforming laws, street-fights for equality, and a national assimilationist politics of citizen rights is eventually based on two central pillars of electoral representative-democracy: (neo)liberal humanism and multicultural identity politics that will always strategically re-entrench Euro-American white ascendance and individualism. From this perspective, irrespective of 13th and Right to Vote amendments, plantation slave economies continue to be enshrined to this day through what Saidiya V. Hartman refers to as "afterlife slavery."[115] Since the Jim Crow, Black Codes, and segregation era, slavery is constantly (re)birthed through Stand-Your-Ground laws, police brutality and premeditated extrajudicial killings, routine "Stop and Frisk" policies, "Broken Window Policing," voter disenfranchisement, school-to-prison pipelines, impoverishment and premature deaths, as well as 1994 crime bills which Hillary Clinton and Bernie Sanders voted for and that superfluously target and incarcerate Black youth who are referred to as "super-predators" and "thugs" within a shattered criminal justice system.

In contrast, decolonization and Anarchic Ijtihād center and operate from the premise that (neo)liberal representative democracy, ultimately anchored in capitalist-state structures (whether they are animated as Christian-secular or religious or even as military dictatorships) is a neocolonial product of modernity. Here, the modern-state is taken as a propagator of social terror, indeed one that inherently iteratively thrives on promoting racial/ethnic, classist, gendered, sexual, ableist, as well as sectarian violence and structural discrimination in an endless competition of oppressions between minorities. The state is an extension of an ongoing Euro-American neoimperialist project that we all ceaselessly subordinate ourselves to in non-Euro-American and Euro-American societies. In turn, Anarchic Ijhtihād and decolonial strategies are not focused on the seizure of the nation-state, with the aim of enacting change from within.

Accordingly, Anarcha-Islām's relation to capitalist-states resembles "a clinic" that I, an Oedipal subject, attend to become relatively de-Oedipalized, and to decolonize. Anarcha-Islām seeks to open room for the curing of SWANA Muslim and non-Muslim European Christian-secular and neoliberal fantasies, and strategically enable the countering of white supremacy, cisheteropatriarchy, anti-Black and anti-Indigenous imperialist-settler projects. In this clinic, I live, alongside others sharing similar commitments, permitting me at times to temporarily break free of dichotomous Orientalist/Fundamentalist representations, and instead practice resisting the micro-authoritarian and capitalist practices I internalized and embody by embracing a radically distinct ethical-political orientation and trajectory, through my participation in non-authoritarian and non-capitalist concepts and practices. But, and with the construction of this subjectivity, Muslim anarchist, as any, I realize too that no identity can truly be "free," of (neo)colonial/imperial capitalist and authoritarian practices irrespective of how creative the identity constructed may be; that requires communitarian land-based alternatives.

The absence of substitutes to capitalist-states demands that we ask pivotal questions about how mutual aid land-based practices, gender egalitarian governance and decolonization can and would restructure our spatial-temporal conceptualizations of sexual and non-sexual desire, and liberation. There can be no liberation of the poor, the elderly, the youth, women, gender dissidents, our conceptualizations of masculinities and femininities, the differently abled, and BIPOC without liberating land first, given how land structures desire. In so doing, it is equally essential to explore the practical challenges of creating other forms of solidarity, as the need for an ethics of disagreements, or what I refer to as *Uṣūl al-Ikhtilāf*, given activist micro-fascistic celebrity egos and sicknesses like sexism, as well as Arab and Zionist supremacy, anti-blackness in Egyptian and diaspora SWANA Muslim communities, and anti-Indigenous politics in Turtle Island.

Diasporic SWANA Muslim peoples in settler-colonial societies must contend with having internalized a sense of shame through our adoption of a colonized inferiority complex and gendered Islamophobia, indeed how we are implicated in sustaining settler-colonial Israeli pinkwashing and homonationalist narratives. After all, as diasporic SWANA Muslims many of us reify and mimic anti-blackness and participate in the U.S./Canadian states' settler-colonization of Indigenous peoples. We do so despite the latter radical collective calls for BIPOC to engage in *anarchistic*, horizontalist, egalitarian, and feminist discourses concerned with non-statist, spiritual, conceptualizations of decolonization, indigeneity, and reindigenization. Innumerable diasporic Muslims do this although capitalist-states theologically contradict Qur'ānic non-authoritarian and non-hierarchical principles as I discuss in the following chapter and upon which I construct Anarcha-Islām.[116]

Anarcha-Islām is vital given how franchise post-colonial and settler modes of colonization are historically, materially, and symbolically interrelated.[117] The modus operandi and object of one category of (settler-)colonialism in Euro-American societies *can be* (if not in fact is) the intersectional agent of another (post-)colonialism in non-Euro-American societies. The multiple racial and gendered colonialisms are as entwined as grape vines. Their interconnections are mitigated through the normalized transnational authoritarian and macro-fascistic adoption of capitalist-states as the means through which populations ought be both bio- and necro-politically, spiritually, and economically organized.

3
Anarcha-Islām: An Anti- and Non-Authoritarian Islām

> I am God most of the time when I don't have a headache, when I think of everything and nothing, when I'm not slipping down some Satanic slope...Then I understand quite well that one might settle oneself down in God or that one might settle him on a pedestal. I will not reproach anyone for that.
>
> Félix Guattari (1995, 51)[1]

> While colonialism in its formal sense might have been dismantled, the colonial state has not. Many of the problems of democracy are products of the old colonial state whose primary difference is the presence of black faces. It has to do with the rise of a new ruling class ... who are content with mimicking the colonial masters.
>
> Aimé Césaire (1972, 27)[2]

> To change the outlook of the people and initiate a mental revolution among them through speech or writing is a form of "Jihad". To alter the old tyrannical social system and establish a new just order of life by the power of sword is also "Jihad" and to expend goods and exert physically for this cause is "Jihad" too.
>
> Abul Alā Al-Mawdūdī (1939)[3]

Anarcha-Islām's Osteological Left-Side

In this chapter I affirm Anarcha-Islām's non-authoritarian commitments by demonstrating that Islām is incompatible with modern capitalist-state frameworks.[4] In constructing Anarcha-

Islām, I equally refute two of the misconceptions relating to Islām and Muslims amongst anarchists and more broadly leftists: the impossibility of constructing either an anarchic interpretation of Islām or an Islamic interpretation of anarchism and the impossibility of the co-existence of Muslim and anarchist identities in a single subjectivity.

Anarchic Ijtihād also challenges neo-orthodox and neoliberal Muslim scholars who argue that anarchism is an impractical and immoral Euro-American import.[5] In his essay "Nonwestern Anarchisms," Jason Adam reveals how decolonized anarchistic traditions have been discounted and dismissed by Eurocentric anarchists.[6] Similarly, Maia Ramnath argues that Euro-American anarchist modes of thinking and acting are just one way towards liberation and that "something else" needs to be "a reference point for us ... instead of us being the reference point for everything else ... [which is] a deeply decolonizing move."[7] The dangers of the superficial perceptions that anarchists have of one another is illustrated in Palestinian writer Budour Hassan's discussion of the Egyptian Black Bloc in Cairo street protests in 2013: "[While] the appearance ... triggered gullible excitement in Western anarchist circles. Little thought was given to the Egyptian Black Bloc's political vision – or lack thereof – tactics, or social, faith-based, and economic positions. For most Western anarchists, it was enough that they looked and dressed like anarchists to warrant uncritical admiration."[8] In fact, Egyptian anarchists like Yasser Abdullah have demonstrated that anarchist movements have been active in Egypt since the 1870s.[9]

Doing away with what Gayatri Spivak refers to as "strategic essentialisms," meaning in this context that radicalism embodies a homogeneous ideology, is needed because these holistic essentialisms deny the reality of agential change and choice by BIPOC and radical subjectivities who are heterogeneous, multiplicitous, and fluid in character, given the interchanged migratory transference of ideas, thoughts, and peoples, even when civilizational binaries are reasserted at the macro-level by elites, and are internalized by the masses as constructed worldviews. The reality of history, as noted in the Introduction, is not a binary "East vs West." The truth is "the Left" as an independent identity-based and "sectarian" body with distinct knowledge production mechanisms which did not emerge in the same way in the SWANA region as it did in Euro-America contributes to the widespread geopolitical perception that anarchism and radical politics are a new phenomenon in the SWANA region.[10] One of the few exceptions, situated in the late Ottoman period, contesting this misperception is Ilham Khuri-Makdisi's network analysis of the circulation of radical ideas in local-regional and even global contexts in the "Eastern Mediterranean," and their integration into a global system.[11] By focusing on the expression of radical ideas, not in leftist milieus, but in popular nationalist newspapers and theater, Khuri-Makdisi shows how "these apparatuses themselves served for the formation of radical ideologies and networks in this period."[12] In his review of her work, Akin Sefer argues that by "discovering [journalistic networks in the Beirut-Mount Lebanon area] and displaying the formation of its radical discourse on workers and their practices – especially towards the education of working classes through reading rooms, night schools, and mass media – Khuri-Makdisi, beyond opening up a very useful perspective, also calls on us to reconsider our factual knowledge about the history of the left, particularly regarding the period before World War I."[13] Summing up her work on this and the Italian anarchist network in Cairo, Khuri-Makdisi writes:

> What is evident, though, is that anarchism and anarchist ideas, in Egypt and elsewhere in the Ottoman Empire, far from being confined to marginal and minority groups, were gaining ground and being synthesized in other revolutionary radical or social movements, which included protonationalist, nationalist, trade unionist, and Muslim reformist movements.[14]

Currently, some Muslim scholars are undertaking alternative terminologies to decolonization. Cutting-edge Iranian Muslim anarchist filmmaker Milad Dokhanchi equates decolonization to "detaqutization."[15] Reporting a telling conversation with a prominent Iranian official, Dokhanchi quotes the functionary as saying:

"When the Revolution happened, we kicked the *taqut* out of our country, but not the *taquti* mentality."[16] Dokhanchi continues,

> [L]ater I looked up the term more closely. *Taqut* is a Qur'ānic term that refers to idolatry or to worship anything, including a nation-State, against Allāh. Kings who rebelled against and imprisoned the Prophets are referred to *taqut* in the Qur'ān. In post-revolutionary Iran, the term was used as a reference to the Shah of Iran. I even remember my grandmother referring to pre-revolutionary Iran as *zamane taqut* (the era of the Shah) ... Similar to colonialism, *taqut* does not only manifest itself in a few colonialist individuals. *Taqut* is a state of mind, a way of thinking. *Taqut* embodies its own cultural and political values and produces institutions to reflect, preserve and promote the underlying assumptions of those values.[17]

Dokhanchi proceeds to argue that post-revolutionary Iran is still structured by *ṭaghūti* institutions that were premised on and reify a set of non-Islamic and Euro-American assumptions. He notes that *detaqutization* denotes "the need for an effort to deconstruct and then re-imagine the surface and symbolic reflections of the heritage of *taqut*."[18]

In an article on the crisis of the nation-state, Cairo University political scientist and former member of the Muslim Brotherhood, Heba Raouf Ezzat, reminds readers that anarchism's accurate meaning is closer to a "state-less society" rather than "chaos."[19] In arguing for the renewed elucidation of anarchist ideas, she cites examples such as the rise of internationalist networking and embodied forms of local participatory self-organization and autonomist orientations in Egyptian history. She continues,

> I wanted to explain that anarchists from everything from a liberal to a Marxist background have given a lot of thought to the overweening power accorded the state in the modern age, and that this is a respectable tradition deserving to be revisited. This is one of my main themes [i.e., anarchism]. What I have tried to argue in the Islamic public domain, virtual or intellectual, is

> that ideology has to be taken seriously, not in a dogmatic way, but as part of a neo-Islamic vision, and that we have to build bridges with some of the people with whom we rarely engage. Muslims have been over-obsessed with talking to democrats and liberals who already accept their presence in the Western world, or who accept their parliamentary representation in the Muslim world. They have shied away from dealing with the leftists, the anti-globalisers and the different resistance and protest groups in the West.[20]

Similarly, writing from a settler's perspective within Turtle Island, Adam Lewis argues that (settler)-colonial analyses have been largely absent from anarchist theory and practice, despite the fact that "as a political philosophy and social movement practice committed to resisting all forms of oppression and domination, [anarchism] needs to place [neo]colonialism more clearly and consistently at the centre of its analysis of interlocking systems of oppression," particularly when anarchist praxis manifests "against the backdrop of settler colonial realities and on Indigenous lands."[21] In a similar vein of critiquing the constrained vision of Euro-American anarchists, Black anarchist and former member of the Black Panther Party and Black Liberation Army Ashanti Alston notes:

> we have to look at the fact that most of our understanding of anarchism comes from Europe. [Although] it may have taught us a lot, in terms of another way to live and organise, or how to be open to differences, … coming out of Europe it will also bring us a perspective on class struggle that they pretty much want to adhere to as if it was something Biblical, that if other struggles are anarchistic and they don't come out of working class struggles that does not make them any less anarchists because it is not workers taking it on. It may be peasants taking it on, it may be people tied to the land in other ways. So for me one cannot just read the anarchist classics coming out of Europe, but one has to learn from other people's living experiences and writings on their experiences. Even if those experiences and writings are not from people that say "I am an anarchist". But you can tell

> pretty much from their writings and experiences that these are anarchistic struggles, you know, that play a big part even today in being at the foremost of some of the most challenging struggles against the Empire.[22]

In contrast, anarchist bloggers like Brain-Fear and PJP, as well as innumerable others, insist on a Eurocentric view of anarchism, and dismiss the possibility of Muslim anarchists, premising their views on an essentialization of Islām and Muslims. Brain-Fear and PJP write:

> Any form of religion is thought control – Islam is sexist and homophobic ... If they [Muslims] are serious about anarchism, they would have dropped the sexist and homophobic aspects of the religion and accentuated more libertarian aspects of the religion.[23]

More bluntly, "Burning-man" writes,

> Anarcho-Islam is about the stupidest thing I've ever heard of. Islam is about submission. Slave to Allah and all that crap. It has an extremely rigid set of rules and conduct and, while more enlightened than other monotheistic religions in a number of important ways, it never quite went through anything like the Reformation. It is reactionary, pro-capitalist, pro-slavery, imperialist and misogynist to the core. Just read the fucking Qur'ān.[24]

The Anarchist Federation in London hyperbolically portrays Islām as monolithic, reactionary, homo-trans-queerphobic, and over-simplistically oppressive towards women and "the enemy of all Freedom loving people."[25]

These sweeping dismissals of Anarcha-Islām can in part be traced to lack of clarity on what is meant in the contemporary world by "Islam," including its referents and significations. As Joseph A. Massad has argued,

> European Orientalists and Muslim and Arab thinkers have begun to translate to us "Islam" in numerous ways while seemingly convinced that it possesses an immediate intelligibility that requires no specification or definition. "Islam", for these thinkers, is not only the *name* the Qur'ān attributes to the *din* (often (mis) translated as "religion", though there is some disagreement about this) that entails a faith [*īmān*] in God disseminated by the Prophet Muhammad, but can also refer to the history of Muslim states and empires, the different bodies of philosophical, theological, jurisprudential, medical, ritualistic, scholarly, agricultural, medical, literary, and scientific works, as well as to culinary, sexual, social, economic, religious, ritualistic, scholarly, agricultural and urban practices engaged in by Muslims from the seventh to the nineteenth century and beyond, as well as much, much more.[26]

Euro-American gender, sexual, political science, and historical discourses have produced meanings of Islām that are not "of it," operating from the outside in, contra distinct from the premise of comprehending Islām's own frameworks of reference and engaging it from the inside out. These recurring misperceptions are constantly reified across the political spectrum, as in Andrew Flood's article "The Trouble with Islam":

> The left in general … [but in particular] groups like the British SWP [Socialist Worker Party] have gone so far as to describe left criticism of the Islamic religion as "Islamophobia" echoing the official line of their government which insists "The real Islam is a religion of peace, tolerance and understanding". While there is a real need for the left to defend people who are Muslims from state and non-state victimization in the aftermath of 9-11 this should not at any time imply a defence of the Islamic religion. Freedom of religion must also allow freedom from religion![27]

While I concur with Flood's views that "freedom of religion must allow freedom from religion" and that the "Left ought to possess the right to critique Islam without fear of the accusatory charge of Islamophobia," Flood's argument supports the reductive view of Islām and Muslims as monoliths. Furthermore, Flood, as innumerable Euro-American anarchists, dismisses the possibility of (re)locating an anarchic interpretation of Islām, indeed that there exist resonances between plural worlds to which others belong and whose "Otherness" embodies the potential to contribute to Euro-American circles in unfathomable ways, as per the example of other religious anarchisms.[28] Instead, Flood argues that somehow Islām in its innate nature runs counter to anarchism's commitments to freedom from interlocked oppression(s):

> Anarchists have a long and proud tradition of fighting the power of organised religion, including in countries like Spain fighting fascist gangs formed on a religious basis. While we recognise the freedom of people to hold a religion we also recognise that there has to be a freedom from religion – an idea that runs against the basis of Islam. Anarchists in the Middle East and beyond will need to determine for themselves the most effective ways of counteracting the influence of the fundamentalists there. In the west we can at least make sure their attempts to impose themselves on the immigrant communities are opposed.[29]

Anarchists retain these misconceptions about Islām for two reasons. First, they are influenced by (neo-)Orientalist and (neo-) Fundamentalist Euro-American representations of Islām and Muslims. Second, most Euro-American anarchists have never read the Sunnah, aḥadīths, or the Qur'ān in the language in which they were dictated and written – Arabic. Moreover, these anarchists have never practiced Ijtihād and are ill-versed in interpretative traditions within Islām. A majority of Euro-American anarchists are unaware that within Islām, "everything that is said under the explicit form of the law usually also refers to another meaning."[30] In turn, they remain blind to the reality that there are non-dogmatic possibilities for *mujtahidīn* who engage in jihād and Ijtihād as noted and prescribed.

Socialism – in its broadest of historical interpretations that would include anarchism and that distinguishes the former term from Communism – has and continues to be antagonistic towards religion, despite its own manifested embodiment of faith and "spirituality." Although this hostility to religion *may be* traditionally justifiable, equally this view on "religion" emerges from a particular rooted experience with modern conceptualizations of "institutionalized religion," primarily premised, influenced, and informed by Euro-American crusader forms of distorted Christianities.[31] Building on Jacques Derrida, Jean-Luc Nancy, and Maurice Blanchot, Leela Gandhi discusses the vitality of a *politics of friendship* to solidarity. In *Affective Communities: Anti-Colonial Thought, Fin-De-Siècle Radicalism, and the Politics of Friendship* she examines this divide between faith-based social movements and socialists and provides evidence of historical instances of its transcendence, where shared ethico-political principles informed the former in the name of intersecting anti-imperialist and anti-colonial struggles.[32] She points to the friendship between Charles Freer Andrews – an English-Anglican priest in India in 1904 – and M.K. Gandhi, even the friendship of Manmoham Ghose – a late Victorian, Oxford educated Hindu – with Oscar Wilde.

If socialism is to breach the web of "imperial inhospitality" that has become ideologically rigid within it – and more catastrophically, internalized and embodied by its practitioners and flag bearers – then it must widen its engagement to be inclusive of non-institutionalized forms of radically oriented spiritual and faith-based movements.[33] Particularly, when these anti-institutional faiths have their own similar yet *indigenously* distinct political-theological concepts, experiences, and practices of social justice, beyond the essentialist binary representations of them.[34] These fallacies possess a particularly adverse effect on Muslim anarchists in the newest social movements, as noted in the Introduction. They abandon Muslim anarchists to face doubly marginal ostracization from settler-anarchist circles and mainstream liberal and conservative Muslim communities.

This insight illuminates the strategic limits of identity politics (informed by liberal Enlightenment), and the necessity for "opening up the new world order to a quite different and new world of the multiple."[35] Yet, still there remains no method to eradicate misconceptions entirely. They will indefinitely persist, and stereotypes can only be minimized not eradicated; asymmetrical power relations, indeed, are inescapable. Muslims, anarchists, and Muslim anarchists within the newest social movements still have journeys to travel in enacting inclusive hospitable welcomeness, ethically disagreeing, and unsettling each other in productive ways by interrogating critical misconceptions between them that hinder affined solidarities and collaborations. These misconceptions vary from anarchists sweepingly perceiving Islām and Muslims as being naturally queerphobic, without much, if any, decolonial consideration of their own imperialist settler-colonialist politics while espousing (neo)liberal homonationalist and pinkwashing slogans like "queer rights are human rights." Totalizing assumptions regarding Muslims, Islām, and queerphobia, indicate how indispensable it is that anarchists and socialists equally participate in the project of decolonizing their ethical-political orientations.[36]

In the next section, I construct, using Anarchic Ijtihād, Anarcha-Islām's anti-authoritarian commitments with respect to micro and macro forms of authority. First, I introduce four micro-anti-authoritarian concepts and practices I extract from Islām: *Tawḥīd* (fidelity to anyone but Creator), *Shūrā* (mutual consultation), *Ijmāʿ* (community consensus), and *Maṣlaḥa* (public interest) and show how they inform Anarcha-Islām's resistance to micro forms of authority. From there, I construct Anarcha-Islām's anti-authoritarian commitment at the macro-level, which involves an anti-institutional and anti-statist critique. Anarcha-Islām's anti-institutional commitment is established through a critique of contemporary Muslim clergy, irrespective of the titles they embrace, be they as *Īmāms*, *Khulafā*, or *sheikhs* etc., and that represent nothing but short-hand designations in their "frenzied search for an ideological guarantee for their social and material advantages."[37] After formulating Anarcha-Islām's anti-institutional commitment, I construct Anarcha-Islām's anti-statist commitment. In doing so, I go against the post-Prophetic framework of the Caliphate derived from the Islamic concept of *Khilāfah*, meaning "representation," manipulated by clergy as the context for founding a so-called "Islamic state," and, in general, hierarchical top-down authoritarian rule. Deploying the Qur'ān, I reinterpret Khilāfah to correspond to "identifying human beings in general as God's vicegerents [*Khulafā*, multiple, in a vehement opposition to the singular, *Khalīfah*] on Earth [with] human stewardship over God's creations."[38]

After constructing Anarcha-Islām's anti-statist commitments, I address the "authority" of the Prophet Muḥammad and God. Regarding Prophet Muḥammad's "authority," I argue, using the Qur'ān, that the Prophet Muḥammad is nothing beyond a *Rasūl* (messenger) and *Nabī* (prophet), for a spiritual call, born purely for the sake of conveying Islām's message (*da'wa*) to the world. With respect to the "authority" of God, I first contend that in Anarcha-Islām "there is no compulsion in religion."[39] That is, according to Anarcha-Islām and in line with the previous Qur'ānic verse cited, anarchists and others are not required to accept God, only to recognize the right of a Muslim to believe in the Creator. Second, I argue, in line with Saul Newman, that anarchists have not eliminated God, but "only reinvented [God] in the form of essence."[40] As Talal Asad notes, despite the secular (and in this instance anarchist) stated rejection of transcendence, they are in fact subject (often willingly subject) to transcendental forces such as the market ("which is a crucial part of modern capitalist society") as well as equally beholden to the patriotic forces of Euro-American nation-state citizenship discourses and that would include their "non-religious" transcendental appeal to abstract liberal humanist subjects and projects entwined with the Enlightenment notion of "cultural and moral progress."[41] According to this analysis, anarchists ought to acknowledge that there is a difference between, on the one hand, resisting God and Creation, which arguably represents an extension of themselves, and on the other hand, contending against all manner of authoritarian rule, including organized religion. In this sense, when anarchists misguidedly posit that they are resisting Creator, the truth is God is not the object of their resentment and resistance. Rather, they are resisting institutionalized religion, faith, and spirituality.

In concluding the chapter, I discuss concepts such as the Nation, Waṭaniyyah, Qawmiyyah, the Dawla and the Umma in Arab and Muslim lexicons. Tamim Barghouti argues that in the wake of post-colonial independence movements Arabs and Muslims altered the meanings of their own language to correspond with European definitions, ontologies, and terminologies associated with "the nation" and capitalist-states.[42] I examine the history and consequences of these "translations" and conclude the chapter by reclaiming these terms and constructing an alternative Muslim and non-Muslim vision for a resurgent Umma based on Prophet Muḥammad's Medina Charter (*Mīthāq al-Madīnah*) and the *Treaty of Al-Ḥudaybiyah*, (*Ṣulh Ḥudaybiyah*). I also develop and address a transnational framework for *indigeneity*, *decolonization*, and *reindigenization*.

Arise: An Anti- and Non-Authoritarian Islām

Micro- and Macro-Politics: Shūrā, Ijmāʿ, and Maṣlaḥa

Islām seldom offers concrete guidance in either the Qurʾān, aḥadīths, and the Sunnah regarding macro-politics except through the abstract concept of Umma. Nevertheless, Islām imbues Muslims with pragmatic micro-anti-authoritarian principles that cannot be contravened and are to be collectively applied and internalized. Recognizing the distinction between ethics and morals, discussed in Chapter 2, Islām breeds an alternate sense of individual and collective responsibility amongst all believers and spiritual people through these micro-anti-authoritarian practices aimed at achieving the entwined goals of mutual *raḥma* (mercy) and *taʿāwun* (cooperation or mutual aid) in virtue and piety (*taqwā*). Since there is no concept of chosen-ness in Islām, the Qurʾān encourages these ethical-political commitments as a means of achieving a unified and egalitarian Umma based on taʿāwun amongst Muslims and non-Muslims alike. In one verse, Creator addresses all believers, and emphasizes the vitality of taqwā and taʿāwun through adherence to what is socially just, stating: "O you who have believed … cooperate in righteousness and piety, but do not cooperate in sin and aggression."[43] The Qurʾān repeatedly extols this spirit amongst all believers, even when they adopt different ritualistic paths to the same Creator, yet are united in their monotheism (*Tawḥīd*) and adherence to justice. As the Qur'ān notes, "Indeed, the believers, Jews, Christians, and Sabeans – whoever truly believes in God and the Last Day and does good will have their reward with their Lord. And there will be no fear for them, nor will they grieve."[44]

In order to catalyze Muslims and believers in an anti-authoritarian direction, this Islamic interpretation adheres to the following micro-anti-authoritarian concepts and practices as counter-measures to micro-authoritarian practices: *Tawḥīd* (monotheistic belief), *Shūrā* (mutual consultation), *Ijmā'* (community consensus), and *Maṣlaḥa* (public interest).

The Islamic anti-authoritarian concept/practice of *Tawḥīd* is critical, because, as noted in the Introduction, Muslim scholars continue to tirelessly debate the possibility of being a Muslim nationalist in light of *Tawḥīd* that stresses that the paramount duty of Muslims is to solely recognize the absolute authority of Allāh and not one's ego or a nation, leader, tribe, or state.[45] According to some Muslim scholars, to love one's nation is to divert love away from the Creator. But this comprehension rests on modern neo-colonial understandings of nationhood as opposed to decolonial conceptualizations of it. As argued in the Introduction, the former views represent an overzealous extreme, as one may love the Divine through variant decolonized non-Euro-American and non-statist expressions of community and nationhood that embody the Creator's will and what the Creator denotes. Nonetheless, *Tawḥīd* is a fundamental premise and pillar for Anarcha-Islām, as it condemns fidelity to anyone but a Creator, whether the so-called rulers are referred to as *Īmāms*, *sheikhs*, *Khulafā*, *mullahs*, *muftīs*, *mutakallimūn* (scholastic theologians), *'ulamā* (religious scholars), *fuqahā* (jurists), *qāḍīs* (judges that are deified as "experts"), or any entity such as the modern-state. *Tawḥīd* is the fundamental *'aqīdah* or tenet within Islām that relies on the conceptualization of God as the sole sovereign and protector of rights for all life. *Tawḥīd* is the acknowledgment that the singular authority one pledges allegiance to is Allāh, with the deification of any other referred to as *širk* (polytheism), including the rampant worship of materialism, power, prestige, money. From an Islamic perspective, and as the foundational pillar to all monotheistic spiritualities, *Tawḥīd* is a central anti-authoritarian concept that informs Anarcha-Islām.

From the foundation of *Tawḥīd*, God affords Muslims the right to embrace any macro-political governing structure so long as it does not contradict other Islamic political practices such as *Shūrā* (mutual consultation), *Ijmāʿ* (mutual consensus), and *Maṣlaḥa* (public welfare). God intends this right as a merciful act for Muslims, such that they may adapt to differing geographical, spatial, temporal, and socio-political-economic historical terrains. This is a critical premise in the Islamic anarchistic argument that there is no such thing as an "Islamic state," offering avenues towards decolonized and reindigenized conceptualizations of the Umma, as a global coalitional polity of Muslims and non-Muslims, whose boundaries and identity are premised solely on the existence of identifiable ethical-political-spiritual socially just commitments. This is all the more vital given that the Qur'ān speaks in the language of people of faith (*mūmineen*), and not in the exclusionary context of solely addressing Muslims; the Qur'ān's message is universal. The radical emphasis on *Tawḥīd* offers Anarcha-Islām an anti-authoritarian trajectory akin to Indigenous, feminist, and queer critiques as well as radical SWANA social movements and perspectives that have fundamentally rejected not only playing to a "politics of assimilation or recognition," but rather also have contested the very legitimacy of the modern-state and its rule in exchange for autonomy, horizontalism, non-authoritarianism, and land sovereignty.[46]

The second anti-authoritarian pillar that informs Anarcha-Islām is *Shūrā* (mutual consultation). Shūrā as Anarcha-Islām's cardinal micro-anti-authoritarian concept and practice signifies "'consultation', 'concertation' or 'deliberation'."[47] Shūrā's significance is evidenced by Chapter 42 being named after it, emphasizing its prescriptive practice:

> But what is with God is better and more enduring for those who believe and put their trust in their Lord … [than] those who avoid the heinous sins and indecencies and when they are angry forgive, and those who answer their Lord, and perform

> the prayer, their affair being counsel between them, and they expend of that We have provided them ...[48]

This verse not only emphasizes humility in identifying Creator as the ultimate and actual provider of all, but also upholds the Qur'ānic spirit that envisages "the ... *Umma* as a perfectly egalitarian, open society based on good will and cooperation" as all believers advised to seek Shūrā relative to each other.[49] In other words, through Shūrā, Muslims, individually and collectively, are encouraged to embody, each towards the other, the essence of the practice referred to as *Iṣlāḥ al-nafs* or "the betterment of the self." Iṣlāḥ al-nafs is the acknowledgment and rectification of one's egoistic and micro-fascistic characteristics and actions. As the Prophet Muḥammad stated, "If you see me in the right, help me; if you see me in error correct me ... If any of you sees distortion in my actions, let them rectify me."[50] To beckon for help, to ask for advice, is Islamically tantamount to humbling oneself, without shame, to Others. It contributes to one's maturing, the taming of our superegos, as opposed to parasitically feeding our insecurities and vulnerabilities. In divulging our intimate fears we abandon our pride, envy, our righteous and holier than thou cloaks to facilitate intimacy and familiarity with each Other, who in turn are also undressed and exposed to us.

In contrast to pride and arrogance, which are strongly and repeatedly condemned in the Qur'ān as in Verses 39:60, 39:72, and 40:35, Shūrā facilitates accessibility to the other, indeed strengthens the skills of active listening, and gentle and honest communication because of the immense sense of self-consciousness and association with the Other that it demands in genuinely comprehending the ethical "rights" and the "wrongs" of the self and the delineation of one's own hypocrisy relative to others.[51] Shūrā aims to heal our internalized isolating walls of existence, the palpable loneliness that annihilates our mental health, as well as our festering distrust of others who presumably pose utilitarian ulterior motives. Shūrā vehemently goes against the Weberian Protestant ethic that informs Euro-American capitalism and adheres to the "myth of the self-made-man." Shūrā facilitates the ethical caring for the self as it permits the addressing of our intersecting penalties and privileges as well as our internalized and festering prejudices and fears as opposed to breeding indifference to them, emblematic in the covert (neo)liberal multicultural rubric of "post-racial color blindness." Shūrā is not founded upon confessional guilt, but rather enables individuals and communities to be non-hierarchically accountable and ethically responsible for themselves and each other in the collective binding of our struggles towards strengthening our communal fabric, relying on the cultivation of kindness (*taraḥum*) and cooperation.

Shūrā thus necessitates a "kind of radical personal responsibility" towards what is referred to as the "greater jihad of the self" (*al-jihād al-akbar*).[52] In other words, Shūrā entails an individual and collective dynamic and fluid everyday struggle engaging in molecular insurrections against our inner micro-fascisms.[53] In turn, Shūrā requires respecting and distinguishing between what is mutually obligated (*al-masuliyyatu'al-jamāʿiyyah*) between members of the same polity (*jamāʿat al-mūmineen*) and that which pertains to particularities of an individual's private environment (*khuṣuṣiyāt*). Regarding these internal insurrections, it is related in a ḥadīth (Prophetic Oral tradition) that:

> Imam Ja'far al-Sadiq (a) said: "The Prophet (s) of God dispatched a contingent of the army (to the battlefront). Upon their (successful) return, he (s) said: "Blessed are those who have performed the minor jihad and have yet to perform the major jihad." When asked, "What is the major jihad?" the Prophet (s) replied: "The jihad of the self (struggle against self)".[54]

The greater jihād against one's own micro-fascisms creates room for a revolutionary eco-system wherein Muslims and believers take comfort and refuge in each other. The greater jihād that Shūrā dictates, facilitates the germination of an egalitarian sanctuary in which equality (*musāwāt*) and justice (*ʿadalah*) can thrive in relation to all nonhuman life. The genuine humility and consistency bred through Tawḥīd and Shūrā that are enjoined and entrusted to all Muslims possesses radiating effects that extend to all intents, purposes, actions relative to all life-worlds.

Significant chapters in the Qur'ān are named after creation and nonhuman life as the Chapters of "the Moon," "the Sun," "the Thunder," "the Spider," "the Light," "the Sand Dunes," "the Smoke," "the Mountain," "the Stars," "the Jinn," "the Night," "the Fig," "the Elephant," "the Bees," and "the Ants." These Qur'ānic chapters are meant to remind and inspire complex reflections and communal deliberations, based on Shūrā, relative to our symbiotic relations to plant and animal nations in our temporary transits across this spiritual realm, regardless of how presently rooted in place we are. This way, Shūrā is not solely prescribed to an assembly of individuals, but must also be enacted in all our relations and with appreciation for Creator's magnanimous creation. In this sense, Shūrā's prescription is for an everlasting liberating engagement by our entire communities with all that undeniably belongs to and is an extension of the Divine. After all, partaking "in working towards the reconstruction of human relations at all levels of the socius, [a] 'social ecology' cannot simply take up a position of external opposition – as do, for example, existing trade union and political practices," but rather these intimacies must extend in biodiverse relation to all that defines, precedes, and determines our petty existence and which our species' survival is dependent upon.[55]

Anarcha-Islām's micro-anti-authoritarian stance is constructed on "the Qur'ānic understanding of Shūrā [as] a process of mutual advice through mutual consultation."[56] This ability to trust other Muslims, and arguably non-Muslims, demands individual and collective Muslim consciousness regarding our individual ethico-political commitments relative to ourselves and others. Shūrā's practice on an individual and collective level becomes a process and a promise of self that facilitates our constant evolution, metamorphoses, and becoming to minimize domination and oppressive micro-authoritarian power relations manifesting at the myopic level. Because Islām distinguishes between what is seen (*ẓāhir*) and hidden (*bāṭin*) which leads to a distinct understanding of private and public spheres, when a believer chooses to engage in non-compulsory Shūrā, this enhances trust (*thiqa*) in oneself and others while also working to minimize bigotry, the suspicious need for *tagassus* (spying and invasiveness), as well as *balbala* (scandalous publicity) and *namīma* (tale bearing gossip or backbiting) that often tears families, friendships, communities, indeed nations apart.[57] This further preserves each individual's dignity (*karāma*) and respect (*ihtirām*), and re-emphasizes an individual's rights to privacy (*khuṣuṣiyāt*) and *satr* (covering up faults), and delineates defamation, liability, and re-enacted states of injury. As the Qur'ān states,

> O ye who believe! Avoid suspicion as much (as possible): for suspicion in some cases is a sin: And spy not on each other behind their backs. Would any of you like to eat the flesh of his dead brother? Nay, ye would abhor it ... But fear Allāh: For Allāh is Oft-Returning, Most Merciful.[58]

In encouraging Shūrā, Islām targets micro-fascisms by recognizing micro-power's passing through the hands of the mastered no less than through the palms of the masters. In the contemporary and given that our positionalities are informed by innumerable identity crises wrought by internalized white-supremacist (neo)liberal identity politics, no singular individual or collective is immune to micro or macro-fascisms, particularly given that "fascism has already won" and is crystallized at the center of all our hearts and actions vis-à-vis the asymmetrical privileges and penalties we possess and enjoy in relation to others across dynamic and malleable intersectional matrices of race/ethnicity, class, gender, sexuality, age, ability, etc.[59] Therefore, in its collective application, Shūrā proffers a committed sense of communal cohesiveness, rebirth, and renewal. It breeds and manifests in a community a shared ethic of reciprocity and conjoint responsibility.

The collective mutual aid inherent in Shūrā is Anarcha-Islām's second micro-anti-authoritarian concept and practice: *Ijmā*ʿ. Ijmāʿ is the practice required by a Muslim community in seeking "consensus" in matters pertaining to the community.[60] Ijmāʿ emphasizes compassionate, emotionally intelligent, good-faith, knowledge-based, and horizonless open debate that is the cornerstone of any healthy community. Debate and differences are natural and to be expected in Islām for our collective enhancement. Contrary to dogmatists, the Qur'ān itself states, "for every one of you did We appoint a law and a way, and if Allāh had pleased He would have made you (all) a single people, but that He might try you in what He gave you, therefore strive with one another to hasten to virtuous deeds."[61] The right to Ijtihād as a continual mechanism in facilitating what Félix Guttarati calls "dissensus" acts as a means for subjects to critically engage in issues over which there is no consensus. Indeed, the former alongside Shūrā enables the possibility and room for Ijmā' to be attained, by keeping open avenues for the re-visitation of concerns over which there are dissident opinions. Islām unequivocally encourages and engenders informed debate, particularly when the express *niyya* (intent) is not an individual's ego, but rather driven by the community and collective Umma's *Maṣlaḥa* – Anarcha-Islām's third micro-anti-authoritarian concept and practice.[62]

Given the multidimensional composition of an Umma of Muslim and non-Muslim believers, Maṣlaḥa is a community's path towards its ideal aspirations: minimizing asymmetrical power relations and realizing egalitarianism. Maṣlaḥa is "the principle of … 'public interest'."[63] In the absence of Ijmā' (consensus) regarding issues that pertain to the Umma's Maṣlaḥa, Islām also establishes an ethics of disagreements (*Uṣūl al-Ikhtilāf*) and an ethics of hospitality (*Uṣūl al-Ḍiyāfa*) to create a bridge between members of a polity and community in the event of disagreements over ethical-political tactics or approaches.[64] *Ikhtilāf* is an "Arabic term … [meaning] taking a different position or course from that of another person either in opinion, utterance, or action." [65] *Uṣūl al-Ikhtilāf* is the recognition that dissention is an inevitable part of any relationship, but should never be engaged in for its own sake. It is critical that both parties ask of themselves and each other the question: "Was there a moment I missed to push the disagreement and negotiation of difference(s) between us forward, little by little, till the moment we could see eye to eye on our disagreement"? This is because Maṣlaḥa has to "provide benefit to individuals and the community as a whole and not only to a class [any subset of the community,] or an individual."[66] Maṣlaḥa re-emphasizes the paramount Islamic pursuit of egalitarianism, particularly if the community already offers support to each other in concert with an ethics of hospitality (*Uṣūl al-Ḍiyāfa*), and consensus exists on overarching strategic ethical-political commitments shared by all.[67]

As a micro-anti-authoritarian practice Maṣlaḥa is "at the essence of Islamic commands" and communal principles.[68] Ijmāʿ, as a required dictum and practice, represents a binding social conduct in light of the community's collective pursuit and struggle for not merely its cohesive existence, but rather its wholesome thriving as a vigorous and rigorously egalitarian community.[69] This commitment to thrive is born from the acknowledgment that egalitarianism and decolonial social justice are never-ending aspirations to be paradoxically sought yet never attained, irrespective of the quantity, quality, and intensity of Shūrā, Maṣlaḥa, and Ijmāʿ's iterations as micro-anti-authoritarian practices. However, if there is hope in Islamically transcending modern identity politics and the unequal power distributions that inform our relations, then the coalescing, multiplication, and amalgamation of the aforementioned commitments as ethical-political compasses and as part of our *thaqāfa* (critical cultural consciousness and intellect) facilitates attaining this collective anti-authoritarian horizon.

The above anarchic reading of the concepts and practices of Shūrā, Ijmāʿ, and Maṣlaḥa collectively constitute an ushering in of Anarcha-Islām's micro-anti-authoritarian principles, unveiled using Anarchic Ijtihād. Over these principles there is no compromise.

Prior to discussing Anarcha-Islām's macro-anti-authoritarian principles, it is essential to clarify a few matters. In general, there is little concrete guidance in Islām regarding macro-politics. Qur'ānic commentary is offered solely with respect to paramount abstract principles, the foremost of which is the Umma.[70] Nevertheless, there is no debate regarding the fact that any "hierarchical, dictatorial system has been condemned as non-Islamic."[71] Any tyrannical or authoritarian system is Qur'ānically forbidden. In innumerable verses, the Qur'ān states, "And [all] faces will be humbled before the Ever-Living, the Sustainer of existence. And they will have failed whomever carries injustice."[72] Another verse notes, "O you who have believed, do not consume one another's wealth unjustly but only [in lawful] business by mutual consent. And do not kill yourselves [or one another]. Indeed, Allāh is to you ever Merciful."[73] And yet another verse recalls, "And remember when He made you successors after the 'Ad people and settled you in the land, [and] you take for yourselves palaces from its plains and carve from the mountains, homes. Then remember the favors of Allāh and do not commit abuse on the earth, spreading corruption."[74]

The underlying premise for the macro-political condemnation of all tyranny is the revolutionary conceptualization of God as the sole sovereign and protector of rights for all beings. In Islām, righteous "deeds ... recognized are not the monopoly of any single competitor ... as the judge God, has to be above the narrow interest of participants ... [and] claims of familiarity with the judge [God] with any particular 'team' will not avail the participants."[75] *Al-Ḥaqq* means "The Just," from whom the plural Islamic concept of *ḥuqūq Allāh* (divine rights) is derived. All possess the right to access *ḥuqūq Allāh* as well as the inherent unchangeable (*ittibā*ʿ) right to access it as individuals, communities, and Adam's peoples (*ḥuqūq al-ʿIbād*, *ḥuqūq al-nās*, or *ḥuqūq Banī-Ādam*).[76] Even Prophet Muḥammad was warned by God not to exceed God's adjudication over this divinely decreed right to access.[77] Through the emphatic pillar and reminder of *Tawḥīd*, Islām consistently subscribes to the minimization of repression (*qahr*) and emphasizes social justice (*ʿadāla ijtimāʿiya*) as a foundation against oppression (*ẓulm*). It is through the creed of *Tawḥīd* that God affords Muslims the right to embrace any macro-political arrangement that Muslims deem fit. In other words, this right to orient macro-politically is entrusted to a Muslim community, yet contingent upon the guarantee that the macro-political structure chosen by believers does not contradict the concept of Tawḥīd and the micro-political practices of Shūrā, Ijmāʿ, Maṣlaḥa, and accompanying Islamic ethics.[78] God intends and appoints this right as a merciful act for our species such that they may adapt to differing geographical, spatial, temporal, and socio-political-economic historical circumstances and terrains.

Unlike the capitalist-state and its hierarchical Euro-American secular-Christian institutions, disciplinary, and controlling mechanisms, in which power assumes more crystallized, hegemonic forms, pre-modern Islām acknowledged the right of any Muslim to engage in Ijtihād as a continuous method of facilitating dissent in the face of injustice. However, in the aftermath of the Prophet's death and particularly following the initial "Golden Era of Islam" period, with each successive generation there was an incremental withering away of Ijtihād, Shūrā, Ijmāʿ, and Maṣlaḥa as public practices replaced by the gradual rise of authoritarianism. In the Golden era, the initial four "Rightly Guided Caliphs" – Abū Bakr al-Ṣiddīq (r.632–634), ʿUmar ibn al-Khaṭṭāb (r.13–23/634–44), ʿUthmān ibn ʿAffān (r. 23–35/644–56), and ʿAlī ibn Abī Ṭālib (r. 35–40/656–61) – did not consider themselves "rulers" in the formal understandings of the word. They represented a tight-knit circle of fallible and close companions to the Prophet (*Ṣaḥābah*), all foretold of their acceptance into heaven without permitting this revelation to feed into their hubris; each possessed distinctive personal traits that complemented the qualities of the others. All four were exceedingly humble, accountable, accessible, courageous, generous, righteous, deeply reflective, and embodied the revolutionary Tawḥīdic spirit, having internalized Islām's social justice foundations and pillars. While Abū Bakr was revered for his extreme honest compassion (*al-ṣādiq*), ʿUmar was resolute and prudent (*ḥāzim*), and whereas ʿUthmān was extremely generous (*sakhy* or *karīm*), the remarkable ʿAlī was distinguishable from the rest in his profound knowledge (*ʿilm*). None coveted power and they were all hesitant to become caretaking leaders as they accompanied each other, and assigned responsibilities to one another while binding themselves and Muslims to Ijmāʿ, Shūrā, and Maṣlaḥa. After all, as will be discussed, according to the Qurʾān our entire species are regarded as equal Khulafā (Caretakers and stewards) of the Creator on earth. What led to the gradual development of tyranny and decadence, in fact, is the collective Muslim abandonment of the revolutionary anti-authoritarian spirit of the micro-anti-authoritarian principles that informed the nascent period.

Thus, Anarcha-Islām rejects the exhausted, sectarian debates about the Prophet's "successor" for a number of reasons. First, as Anarcha-Islām and the Qur'ān argue, designating any "successor," particularly a family member, was and remains a nepotistic sign of kingship (*taghūt*), whereas the Prophet consistently endorsed the practices of Ijtihād, Shūrā, Maṣlaḥa, and Ijmāʿ as communal affairs given the Islamic expectation of their internalization and practice by all Muslims. This point is often neglected by most mainstream Muslims, particularly the major sects, Sunnis and Shi'ites alike, if not across the board in contemporary Islāms. On the one hand, a majority of Sunnis, past and contemporary, claim that the Prophet's deathbed statement, that his dearest friend and father-in-law, Abū Bakr al-Ṣiddīq, lead prayers (and merely that) as evident claim to the former being regarded a single rightful political "heir," although narratives of inheritance are forbidden. On the other hand, and in a similar dismissal of the implications of nepotistic ṭaghūt based on kinship relations, the majority of Shi'ites argue that the Prophet's cousin and son-in-law, ʿAlī ibn Abī Ṭālib, ought to have led, citing his presence beside the Prophet on his deathbed and the theological permission (due to his familial proximity) that he assist in the washing of the Prophet's body turned cold. Shi'ites insist on their narrative by way of contending that Abu Bakr and Umar coveted power. For though the latter were present at the Prophet's funeral, they were absent from his bedside, and instead were at a roofed building *Saqīfat Banī Sāʿidah* where a dispute erupted. What the Shi'ite narrative elides is that sedition had already emerged at Saqifah between the *muhājireen* (Muslims in Mecca who migrated to Medina with the Prophet Muḥammad to Medina) and the *anṣār* (who were originally from Medina) as to the vacuum the Prophet's death was about to create. In insisting on a single Muslim successor, Sunnis and Shi'ites ignore not only Ijtihād, Shūrā, Ijmāʿ, and Maṣlaḥa as public practices, but also dismiss what *made* these "Rightly Guided Caliphs" collectively and not merely individually exceptional – as in the *Bayʿah* (pact) they made to guide each other and Muslims through the Qur'ān during the initial tumultuous period that led to the assassination of three of the four of them. None of them sought revenge for the others' deaths given the Creator's warning in the Qur'ān about the dangers of sedition (*fitnah*).[79] Maṣlaḥa and the public good were above any and each of their personal whims and desires.

Thus, Anarcha-Islām challenges the classical scholarship on Muslim governance that argues for the belief in a singular "Khalīfah ," often strictly interpreted as individual "successor." The Qur'ān evokes the plural form of *Khulafā* to indicate the need for our species to recognize our collective and obligatory responsibility for the cultivation and caretaking of this earth together. Even pre-modern and modern scholars who argue for the need of a single human Īmām as a "symbol whose presence is necessary for the welfare and protection of the Umma," always affirm that this human leader must "be subordinate, in one sense or another, to those supreme textual Imams," the Qur'ān, aḥādīth (the Oral Tradition), and Sunnah (Prophetic practice).[80] In turn, I argue that the singular form of Khalīfah obscures a far more complex and radical vision that coincides with *anarchistic* values of freedom, equality, responsibility, mutual aid, consensus, and resistance to injustice and tyranny.

The gradual Muslim abandonment of their original micro-non-authoritarian principles was parallel to the long rise of Muslim arrogance and nepotism, the Euro-American Crusading eviction of Muslims and Jews from Andalusia Spain in 1492, the beginning of the collapse of the Ottoman Empire in 1798, and the Sykes-Picot European imperialist fragmentation of predominantly Muslim societies. It facilitated the Umma's contemporary diminishment as pre-modern Muslim clergy introduced "non-Islamic dynastic notions" into Islām, while modernity ushered in European capitalist-states that spawned a reactionary transition towards post-colonial nationalism (*Waṭaniyyah*).[81] With the arrival of post-colonial elites, a new generation of self-righteous Muslim clergy arrived to (further) institutionalize Islām and affirm illegitimate dictators and monarchies. For example, in the contemporary, as an authoritarian institution, Al-Azhar University – a pre-eminent institution for Islamic religious studies – has been complicit with whichever pharaoh and demagogue has arisen in Egypt. These newer generations of Muslim clergy collaborating with dictators are as abominable as the generation of the tenth century that purportedly attempted "to shut the door of Ijtihād" during the ʿAbbāssid era.

As Maxime Rodinson argues:

> With the coming of [nationalist] independence … gradually … [rose] on the social scale ... [alongside] the (more or less exploiting) upper strata [who] increasingly proclaim[ed] their "attachment to Islam, in a frenzied search for an ideological guarantee for their social and material advantages".[82]

Vastly different from pre-modern, egalitarian circles of scholarship such as *Bayt Al-Hikmah* (The House of Wisdom), a library and research centre for Ijtihād, inaugurated by Hārūn al-Rašīd, in the early ninth century and culminating during al-Ma'mūn's reign, contemporary Islamic institutions began to domesticate Islamic knowledges and separate them from worldly affairs in an attempt to emulate segregated and hierarchical European knowledge systems. Modern clerics overarchingly dismiss the imperative of Shūrā, Maṣlaḥa, and Ijmāʿ as public doctrinal ethico-political practices to be exercised in public assemblies, open forums, informal colloquiums, symposiums, and rallies, in turn violating the "right to access" decreed by God for Muslims to individually and collectively partake in the rigorous questioning and interrogation of their own sense of self, each other, as a community and their interconnected Islamic knowledge(s).[83]

For example, unlike the neoconservative and cisheteropatriarchal perspectives of contemporary Al-Azhar, medieval Islamic jurists considered mental health crises and medical ethics to be related to social justice. Such connections can be seen in the works of the medieval Muslim scholars who addressed gender and sexuality relative to mental health, obsessive-compulsive disorders, grief, substance abuse, depression, anxiety, and suicide from spiritually meditative, aroma-therapeutic, bio-psychosocial, and musical perspectives. They did this with group therapies that did not stigmatize patients. Re-establishing this perspective would require the decolonial reintroduction of spirituality's relationship to healing and queer-feminisms. However, in light of taboos regarding queer-feminisms, Al-Azhar is disinterested in these pre-modern methods that exist in works such as Abū Bakr Muḥammad ibn Zakariyyā' al-Rāzī's (854–932) book *El Mansuri' dan 'Al Tibb al-Ruhani*, as well as others like Al-Farabi (870–950) and Ibn Sina (980–1037).[84]

Contemporary Al-Azhar is too keen to preserve the dominant cisheteropatriarchal social, cultural, and religious order that exists in Egypt, rather than exploring alternative Islamic conceptualizations of gender. Innumerable scholars have also identified the contemporary destructive legacy of (neo)liberalism on academic intellectualism, the absence of *Ijtihād* and *thaqāfa* (critical intellectual consciousness), and social diseases such as poverty and illiteracy as factors that influence contemporary SWANA perspectives on discourses now regarded as anathema, particularly as the conflation between intersex and transgender people.[85] In this example, the general Egyptian and Muslim disarray is also informed by the political co-optation of gender and queer significations. Military-ethnonationalist and Islamist forces, engaged in cultural and religious wars, politically co-opt gender/queer significations as each seeks to be the true representative and moral guardian of Islām and Egyptian identity.[86] After all, *fatwās* (religious jurisprudential adjudications), issued by institutions as Al-Azhar on gender egalitarianism and sexual ethics, are both religious documents and inherently political. Fatwās and the publicity around them distract from far more pertinent interrelated social injustices (*maẓālim*) in predominantly Muslim societies such as racism/ethnocentrism against the Sudanese, Sinai Bedouins, Ethiopian, Somali, Iraqi, and Palestinian refugees in Egypt, as well as indentured labor and enslavement, debt bondage, sexual- and gender-based harassment, domestic abuse, and the continuous clampdown on political expression.[87] Respectively, religious institutions are more keen on maintaining strict gender boundaries and other dominant power structures, without considering broader implications of these structures, despite their purported concern for social harmony and the social fabric. Religious institutions seldom offer grounded solutions to skyrocketing Egyptian divorce rates or the disease of gender-based sexual harassment or the emasculating crises of poverty that Arab and Muslim youth experience.[88] Rather, they are often content with casting women and gender dissidents as the mainspring from which Egypt's crises emerge, not colonialism/imperialism or corruption.

The contemporary absence of genuine Ijtihād is critical considering that it is reported, through Anas Ibn Mālik, that the Prophet Muḥammad stated: "Seeking knowledge is incumbent on every Muslim; they who offers knowledge to those who do not appreciate it, is like the one who decorates pigs with precious stones, pearls and gold."[89] This Qur'ānic public right violated by clerics is one which "no authority, no leader, no government, no assembly can restrict, abrogate or violate in any way."[90] The clergy's corruption, besides their aspirations to wealth, pious status, loyalty, and the propping up of monarchies and dictatorships, local and foreign, has led to the consolidation of authoritarian interpretations of Islām.

For example, the Islamic concept *Khilāfah* has been exploited by the sheikhs and clerics who use it to justify their adoption of the Eurocentric notion of modern-states in the name of safeguarding Islam and the so-called moral purity of predominantly Muslim societies. Yet, Khilāfah, which literally "means 'representation'... [with] the connotations of ... a deputy [or] representative," does not indicate a particular type of government and the Prophet Muḥammad never called himself *Khalīfatullah.*[91] His immediate successors, noted above, were each known as the Prophet's successors (i.e., *Khalīfat al-Rasūl*), but this ascription was not associated with a particular form of government rule. The singular form, Khalīfah, appears in the Qur'ān in Verses 2:30, 38:26, 10:73, and 35:39. However, the plural form, that is, Khulafā occurs more often in 7:69, 7:74, 27:62, 6:165, and 10:14. Neither the singular nor plural form of Khulafā in the Qur'ān in any way indicates what form of governance, as that would negate and render unnecessary the public and collective practices of Ijtihād, Shūrā, Ijmāʿ, and Maṣlaḥa.

Even the classical schema for choosing a singular Khalīfah or "deputy," developed during the medieval period and accepted by most contemporary Muslim scholarship, noted that the choice is to be governed by three binding criteria. First, any selection process is acceptable, as long as the non-negotiable tenets of Shūrā, Ijmāʿ, and Maṣlaḥa are maintained.[92] Second, the choice must occur in "conditions that [would] allow Muslims the opportunity to choose with *full knowledge of the facts*" be it in relation to political candidates and the transparent processes entailed in their selection.[93] Third, there can be no coercion of any kind, in itself an impossible condition to guarantee, even in the grandest well-renowned "democracy" in the world. But, in turn, how can this influence be reconciled with contemporary political campaigns that are inherently coercive and tainted by a rigged electoral college system often pegged against the popular vote, as well as 2010 Citizen United and "*McCutcheon v FEC*" verdicts that give special interest groups unlimited influence over politics.[94] This is to say nothing with respect to dark money ads, corporate and non-corporate, labor union lobbying, partisan gerrymandering, multi-billion dollar advertising industries, neoliberal mainstream fourth estate media, that all represent gatekeeping mechanisms in collusion with one another, with each election cycle recommencing arguments on racial redistricting, gentrification, territorial remapping, and voter disenfranchisement.

These criteria, well established by scholars such as John Esposito, including this Islamic interpretation's anchorage in consultation (Shūrā), consensus (Ijmāʿ), and independent interpretative judgments (Ijtihād), do not fit within narrow European definitions of self-governance.[95] In light of prevalent ignorance, illiteracy, the appalling fermentation of poverty, corruption, and misery, and other social phenomena rampant within all societies, there can be no doubt that such criteria cannot be Islamically fulfilled in existing political forms. This is a vital point, particularly when it is reported that the Prophet said:

> The Prophethood will remain amongst you for as long as Allāh wills it to be. Then Allāh will raise it when He wills to raise it [meaning the prophet will die]. Then there will be the Khīlāfa *upon the Prophetic methodology*. And it will last for as long as Allāh

> wills it to last. Then Allāh will raise it when He wills to raise it. Then there will be biting *monarchical kingship*, and it will remain for as long as Allāh wills it to remain. Then Allāh will raise it when He wills to raise it. Then there will be *tyrannical* (forceful) *despotic kingship* and it will remain for as long as Allāh wills it to remain. Then He will raise it when He wills to raise it. Then there will be a Khīlāfa *upon the Prophetic methodology*. Then he (the Prophet) was silent.[96]

In the absence of the conditions required for a singular Khalīfah and the "non-binding nature of the idea itself," Anarcha-Islām's anti-statist and anti-institutional commitment proposes a radically different ethical-political territory and trajectory.[97] Anarcha-Islām does away with the desire to seek a single representative of the Umma, who has supreme religious institutionalized authority, given too that the concept of a so-called "Islamic state" does not exist in Islām. In resisting and combating the classical singular perceptions of Khalīfah, I contend that Muslims are collectively stewards or Caretakers of each other and their affairs, and that the concept of "caretaker" is pluralistic. As John Esposito notes, it is "possible to interpret ... the Qur'ān as identifying human beings in general as God's vicegerents [Khulafā, multiple, in opposition to the singular, Khalīfah] on Earth ... [with] human stewardship over God's creations."[98] This reading is in line with Muslim feminist scholars like Amina Wadud, Asma Barlas, and Kecia Ali who have also argued that not all interpretations of Islām and Muslims embrace the authoritarian, capitalist, transphobic, conservative, and essentialist positions that have emerged in contemporary expressions of Orthodox/Fundamentalist Islām.[99] This way, Anarcha-Islām is also inspired by scholarships like Zahra Ayubi's *Gendered Morality: Classical Islamic Ethics of the Self, Family, and Society* (2019) and Sarra Tlili's *Animals in the Qur'ān* (2012) in reinterpreting the concept of Khulafā (Caretakers) in its plural form to emphasize "empathetic responsibility" across genders towards recognizing anti-authoritarian egalitarianism amongst our collective species. In this reading, Khulafā disrupts the mantle of male leadership and its paternalistic hegemonic constraining in the hands of a single leader.

Ironically, this conceptualization of Khulafā as pluralistic is confirmed in Islām's *Universal Declaration of Human Rights* (1996) that emphasizes "that the ultimate objective of the Umma ... is to reach the level of self-governance."[100] In turn, Anarcha-Islām's anti-statist commitment is grounded in the reinterpretation of Khalīfah from a singular to multiple "foundation for concepts of human responsibility ... of opposition to systems of domination."[101] Furthermore, Anarcha-Islām's anti-statist commitment is informed by two positions or locales. First, an acknowledgment of human responsibility, whereby individuals are responsible for themselves, for each other, and this earth; second, an opposition to Eurocentric systems and orders of domination embodied in the contemporary frameworks of the modern-state, as they easily facilitate the contradicting of the creed of *Tawḥīd*. It is solely with Anarcha-Islām's anti-statist commitment that there may truly be a "transfer of power of Ijtihād from individual representatives of schools to Muslim legislative assemblies which in view of the growth of "opposing" sects is the only form of" Ijmāʿ possible.[102] This type of Ijmāʿwould permit flourishing contributions to and discussions from lay Muslims who desire, possess, and have a right to publicly participate in political decision-making processes, if only to reclaim, rewrite, and reconceptualize our histories.[103]

The desire for a singular authority figure and leader, which Anarcha-Islām challenges, involves an internalized messiah and savior complex that can be seen in another non-binding Islamic concept and practice that Muslim clergy have also manipulated and at times used interchangeably with Khilāfah: "Īmām[ah]."[104] Mostly emphasized in the ethos of Shi'ite "Imamology," or prophetic philosophy and eschatology, Īmām as a term has diverse meanings.[105] According to Al-Barghouti, "etymologically as well as theoretically and historically the Imam means a book, a guide, one that is followed by a group of people: 'and the Qur'ān is the Imam of the Muslims ... and God said [referring to the Day of Resurrection] *Yawma nad'ou kulla unasin be'Imamihim* (the Day we'll call upon every people by their Book)'."[106] This is consistent with my argument that there is no Islamic macro-formulation of governance, besides the emphatic and stringent emphasis on the identified micro-anti and non-authoritarian concepts, commitments, and practices. Īmām may possesses other connotations. As Al-Barghouti writes,

> The Imam also means the person followed: The Messenger of God is the Imam of his Umma and they all have to follow [the verb used here is *etimam* which is a participle of *Amm*] his way [*Sunna*]'; the Imam means the ideal, "the Imam is every ideal to be followed"; the Imam is the rope or piece of wood by which the equilibrium of any building is measured; "the Imam is the way or the road (*al-Imamu al-Tareeq*)".[107]

The term Īmām is often used to refer to a singular individual. For example, it is commonly used in denoting the individual who leads other Muslims in a required or supplementary prayer. However, this obscures the fact that whoever leads prayers is subject to fellow worshipers and more principally that choosing who will lead prayers involves a re-affirmation of Shūrā, Ijmā', and Maṣlaḥa, and does not do away with them. Muslims always reserve the right in their collective decision-making to accept or reject a particular individual leading them, even during prayer, and on any occasion, for that specific instant and moment in time.

However, the paramount connotation of the concept is that "'the Imam is the Umma'."[108] The implication of this is that both the Īmām and the Umma are a collective image or understanding of themselves that guides Muslims to govern in specific ways. Accordingly, each of us acknowledges ourselves and each other as Khulafā who together are engaged in the collective combating of our individual and collective micro- and macro-fascisms. In this instance, it is the Qur'ān that acts as the sole spiritual guide, as the Qur'ān is what collectively safeguards us as believers (*mūmineen*) from derision. Again, in this occasion, our collective mode of socio-political and economic organization could very well be anarchism, and the Anarcha-Islamic ideals that we, individually and collectively, aspire towards, as derived from Islām and our holy and traditional texts. This is further affirmed in that there is no obligatory theological, moral, ethical, or political justification in Islām that conclusively and compulsorily mandates the exclusivity of the latter singular definition of Īmām.

As with pre-modern conceptualizations of Dawla (discussed in the following sections), Īmām and Khalīfah are therefore non-binding, dynamic, and temporally not static concepts, indicating the inherent revolutionary cyclical character of political Muslim subjectivities and governance. The fluidity of the former non-compulsory concepts also indicates the fact that, doctrinally speaking, the Qur'ān acknowledges that power is always "lively," in line with post-anarchistic conceptualizations of power. The penultimate justification behind this conceptualization is to delineate power's concentation, and illuminate that everyone always already possess agency regardless of how oppressed we may perceive ourselves to be. Arguably, this is the reason that the radically democratic "Kharijites (the *Najdat*), ... argued that if people obeyed the rules of the Qur'ān and the Hadith, that is, the textual guides, there would be no need for a human guide, or any kind of authority."[109]

Similar to the terms Īmām and Khalīfah, the contemporary meaning of the term *siyāsa* (the Arabic term for "politics" or the "art of governance") and its relationship to Muslim theology has varied widely. As Muhammad Khalid Masud discusses in *The Doctrine of Siyasa in Islamic Law*, siyāsa's etymological history ranged from training a horse to punishing a criminal before it came to generally mean the art of governance.[110] There are ample divergent medieval doctrines of siyāsa (politics) by pre-modern Muslim scholars such as Abu'l-Hasan 'Al-Mawardi that show the debates over the concept and that contributed to differing Ash'arite and Mu'tazillite perspectives over who and what constitutes a Muslim, particularly when it pertinently relates to matters of disagreement and conflict amongst Muslims themselves, as well as in relation to other non-Muslim believers (*mūmineen*) as enunciated in the Qur'ān.[111]

Unfortunately, with time, siyāsa in contemporary Islamic law came to mean a ruler's discretion over *fiqh* (Islamic jurisprudence).[112]

Al-Mawardi was a *qāḍī* (judge) who sought to restore Sunni orthodoxy against the Shi'i Buwayhid Sultans.[113] In his seminal work *al-Ahkam al-sultaniyya wal-Wilayat al-Diniyya* he outlined "the rules of political authority according to Islamic law."[114] Although he sought to unite religious and political authority within a single system, it is already possible to see within his work the false binaries between religion (*dīn*) and politics (*siyāsa*) that followed the Prophet's death and that of the first four Caliphs. Al-Mawardi recognized siyāsa's binding nature to Islām and argued that rulers should hear cases having to do with Islamic law, under the prerogative that "al-qawanin al-siyasa ["laws of politics and governance"] were necessarily related to the protection of the community."[115] On the other hand, scholars such as Abū ʿAbdillāh Muhammad ibn Idrīs al-Shāfiʿī argued for the distinction "between the rights of God and the rights of [hu]man[s]."[116] He argued that neither the Khalīfah nor the Īmām be permitted "to hear the cases relating to the rights of God."[117] Others like Muhammad al-Ghazali's (d. 1111) drew on Muslim philosophers who followed the Aristotelian concept of "Politics" in conceptualizing siyāsa.[118] He distinguished between the siyāsa of the "ulama" and "fuqaha" (Muslims learned in Islamic jurisprudence) and the siyāsa of rulers, noting that the latter in particular "refers to social organization and cooperation with reference to economic resources and their control."[119] And yet, other Shafi'ite jurists like the Hanbalite Abu al-Wafa Ali Ibn ʿAqil (d. 1119) debated the relationship between siyāsa and Islamic law arguing that siyāsa is not entirely independent of sharīʿa.[120] In so doing, Ibn ʿAqīl drew on three practices of his day that included: (a) when theological "philosophers (alhukama' al-ilahiyyun)" can opt for "hikma [i.e. wisdom]" in determining the appropriate conditions in which sharīʿa *can* be suspended; (b) second, when "jurists (*al-futana* or the wise)" can subject reason to sharīʿa; and (c) finally, how a ruler's "governing of worldly affairs," including the management of daily decisions can occur, "where no text of the sharia was available."[121] Ibn ʿAqīl concluded that a ruler is permitted to engage in *al-siyāsa al-sharʿiyya* (Islamically legitimized politics), and hence that rulers have the discretion to fuse theological-political power so long as the ruler's siyāsa is in accord with sharīʿa.[122]

Ibn ʿAqīl legitimized this view by contending that siyāsa is a tool for improving people's welfare and can easily be entwined with theology, although the idea of a singular Khalīfah, let alone what their relationship to sharīʿa ought or should be, even if the former were regarded as a legitimate governance model, is not stated in the Qur'ān.[123]

By the time Muslim scholars like Ibn Taymiyya (d. 1328) and Ibn Qayyim (d. 1350) were writing about siyāsa, Ijmāʿ, Shūrā, and Maṣlaḥa had already been abandoned as public practices. Masud argues that facing the Mongol invasions from without and sedition from within, these scholars, including historians such as Ibn al-Tiqtiqa (b. 1262), redefined siyāsa as "the chief resource of the king, on which he relies to prevent bloodshed, defend chastity, prevent evil, subjugate evildoers and forestall misdeeds which lead to sedition and disturbance."[124] Similarly, the Hanbalite jurist Ibn Taymiyya, given the Mongol aggressions, argued that siyāsa, should be assimilated the into *sharīʿa*, because a forceful ruler was needed to uphold Islām's pillars of jihād and *Ḥudūd* (Islamic penal codes and punishments).[125] Ibn Taymiyya's "doctrine of al-siyasa al-shariyya [or the "political discretion of rulers"] went further than other jurists in allowing the right of siyāsa to the ruler," given how he refused to distinguish between the political authority of a ruler and that of religious courts.[126] In contrast, Ibn Qayyim argued that siyāsa should be independent of *sharīʿa*, as "siyasa [as practiced by rulers] could be unjust or just."[127]

Ibn Nujaym (d. 1562) tried to resolve this debate by defining siyāsa as a delicate balance between matters of spirituality and politics.[128] Ibn Nujaym's view was first posited by scholars like Taqī al-Dīn Aḥmad Al-Maqrīzī (d. 1441) who feared the influence of the Mongolian *yāsā* customs along with other foreign influences during this period on Muslims.[129] As Masud notes, "al-Maqrizi explains that after Turkish rule in Egypt, two types of law began operating, shari'a dealt with religious matters such as prayer, Hajj, fasting and other pious acts, whereas qanun [formulated and derived laws] governed the matters relating to public interest and management of properties."[130] Al-Maqrīzī saw these as meeting in siyāsa, which he understood as "seeking the welfare of the people by leading them to the way of success in this and other world. The siyāsa of the Prophet focused on everyone, high and low and in spiritual and mundane matters, the siyāsa of the rulers concerned mundane matters of everyone, the siyāsa of the *ulama* [i.e., "scholars"] dealt only with the spiritual matters, but not for everyone."[131]

In modern times, the impact of colonialism caused further alterations to siyāsa's conceptualization. Rifāʿah Rāfiʿ aṭ-Ṭahṭāwī (d. 1873) used siyāsa as the translation for *loi, règlement*, in his Arabic translation of the French constitution of 1830.[132] Egyptian jurists such as Abd al-Wahhab Khallaf and Ahmad Fathi al-Bahnasi defined siyāsa as the management of public affairs in an "Islamic state that could mean the dispensation of the rulers to take judicial-theological actions in the name of public interest, although they both argued it could not be contrary to Islamic principles and maintained that political ruling is distinct from Islamic jurisprudence."[133] Masud contrasts these definitions of siyāsa with that of the Algerian jurist Abu 'Abd al-Fattah 'Ali ibn Hajj, who distinguished between ordinary siyāsa and al-siyāsa al-sharʿiyya.[134] According to Masud, ibn Hajj's discussion of al-siyāsa al-sharʿiyya is more focused on "political affairs (hukm al-Imamah, dealing with matters relating to governance)."[135] For ibn Hajj, "[al-]siyāsa [al-] shar'iyya [that] originated with Prophet Muḥammad, [represented] two aspects of siyāsa [that] were combined in his person: tabligh [conveying the message] and Imama [guiding the polity]."[136] Here it is rather clear how the Prophet Muḥammad saw faith as inherently political, Khilāfah as multiple, and Shūrā, Ijmāʿ, and Maṣlaḥa as public practices. For ibn Hajj, "the rules of siyāsa relating to tabligh are universal and immutable" and "the rules relating to Imama, on the other hand, are subject to change."[137]

These views represent a brief overview of the fluid, even false, dualities at play in the equation of siyāsa and Muslim (political) theology. Despite their malleability, the continual concerns of pre-modern and contemporary scholars is a recognition of their inseparability. It is for this reason that Anarcha-Islām adopts the view that politics and spirituality are inseparable and even indistinguishable. They may only be momentarily separated in so far as what constitutes pure "ethical" and "moral" realms, especially with respect to the former's correlations to *ifrāṭ* (the expansion) and *tafrīṭ* (restriction) in the appropriate interpretation of God's word and what the Creator expects of us, but the delineations represent a fine line.

For this reason, Anarcha-Islām maintains that Ijtihād, Shūrā, Ijmāʿ, and Maṣlaḥa ought to be collective, communal practices, particularly in the absence of a monolithic Islām. Anarcha-Islām also contends that secularism is non-existent in the contemporary, given the inseparability of any faith and spirituality. The ethics and siyāsa that inform any ideology or political identity formation is a form of spirituality. Euro-American societies have striven to forcibly transplant and project a Christian-secular experience upon SWANA societies that the Europeans themselves have never concretely nor successfully established. This process can be seen in the work of innumerable liberal scholars like Tariq Ramadan and other "American-Muslims" noted in the Introduction, who shallowly grapple with fraudulent concepts such as a "European-Islam," as they seek to legitimate assimilation into a white-supremacist civilizational colonial present.[138] The hypocrisy is most clear when Ramadan draws upon the examples of Mustafa Kemal Ataturk and Gamal Abdul Nasser as secularists in Muslim-majority societies. Although Ramadan rightfully identifies that their secular "history took a different course" than it did in Euro-America, he does not offer the same reflective courtesy to digest the teachings from the initial period of the Prophet and what exceptionally characterized it.[139] Ramadan draws on "Alain de Libera," and selectively chooses pre-modern scholars to support his position on legitimizing Islamic "secularism" based on the siyāsa and related theological debates above, while ignoring the role spirituality still played then, and the implications of the fact that neither racial capitalism nor nation-states existed prior to medieval times. His evidence actually undercuts the argument that an "Islamic state" supposedly existed in medieval times, a view espoused by militant Muslim movements, despite the fact that the macro-political framework was that of the Umma. This is most notable, when Ramadan argues that the dominant position of pre-modern Muslim scholars was to reject "any attempt by the state to impose any particular school of jurisprudence."[140] In so doing, Ramadan cites pre-modern Muslim scholars such as Malik ibn Anas (711–95), and Ahmed ibn Hanbal (780–855) who "resisted attempts by the state to impose a single doctrine on the createdness or uncreatedness of the Qur'ān."[141] This dehistoricized view is one which Ramadan excessively repeats and promotes, and indeed conflates the medieval conceptualization of Dawla with misinterpretation as "the State," although, as I have argued above and highlight further below they are not synonymous. Furthermore, contemporary scholars and activists like him do not critically engage or offer a strategic vision of an overarching project of decolonization that would pave the way to liberation from neoliberalism. Ramadan's vision of a "Euro-American Islam" is emulated by many like the Zaytuna Institute and scholars like Sherman Jackson, Hamza Yusuf, and Zaid Shakir, as well as Muslim celebrity activists and politicians like Linda Sarsour, Dahlia Mogahed, Omar Suleiman, Ilhan Omar, and Rashida Tlaib. While the latter activists and professional politicians are more attentive to social justice concerns, they incoherently and selectively fetishize certain causes relative to historical Muslim political-theological debates, in justifying their unapologetic insistence on Euro-American identities, transforming them into ambivalent but complicit upholders of settler-colonialism and Indigenous dispossession. While they address Black, anti-Zionist and feminist struggles, they generally ignore queer-feminist and Indigenous issues, as the latter causes would disavow them of their Euro-American Muslim identities as well as disrupt the myth of the immigrant dream, and imply paying more than lip-service to their decolonial responsibilities in intent, purpose, and action as settlers of color to abolitionist stances and the rematriation of Indigenous land.[142] Such a decolonial acknowledgment would also imply that they would have to address the fact that cisheteropatriarchy is a pillar of the modern-state which renders their Women's Marches empty from even a gestural standpoint. After all, one can confidently claim that the farce that is Christian-secularism, at best, amounts to a superficial melting-pot multicultural liberalism that still retains its Euro-American crusading and Protestant missionary trajectories, which innumerable decolonial and radical Indigenous and non-Indigenous social movements have critiqued.[143] Liberal multiculturalism in Euro-America continues to deny the rights of Indigenous peoples to land, and their demands for sovereignty, self-determination, (non-statist) nationhood, and autonomy.[144] Capitalist-states are incapable of reconciling the rights of their minority constituents, subjects, and citizens, as these rights are attained and achieved at the unacceptable expense of innumerable other minorities.

In contrast, Anarcha-Islām is based on interpreting politics as the affective condition and natural mode of existence since time immemorial, whether we have actively chosen to acknowledge our political participation or passively claim that politics has nothing to do with spirituality, hence denying our own mobilization and agential complicities in power and its oppressive dynamics. Politics is inseparable from Islamic principles, and the question of social justice from its inception has been related to spirituality, faith, and religion. We are never "outside" the manifold of politics even if we may naively claim to be "apolitical" or "nihilist." Politics not only defines our relationship as a species, but is implicit in our connection with nonhuman life. This is how an anti-statist Anarcha-Islām, an egalitarian Islām, becomes conceivable and possible.

The "Authority" of Prophet Muḥammad and Creator

Given the preceding discussion of the weak foundation for the singular conceptualizations of authority relating to classical understandings of Khilāfah and Īmāmah, the two remaining authorities are the Prophet Muḥammad and God.[145] Clearly, Muslims ought to appreciate everything that Muḥammad taught. However, a prophet signifies prophecy, nothing else. Accordingly, Prophet Muḥammad – upon him be peace – is not a sultan, sheikh, or God. He is a *Nabī* (prophet) and *Rasūl* (messenger) whose duty is to convey religious prophecies and teachings, purely for the sake of the call, as guided by Allāh and on behalf of Islām. Muḥammad is not to be deified or worshipped and was also, though unlike us, fallible, as were Moses and all the other prophets and messengers. This is evident in at least three Qur'ānic verses. The first verse is: "Say (O Muḥammad) that I am only a mortal like you."[146] The second verse is 41:6: "Say I [Muḥammad] am nothing but a mortal: It is revealed to me by Inspiration, that your Allāh is one Allāh."[147]

The third verse directly addresses the scope of Prophet Muḥammad's authority:

> For those who take as *Awliyâ* [guardians, supporters, helpers, protectors, etc.] others besides Him [i.e., whom take other deities, other than Allāh as protectors, and worship them, even then] Allāh is *Ḥafīẓ* [Protector] over them [i.e., takes care of their deeds and will recompense them], and you [O Muḥammad] are not a *Wakîl* [guardian or a disposer of their affairs or have say] over them.[148]

Thus, God is the Absolute Authority, and Muḥammad is forbidden from becoming, or performing even the role of a *Wakîl* (guardian) and disposer of affairs and claims over non-Muslims. Accordingly, beloved Muḥammad's "authority" ought to be put to rest.

As for the "authority" of Allāh, it is pivotal to first understand that in Anarcha-Islām, as the Qur'ān itself states, "Lā īkrāh fi'al-dīn."[149] To express it more explicitly, as the Qur'ān states, "There is no compulsion in religion." Anarcha-Islām is not concerned with "vanguardism," "conquering," or "converting" anarchists or anyone for that matter to either Islām or Anarcha-Islām. As noted in Chapter 2, Anarcha-Islām distinguishes between ethics and morals, and redefines who is Muslim and non-Muslim according to Qur'ānic distinction between religion, faith, and spirituality.

A key verse is as follows:

> "And they say, Be Jews or Christians, then you will be guided." Say (to them, O Muḥammad Peace be upon him), Nay, (We follow) only the religion of Ibrāhīm (Abraham), Ḥanīfa [Islamic Monotheism, i.e., to worship none but Allāh (Alone)], and he was not of Al-Mushrikūn (those who worshipped others along with Allāh; Say (O Muslims), We believe in Allāh and that which has been sent down to us and that which has been sent down

> to Ibrāhīm (Abraham), Ismāʿīl (Ishmael), Isḥāq (Isaac), Yaʿqūb (Jacob), and to Al-Asbāṭ [the twelve sons of Yaʿqūb (Jacob)], and that which has been given to Mūsa (Moses) and ʿĪsā (Jesus), and that which has been given to the Prophets from their Lord. We make no distinction between any of them, and to Him we have submitted (in Islam). So if they believe in the like of that which you believe, then they are rightly guided, but if they turn away, then they are only in opposition. So Allāh will suffice you against them. And He is the All-Hearer, the All-Knower; Say, Belief in God and following the guidance of Islam are God's means of purification for us. Islam is the baptism of God. No one is a better baptizer than He and we Muslims worship Him; Say (O Muḥammad Peace be upon him to the Jews and Christians), "Dispute you with us about Allāh while He is our Lord and your Lord? And we are to be rewarded for our deeds and you for your deeds. And we are sincere to Him in worship and obedience (i.e. we worship Him Alone and none else, and we obey His Orders)".[150]

Here, the very definition of Islām is revealed seeing that "Islām" is often mistakenly depicted in Euro-America as distinct from Judaism and Christianity, and misinterpreted as meaning "submission" (the Arabic term for which is *khuduʿ*), rather than willful and engaged surrender, or choice-based deliverance (from the root *s-l-m* or peace and verb *u-sa-lim* and hence to offer or hand oneself over by informed consent).[151] There are innumerable paths to the same Creator, with hundreds of thousands of prophets unnamed in the Qur'ān regarded as *ʿala millat Ibrāhīm* ("on Abraham's path"). For this reason, Anarcha-Islām is not interested in whether anarchists or anyone else chooses to believe in God, Prophet Muḥammad, or Islām, let alone the compulsive practice or institutionalization of dogmatic rituals. Anarcha-Islām is not concerned with giving rise to mass-produced anarchist converts, nor does it require that others become missionized and conquered colonial Muslim subjects in expansionist projects according to austere and literalist Fundamentalist interpretations of Umma.[152] Rather, Anarcha-Islām is determined through exchange and the offering of an extended arm of hospitality to individuals and communities who espouse ethico-political commitments that resonate with those of this interpretation of Islām.

Second, as Saul Newman argues, anarchism has "not ousted God … [as anti-religious anarchists would have hoped because] the place of authority of the category of the divine remains intact, only re-inscribed in the demand for presence … Atheism changes nothing in this fundamental structure."[153] Accordingly, anti-religious anarchists who chant "God is dead" should recognize the right of religious anarchists to argue for the possibility and the usefulness of a divine presence within their lives, and that we should not remain bootstrapped in debates about the unverifiable empirical evidence of either God's life or death. Such discussions merely enhance micro-fascist tendencies internalized amongst religious and anti-religious anarchists, and expound our demagoguery as a species. Instead, we can choose to cherish social justice sensibilities and mutually resist common enemies in line with an ethics of disagreement and hospitality noted earlier.[154] According to this analysis, every politically and ethically committed individual is a rightful bearer of "the trust" in themselves and the community. Whether we believe in God or not is irrelevant. Rather, the question is what does believing and disbelieving imply in our collective responsibilities to ourselves, each other, and nonhuman life. This issue of God's authority ought be put to rest.[155]

Modern Uses of Waṭaniyyah, Qawmiyyah, and Dawla and Decolonized Vestiges of Umma and Īmāmah in Arab and Muslim Lexicons

In Islām, all humans descend from Ādam and *Hawā* (Eve), but *Qawm* (a people) is utilized in the Qur'ān to distinguish between different peoples, usually in reference to their historical geographies, and relates a people's intimate relation to land-based practices and commitments to nonhuman life. A Qawm consists of a group of *Shuʿūb*, the plural form of *Shaʿb* (great tribe), which are themselves formed from smaller tribes referred to as *Qa'bā'il*, the singular form of which is *Qabilah*. Again, all these terminologies are mentioned in the Qur'ān.

In contrast, the term Qawmiyyah (the modern sentiment of peoplehood or regional nationalism) is not an Islamic concept, and only relates to Islām through the Arabic noun. Qawmiyyah, which developed in the late nineteenth and early twentieth centuries with the rise of pan-Arab nationalism and pan-Africanist movements for post-colonial independence, refers to a collective peoples' regional belonging, though it is interchangeably used, though less commonly so, to refer to specific local rootedness, as in *al-Qawmiyyah al-Missriyya* (Egyptian peoplehood).[156] Qawmiyyah is primarily used to refer to the contrived regional racial/ethnic pride of a group of people and what they presumably mutually experience and perceive to share, across territories, language, history, and religion (etc.). In other words, Qawmiyyah emerged as a particularly *Arabized* anti-colonial and anti-imperial, yet conformist and regionally nationalist and statist, unified reactionary response to (neo)colonialism/imperialism, and specifically to events such as Sykes-Picot in 1916, the French-British collaboration to divide and establish borders between what are predominantly Muslim peoples. Qawmiyyah focused on Arab Qawmiyyah (pan-Arab regionalism) and is a consequence of Arabs having to choose whether their loyalty lies exclusively with identifying as Arabs or as Muslims, premised on the racial-spiritual and sectarian divides the Enlightenment incepted. This represents a false binary and divisive choice that was imposed and continues to be internalized, in particular, by both Arabs and Muslims and is echoed in the reactionary Islamist and secular-nationalist trajectories they spawn. As Al-Barghouti writes, "while still void of any indication of the form of government," Qawmiyyah, "is closely associated with political identity" and the term is usually followed by an adjective that indicates "the group of people referred to [as per the example of] *Al-qawmiyyah Al-missriyya* [to denote] Egyptian local nationalism, [and] *Al-qawmiyyah Al-Arabiyya* [as] pan-Arab nationalism, and so on."[157] In the former example, "Qawmiyyah means to belong to a certain group of people, 'a qawm', and is therefore usually associated with Arab nationalism; Arabs have the same origin, the same language, and the overwhelming majority of them have the same religion and the same collective memory."[158]

This colonial understanding of Qawmiyyah is radically distinct from Islām's trajectories of seeing the world in a distinct light, whereby Allāh states in the Qur'ān: "We created … and made you into Shuʿūb (big tribes) and Qa'bā'il (smaller tribes)," with the intent that these Shuʿūb and Qa'bā'il "might come to know each other."[159] According to the Qur'ān, this creation and our species are composed of differing Qawm that are to know one another beyond individualist and isolated national or regionally rigid geographies, constructed around sterilized notions of ethnicity/race, or any other social bond for that matter. After all, as discussed above, when taken to an extreme, nationalism as patriotism is contrary in spirit to this interpretation of Islām, given what often accompanies it is puritanical xenophobic and cisheteropatriarchal beliefs of racial/ethnic superiority and inferiority complexes in relative degrees to internalized cultures of whiteness. Modern nationalism reinforces divisionary racial/ethnic zeal that goes against and contradicts the very spirit of Muslim ideals.

Although most Islamists are skeptical of nationalism, some still recreate nationalism's racial/ethnic hierarchies that manifest anti-Black and anti-Indigenous politics as in the case of Egypt. For most Islamists, this often translates to the *Arabization* of Islām based on Arab supremacist authoritarian institutionalized interpretations of Islām. Even those who subscribe to an anti-statist Islamist agenda manifest, embody, and reify these racial/ethnic insecurities and prejudices within our communities. This approach blatantly contradicts Islām's ethico-political commitments, given Arab supremacist perceptions in relation to non-Arabs, which are often cast as inferior. This Arab ethnocentric sentiment is informed by aspirations to identify as "white" as well as a colonially/imperially influenced contemporary hegemonic authoritarian struggle in the search for a dehistoricized so-called authentic Islām. Arabs have been legally constructed as white in the settler-colonial U.S. and not merely in Egypt.

None of this is meant to claim that prejudices and oppressions did not exist amongst Muslims during pre-modernity, but they manifested in distinct forms from those created by modern identity politics based on white-supremacist ideals. Arabs often rely on access to Arabic and pertinent linguistic skills and religious texts in justifying their supremacy. Indeed, Arabs use their knowledge of Arabic to lay claim and determine what is legitimately Muslim and what is not. Arab supremacy is exacerbated in the contemporary by asymmetries of power that coincide with the individualist rise of modern nationalism and vexed identity crises amongst Muslims more generally. This Arab attitude delineates valuable non-Arab contributions to Islām as well as the fluid space that Islām is capable of incepting for all people, irrespective of their race, gender, spirituality, and descent. The misfortune of Arab supremacy is that Prophet Muḥammad addressed it in *Khuṭbat al-Wadāʿ* (farewell address) and stated:

> All humankind is from Adam and Eve, an Arab has no superiority over a non-Arab nor a non-Arab has any superiority over an Arab; also a white has no superiority over black nor a black has any superiority over white except by piety and good action. Learn that every Muslim is brother and sister to every Muslim and that the Muslims constitute one Umma. Nothing shall be legitimate to a Muslim, which belongs to a fellow Muslim unless it was given freely and willingly. Do not, therefore, do injustice to yourselves.[160]

Quite contrary to pan-Arab nationalism (*Al-Qawmiyyah Al-Arabiyya*) then, both God and Muḥammad's antecedent testimonies and egalitarian visions demonstrate not only that Muslims are required to believe in different peoples, but also that they ought to abide by the respectful rights of and responsibilities towards all peoples whether they are Muslims or non-Muslims, Arabs or non-Arabs. In this sense, respecting a collectivity's self-determination, irrespective of their size, through quantitative qualifiers such as Qawm, Shuʿūb, and Qa'bā'il. Arab Qawmiyyah, in the contemporary context, is equally fraught because as a racial/ethnic category it assumes that there indeed exists an authentic, timeless, Arab identity despite historical realities that led to complex hybridity and polyandrous interracial/ethnic interactions between Arabs and non-Arabs alike.[161] This modern understanding of Shuʿūb, impacted by colonialism/imperialism, birthed local Egyptian, Syrian, Palestinian (etc.) identities and nations as subsets of Qawm. If the collective Shuʿūb of Egypt, Syria, and Palestine (etc.) compose an Arab Qawm, then in this instance, the Berbers of the Siwa Oasis or Arab Bedouin tribes of the Sinai Peninsula – if one were to specifically speak of the local context of Egypt – constitute Qa'bā'il or smaller subsets of a Shaʿb (singular form of Shuʿūb). After all, there are inter-religious/ethnic minorities in Egypt itself as per the example of Coptic Christians, Nubians, or the Beja and Dom, and even other Arabs such as Palestinians, Syrians, and Sudanese who possess deep historical ties to Egypt. From a Muslim perspective, all peoples, irrespective of their Qawm or whether they constitute a majority or minority, are to know each other without acting hegemonically and authoritatively in relation to each other and hence through a determinable shared set of ethical-political and spiritual principles and affinities between them, without compulsion as the Qur'ān commands, and hence with dignity and respect.

Wael Hallaq argues in *The Impossible State* that the Prophet Muḥammad himself created a mega-tribe of Muslims and non-Muslims alike, known as an Umma in Medina, which included *Ahl al-Kitāb* (People of the Book). The Medina Charter created a tribal multi-faith community premised upon the interplay between the spiritual principles of social justice, political unity, and equity of non-Muslim believers (*mūmineen*) and those Muslims of Quraysh and Yathrib (present day Medina).[162] Emphasizing the *ʿaqīdah* (creed) of faith (īmān) as an anchor, the Charter advocated mutual co-existence, cohabitation, co-mingling, and the freedom of all to exercise rights to property, rituals (*ʿibādāt*), laws, and beliefs under the collective protection and sovereignty of a single Creator. The Charter emphasized that non-Muslim believers (*mūmineen*), and in this particular instant numerous Jewish tribes amongst which included the Jews of *Bani ʿawf*, *Bani'al-ʿAws*, *Bani ʿAmr*, *Bani'al-Nabeet*, *Bani'Harith*, *Bani'Saeeda*, and *Bani al-Najjar* "are an Umma with the believers [*Umma Wāhidah*]."[163] The Charter can also be interpreted as meaning that non-Muslim believers form an independent Umma that is equal to that of the Muslim Umma and are thus to be "treated as one community with the believers."[164] The conjoining of Muslims and non-Muslims alike created a "brotherly[/sisterly] Umma [*Umma mutākhiyya*]" constructed upon the "principles of decent manners (*al-qawā'id akhlāqiyya*)."[165] The second treaty, the *Pact of Al-Ḥudaybiyah*, emphasized the necessity of striving for peace and upholding social contracts and covenants even with pagans, even if they are unjust towards Muslims, as the Qur'ān commands in numerous verses such as 4:90, 9:4, and 9:7.

Since there is no concept of "chosen-ness" in Islām, the Qur'ān declares that people are created inherently equal and differ only based on their *taqwā* (piety). The Qur'ān states, "Verily the most honoured of you in the sight of Allāh is (he who is) the most righteous of you. And Allāh has full knowledge and is well acquainted (with all things)."[166] Anarcha-Islām abides by an understanding that piety is an expansive concept in which who and what is a spiritual believer is contingent on the ethical-political commitments and practices we all follow despite our diverse traditions and paths to the same Creator. In this sense, I argue, it is irrelevant from a Qur'ānic perspective whether or not individuals and communities explicitly identify as Muslim or not. Besides the Qur'ānic injunction that there "is no compulsion in religion," in numerous verses such as 2:251, 7:56, 7:74, 8:73, 11:116, 12:73, 13:25, 26:152, 27:48, 47:22, etc., the Qur'ān explicitly describes disbelievers, amongst many other facets, as those who dabble in "excess," dismiss responsibilities towards "women, orphans, travelers, wayfarers, and the poor," as well as uphold "injustice," spread "mischief," and "corrupt the earth." Once again, this affirms the necessity of not only recognizing that all our identities have been impacted by white-supremacist (neo)liberal divide-and-conquer politics in the contemporary but also the decolonial necessity of strategically recentering identities around ethics and politics to facilitate possibilities of re-envisioning their rootedness and reconfiguration in practices that impact our knowable relations to each other as Muslims and non-Muslims alike, that is, if we are to collectively resurrect a collectively based Umma premised on social justice.

In this sense, the emphasis in Islām, in the Qur'ān, is on the radical and decolonial non-racialized and non-territorial Islamic concept of Umma, which has problematically been misinterpreted to strictly refer to a community of Muslims irrespective of borders, cultures, and nationalities, despite the fact that Prophet Muḥammad's original Umma was constituted by Muslims and non-Muslims alike bound by spiritual ethico-political principles and commitments to each other. While modern (neo)conservative Muslim thinkers such as Abul Alā Al-Mawdūdī (1967) tend to advocate for misogynistic, patriarchal, restrictive, and exclusive literalist scripturalist interpretations of Umma strictly confined to Muslims, similarly Arab nationalists usurped its Islamic connotations to refer solely to Arabs; that is, an *Arab Umma.* Etymologically and from an Islamic and arguably Islamist perspective, Umma, however, is designated in *Lisan al-Arab*, one of the foremost authoritative Arab dictionaries written by Mohammad Ibn Makram Ibn Manzhour Al-Ansari (1233–1311), as emanating from the root "*Amm* which, as a verb, means to head for, to quest, to lead, to guide, or to mean and to intend … [while] as a noun means destination, purpose, pursuit, aim, goal and end."[167] As Al-Barghouti writes, the "physical existence of individuals is called an Umma … when these individuals have an image of themselves as a collective, and when this image is guiding them to do things in certain ways distinct from others."[168] Furthermore, it is to be understood that "Umma could be only one person, if that person had a creed by which they defined themselves and that was expressed in their actions, even if no one followed them in their quest."[169] Prophet Abraham (peace be upon him) is illuminated in the Qur'ān as an Umma onto himself, when Allāh states, "Surely Ibrahim was an Umma obedient unto God a man of pure faith and no idolater."[170] No less critical to comprehending Umma is the essential fact that this concept is not constrained or solely applicable to Muslims, when Muḥammad stated in the Medina Charter that the Jews of *Bani 'awf* and *Bani Najjar* "are an Umma with the believers (Muslims)."[171] Prophet Muḥammad's statement can also be understood as meaning that the Jews of Bani ʿawf and Bani Najjar form an Umma that is equal and alongside their fellow Muslim kin, each maintaining their own faith, laws, and traditions. The issue, therefore, is not a matter of Bani ʿawf and Bani Najjar's belonging to a different ethnicity/race for they were Jewish-Arabs, given they were "to be treated as one community with the Believers," as dictated by Prophet Muḥammad in the Charter of Medina.[172]

This revolutionary spirit of the original Umma can also be read as a means by which spiritual communities remind each other of what is ethically-politically "good," without any sense of exceptionalism between them on account of their identitarianism and/or accompanying moralistic, ritualistic belief system. Moreover, a unified Umma of believers from different faiths and spiritualties also disrupts any sense of a homogeneous Muslim, Christian, Jewish, or any other spiritual identity, given that a non-Muslim could very well embody ethical-political Muslim values and characteristics, even if they do not subscribe to Islām, particularly if the roots to Islām exist prior to Islām's emergence and naming as such. After all, the original Treaty of Ḥudaybiyah that bound Prophet Muḥammad's Umma entailed the creation of revolutionary subjectivities who understood their spiritual and ethico-political rights and responsibilities in relation to each other. As the Qurʾān itself states, "Allāh does not forbid you from those who do not fight you because of religion and do not expel you from your homes – from being righteous toward them and acting justly toward them. Indeed, Allāh loves those who act justly."[173] Moreover, the Qurʾān emphasizes complete freedom of choice as to whether one chooses to believe explicitly in Islām or not, when Allāh states in, at least, two verses: "Say, 'O disbelievers' … You have your religion and I [a Muslim] have mine" and "Proclaim [O Muslims]: 'This is the truth from your Lord', then Whoever wills let them believe, and whoever wills let them disbelieve."[174] This reiterates my former assertion, that even Prophet Muḥammad was warned not to exceed these limits and to rather simply deliver a reminder that our species possesses similar and interconnected spiritual ethico-political responsibilities of existence towards life. Allāh states in the Qur'ān: "You [O Muḥammad] shall remind, for your mission is to deliver this reminder. *You have no power over them.*"[175]

Similar to the way in which Qawmiyyah has been Arabized in modernity, in the wake of post-colonial independence movements Arabs altered the meanings of their own language to correspond with European definitions, ontologies, and terminologies associated with "the nation" and capitalist-states.[176] For example, Dawla is the post-colonial term used by Arab nationalists to refer to each individual Arab and Muslim state, and has been deployed by movements such as ISIS in the form of *al-Dawla al-Islamiyya* (the "Islamic State"). This is a distortion of Dawla's meaning and violently forces its discursive correspondence with European liberal and patriarchal nationalist projects, globally, regionally, and locally. Dawla "stems from the verb *dal* which morphologically, as well as semantically, falls between the verb *dar* (to rotate) and the verb *zal* (to go away, or fall)."[177] The pre-modern meaning of Dawla as a matter of fact revolves "mainly around the notions of temporality, change and rotation … [as opposed to] a fixed order in which a nation aspires to organize itself (if the nation predated the state) or a fixed order of things in which the nation should aspire to organize itself (if the state predated the nation)."[178] Temporality and succession are thus essential connotations of Dawla, with anything circulated from one hand to another referred to a Dawla, as much as it can also signify "the condition of well-being, for one person or a group of persons, since such condition will sooner or later end, by the death of the people who are enjoying it, if not by any other means."[179] The 59th chapter of the Qur'ān, Chapter of "The Gathering," Verse 7, for example, speaks of the Prophet's distribution of the spoils of war to those in need, "so that it may not just make the circuit (*dulatan*) among the wealthy of you."[180] Analogously the third chapter of the Qur'ān, the Chapter of "the Family or House of Imran," Verse 140, discusses the cyclical nature of human vicissitudes, such that triumph one day is replaced by defeat another day. As a pre-colonial and pre-modern Muslim term that remains distorted by Arabs, Dawla therefore refers to any political arrangement, as long as it is temporary and not territorially fixed, with sovereignty lying in the Ummah, and not the Dawla.

In this sense and from a Qur'ānic standpoint, Dawla extends from the root D-W-L, used in the Qur'ān and which in fact signifies and means to "turn," to "alternate," or to "come around" in a cyclical fashion. Within Islām's pre-modern history there even existed a multiplicity of Dawlas within one Dawla, loosely resembling a confederacy. Examples of this include the Hamadanite, Buwaihid, Ekhsheedi, Ayyub and Mamloui Dawlas within the *Abbasiyyan* period and Ummah, and Mohammad Ali and Ali Bey al-Kabir's Dawlas within the *Uthmaniyyan* period and Ummah.[181] In medieval times the "'Ummayyad Caliphate' having a seat in Damascus did not mean there was a 'Syria'," and by the same token that a "'Abbassid Caliphate' with a seat in Baghdad never meant it was an 'Iraqi' caliphate."[182] It happened that with the Abbassid turn in power, as with the Umayyids before them, the Abbassid house became entrenched in power, as the dynamic sense and essence of Dawla became conflated with the elitist notion that a single family ought to rule. Though the "Abbassid Dawla derived its legitimacy directly from the Ummah" it did this by abusing a "certain interpretation of some of the inheritance verses in the Qur'ān, as well as on a set of sayings by the Prophet showing the virtues of their ancestor al-Abbas, the Prophet's uncle" in legitimizing its claims to authority and stronghold maintenance of power.[183] This impression of an alternating aeon of fortune and misfortune led pre-modern Arab and Muslim scholars to use Dawla in reference to dynastic succession, particularly in the period following the rise of the Abbassids. Thus Dawla, unlike the static notions of modern-states with their fixed imagined borders, serves as a reminder of the fact that what is construed as a uniform bounded-identity strictly based on colonially produced geographic-societal characteristics or traditions are actually temporal. In Islām's pre-modern period, Dawla could be any political arrangement, as long as it was temporary and not territorially fixed, with sovereignty lying in the Umma, and not the Dawla.

Furthermore, some medieval Muslim scholars and rulers conflated Dawla with the rise and fall of dynasties, as documented by fourteenth century historiographer and sociologist Ibn Khaldūn's usage of the term, when he writes: "a state exists only insofar as it is held together and ruled by individuals and the group which they constitute, that is, the dynasty. When the dynasty disappears, the state, being identical with it, also comes to an end."[184] Ibn Khaldūn put forward arguments regarding the circular nature and indefinite reconstitution of *ʿassabiyya* (social and tribal solidarity), and the rise and fall of princedoms, in which a revolving "ethic developed because of the nomadic forms of production and social organization, and that it enabled nomads to invade settled societies, at which point they gradually turn into settled communities themselves, allowing tribal bounds to loosen, forming a specialized economy, where defense is delegated to mercenary forces, thus making them vulnerable to fresh nomadic invasions."[185] As Al-Barghouti writes, the legitimacy of a Dawla, in pre-modernity, was not gauged "by the welfare the Dawla provides to its own inhabitants regardless of the Muslims or regardless of the ideal image of the Ummah, rather it is measured by both, the welfare of its inhabitants as the welfare of other Muslims and the service of that ideal image."[186] In fact, Al-Barghouti states, Dawla, pre-colonially, was neither associated "with supreme power" nor "sovereignty" as that tied with the Euro-colonial idea of "nation."[187] After all, both supreme power and sovereignty lay with the Umma. However, the crisis of meaning regarding Dawla truly exacerbated during the nineteenth century, as Euro-American colonial/imperial distinctions filtered into Muslim societies and led Dawla to become increasingly disentangled from its nuanced connotations, until it has now practically become exclusively abused in the sense of the modern-state – a completely disfigured paradigm shift of what it represents in the Qur'ān. Colonial/imperial influences skewed the understanding of Dawla from a metaphorical image of the Umma to an identity that is territorially bound by rigidly fixed borders and enclosures. The political consequence of this alteration in meaning was the creation of post-colonial states formed of remnant and residual nations composed of various Shuʿūb and smaller Qa'bā'il, creating a setting in which "the colonial redefinition of Arabs and Muslims had two contradictory foci of loyalty, two mutually exclusive images to serve; one was the colonially imposed focus of loyalty, the nation-State: Egypt, Jordan, Palestine, Qatar, Syria, Lebanon, etc and so on, and the other was the Umma."[188] The contradiction and "paradox of the Arab Muslim state, thus, is that its very independence is the expression of it being under the power of colonialism; its very sovereignty is the sign of its servitude."[189] This way modern "nationalisms created by colonization are only those whose foci of loyalty were the colonially created states, or whose ultimate purpose is to found a nation-State similar in form and content to the colonially created one, only with adjusted borders."[190]

The pertinence of decolonizing these concepts, practices, and connected logics ought be to crystal clear. As Al-Barghouti argues, in line with Edward Said's *Culture and Imperialism* (1994), resisting colonialism and imperialism ought to mean resisting colonial, Eurocentric, and Orientalist conceptualization of the nation and an acute attentiveness, as already noted, to what Gayatri Spivak, Saba Mahmood, and Joseph Massad refer to as a "politics of translation." I further argue that decolonization and resisting Eurocentrism requires dismantling the *very foundations* and framework upon which nationalism rests, i.e., the modern-state, particularly given the collective prejudices and injustices that accompany its racial/ethnic capitalist formulations. Unfortunately, today's Muslim societies "are but [mere] extensions and mirror images of" a socio-politically and economically emulated Euro-America.[191] Part of this dismantlement includes the Orientalist Euro-crusading narrative that Islām was primarily spread by the sword, which numerous scholars such as Albert Hourani's *A History of Arab Peoples* (1991), Marshall Hodgson's *The Venture of Islam: Conscience and History in a World Civilization* (1977), Edward Said's *Covering Islam* (1980), Karen Armstrong's *Fields of Blood: Religion and the History of Violence* (2014), Hugh N. Kennedy's *The Great Arab Conquests: How the Spread of Islam Changed the World We Live In* (2007), Youssef Aboul-Enein's *Islamic Rulings on Warfare* (2004), Ira Lapidus' *A History of Islamic Societies* (2014), Thomas Arnold's *The Spread of Islam in the World* (2008), and others have long debunked. While no one can deny injustices committed in the name of Islām over 1443 years, Islām's spread, as Esposito writes, was "driven by the economic rewards from conquest of richer, more developed areas, united and inspired by their new faith, Muslim armies proved to be formidable conquerors and effective rulers, builders rather than destroyers."[192] In other words, by majority, upon arrival Muslims tended to replace "the conquered countries, indigenous rulers and armies, but preserved much of their government, bureaucracy, and culture."[193] What subsequently distinguishes medieval Muslim societies from numerous other pre-modern Empires is that "for many in the conquered territories, it was no more than an exchange of masters, one that brought peace to peoples demoralized and disaffected by the casualties and heavy taxation that resulted from the years of Byzantine-Persian warfare."[194] By majority, "local communities were free to continue to follow their own way of life in internal, domestic affairs" and in many ways, local populations finding "Muslim rule more flexible and tolerant than that of Byzantium and Persia."[195] Esposito further notes, "religious communities were free to practice their faith to worship and be governed by their religious leaders and laws in such areas as marriage, divorce, and inheritance" and often enjoyed lower taxes "greater local autonomy, rule by fellow Semites with closer linguistic and cultural ties than the hellenized, Greco-Roman élites of Byzantium, and greater religious freedom for Jews and indigenous Christians."[196] While "most of the Christian churches, such as the Nestorians, Monophysites, Jacobites, and Copts, were persecuted as heretics and schismatics by Christian orthodoxy," as Esposito writes, "the conquests brought a Pax Islamica to an embattled area" that was keen on destroying little and suppressing "imperial rivalries and sectarian bloodletting among the newly subjected population."[197]

Therefore, Anarcha-Islām is predicated on comprehending that the true problem of nationalism is not its limitations as a communitarian experience, but rather that it normalizes the erasure of dissident experiences by promoting patriotism relative to the modern-state, itself a colonial product of Enlightenment visions. As Al-Barghouti notes, this conflation is also seen relative to how nation and patriotism are translated into English. In other words, both Qawmiyyah and Waṭaniyyah are interchangeably translated into English as "nation." Waṭaniyyah "stressed local patrimony over wider loyalties – [and that] the Egyptian Taha Hussein emphasized his country's pharaonic past and saw Arab and Islamic influences as contingent; and the Lebanese Antoine Saadeh's 'phoenicianism' extolled 'Syrianness'."[198] Proving the need for their decolonial situating, even "the late departed Saddam Hussein at different times used both ideologies, proving that Waṭaniyyah and Qawmiyyah need not be mutually exclusive."[199] For this reason, Anarcha-Islām distinguishes between the two. I take Qawmiyyah to refer to a regional belonging of "a certain group of people (qawm)" and "Wataniyyah [to] mean belonging to the homeland, to a certain territory: 'watan'." [200]

It is in this typical paternalistic patriotic logic, that Waṭaniyyah came to mean "local patrimony over wider loyalties."[201] Since 1798, this has been the preliminary strand of (neo)colonial Arab and Muslim political discourse. As Al-Barghouti writes,

> In a pamphlet distributed in Alexandria one day before the city fell into the hands of French troops, Napoleon's translators introduced the expression "al-Umma al-Misriyya" (the Egyptian community or nation) for the first time to the Arabic language. Napoleon claimed to be liberating the Egyptians from the Mamlouks, who were foreigners; he was a savior rather than an invader. Of course, to the people of Cairo, the Mamlouks and the Ottomans were no foreigners; Islam, not nationalism, was the basis of political identity. "Al-Umma al-Islamiyya" (the Islamic community, sometimes translated as the Islamic nation) was the only Umma around, especially when it came to dealing with Europe."[202]

But Napoleon's discursive incursion did not end there. Al-Barghouti further notes,

> Napoleon was quick in understanding that his invention did not work, so he swiftly changed his discourse. In order to avoid the inevitable comparison between his campaign and the Crusades, he kept asserting that he himself was not a Christian and that he had attacked the Pope's seat in Rome. In his meeting with

> the notables of Cairo and the sheikhs of Al-Azhar University in July 1798 he claimed to be a Muslim himself … [Only to appoint] Fourteen sheikhs of Al-Azhar university [who] were now the administrative government of Egypt under French occupation … [And] even made this council of 14 issue a fatwa (a religious edict) stating that Napoleon was the awaited Mahdi, a religious figure, whose appearance, Muslims believe, would fill the land with justice just as it has been filled with oppression. They claimed that 20 verses of the Koran implicitly referred to Napoleon![203]

Today, proponents of Arab unity argue that the sole route to Arab and Muslim self-fulfillment is through a horizon of unification. Arabs argue that Arab identity ought to take precedence over Muslim identity because they dread Islām's zealots and sectarian interpretations. Nevertheless, since this vision's modern inception in the late nineteenth to early twentieth century and through the subsequent *Nahḍa* (Arab Awakening and Renaissance), pan-Arabism has failed to materialize. Even if moved towards egalitarian socialist intents, the horizon is still based on neoliberal modern-state paradigms and produces ethnic elite nationalists and nationalism.

In fact, the de facto dominance of neoliberalism immediately puts into question all forms of so-called "post-colonial" liberations that seek to appropriate the modern-state as an instrument of revolutionary liberation. The premise of neoliberalism is that governing in modern capitalist-states "no longer" occurs through "reconstructing a (political-mechanical) logic, but on analyzing a form of human action governed by a specific, unique (abusive economic) rationality … [that] essentially includes all forms of human action and behavior" beginning with the very realm and dominion of "the political."[204] And so while "classic liberalism had called on governments to respect the form of the market, in the neoliberal approach the market is no longer the principle of self-delimitation by government, but instead the principle against which it rubs, or as Foucault calls it 'a kind of permanent economic tribunal'."[205]

Neoliberalism's seemingly irreversible effects imply that the state is beyond rescue or reform by either Muslims or non-Muslims alike.

Instead of working within the framework of the contemporary modern-state, Anarcha-Islām adopts and builds on traditional orthodox non-conformist Islamist thinkers who generally have adopted a Fundamentalist stance against Waṭaniyyah and the modern-state (not to be confused with Dawla), in favor of an Umma. Where I diverge from them is on both who and what ethically-politically constitutes an Umma, as their exclusionary vision verges on pure totalitarianism. For Anarcha-Islām, and given the spirit adopted here, this egalitarian ideal ought to culminate and configure itself as an Umma constituted from Muslims and non-Muslims alike and who regard each other as ethico-political spiritual believers with faith (*mūmineen*) irrespective of their belonging to different Qawm, Shuʿūb, or Qa'bā'il. After all, as the Qur'ān argues and Joseph Massad rightly identifies, the Qur'ān refers to people as mūmineen (believers) far more often and more explicitly than *Muslimeen* (Muslims). Inclusion within this Umma is contingent on the existence of ethical-political orientations towards non-authoritarian and non-capitalist ethical and political pillars that must be established by each of its constituents.

It is in reorienting the contours of Islām, the identity Muslim, and what a Muslim and non-Muslim Umma espousing anarchic ethical and political commitments would mean to itself, as well as in relation to the newest social movements and all life, that decolonized possibilities for liberation and the transcending of binaries arrive. Moreover, it is in this sense that nationalism possesses limits, as is the case with authoritarian and exclusionary interpretations of who and what is a Muslim, and their incumbent responsibilities. In the absence of such ethical-political commitments one does not belong to an Umma, as is similarly the case with anarchism. After all, as argued throughout, our identities should not just revolve around abstract (neo)liberal identity politics and their identitarian claims, and hence because one identifies as a Muslim or as an anarchist does not denote immediate belonging to these specific communities. Rather, it is the ethics and politics lived, as well as the shared commitments established, that ought to ground any identity, and must assume greater, paramount relevance than any identitarian label. It is what is believed, followed through in ethical-political principles and practices, that affirms, indeed identifies and gives meaning to, identities as well as the contours of, in this case, a relationship to the three: Umma, Islām, and anarchism.

Muslim and Non-Muslim Glossaries of Indigeneity Towards a Resurgent Umma: Anti-Blackness and Anti-Indigenous Politics

Settler-hood, anti-blackness, and Arab supremacy fester within Muslim communities in Egypt and the U.S./Canada. While post-colonial literatures can illuminate the ties that undergird the dynamic relationship between these franchise and settler-colonial societies, post-colonialism is also limited. In advocating for decolonial trajectories, Gustavo Esteva argues that revolutionary changes require our coming "together and moving to create a society that is beyond our current reality," not an identical society with different professional operators.[206] Uprisings are not about seizing power, but rather knowing what to do with the power seized and ought to entail practical questions of how will we organize socially, politically, economically, indeed our communities, and according to a renewed social contract reconstructed upon reoriented, cohesive ethico-political principles.

Hence the demand to seriously examine concepts of non-statist decolonization/reindigenization within Indigenous discourses, particularly in relation to what community means to Muslims through the Islamic concept of Umma. As radical trajectories within Indigenous studies illuminate, decolonial movements ought to collectively strive to unsettle the rigid, dogmatic, and limiting ways of conceptualizing liberation through an adherence to civil and human rights paradigms or a "politics of recognition" through the constant decolonization of our paradigms.[207] It is decolonial frameworks and social movement histories and theories that link advocacy for land-based struggles and the necessity of constructing alternatives in Egypt, to similar trajectories by radical

Indigenous and Black trajectories that ought to be embraced by SWANA diasporic settlers in Turtle Island.[208]

Post-colonial societies such as Egypt never decolonized beyond limited agrarian and superficial women's rights reforms; they merely adopted the European capitalist-state model, including their security and surveillance apparatuses and their political, economic, social, medical, and judicial systems. Post-colonial nation-states even emulate the architectural and spatial-temporal construction of the colonizers, including the casting of "peripheral" rural terrains as inferior and savage. Their embrace of neo-developmentalist frameworks that mold their urban-metropoles in the image of Euro-American city-states not only disconnects native-subjects from land and their responsibilities to nonhuman life, in authoritarian, hierarchical, and materialist ways, it also restructures gender/sexual practices, as well as perceptions of the private/public.

This book deploys the work of post-colonial feminists who have "contributed greatly to the discussion of the 'double marginal' and have challenged other feminists to consider the intersections of gender with other axes of difference."[209] But even post-colonial feminists and critical race theories can reproduce colonial discourses through their adoption of nation-state frameworks.[210] In so doing, they ignore the "gendered dispossession of Indigenous lands and sexist neoliberal and neo-racist migratory structures and processes."[211] Eve Tuck and K. Wayne Yang affirm this when they note that racism and colonialism are not just symptoms and technologies of racial capitalism but are also a product of the organizing principle that is the nation-state, whether capitalistic or Marxist.[212] Sandy Grande notes, "both Marxists and capitalists view land and natural resources as commodities to be exploited, in the first instance, by capitalists for personal gain, and in the second by Marxists for the good of all."[213]

Jodi Byrd and Michael Rothberg argue that it is the misleading emphasis on "post" in post-colonialism that has meant that post-colonial studies have largely ignored the specificities of settler-colonialism and Indigenous studies, and hence avoided a critical engagement with the material oppression and the settler-colonization of Indigenous peoples.[214] Similarly, Tuck and Yang note that the reliance in post-colonial scholarship on anti-colonial critique is not remotely equivalent to a decolonizing framework.[215] An anti-colonial stance celebrates the transfer of power to post-colonial subjects, whereas a decolonizing stance seeks to subvert and remake the colonial system.[216] In this sense, the "postcolonial pursuit of resources is fundamentally an anthropocentric model, as land, water, air, animals, and plants are never able to become postcolonial; they remain objects to be exploited by the empowered postcolonial subject."[217] Furthermore, as argued in Chapter 2, Tuck and Yang note, though the strict "pursuit of worker rights (and rights to work)" by Marxist-Leninist movements like the revolutionary socialists in franchise-colonial societies and "minoritized people's rights in a settler colonial context can appear to be anti-capitalist," "this pursuit is nonetheless largely pro-colonial" as both approaches and their respective movements are still anchored in the anthropocentric idea that "land is property; land is/belongs to the United States; land should be distributed democratically."[218]

Critiques of settler-colonialism are therefore indispensable to Anarcha-Islām. Anarcha-Islām recognizes that Indigenous and Black subjugation are integral to white settler-colonialism and both are interrelated projects.[219] Scholars like Rita Dhamoon and Patrick Wolfe have noted that discourses on race and religion are deployed in settler-colonialism to provide access to land.[220] Wolfe argues that the expropriation of land is the basis for physical, spiritual, and cultural genocide that contains and kills Indigenous peoples, which in Canada takes the form of the Indian Act, blood quantum politics, and their continued treatment as children under the paternalist wardship of the nation-state.[221] Scholars in Indigenous studies have long argued that policies of "inclusive" integration into the nation-state erases native and Indigenous ontologies/epistemologies, sovereignty, and the intimate relationships that all people living on Indigenous territories must bear to land, culture, spirituality, egalitarian self-governance, and values. Moreover, they have called on those who become assimilated citizen-subjects to challenge the "constructions of land as extractable capital," given the ways in which this denies Indigenous sovereignty and Indigenous views on the integration of cosmological, ecological, spiritual, and non-statist, feminist, ethical-political commitments to land.[222]

At the same time, as Tuck and Yang note, settler society participates in what Philip Deloria refers to as "playing Indian," or what Sherene Razack refers to as a "race to innocence."[223] As Tuck and Yang note, these strategies, practiced by white and Brown settlers, are attempts to relieve feelings of guilt without giving up land, power, or privilege.[224] These moves to innocence like that of Elizabeth Warren and Nancy Reagan include evoking Indian blood quantum narratives, registries and policies, gendered settler-nativism, and Indian grandmother complexes that ignore the implications of sexual violence and the continual attempted eradication of Indigenous peoples. Audra Simpson writes that settler-colonialism thrives on bypassing Indigenous peoples and creating an environment in which Indigenous peoples are just another oppressed group.[225] Similarly, using an anti-imperialist approach, Byrd argues that the logic of settler-colonialism is replicated throughout the U.S. Empire, transforming "those to be colonized into 'Indians'," who are politically erased physically and culturally.[226]

Unlike post-colonial movements, non-statist decolonization suggests there is no single framework for decolonization or for Indigenous sovereignty, although there is some agreement that "decolonization requires, at a minimum, the repatriation and the rematriation of land."[227] Dene critical theorist Glen Coulthard states that land is the ethico-political criterion for Indigenous peoples' identities. He argues for Indigenous conceptions of autonomy to focus on land as an "ontological framework for understanding relationships" in non-individualist and non-exploitative ways, which will facilitate renewed interconnections between Indigenous and non-Indigenous peoples, and their mutually shared environments.[228]

After all, as Achilles Mbembe writes in *Necropolitics*, colonialism is always associated with "seizing, delimiting, and asserting control over a physical geographical area – of writing on the ground a new set of social and spatial relations."[229] Indeed, modern colonial/

imperialism's success rests on the disciplining and control of local populations and their relationship to land. The rewriting of spatial relations and the upending of local relations to land was the primary part of the reclassification of people and resources and finally "the manufacturing of a large reservoir of cultural imaginaries."[230] As Mbembe writes, sovereignty meant disconnecting the natives from their land and then using this disconnection in the construction of the rurality as backwards, savage, and underdeveloped according to Euro-American civilizational theories of development.[231]

It would be a grave mistake to think that settler-colonialism's manipulation of race/ethnicity as a site through which whiteness orients and replicates internal and external racializing, genderizng, and sexualizing projects as affecting only settler-societies. Due to imperialist projection and transference of its effects onto franchise-colonialism, both types of colonialism uphold each other. Therefore, in light of the intertwinement of gendered and racial colonialisms, social movement scholars/activists should strive to examine the intersections between "the comparative racialization projects of U.S. orientalism and U.S. settler colonialism."[232] Settler-colonialism, homonationalism, and cisheteropatriarchy not only systemically racialize and sexualize all people within settler-colonial states, they also forcibly *queer* people in post-colonial nations.

Anarcha-Islām is founded on the principle that decolonization in franchise-colonial societies entails abandoning capitalist-state paradigms, as well as the inferiority complexes and cultures of whiteness that we, as BIPOC, have internalized. It involves a complete reconceptualizing of our utilitarian and exploitative manipulation of natural resources, land, and nonhuman life, and the construction of non-statist and non-capitalist, non-cisheteropatriarchal, egalitarian social justice land-based alternatives that are premised on our own spiritual and cultural traditions, and are characterized by our own notions of public/private as well as our gender/sexual-based intimacies, encounters, and relations. Decolonization facilitates the assertion of dignity and respect, as it offers alternative ways of interpreting taxonomies of SWANA Muslim sexual and non-sexual desire in relationship to self, community, kinship, family, and territory. Decolonization in settler-colonial societies implies being guided by an "ethic of incommenserability" that entails the repatriation/rematriation of Indigenous land, and hence is not just a toothless metaphor for reconciling with modern-state paradigms.[233]

It is paramount to note, as Tuck and Yang do, that decolonial struggles in post-colonial and settler-colonial societies intersect but are distinct.[234] As Manu Vimalassery, Juliana Hu Pegues, and Alyosha Goldstein argue, decolonial movements in post-colonial societies can "potentially reproduce precisely the effects" they are contesting.[235] Thus, decolonization does not mean adopting civil/human rights-based approaches, nor does it mean that we simply improve our school curriculums or deploy liberal-multicultural social justice paradigms. Radical autonomous and Indigenous non-statist conceptualizations of decolonization involve comprehending that white settler states engage in and benefit from constructing, collapsing, and reshuffling the taxonomic borders "between Native, enslavable Other, and Orientalized Other[s]."[236] This divide-and-conquer strategy sets "model" and quasi-assimilable minorities in competition with each other. Radical understandings of decolonization, based on the understanding of how settler-colonialism fuels imperialism, can therefore illuminate the co-dependence and constitutive natures of gendered colonialism and racism. It can also demonstrate how white anti-racists, allied decolonialists, and BIPOC activists can and must explore ideas and practices that abstain from reinforcing "model minority" myths. As Amy Brandzel suggests, we decolonize by focusing "our energies toward queering – as in, denaturalizing – the disaggregation of race and colonialism [and hence embracing] a politics that is against citizenship – one that refuses both futurity-as-inclusion as well as retroactive and restorative political visions of the past, in order to enact a coalitional, intersectional, and decolonial politics in and of the present."[237]

Linda Tuhiwai Smith (née Mead), as well as others, including the Mi'kmaq scholar Bonita Lawrence and Enakshi Dua, call for settler-accountability from the margins.[238] Urging non-native POC to abstain from seeking settler-colonial administrative inclusion within the specter of American/Canadian citizenship-belonging and instead decolonize their anti-racist and feminist movements, and to make returning to the land a priority of their agendas, Lawrence and Dua have helped spawned discourses between Indigenous, Black, and anti-racist POC on the varying typologies and differential placements that occur as a consequence of both historically forced and willful displacements and migrations to North America.[239]

Although the term "settler" is linked to the Euro-American colonial project, non-native POC can be complicit in settler-colonialism that thrives on settler-national imaginary to justify the inclusion of transnational diasporas at the expense of Indigenous peoples and sovereignty.[240] However, Jodi Byrd notes that "it is all too easy, in critiques of ongoing U.S. settler colonialism to accuse diasporic migrants, queers, and POC for participating in and benefitting from indigenous loss of lands, cultures, and lives … as if they could always consent to or refuse such positions or consequences of history."[241] In her efforts to destabilize the construction of "Indianness" and the notion of a "pure" authentic indigeneity, whether in the context of Indigenous peoples or the general colonized Other, Byrd introduces the category "arrivants," borrowed from Barbadian poet Kamau Brathwaite "to signify those people forced into the Americas through the violence of European and Anglo-American colonialism and imperialism around the globe, but who have functioned within and have resisted the project of colonizing the 'New World'."[242] Hence, arrivants include racialized non-European immigrants, migrants, and refugees as newcomers to Turtle Island.[243] She argues that "to make visible what imperialism and its resultant settler-colonialisms and diasporas have sought to obscure," settlers, natives, and arrivants must all reconsider their own position within mutually constitutive colonial frameworks and in relation to each other.[244]

A growing body of research addressing the solidarities between Indigenous and Black peoples is illuminating how white settler-colonialism is, was, and continues to be contingent on not only Indigenous genocide, dispossession, and the denaturalization of their relationship to land, but also fundamentally continues to co-depend on anti-blackness as illuminated in the work of Tiffany Lethabo King, Alaina E. Roberts, and others.[245] Settler-colonialism, as these authors describe, relies on the racial and gendered-sexual economies of the Middle Passage, as well as the abduction and sustaining of transatlantic chattel and plantation colonial enslavement of Africans as indentured labors and property. It also relies on what Saidiya Hartman refers to as contemporary colonial/imperial "after-life slave" projects that continue to dehumanize POC whether through white-liberal humanist laws that are purportedly impartial and objective, or the usurping modus operandi of global racial capitalism across what Katherine McKittrick refers to as a vast "landscape of systemic 'blacklessness'."[246] Indigenous-Black relations are marked by white settler-colonialism, whose divide-and-conquer strategies pit native against native and Black against Black. Whereas historically both entities were mutually engaged through treaty and other forms of cooperative relationships. The impact of white colonialism resulted in fraught conflicts as some Native people enslaved Black people, and some Black people participated in Indigenous extermination, expulsion, and land theft. And yet, in other instances, we see fused identities like the Black Cherokees in Oklahoma and Black Mi'kmaq peoples in Nova Scotia, who are a living embodiment of these two worlds and the intertwining of Indigenous and Black peoples' fates and futurities.[247]

The entanglement of Indigenous and Black histories emerges not only in the context of the U.S., but Canada as well. This is despite the myth of Canada's multicultural inclusiveness and innocence, for example as a haven to runaway slaves. Scholarship by Rinaldo Walcott and Afua Cooper documents the invisible history of the slave trade and argues that the reality is:

> First, that Canada was a colony of France and Britain, two of the largest slave traffickers. Second, because the Atlantic slave trading activities connected diverse economies, for much of the slavery period, there was a brisk trade between the capitalists of eastern Canada and the slaveholders of the Caribbean. Third, recent scholarship discovered that at least 60 of the slave

ships used in the British slave trade were built in Canada. Most important, enslavement of Africans itself was institutionalized in Canada. The enslavement of black people existed from at least 1628 to 1834.[248]

The complicated nature of Black-Indigenous relations is evident when one considers how Nubian Egyptians or even Sudanese Egyptians, on account of the hyper-visibility and invisibility of Blackness and Arab supremacy, can shun their Arab identity in exchange for a perceived globalized Black and African identity. Similarly when Arab Egyptians shun their African identity in exchange for embracing Arab supremacy. Such an essentialization of "blackness" can both erase the ongoing effects of the Middle Passage and contribute to the promotion of narratives that Islām was "spread by the sword" and that "Muslim slavery is akin to Euro-American slavery." Further complicating race-ethnic politics is the reality of Black-on-Black prejudices, and the difference between diasporic Black experiences in the U.S./Canada and the unique position of transatlantic descendants. This occurs despite how contemporary militarized policing allocates Black bodies, irrespective of their origins, to prison industrial complexes.[249] These accounts echo the call to acknowledge how settler-colonialism benefits from conflating historical experiences, and hence the need to expose the power relations, cultural logics, and subjects that have co-opted and erased radical Indigenous and Black trajectories. Blackness is further complicated when it intersects with Islām as many Middle Passage slaves were Muslims who were forcibly Christianized.

Slavery (*ʿubūdiyyah*), Arab supremacy, blackness, and Islām indicate the need for conversations about how neocolonialism and neoimperialism produce reactionary subjects and colonized subjectivities that are simultaneously racialized, sexualized, gendered and internalize authoritarian and individualist-materialist characteristics. Racialization demands that discussions about anti-blackness within a yet to be reborn Muslim and non-Muslim Umma first recognize, as Khaled Beydoun writes, that "slavery and its incidents are far more complex than Arab versus Black."[250] Kecia Ali notes, "Muslim history reflects a wide variety of historically specific patterns of enslavement, slaveholding, manumission and abolition."[251] Pre-modern slaves from "Europe, Asia and the Caucasus as well as Africa" might be "conscript-convert Janissary troops, cooks, nannies, Mamluk military rulers, salt miners, pearl divers, craftsmen [who are] allowed to keep part of their wages, mothers of Ottoman sultans and the drudges who cleaned the royal harem quarters."[252] Such oversimplifications then are frequently associated with the false Orientalist and ahistorical narrative that sword-wielding Arabs spread Islām, and that Arab slavery is indistinguishable from its European plantation counterpart. However, unlike the market-driven cotton plantations, slavery during the medieval Muslim period was not a central component of the political economy of Muslim societies, and identity politics that rely on the supremacy of whiteness and capitalist nation-state paradigms did not yet exist.[253]

This is a significantly different form of slavery than one based on racial hierarchies. In fact, Islām sought to acknowledge but also transcend tribal loyalties based on racial/ethnic affiliations when the Holy Prophet on the occasion of his last pilgrimage declared: "All beings are like brothers and sisters: a Black has no superiority over the Red, nor has an Arab any preferential claim on a non-Arab."[254] This is not to deny or condone the fact that non-Black Muslims continue to perpetrate and perpetuate anti-blackness and Afrophobia. One cannot deny, as Umar Lee writes, the "rampant abuse of workers in the Gulf, the thousands of workers in the Gulf dying on construction sites, the South Asian child camel-jockeys imported into the United Arab Emirates to race camels under harsh conditions, or the horrific conditions of prisoners in the Muslim world (the latest news being 13,000 prisoners executed in Syria)."[255] However, dehistoricizing and conflating modern and pre-modern references to slavery, its contemporary forms, and Islām serves to reify and promote clichéd stereotypes of Islām, while empowering both Euro-American Orientalist views and non-Euro-American narratives, such as those of al-Qaeda or ISIS. Many Qur'ānic passages specifically describe releasing slaves: "pious are those who believe in God, the Last Day, the angels, the Book, and the prophets; and who gives wealth, despite loving it, to kinsfolk, orphans, the indigent, the traveler, beggars, and for [the ransom of] slaves" (2:177); "*Zakat* [The charitable offerings] are only for the poor, and the indigent, and those working with them, and those whose hearts are [to be] reconciled, and for [ransoming] slaves and for debtors, and in the way of God, and for the traveler: a duty from God" (9:60); "And what will apprise thee of the steep pass? [It is] the freeing of a slave, or giving food at a time of famine to an orphan near of kin, or an indigent, clinging to the dust" (90: 4-13). Other Qur'ānic verses such as 2:177 and 9:60, not only clearly demonstrate a Muslim community's directive to create permanent funds for freeing those in bondage. The Qur'ān indicates that freeing slaves is a means of penance, as freeing a slave is equivalent to fasting (from three days to two months) or feeding or clothing the poor (from ten to 60 people).[256]

Decolonizing anti-blackness within Muslim communities requires understanding that Islamophobia and anti-blackness are not necessarily mutually exclusive; a hardly insignificant portion of the first transatlantic slaves during the Middle Passage were Muslim prior to their forced conversion to Christianity and transatlantic slavery's roots lie in the Iberian Muslim Peninsula. In the contemporary, Black Muslims are not bystanders, but rather allies when both Black people and Muslims are ascribed the epithets thug and/or terrorist as well as act as intersectional subjects of anti-Black racism, poverty, mass incarceration, or police brutality. Noting the similar roots of anti-blackness and Islamophobia is not meant to deny or condone the fact that non-Black Muslims continue to hide behind the Qur'ān, perpetrating and perpetuating anti-blackness and Afrophobia, to the extent that they do not recognize great Islamic civilizations like the Mali Empire, the Songhai Empire, and the Sokoto Caliphate.[257] We must strive to decolonize the intimate inter-racial and ethnic relationships between Northern African Hamitic and Arabian Peninsula Semitic peoples, without neglecting how now Zionist Africans at present are complicit and participate in the ongoing settler-colonization of Black and non-Black Arab Palestinians, in light of Israel's construction of second- and third-rate citizenries that include Sub-Saharan African, Eritrean and Sudanese refugees, and asylum seekers.

Similarly, to unsettle hierarchical frameworks that underlie Arab supremacy and the essentialization of queerness, gender, and blackness, we need to engage in decolonial solidarities that are "an uneasy, reserved, and are an unsettled matter that neither" necessarily reconcile present grievances nor foreclose future conflict in the formulation of uneasy potential alliances.[258] Differences between struggles ought to be politically amplified as opposed to quieted, irrespective of diasporic settler anxieties related to them and across our seemingly contradictory decolonial desires. Decolonization is not merely about reparations but rather repatriation and rematriation of Indigenous land, and as such is not concerned with social justice through civil rights frameworks. Decolonization entails identifying and understanding "co-constitutive dynamics and contingencies that appear to be unintelligible," under colonial/imperial conditions, and how we are implicated in each other's struggles; otherwise we will end up replicating colonial regimes of power/knowledge we seek to unhinge.[259] What is required is our collective respect, self-reflection, and reimagining of our positional relationships (*mu'āmalāt*) within the spirit of honoring Indigenous Treaties in settler-colonial U.S./Canada that have never been fulfilled.[260] Putting Islamic studies, Arab, Northern African, Muslim feminist, Islamic anarchism, and queer scholarship in conversation with queer Black studies, queer South Asian and diasporic critiques, other queer of color critiques in relation to queer Two-Spirit Indigenous critiques is fundamental to liberation and emancipation in both settler- and franchise-colonial societies.[261] Framing the conversation as if Black representation is in opposition to South Asian, non-Black Arab and Black North African representation stifles what could be valuable discussions amongst allies, because the same white supremacy that makes Brown SWANA Muslims invisible relies specifically upon anti-blackness and anti-Indigenous oppressive realities to function. Given intersections between white supremacy, law and racial hierarchies, it is vital to increase an understanding of how racism and Islamophobia/Salafiphobia intersect given the systemic oppression and daily microaggressions that BIPOC are exposed to, and that hinder their solidarities.[262]

Recent diasporic migrations of POC render the notion of settler-hood even more complicated. There can be little doubt that arrivants, and in particular Brown POC who have embraced and promote a culture of whiteness, have knowingly or unintentionally accepted a permanent invitation to appropriate Indigenous land.[263] An ethic of healing must be embraced, but this cannot happen without acknowledging and being accountable for the ways that we, as BIPOC, and all that is in between, collectively hurt each other. White supremacy must be recognized as a "key pillar of the settler colonial state" and this knowledge can be "mobilized as common ground for solidarity among [colonized] people."[264]

Many SWANA Muslims emigrate to Euro-America, particularly to the U.S./Canada, as a consequence of their repression and in pursuit of the fantasy of interminable happiness that always arrives at the expense of others. It is therefore critical to examine Byrd's category of arrivant relative to the concept of indigeneity. I concur with Sara Ahmed that Byrd's arrivant is not "a third position somehow located between settler and native," but rather a productive means to "destabilize the settler/native binary."[265] The emphasis on arrivant can potentially disrupt the imperial/colonial categories that separate labor and bodies from land.[266] This requires, as Byrd notes, settlers, natives, and arrivants to each first acknowledge their positions within the imperial system of relationships and then to reconceptualize them. There are two means through which this can be achieved. The first is through mobilizing Sara Ahmed's insights in *Queer Phenomenology*. She discusses the process of arrival and "migrant orientation" that operates against the logics and dynamics of invasion while also reifying one's position as a colonial product now engaged in the colonization of others.[267] The second is through mobilizing the concept of *indigeneity*, especially given how a majority of non-Indigenous Muslims from franchise-colonial nations do not identify as settlers of color and abdicate their responsibilities to Indigenous peoples.

Ahmed reflects on the process of arrival by noting that what is transplanted or arrived "is shaped by the conditions of its arrival, by how it came to get there."[268] Understanding the migrant's orientation is critical for the purpose of relating across our mutual struggles, because, as Vimalassery, Pegues, and Goldstein note, both the "arrivant and Indigenous positions alike certainly speak to 'lost homes', but neither seems to inhabit home in the mode of 'not yet'."[269] For this reason, a too-neat settler/native binary not only compromises the project of Black liberation, but also the futurity of settler POC.[270] Furthermore, non-Indigenous peoples cannot miss out on the productive opportunity to dismantle imperialist conditions in franchise-colonial societies. Taking into consideration the migrant orientation and constructing relational opportunities should not mean, as Tuck and Yang note, "that Indigenous peoples or Black and Brown peoples take positions of dominance over white settlers; the goal is not for everyone to merely swap spots on the settler-colonial triad, to take another turn on the merry-go-round," but rather "the goal is to break the relentless structuring of the triad – a break and not a compromise."[271] Instead, non-Indigenous settlers of color must build decolonial relationalities through situating their struggles in one another's narratives. Dismantling settler-colonialism "here" means eradicating franchise-colonialism "elsewhere," because both colonialisms are informed by liberal universalism and modernism that regenerate the social formations of empire.[272] Any thesis on decolonization must address Indigenous sovereignty and take into account the settler-responsibility of unsettling and de-occupation of land. To do otherwise constitutes an equivocation.

I disagree with Nandita Sharma and Cynthia Wright, who argue that POC are not settlers. They also critique all nationalisms for being cisheteropatriarchal and hierarchical products of colonialism, and assume that Indigenous nationalisms are antithetical to decolonization, by suggesting that they are premised on Euro-American ontologies of the nation.[273] By problematically essentializing Indigenous understandings of the nation, Sharma and Wright's analysis denies and depoliticizes, as Rita Dhamoon notes, the "differences between Indigenous peoples and other non-whites."[274] In fact, like the Islamic concept of the Umma, Indigenous approaches offer ontologies of nation that refuse hierarchies of power and open decolonial modes of governance. By adopting a perspective that pits claims of oppression against one another, Sharma and Wright misconstrue settler-colonialism and Indigenous nationhood, and interpret the latter as implying the expulsion of non-Indigenous peoples.

In response to Sharma and Wright's model, Dhamoon argues that the crisis of collective liberation is "not so much about whether migrants are settler colonists, but rather how migrations and the movement of non-whites are enabled and regulated by a global system of nation-states and corporations in the service of settler colonial projects and vice versa."[275] Drawing on Melissa Phung, Robinder Sehdev, and Beenash Jafri, Dhamoon argues that the differing effects of racial colonial structures on their lives mean that not all non-Indigenous residents of Turtle Island can be categorized as one.[276] The call here is for allies across the vast array of racialized arrivant-communities, who bear distinctive historical trajectories from both Indigenous peoples and white settlers, to adopt or at least engage Indigenous conceptualizations of treaty. Seeking to distinguish between settler-privilege and settler-complicity as well as arrivant-privilege and arrivant-complicity is necessary because privilege and complicity do not circulate in the same way. Racialized subjects who have been marked as white may not benefit from the former, but cannot disavow the latter. Beenash Jafri states,

> When people refer to "settler privilege", they are referring to the unearned benefits to live and work on Indigenous lands, and to the unequal benefits accrued through citizenship rights within the settler state. However, for people of colour the benefits of being a settler are accrued unevenly. These privileges or social advantages are contingent on things like nationality, class, gender, and migration status. When we account for systemic inequities, underemployment and the racialization of poverty, for most people of colour there are few "benefits" associated with being a settler. Thus, if we follow the logic of a settler/non-settler binary, an argument about people of colour having settler privilege quite easily falls on its face. Many people of colour are settlers without (or with limited) settler privilege.[277]

If BIPOC communities seek to transcend the triadic structures of settler-native-arrivants to offer a horizontalist unconditional hospitality that is still paradoxically conditioned on the existence of conditional shared ethical-political decolonial commitments, then, I argue, that beyond an honest action-based acknowledgment of our complicities and privileges relative to each other, as well as Byrd's category of arrivant, and Ahmad's migrant orientation, there is a need to activate what Byrd, Jeannette Armstrong, and Robert Lovelace refer to as indigeneity.

Byrd and Michael Rothberg argue that in this time of volatile borders and massive displacements of people, "'indigeneity' holds the promise of rearticulating and reframing questions of place, space, movement and belonging."[278] They see post-colonialism and indigeneity as overlapping and opposing positions that can illuminate each other, and they point to Gaurav Desai and Supriya Nair as rare examples of academics exploring this area.[279] Byrd and Rothberg also note the reluctance of some Indigenous scholars to adopt post-colonial perspectives as they are confronting ongoing colonization and are reluctant to adopt positions that suggest this is a thing of the past.[280] Moreover, although post-colonial studies have provided important tools for Indigenous scholars, it is unclear whether the models developed to describe European colonization of the Indian subcontinent and Africa are suitable for understanding the settler colonies in the Americas, Australia, New Zealand, and Palestine.[281] This problem is seen in the relationship between the terms "subaltern" and "Indigenous." Gaurav Desai explores this issue in his case studies and travel narratives on the Otavalo and Cotacachi, two Indigenous communities in Ecuador. He suggests that the term "diaspora" is key to understanding the relation between subalternity and indigeneity.[282] Byrd and Rothberg note, "Desai calls for a 'located' consideration of the significance of indigeneity and uses the category of subalternity as a lever for revealing power relations that cluster around different experiences of tradition, place and movement."[283] However, Byrd and Rothberg also direct our attention to how Desai rightfully argues that indigeneity can become nativist and have genocidal mutations such as "Hindutva in India and Hutu Power in Rwanda."[284] The objective, as Byrd and Rothberg interpret Desai, "is not to relativize the emphasis on distinctions of power that subaltern studies and Indigenous studies share, but rather – in the spirit of Desai's call for a located critique – to trace the shifting meanings that indigeneity has had and continues to have in colonial and neocolonial imaginaries."[285]

Syilx Okanagan scholar/activist Armstrong notes that through sacred activism and spiritual paths of service, indigeneity can become a social ethic in which "[l]ife practices intent on TEK, and knowledge of the land's local realities and regenerative capacity, become the guiding force for human occupation."[286] Moreover, Ardoch Algonquin elder Robert Lovelace notes that indigeneity or becoming indigenous is not synonymous with nor is it a politically charged euphemism for Aboriginal, Native, or Indian.[287] Nor does it follow from archetypical multicultural liberal UN declarations, articles, and racial definitions of Indigenous peoples. To Lovelace, indigeneity and becoming indigenous cannot take place in the domesticated corridors of a cordoned neoliberal academy that has a transactional relationship with corporations and the state. Lovelace states, "re-indigenization and indigeneity entail a return to the expectations of the womb [and] every infant in the womb has an expectation that he or she will emerge into a thoroughly indigenous world."[288] Indigeneity can only manifest and unfold through anti-colonial/anti-imperial sacred and decolonial, place-based, ecologically literate, symbiotic relation to land and life. To do so demands that peoples develop trust, an ethic of hospitality and disagreements towards each other, and enhance cognitively, spiritually, politically, and metaphysically each other's relationship to land. This allows settlers and non-settlers alike to engage in *becoming* indigenous. Nonetheless, this entails decolonially teaching, learning, and listening to each other as we discover what it means to become human again in a world in which we are mere migrating travelers, witnesses to each other's worlds during our temporary transit(s).[289]

Lovelace emphasizes that we are not our ancestors and hence there is no return to an authentic and pure notion of self. He writes,

> re-indigenization focuses interest on a complex set of contingencies. Knowledge of Indigenous technologies is certainly part of it. Exploring the theoretical underpinnings of technological, social, political, economic, artistic, psychological and philosophical development within Indigenous societies as they may be applied to real life collective decision making connects knowledge to practice ... [reindigenization is] about present decision making, forming intentional communities and engaging in actual earth based work.[290]

Amadahy interprets and expands on Lovelace's views, arguing that non-Indigenous people should do away with settler-guilt syndrome in exchange for our collective embracing of healthy minds and living well.[291] As an Algonquin-Muslim, Lovelace teaches, "anyone can become indigenous to a place" and this does not mean "everyone has to 'become Indian'" or that we engage in white Orientalized projects that entail our collective return to innocence.[292] At the core of Lovelace's understanding of decolonization/indigenization, Amadahy notes, "is not bloodlines, skin colour, or cultural heritage."[293] Rather, Lovelace argues for fulfilling acts of compassion (*raḥma*), goodness (*iḥsān*) and intelligence, and adhering to non-statist, innate communal bonds and ethical-political, spiritual commitments. These are all synonymous with Islām's notion of *fiṭrah* (the originary nature of individuals to be born in a condition and incline towards all that is communal and good) and associated with achieving an anarchistic interpretation of a global Umma and pluriverse-spiritual world. As discourses on Islamic anarchism have discussed through the concept of Umma, "there are existing ontologies of nation that refuse hierarchies of power and still open decolonial modes of governance."[294] A pluriversal vision of an Umma (global Muslim and non-Muslim polity) is premised on the acceptance and not mere tolerance, in a multicultural liberal sense, of the Other, and is composed of participants bound by variant spiritual belongings, faiths, and religions interwoven with shared decolonial ethico-political values derived from their own paradigms. This occurs even if those composing the Umma differ from each other in their cultural and ritualistic performances and traditions.

Through Lovelace and Armstrong, and a conceptualization of ethics within decolonial understandings of Islām, I seek to go beyond Byrd's understandable trepidation regarding indigeneity. This is done by offering indigeneity as a non-racial/ethnic transnational category and a spiritual-ethical-political decolonial coordinate in relation to land. After all, seeing that there is no concept of "chosen-ness" or "original sin" in Islām, the Islamic concept of *fiṭrah* can be conceived of as a global form of indigeneity, such that we may return to our species' original purpose of fulfilling ethico-political acts of compassion, intelligence, and iḥsān. Or, in other words, striving towards that which communally, ethically, politically, and responsibly connects us as a species to each other and Creation, land, or non-human life; perhaps, we may discover our purpose, and if so, a Creator. Fiṭrah conceived this way is similar to the core values informing Armstrong's as well as Amadahy and Lovelaces' understanding of indigeneity as going beyond bloodlines, skin color, or cultural heritage and centering instead on non-statist, non-capitalist, ethical-political, spiritual commitments towards a global Umma and pluriversal world.[295]

If Muslims are truly keen on resurrecting an egalitarian, non-statist Umma, which they are theologically bound to, then this means understanding that the condition of being indigenous or indigeneity allows us to mobilize as an international collective of multiple anti-imperialist, anti-racist decolonial communities that can build solidarities with Indigenous Peoples in Turtle Island and in settler-colonial societies found in Australia, New Zealand, and Palestine. Since decolonization is a spiritual act, arrivant Muslims must engage decolonial scriptural interpretations, as those emergent from Islamic anarchism, to locally connect and correspond with spiritual, decolonial visions of indigeneity.

Having thus addressed questions regarding decolonial anti-authoritarianism in this interpretation of Islām, in the following chapter I return to the conceptual and practical inscriptions of Islām, where we may discover, utilizing Anarchic Ijtihād, an ensemble of fundamentally interconnected anti- and non-capitalist concepts and practices that complement this interpretation of Islām's anti- and non-authoritarian stances, positions, and leanings.

4
Anarcha-Islām: An Anti- and Non-Capitalist Islām

In order to defend this senseless manufacture from all competition that could not fail to arise on all sides, one must have soldiers, armies, airplanes, battleships, hence this sperm which it seems the governments of America have had the effrontery to think of. For we have more than one enemy lying in wait for us, my son, we, the born Capitalists, and among these enemies Stalin's Russia which also doesn't lack armed men.

Antonin Artaud (1976, 556)[1]

If Poverty were a Man, I would have slain him.

Al-Shaheed Alī ibn Abī Ṭālib (601–61 AD)

Anarcha-Islām's Osteological Right-Side

In this chapter, I use Anarchic Ijtihād to construct Anarcha-Islām's resistance to racial capitalism through non-capitalist concepts and practices extracted from Islām. These concepts include Islamic conceptualizations of *Property*, *Communal* and *Individual Caretakers*, *Muḍārabah/Mushārakah*, *Ribā*, *Zakāt*, *Ramaḍān* (or *Ṣawm*), *Ṣadaqat Al-Fiṭr*, and *Islamic banking*. First, I offer an anti-capitalist reading of the concept and practice *Property (or mulk)*. In Anarcha-Islām, property is interpreted as belonging solely to God, with human beings acting as mere *Caretakers* of God's property. Property is therefore publicly shared amongst Caretakers and is not to be privately hoarded. Second, I offer an anti-capitalist reading of the concept and practice of *Caretaking*. A Caretaker is a temporary beneficiary and a trustee or borrower of God's property. A Caretaker's role is thus radically different from that of an absolute owner under capitalism. There are two types of Caretakers: *Communal* and *Individual*. Communal Caretakers are defined as Caretakers engaged in economic unity and who are in collective partnerships as a community. However, though Communal Caretakers in Islām are preferred, Individual Caretakers are permitted because the "construction of healthy communities begins and ends with unique personalities, that the collective potential is realized only when a singular is free."[2] However, there are three restrictions placed on Individual Caretakers to establish equilibrium between the ambitions and rights of an individual and critical ethical-political responsibilities to their community. The first restriction is that they are forbidden from caretaking for natural resources. That is, natural resources like water, wood, wind, gas, fire, and oil, indeed land within itself, belong to the whole community, and all its members have equal shares and rights of responsible access to these resources. Second, if their caretaking of property is done in an ignoble, indignant "manner, which damages ... others" then the community intervenes to prevent them from causing further damage.[3] Third, if "a segment of society is without shelter, clothing, food, and adequate economic opportunity, then societal needs ... take priority over" the Individual Caretaker's rights by virtue of Maṣlaḥa.[4]

Having offered an anti-capitalist reading of Caretaker and distinguished between Individual and Communal Caretakers, I read *Muḍārabah/Mushārakah* as Anarcha-Islām's third anti-capitalist concept and practice. Muḍārabah/Mushārakah in Anarcha-Islām is interpreted as a communally established anti-monopolistic and anti-oligopolistic external financial dynamic, completely devoid of interest and with the role of encouraging joint ventures amongst existing Caretakers and new Caretakers.

Having read Muḍārabah/Mushārakah as an anti-capitalist concept and practice, I read *Ribā* as Anarcha-Islām's fourth anti-capitalist concept and practice. Ribā, interest, is a fundamental pillar of capitalism and in Islām its "collection ... was and is forbidden because it ... [serves] as a means of exploiting" all those who undergo dire and bare poverty.[5] Having read Ribā, as an anti-capitalist concept and practice, I read Zakāt as Anarcha-Islām's sixth anti-capitalist concept and practice. Decreed in the Qur'ān, Zakāt is interpreted as an obligatory charity. I then read Ramaḍān and its associated Ṣadaqat Al-Fiṭr as Anarcha-Islām's fifth and sixth anti-capitalist concepts and practices. Ramaḍān is interpreted as an "act of worship ... [existing to] lead Muslims to perceive, to feel inwardly, the need to eat and drink and by extension to ensure that every human being has the means to subsist."[6] Finally, I interpret Islamic banking as Anarcha-Islām's seventh anti-capitalist concept and practice. Islamic banking in Anarcha-Islām is interpreted as an anti-capitalist concept and practice that offers unrestricted access to financial resources in banking systems without reference to the criteria of "creditworthiness."[7] Similarly, Islamic inheritance laws are aimed at the wide distribution of a deceased's wealth as opposed to furthering hoarding and nepotism. In concluding the chapter, I clarify that it is the anti-capitalist concepts and practices of Property, Communal and Individual Caretakers, Muḍārabah/Mushārakah, Ribā, Inheritance, Zakāt, Ramaḍān, Ṣadaqat Al-Fiṭr , Islamic banking and inheritance laws that now conjunctively form Anarcha-Islām's anti-capitalist position of resistance to capitalism.

Awaken: An Anti- and Non-Capitalist Islām: Micro- and Macro-Economics

The first anti- and non-capitalist concept and practice we must discuss is *property*, particularly as it relates to "ownership" (*mulk*).[8] In Islām, this world and hence all property belongs to God. Nothing belongs to our species, including our health, nor is what we "possess" a product of our will or our own "making." This understanding of property is distinct from Euro-American secularized-Christian Protestant, individualist conceptualizations that see "individual wealth ... as a sign of divine selection."[9] In other words, *al-mulk lil-Allāh*, "all (im)material matter belongs to God," and human beings are merely stewards, *Khulafā*, or *Caretakers* of God's property, for which we are all accountable and responsible.[10] The Qur'ān states:

> O believers, expend of the good things you have earned, and of what *We have produced* for you from the earth; and intend not the corruption of it for your expending, for you would never take it yourselves … Those who expend … night and day, secretly and in public, their wage awaits them with their Lord, and no fear shall be on them; neither shall they sorrow.[11]

Thus, property is ultimately created and owned by God, even when earned.[12] Creator's maxim and intent is for property to be shared among Caretakers whom God has entrusted with God's property in an effort at establishing *mūsāwāt* (equality) and socio-political and economic *'adālah* (justice).[13] No Caretaker may deprive another Caretaker of property, because the right of access to property is a sacred right decreed by the Creator, and is amongst a set of other divinely ordained rights referred to as *al-ḍaruriyāt al-khams* (the fundamental qualities of life).[14] Two of the five *al-ḍaruriyāt al-khams* are access to property and life.[15] The role of our species is the temporary care of God's property according to decreed ethical-political commitments. As the Prophet explicitly stated, "people are partners in water, pasture, land, and fire."[16] The Qur'ān itself teaches, "And tell them the water is to be divided amongst them each [day of] drink attended [by turn]."[17] On the Day of Awakening, God is the Witness and Absolute Judge of our role in the Caretaking partnership and pact we have with the Creator. Creator will decree whether we, as Caretakers, have betrayed and corrupted the entrusted property or not. Property is thus publicly relegated, owned by The Self Sufficient and The Enricher (*Al-Ghāni* and *Al-Mūghni*) Allāh, to be collectively and equitably shared by Caretakers and not privately hoarded. Read in this manner, property is an anti- and non-capitalist concept and practice.[18]

With property absolutely possessed by God, a singular economic relationship emerges: God-Caretaker. A Caretaker is a provisional "beneficiary," a "trustee," or borrower of God's property, which includes our bodies and selves; after all, in Islām, our genesis, existence, living breath, sight, hearing, and all oratory faculties are due to The Creator of All Power (*Al-Muqtadir*) Allāh. A Caretaker is not an absolute owner as under capitalism. A Caretaker cannot become a capitalist if the Caretaker is to fulfill the concept and practice of caretaking.[19] Rather, a Caretaker has economic relationships with God and with other Caretakers in a community. A Caretaker can become a *Sole* and/or a *Communal* Caretaker.

Akhtar Awan describes Communal Caretakers as Caretakers who engage in economic alliances and collective, cooperative mutual aid partnerships, building their livelihoods by shared use of borrowed property from God.[20] Communal Caretakers operate through the virtue of Shūrā, Ijmāʿ, and through Maṣlaḥa, as in the collective good of the broader community in mind.[21] According to Awan's analysis, small cooperatives or projects based on co-borrowing by Communal Caretakers from God, based also on Ijmāʿ (consensus) from the broader community, are radically different from worker-owner relationships under capitalism. This Muslim perception of a healthy economy is distinct from their regimentation and regulation by monopolies and oligopolies that subjugate our species and nonhuman life into commodities under capitalism. Instead, in Islām, economies ought to be decentralized so that resources are not concentrated in the hands of an elite few. Generally speaking, Islamic economies are meant to be structurally comprised of a multiplicity of decentralized small cooperatives co-borrowing from God. The collective and mutual partnership in each small cooperative is continually transforming, and rupturing, through the entry and exits of other Communal Caretakers within a community into the small cooperative.[22]

Communal Caretakers from this Islamic perspective are expected to be conducting their affairs collectively in *Shirākah* (partnership) with God and with each other.[23] It is under the communion of Shirākah and this decentralized, abstract, Islamic economic structure that Communal Caretakers in Islām can truly become worthy beings capable of deciding whether to participate in a small firm of their choosing.[24] With all Communal Caretakers equal before God, each Communal Caretaker's voice contributes to the decision-making processes of the small cooperative as each Communal Caretaker's voiced concern is dignified and respected, empowering everyone with a sense of purpose.[25] Therefore, Communal Caretakers in Islām are afforded and disposed "a dignity in keeping with … [their] status as … vicegerent[s] of God on earth … [whose] return[s] can take the form of … a share in the useful" benefits of the "enterprise."[26]

Although Communal Caretakers are preferred in Islām, Sole Caretakers are permitted, as Islām offers room for and appreciates the arrival and survival of the unique and the singular, the stem of every collective root, that is, the Caretaker as an autonomous individual.[27] The logic justifying Sole Caretakers is that an individual must not be compelled to live in servitude, or obliterated and disremembered by the caprice of a community. As Félix Guattari and Antonio Negri argue: "The most important lesson is that the construction of healthy communities begins and ends with unique personalities, that the collective potential is realized only when a singular is free."[28]

In Islām, it is unnecessary to privilege the merited right of the community over the individual, or the legitimate right of the individual over the community, as they are interdependent upon each other. In Islām, "the death of the individual" and "the death of the communal" denote extremes and excesses. Islām pursues equilibrium, and thus advocates for moderation, preserving an individual's right to introduce new innovative desires into the individual's social field, while maintaining the centrality of a community's Maṣlaḥa. In other words, an individual's creative desire does not have to follow their community's desire, otherwise inspiration dies. It is equally unnecessary that an individual's desire be motivated by narcissistic and individualistic pursuits of the ego that would ultimately result in that person's exploitation of their Umma and community. Rather, an individual's desire may be accompanied and marshalled by an individual's earnest quest for a community's Maṣlaḥa.

Thus, Sole Caretakers may prosperously and ethically operate their own innovative initiatives. However as with Communal Caretakers, a Sole Caretaker's venture must also be accessible for other Caretakers in the community to partake in, in the future, to delineate monopoly. Nepotism then is lethal to a community's healthy existence, since nepotism usurps and strips individual self-determination. In other words, while Sole Caretakers have the right to exist and flourish, they are restricted by three impediments. These impediments exist because it is expected that differences in *māl* (money) between Caretakers will naturally arise, as a consequence of the reality of differences in productivity and work ethics between Caretakers.[29] As anthropologist and self-identifying anarchist David Graeber writes: "Divine providence has arranged us to have different abilities, desires, and inclinations," with the market and mercantilism intelligibly being "one manifestation of this more general principle of mutual aid, of the matching of, abilities (supply) and needs (demands)."[30] In this sense, some Caretakers may derive joy working ample days and hours, while others may not be able in the same way or may, even, prefer laboring less. Nonetheless, none of them should be economically deprived and punished on account of their abilities relative to what constitutes productivity, or for that matter their choices. By the same token, there is no reason that anyone should or will necessarily earn an equivalent quantity of *māl* if the wellspring is sustainably fair to assure our divinely decreed qualities of life, especially if the source is *ḥalāl* (lawful). Variation in *māl*, alters nothing with respect to the preservation of everyone's right to a decent quality of life in light of al-ḍaruriyāt al-khams be it in shelter, health, nourishment, and sustenance.[31]

The first impediment is that Sole Caretakers may not claim basic or natural resources as their own, because this contradicts the Qur'ān and Prophet Muḥammad's previous commandments and claims.[32] Rather, a Sole Caretaker is only permitted to borrow particular types of resources. As Cummings, Askari, and Mustafa argue, a Sole Caretaker is forbidden from claiming:

> Natural resources in the universe, such as land, capital, general circumstances such as shortages for reasons of war or disasters as well as laws of nature, all these belong to the whole of society, and all its members have equal shares and rights of access to them.[33]

The second impediment is that if a Sole Caretaker's treatment and management of the property or the resources they use damages resources, then the community possesses the immediate right to intervene to prevent that Caretaker from inflicting further abuse and mischief.[34] The third impediment is that a Sole Caretaker must accept responsibility for the community such that if "a segment of society is without [the qualities of life which include] shelter, clothing, food, and adequate economic opportunity, then societal needs … take priority."[35] In other words, yet again, a community is obligated to intervene in a Sole Caretaker's economic affairs by virtue of the ethicality of Maṣlaḥa. Read in this manner, the concept of Caretaker, Communal or Sole, is anti- and non-capitalist in principle and practice.

The third anti- and non-capitalist concepts and practices reread for Anarcha-Islām are the interrelated *Muḍārabah/ Mushārakah*. Muḍārabah/Mushārakah is a communally founded anti-monopolistic and anti-oligopolistic financial mechanism that is void of interest and speculation (*Ribā*), which are Qur'ānically forbidden in Islām. The purpose of Muḍārabah/Mushārakah is to cultivate and encourage joint ventures amongst existing Caretakers and new Caretakers. In this sense, Muḍārabah/Mushārakah restricts attempts by Caretakers to hold unbridled control of small cooperatives for themselves. Muḍārabah/Mushārakah obstructs the development of monopolies or oligopolies by extending existing Caretaker relationships. That is, it creates occasions and opportunities for new Caretakers and new small cooperatives to flourish and emerge as independent offshoots of existing Caretaker partnerships and small cooperatives.[36] There are three beneficiary effects of Muḍārabah/Mushārakah:

1. The creation of other diversified autonomous small firms for new Caretakers. This tactical move not only assists in creating room for new Caretakers but also reduces animosity amongst new and existing Caretakers. In this sense, Muḍārabah/ Mushārakah promotes equitable opportunities for sharing between both new and existing Caretakers, as well as *Iḥsān* (compassion and generosity), by justly spreading resources between Caretakers of a community.[37]

2. The minimization of stockpiling and waste or otherwise what is referred to in Islām as *iṣrāf*.[38] In other words, since Muḍārabah/Mushārakah's objective is the constant recirculation of resources, Muḍārabah/Mushārakah minimizes waste in production, consumption, and commodity exchange values.[39] In so doing, Muḍārabah/Mushārakah prevents unnecessary depletion or destruction in production and consumption once a threshold is reached.[40]
3. Muḍārabah/Mushārakah is guided by the Islamic principle of *Huqūq al-ʿIbādah* (the dutiful responsibility) to new Caretakers and *Huqūq al-Allāh* (duties to God) that are meant to reaffirm God's intent for the minimization of *tabzeer* (waste) and *iṣrāf* (extravagance), in exchange for the promotion of communal solidarity (*akhawiya*) and mutual aid (*taʿāwun*) that are centered on abiding by what is ethically and politically good and just as well as the warding off of injustice and evil (*al-amr bi al-maʿrūf wa al-nahy ʿan al-munkar*).[41]

There are two arrangements in Muḍārabah: *Al Muḍārabah Al Mūqayyadah* (restricted Muḍārabah) and *Al Muḍārabah Al Muṭlaqah* (unrestricted Muḍārabah). In the former, an individual or a group of Caretakers, the *Rabb-al-māl*, express interest in a particular venture that the *Muḍārib(een)*, or new venturer(s), may undertake or partake in.[42] In the latter form of Muḍārabah, *Rabb(āt)-al-māl* (plural form of Rabb-al-māl) possess no claim as to the nature of the venture because the liberty of choice (*ikhtiyār*) resides with the new Muḍārib(een). While old(er) venturers have no right to determine the nature of the projects undertaken by new venturers, new Muḍāribeen (whether sole or communal) cannot accept other new Muḍāribeen or venturers in their midst without the consent of Rabb-al-māl or older venturers and caretakers. Moreover, the new Caretakers or venturers who relied on those older to facilitate their new ventures are also not permitted to amalgamate their own personal investments with that particular Muḍārabah or new venture.[43] The logic of these restrictions is that the spirit of the social bond cultivated and the new pool of resources gathered amongst new and old is based on a "contract" that must be honored. A new Muḍārib (or venturer) is entrusted as an *Ameen* (honest trustee) whose reputation is determined by guarding what has been left entrusted to them (the *amāna*) by older innovators.

In Al Muḍārabah Al Muqayyadah, or restricted Muḍārabah, a Muḍārib's privileges may extend to becoming a *Wakīl* (agent of Rabb-al-māl), who purchases products for trade or assists in the establishment of a new venture. A Muḍārib may also become a *Sharīk* (partner) to the original Rabb(at)-al-māl, and therefore entitled to a portion of the benefits reaped according to a predetermined ratio between the two if indeed a profit is procured. Alternatively, a new innovator may also become a *Ḍāmin* (liable guarantor) relative to Rabb(at)-al-māl if the venture fails or experiences losses, especially if this loss is proven to be due to negligence, abuse, or misconduct, in which case a Muḍārib is obliged to provide compensation. It ought to be clear thus that the relationship between Rabb-al-māl with Muḍārib(een), even in restricted Muḍārabah, is an interwoven relationship based on Shirākah (co-partnership based on sharing).[44] The position that assigns least responsibility possible for a Muḍārib in restricted Muḍārabah is for them to become an *Ajīr* (temporary borrower or helping caretaking partner), who innovates in a new short-term venture, in which case should the venture of Shirākah become void for whatever circumstance or reason, the Muḍārib remains entitled to beneficial rights, the minimum of which is a "fee" for services rendered. In all cases these agreements must be initially established between the two parties. It is pertinent for the validity of Muḍārabah that the parties involved agree from the beginning as to the conditions of the contract, their responsibilities, and what each is entitled to, given that both parties can Islamically share any ratio of the rewards between them that they agree upon.[45] In instances where parties enter into an agreement without mention of the proportions of the rewards from the new venture, they are presumed to share the rewards equally.[46] Apart from the agreed upon proportion of the rewards or profits in Muḍārabah, but particularly in Al Muḍārabah Al Muṭlaqah (unrestricted Muḍārabah), a Muḍarib is not entitled to claim a periodical salary or remuneration from Rabb-al-māl towards a venture they have wilfully chosen to initiate and partake in. After all, the Muḍārib is neither working for a corporation or governmental organization, or Rabb-al-māl for that matter, but rather functioning alongside themselves and other members of their community on their own, even if they were initially dependent on Rabb-al-māl to help them start a new venture. Neither the Muḍārib(een) nor Rabb-al-māl may allocate a lump sum of profit for a "third" or foreign party outside the purview of the parties involved. Neither can determine the share of the profit of Muḍārabah at a rate tied with the capital that an initial Rabb-al-māl invested for the venture.[47] As for when the venture incurs losses in a portion of transactions and succeeds in others, the profits are directed towards offsetting the loss first, with what remains of the profit distributed between the Muḍārib(een) and Rabb-al-māl according to the consensually determined ratio.[48] Either party may terminate both forms of Muḍārabah at any time, and it is therefore permitted that either party can enter and exit at different dates, provided adequate notice is arranged in advance. If Muḍārabah is allocated for a particular term and is for a determined maximum period, it concludes with the termination of the term, meaning that the Muḍārib(een) may not purchase new products related to the venture following. However, they may benefit from selling products purchased prior to the termination of the term. Neither party possesses the right to specify a minimum term of Muḍārabah, as the emphasis should always be on the success of the venture of Muḍārabah and the shared Shirākah (partnership) it precludes following a maximum period.[49] Depending on the extent of financial liquidity at the term's termination, resources accumulated are liquidated, and the profit determined, such that rewards to each Caretaker may be directed and redistributed towards other ventures and even newer Caretakers. Of course, if no profit exists, the Muḍārib(een) and Rabb-al-Māl receive nothing.[50] The quantity of profit gained by either party is independent of the initial capital, and therefore solely dependent on the absolute gross profit realized by the commercial enterprise itself. In other words, the profit assigned to either party is not a percentage of the capital contributed, as that constitutes a fixed return, *Ribā* (or interest) that is forbidden in Islām. The profit assigned to either party cannot be an agglomerated sum either as that too constitutes interest.[51]

What distinguishes Muḍārabah and Mushārakah from each other is that Muḍārabah denotes a particular form of partnership where one or multiple Caretaker(s) collaborate co-equally together in a commercial venture in which all contribute equal resources.[52] Mushārakah entails *Shirākat-al-Amwāl* (partnership in "capital" where all Caretakers contribute to the venture), *Shirākat-ul-'amal* (partnership in labor), and *Shirākat-ul-Wujooh* (partnership in goodwill). In contrast, in Muḍārabah, resources are provided exclusively by the Rabb-al-māl. Further to this, in Musharakah, all the associated Caretakers participate in the affairs of the venture, and contribute and co-equally share responsibility in laboring in it.[53] Whereas in Muḍārabah's unrestricted form, Rabb-al-māl possesses no right in managing or participating in the venture's affairs which is the sole responsibility of the Muḍāribeen who are the *Umanā* (trustees) in Mushārakah. On the occasion of a loss, all Caretakers partaking in Shirākah (partnership) uniformly share the loss, because, again, they ultimately are Umanā of Allāh's property.[54]

Musharakah is different from Muḍārabah where the loss, should any exist, is incurred solely by Rabb-al-māl, due to the fact that the Muḍāribeen do not invest or possess the initial resources, beyond their labor, will, ingenuity, and creativity, to begin with. Of course, this allocation of sole and social responsibility upon Rabb-al-māl is conditional on due diligence: if the Muḍāribeen are proven to have acted negligently or dishonestly, they become liable for the loss wrought forth by their irresponsibility, given the necessity for accountability.[55] Liability for Caretakers in Mushārakah is normally unlimited; if liabilities exceed the venture's assets and there exist few options but to liquidate, then all liabilities become the responsibility of the collective. Nevertheless, if all Caretakers in the collective consent that no Caretaker should incur any debt during the course of the venture, then exceeding liabilities will be borne by the sole Caretaker who is answerable for incurring a debt on behalf of the venture, having violated the aforementioned condition.[56] However, in Muḍārabah the liability of the Rabb-al-māl is restricted to the resources or "capital" they invested, unless they permitted the Muḍārib(een) to incur debts on their behalf, which is also acceptable. Accordingly, in Mushārakah, as soon as partners mix their financial resources or capital together, the entire assets of the Mushārakah become the joint responsibility and care of the collective according to the proportion of their respective pledge, and the predetermined dutiful engagements and resources that were contributed and contractually agreed upon.[57] This way, each Caretaker may benefit from the appreciation in value of the venture's assets, even if profit has not accrued through sales.[58] However in Muḍārabah, all that is purchased by the Muḍārib(een) belongs to Rabb-al-māl, while the Muḍārib(een) earn their share of the profit solely through the operation of a venture; thus, Muḍārib(een) are not entitled to claim their share in the venture's assets, even on the occasion that their value increases. Therefore, Muḍārabah/Mushārakah represents an anti- and non-capitalist concept and practice.

The third anti and non-capitalist concept and practice is *Ribā* (interest) whether in the form of gambling on the stock market, bank loans, or extra charges on products (produce for instance), rent hikes, mortgages, or insurance schemes. Ribā is prohibited in the strictest, indeed severest, terms in the Qur'ān:[59]

> Those who benefit from interest shall be raised like those who have been driven to madness by the touch of the Devil; this is because they say: "Trade is like interest" while God has permitted trade and forbidden interest.[60]

Generally speaking, in Islamic banking and finance, there are three categories of Ribā goods, foodstuffs, precious metals, and money.[61] Ribā can take the form of *Ribā al-faḍl*, *Ribā al-nasiah*, or *Ribā al-diyūn*. According to the Institute of Islamic Banking and Insurance, Ribā al-faḍl is defined as: "A sale transaction in which a commodity is exchanged for the same commodity but unequal in amount, such as unequal exchange involving larger amount of low quality goods with smaller amount better quality goods, resulting in an excess in exchange."[62] Such transactions may involve the exchange of one currency for another at an unequal rate, or any exchange where one party has an "excess" gain.[63] Other forms of Ribā include *Ribā al-nasiah* or *Ribā al-diyūn*, which are Ribā of delay. According to the Institute of Islamic Banking and Insurance, a "Riba of delay or usury of debt, is due to exchange not being immediate with or without excess on one of the counter-values," that is, an "increment on the principal of a debt or loan payable by the borrower."[64] In other words, any transaction is based on the expectation of higher returns.

Ribā in all its forms was forbidden, because it is seen as a form of vicious exploitation of the poor on account of their economic strata.[65] It is a means by which money is cumulatively incurred when nothing, in fact, is produced; money that results in more virtual money. Ribā abuses the notion of debt. Ribā is repugnant of the spirit of Islām, as it contradicts the philosophies of *al-'adl wa'l-iḥsān* (justice and benevolence).[66] The Qur'ān itself advises, if not commands, debt forgiveness. For instance, we can read the following verse: "If the debtor is in difficulty, grant them time till it is easy for them to repay. *But if ye remit* it by way of charity, that is best for you if ye only knew."[67] If you "remit" in this verse here is the key towards the conceptual idea of "forgiving debt," if not advocacy for its complete cancellation in Islām.[68] The prohibition against Ribā too is an anti- and non-capitalist concept and practice.

The fourth anti-capitalist concept and practice reread for Anarcha-Islām is *Zakāt*, or obligatory alms. Zakāt is the *ḥaq* (right) of the poor over the rich, since all *mulk* belongs to the Creator.[69] The Qur'ān is rather unambiguously clear that Zakāt is ordained and to be interpreted as such:

> The offerings are for the poor and needy, those who work to collect them, those whose hearts are brought together the ransoming of slaves, debtors, in God's way, and the traveller; so God ordains.[70]

Zakāt radically keeps social equity integrated in the broader social field. As the third of Islām's five pillars, Zakāt is not just a concept and practice nor is it philanthropy but it is a divinely decreed necessity for a Muslim to attain salvation.[71] Zakāt is a reminder of social responsibility, of who truly owns property, and is an act of expiation for the sins and shortcomings of a Muslim. In this respect, Zakāt is the temporary minimization of micro-fascistic privileges that arise as a consequence of class privileges and dynamics. Significantly, a payer of Zakāt must not be arrogant or disappointed when paying it, because this negates the act of its payment. The Qur'ān is rather clear with respect to the attitude and mannerism of the individual payment of Zakāt:

> As does they who spend of their wealth only to be seen and praised by others … theirs is the parable of a smooth rock with [a little] earth upon it – and then a rainstorm smites it and leaves it hard and bare.[72]

This recurring repayment of Zakāt every year further "demands … knowledge of the environment, the community, and the social and economic situation," which has the further spirited effect of emphasizing and reinforcing communal commitment and a sense of social responsibility and solidarity.[73]

Thus, Zakāt is the ordained act of giving, face to face, and not through an NGO or third party, so that the better off may actually see and affectively feel the plight of the poor, and in turn adequately provide to them what is already justly and rightfully theirs and is due. In this sense, someone who willingly pays Zakāt is someone who has chosen "to bear faith … to bear responsibility for social commitment at every moment … to possess is [tantamount] to have the duty [and obligation] to share."[74] Zakāt understood this way is an anti- and non-capitalist concept and practice.

The fifth and sixth anti- and non-capitalist concepts and practices for Anarcha-Islām are *Ramaḍān* and *Ṣadaqat Al-Fiṭr*. Ramaḍān is a fast (*Ṣawm*), from dusk till dawn, for a lunar month every year, for those able. Ramaḍān is an "act of worship … [decreed by God, and designed] to lead Muslims to perceive, and to feel inwardly, the need to eat and drink and by extension to ensure that every human being has the means to subsist."[75] The function of fasting during Ramaḍān is the purification of the faster's mind, heart, body, and soul from all physical and material possession. Indeed, fasting is an act of expiation in the voluntary cleansing of a faster's internal and external sins and shortcomings for the previous year. Ramaḍān is meant to reduce surplus, excessive acts of production and consumption, and the waste of property entrusted to a faster by God. Ramaḍān, in essence, sanitizes and purifies a faster's body and the property they are entrusted with not only for the spiritual month of Ramaḍān, but rather for the forthcoming year. Ramaḍān acts as a profound rooted reminder to the faster of their inseparable ethical and political commitments as a Muslim, preparing them to maintain the following year's diligent practices and which they cultivated during Ramaḍān. After all, faith is as a sea's waves at times moving calm, and yet at other times raging, but never, in truth, stagnating. Upon Ramaḍān's conclusion *Ṣadaqat Al-Fiṭr* is another obligatory alms to be paid. Ṣadaqat Al-Fiṭr exists in connection with Ramaḍān and is therefore:

> Related to property and is obligatory on every Muslim that possesses more than the prescribed amount of provisions after giving the charity … [and is] to be given in person into the hands of those who are eligible to receive … [not] the wealthy.[76]

Like Zakāt, Sadaqat El-Fitr is to be offered face to face and in discretion, without any state or institutional intervention. Ramaḍān and Ṣadaqat Al-Fiṭr, read in this manner, are anti- and non-capitalist concepts and practices.

The seventh anti- and non-capitalist concept and practice for Anarcha-Islām is *Islamic banking*. Although Islamic banking is based on pre-modern credit instruments that were developed by Muslims during the medieval period, Islamic banking's modern form is problematic given its reliance on a worldwide-integrated capitalist system which even Islamic banks cannot transcend. The modern forms of Islamic banks began to surface in

> The mid-nineteenth century … [and consist of] funding trading activities … [opening] saving accounts with no interest … [and]

whose patrons participate in investments and either earn a share of the profit on the return or suffer a portion of the losses sustained by the bank.[77]

The practices are based on pre-modern credit instruments that facilitated trade.[78] Credit instruments during Muḥammad's life took the native form of *Bayt al-Māl* (the Distributive House of money or wealth), which was developed in recognition of the right of Muslims to possess free necessary sustenance, or borrow money and have access to resources without humiliation or discrimination.[79] *Beyūt al-Māl* (plural for Bayt al-Māl) were constituted, in part, from the excess money collected from Zakāt and *Ṣadaqa* (alms) like Ṣadaqat Al-Fiṭr, and were distributed to meet the basic needs of "the destitute," those weaker, or "under hardship of insolvency," and "those in need of special attention and kind treatment."[80] For medieval Muslims, their intention was to prevent banking activities from becoming a full-time occupation. As David Graeber writes, it was much later during the medieval period that "promissory notes were" developed and called "sakk, 'checks', or *ruq'a*, 'notes'" in Muslim markets whose initial premise was "cooperation rather than competition."[81] This is because "while Muslim economic thinkers did recognize and accept the need for market competition, they never saw competition as its essence" making "the moral implications … very different."[82]

In the twentieth century, there were efforts to establishing Islamic banking as a credit instrument.[83] A number of studies have discussed the founding of small Islamic banks in Malaysia and Pakistan in the wake of post-colonial independence movements, but the first "successful" Islamic bank was established in the Egyptian village of Mit Ghamr, in 1963.[84] Other Islamic banks followed and include intergovernmental Islamic Development Bank in Jeddah in 1975 and commercial banks such as the Dubai Islamic Bank, the Kuwait Finance House, and the Bahrain Islamic Bank, in the 1970s and 1980s.[85] However, conditions became less favourable in the latter part of the 1980s for Islamic banking movements, and the number of new Islamic banks started decreasing with the advent and intensity of neoliberalism.[86] Nowadays, there are conflicting statistics and reports about the size and total number of Islamic financial institutions (not strictly banks), with figures in 1998 placing them around 170 banks with U.S.$ 137 billion in assets.[87] The "International Financial Services of London, an independent financial industry trade group in the U.K., estimates that as of the end of 2007, there were 280 Islamic financial institutions globally with total assets of U.S.$ 729 billion."[88] At present, Islamic banks exist in not only predominantly Muslim societies, but also in Euro-American nations. In addition, many "'traditional' banks offer Islamic services to Muslim clientele."[89]

Despite the apparent innovativeness of Islamic banks, they face overwhelming limitations given the reach of capitalism's tentacles and the inescapable grasp of neoliberalism. Nevertheless, Islamic banks with their fundamental conceptualizations and native foundations can act as radical form of resistance and dissension if a more holistic approach is taken and they are grounded further in the fundamental pillars established here for Anarcha-Islām. Unlike extreme critics such as Nimrod Raphaeli who claims that Islamic banks are another product of capitalism that is repackaged with Islamic terminologies, I argue that the idea of Islamic banks in the form of Beyūt Al-Māl is not inherently capitalist. Pre-modern Islamic banks are based on a pre-modern egalitarian conceptualization of social justice and their modern formation is more than an attempt to "Islamicize" capitalism from within.[90] Modern Islamic banks differ from non-Islamic banks in three fundamental ways.

First, because of the aforementioned Islamic non-capitalist and non-authoritarian concepts, precepts, and practices, the mission of Islamic banking is the same as what was formerly known as Beyūt-al-Māl.[91] After all, in discussing "debt forgiveness" in *Debt: The First 5000 Years*, David Graeber points to the fact that the principles that guided pre-modern Muslim commercial markets include the idea of banks operating based on the principle of "networks of trust" and "partnership of good reputation" as part of the ethical-political conduct expected at the time.[92] Indeed, trust and reputation compose a component of Islamic ethics that would have to re-inform Islamic economics relative to contemporary practices of debt and borrowing.

The second fundamental difference between Islamic and non-Islamic banks is the nature of products and services a modern Islamic bank may offer resources to or finances for.[93] Islamic banks do not finance trade in pork, alcohol, gambling, drugs, or pornography, and offer no interest-bearing products or services. They are oriented towards risk-sharing products and more fundamental services for the communities they cater to, including social and infrastructural projects. Islamic banks also do not invest in "shareholder-ship in firms that are in any way involved with interest-based financing."[94] In practice, Islamic banks offer "costless loans for humanitarian and welfare purposes," upon which following the agreed upon period, the debtor repays the loan, unless financial distress emerges in which case the repayment of the loan "may be postponed" at no additional charge, and in line with Islām, perhaps altogether cancelled.[95]

Third, in their modern organizational forms, it is assumed that Islamic banks have a religious advisory board to monitor and ensure that the bank's practices are according to a socially just interpretation of Islām. The theoretical purpose of this is to preserve social cohesion and to delineate Caretaker divisions within the community, while ensuring the preservation of all the aforementioned principles, where profit or gain is the consequence of an honest effort performed, or (partial) liability, depending on the financial success or loss of a venture.[96] Islamic banks unlike modern banks are premised on a shared risk between the parties, the bank and "client"/Caretaker, such that, should one party lose, the other also experiences a loss, and should the venture be blessed there is benefit to both.

An Islamic bank's Shūrā council of scholars' task further extends to ensuring that profit or gain is not the consequence of property begetting property, or money producing money from nothing, that constitutes Ribā. This certainly is dissimilar to interest-based financing that informs the foundation of Euro-American banks, where a venture could be extremely profitable, yet still yield only a small reward for the lenders. Yet, on the other hand, it could also generate high losses, but the lenders would still receive a share of the reward, that adds up to Ribā.[97] As noted, Ribā is a condemned practice that Islām considers unjust, since the unconditional reward of investors should not be absolutely tied to the result of the investment, with this idea referred to as "profit and loss sharing" (PLS). PLS is not based on Eurocentric conceptions of speculation but rather acceptable shared liability and risk among those partaking and involved in the venture.[98] In PLS, a "client"/Caretaker first presents a detailed investment proposal to an Islamic bank, and the bank proceeds in deciding whether or not to participate.[99] If the bank decides to partake, "it will usually do so on the basis of trust financing, assuming the role of financing partner so as not to be involved with the actual management of the venture."[100] While devising the contract between bank and client/Caretaker, what further distinguishes Islamic from Euro-American banks is that "not only should the contract clearly stipulate the partners' responsibilities and the profit sharing ratio," but rather also that the nature of the contract differs, given the networked trust established between parties, bank and "client"/ Caretaker.[101] That is, contracts in Islamic banks are devised so as not to be too restrictive and detailed unlike the complexities of bureaucratic clauses, forms, and stipulations obligated to be filled with non-Islamic banks.[102]

Thus, Islamic banks could be a means of reopening the creditworthy asylums by setting up real land-based ventures and alternatives and encouraging individuals and communities to engage in inter-communal economic cooperation and participation.[103] When read in this manner, Islamic banks possess the capacity of restoring agency to every individual and collectively within the community of Islamic banking, and represent an anti-capitalist concept and practice.

Finally, the eighth anti- and non-capitalist pillar of Anarcha-Islām is Islām's own inheritance "laws" (*mirāth*). Extremely complicated, as they vary with different familial compositions, inheritance jurisprudences' mechanisms are generally aimed at ensuring the wide distribution of wealth among the deceased's relatives and the community, preventing hoarding.[104] This occurs through a displacement of the individual deceased's desire, in exchange for maintaining the community's fabric of Maṣlaḥa, which is placed "ahead [of and above] the emotional whims of the deceased … [and that leads to] a dispersal of wealth from the one to the many, instead of channelling wealth from the many to the one."[105] The Qur'ān states: "Never let those who hoard the wealth which God has bestowed on them out of His bounty think it good for them: indeed it is an evil thing for them. The riches they have hoarded shall become their fetters on the Day of Resurrection."[106] It is with this express purpose and these ethics in mind that I reject superficial and neoliberal, reformatory, impractical "fixes" as that which has been proposed by the likes of Thomas Piketty's "global tax on the wealthy." After all, there are ample critiques of how Piketty's position sustains neoliberalism and only serves to reinvigorate and restore capitalist economies, in the absence of land-based struggles.[107]

If inheritance laws and the former non-capitalist Islamic currents are to be re-envisioned and indeed transnational decolonization engaged, then we also need to understand that colonialism and imperialism radically altered BIPOC's access and relationships to land, desire, and the metropolitan city. Diasporic SWANA communities must decolonize and act as allies relative to their settler-of-color positionalities, paradigms of reference, and knowledge systems and translate them into engagements with land-based struggles. Decolonization means moving radically beyond Ta-Nehisi Coates' framework for reparations modeled on European restitutions to Zionist Israel for the Holocaust. Coates' schema and logic denies Indigenous and in this case too Palestinian dispossession and nonsensically relies on a capitalist insurance tabulate of dollar cent figures in the devalued redressing of human misery and death, which no price tag can be assigned to. What of after-life reparations to the ongoing slavery enacted through Zero-Tolerance law enforcement, police maiming and calculated extralegal executions, routine racial profiling, stop-and-frisk programs, "Policies of Broken Windows," voter disenfranchisement, and a shattered criminal justice system?[108] What of reparations to Mexican Americans, deprived by the Mexican-American war of the right to migrate into what was then half of their former nation? What of

Japanese Americans, interned during World War II and Chinese Americans and their sufferings under the Oriental Exclusion Acts? In this instance, decolonization ought to mean following the lead of nascent movements such as the Dream-Defenders in linking Black and Indigenous struggles to Palestinian liberation. There is no free Palestine from the River to the Sea until Indigenous and Black peoples are liberated of settler-colonialism in the U.S./ Canada, and vice versa.

Revisioning inheritance laws and engaging in transnational decolonization means understanding how post-colonial subjects such as the 9/11 high-jacker Muhammad Atta are the product of traumatic post-Ottoman encounters. Atta's expressed anti-modernist stances explicitly indicate a rejection of neocolonial urban planning projects associated with phallic towering buildings, which architecturally symbolize European superiority and arrogance. Atta's master's thesis addressed how lofty and erect structures erased and ushered "chaos to the spatial ordering of gender and class, public and private, global economy and Islamic culture."[109] Echoing a prophetic apocalyptic hadith that cites the emergence of towering buildings as a sign of the end times, Atta argued that modernity generates "male *fitna* (meaning strife stimulated by sexual and ethnic difference)" and threatens perceived cultural values, which Atta problematically construed as eternally static.[110] This is akin to Saudi Arabia's unholy destruction of Islamic heritage sites and the construction of *Burj al Mamlakah*, known as Mile-High Tower, that overshadows the *Ka'bah* (House of Ibrahim). This mania over subduing land and our tamed disconnection from it alongside the cultural vandalism it induces includes the demolition of millennia-old archeological Islamic heritage sites and significant artifacts such as "Bayt al-Mawlid," the "Ottoman and Abasi columns of the Grand Mosque," "Al-Masjid an-Nabawi," "Jabal al-Nour," and the "Green Dome" that covers Prophet Muḥammad's tomb as well as cemeteries where the companions and the Prophet's family lay in *al-Baqi*, to forbid their saintly veneration.[111] Sacrilegious acts such as this are led and approved by a Muslim clergy, and are urged and spearheaded by a corrupt and decadent "Saudi monarchy's insatiable appetite for architectural bling" in transforming Mecca into a Las Vegas for the wealthy having turned "the house of the Prophet's first wife Khadijah ... into a toilet block."[112] The corruption is rampant to the extent that these elites have not only McDonaldized Mecca, but rather have also constructed a "1,972ft" Royal Clock Tower that "soars over the surrounding Grand Mosque," paid for by proceeds of "enormous oil wealth" that never belonged to them.[113] This Holy land, Mecca, "has become a playground for the rich ... where naked capitalism has usurped spirituality as the city's raison d'être" in the name of "infrastructural development" and "a glittering array of skyscrapers, shopping malls and luxury hotels."[114]

Ultimately, transnational decolonization means decolonizing ethical-political commitments relative to land and recognizing its relation to grounded knowledge and agency towards the construction of non-capitalist and non-authoritarian spaces whether pertaining to schools and hospitals, towards making military, neoliberal academies, agro-chemical, medical, humanitarian-developmental, and pharmaceutical industrial complexes obsolete. While protests and direct confrontations with the dominant are necessary they can also be futile in the absence of alternative narratives and visions that can act as viable substitutes for what currently exists. Decolonization this way demands: (1) holistic understandings of transformative justice (dismantling the prison industrial complexes); (2) healing (unmaking the biomedical and pharmaceutical industrial complexes); and (3) ethical frameworks of hospitality and conflict resolution for mitigating our disagreements when and should they arrive (in this interpretation, these are referred to as *Uṣūl al-Ikhtilāf* and *Uṣūl al-Ḍiyāfa*).

As Zapatista public intellectual Gustavo Esteva writes:

> For us to indeed heal ourselves, we need to redefine the body and soul: it is about becoming well, physically, emotionally, and mentally so that we may ourselves renew the nourished capacity to rebel every moment and every day.[115]

Indeed, Esteva continues:

> We are the words that we use. Words have been placed in our heads without our permission being asked and we use these

words without knowing what these words mean; we have to reclaim the words we use [through decolonization and reindigenization]. We have to recover the "we", and in every "we", we are not individuals, we are networks of relations, we are part of different communities."[116] Furthermore, as Esteva, John Holloway and the Zapatistas have shown us, we must recognize that capitalism is patriarchal, and women and the feminization of politics are central to restoring our histories and moving forward into alternative futures.[117]

Anarchism equally entails what Jamie Heckert refers to as "an enduring commitment to sustainability, freedom and equality (in permaculture terms: Earth care, people care and fair shares) … [premised upon] principles of using small and slow solutions, integrating rather than segregating and using and valuing renewable resources."[118] What we transnationally require is an engagement with radical direct democratic praxis, as opposed to the blasé attitudes regarding global warming and climate change, by reconnecting with our lands, in a way that simultaneously addresses the psychosocial and ecological ailments of our communities and through means such as "wilderness therapy."[119] We need to abandon the presumptive idea of a "separate and superior humanity" in relation to the rest of life.[120] Re-envisioning our relationship to land entails what anarchist Peter Kropotkin refers to as "mutual aid" towards reformulating alternative paradigms of "care and support among members of a species" that would directly contribute to our collective well-being.[121] As Heckert writes, citing Paul Goodman, these substitute paradigms mean engaging "anarchist-inspired gestalt" therapies that can help us attain "a natural homeostatic equilibrium" as "an alternative to those therapeutic approaches which emphasised adaptation to a society dependent on domination and ecological devastation."[122] Decolonization entails trusting *al-ghayb* (the divine unforeseen), as noted in Chapter 2, that itself means trusting our bodies, their senses "and the natural environment to solve their problems in their own spontaneous way."[123] As opposed to the civilizational perception that casts land-based movements as primitive, diasporic SWANA peoples need to learn from previous and ongoing inspirational alternatives such as the Zapatistas and *La Vía Campesina* as well as works by eco-psychological figures like Gregory Bateson and "ecofeminist and anarchist philosophers" like Chaia Heller, Emma Goldman, Gary Snyder, novelist Ursula Le Guin, as well as horticulturalist and bioregionalist movements in re-imagining a different tomorrow.[124] Temporary, semi-permanent, and even permanent autonomous initiatives that resituate our relationship to land are prevalent since the Seattle 1999 anti-globalization movement and manifest themselves in "squatters' movements, social centers, indigenous collectives, land-reoccupation [and decolonization] movements ... alternative media centers, communes, activist media networks etc."[125] Sustainable alternative ways of living and resistance even precede Seattle, and are embodied in historical ruptures like the Paris and Canton Communes, the anarchists of Catalonia, movements like the 1936 Mujeres Libres. More recent examples of these insurrectionary revolts rising up against capitalist-states also include the Mapuche Indigenous people's struggle in Patagonia, Argentina, the APPO teacher's uprising and Oaxaca Commune of 2006 in which *Oaxaqueños* took over the entire province of Oaxaca, Mexico, for six months, and organized urban land-based autonomous ways of living that outlived the initial Tahrir Uprising's 18 days in Egypt. The skeptical, patronizing perception by liberal-progressives that life without modern-states and its policing apparatuses and industrial complexes is impossible only need to look to Zapatista rebels of the Lacandon Jungle or the Naxalites whose reach now stretches to Chhattisgarh, Orissa, Andhra Pradesh, and Maharashtra, where they have managed to control territories spanning Jharkhand, Bihar, Uttar Pradesh, and West Bengal. Undoubtedly, there exist innumerable other examples of anti-statist resistance.[126]

The general perception that anarchists are merely concerned with wanton destructive violence ignores their sophisticated contributions to thinking on food sovereignty and housing autonomy, and evident in their influence on direct action initiatives relating to "modern environmental movements ... and green political thought."[127] As much as Muslim anarchists have to teach anarchists, it is also in drawing on "rich and diverse anarchist traditions" with both deep ecological and direct democratic commitments that anarchism can teach SWANA Muslims, affirming decolonial Muslim trajectories towards our collective "development of emotionally and ecologically sustainable political systems."[128] After all,

> Eco-anarchists have disagreements as to the particular forms direct democracy might take. Bioregionalists tend to have a commitment to autonomous communities, self-sufficient through their connection with the immediate landscape. For social ecologists, libertarian municipalism is key with village meetings offering a source of inspiration for decentralised cities and confederated eco-communities with a shared commitment to sustainability and freedom (Davidson, 2009). For green syndicalists, democratic control of labour and the creation of ecological guilds are central (Shantz & Adam, 1999).[129]

Muslims ought to realize our acts are always inherently political and must be related to our responsibilities towards land. Ultimately, as self-identifying anarchist Nicholas Montgomery emphasizes:

> Practices of growing, farming, and eating can politicize aspects of everyday life that seem natural or unproblematic: lawns may be politicized, conceived as archaic residues of European enclosures, requiring a constant regimen of fertilizers, pesticides and maintenance, and constituting active obstacles to the creation of community gardens, permaculture, or rewilding. Dumpster diving politicizes the classification of food as "waste" and the capitalist processes that result in the disposal of millions of pounds of food each day.[130]

Montgomery further affirms that in our collective quest to decolonize we ought to ask ourselves:

> How can these alternatives connected to permaculture and anarchism, be deepened and radicalized by decolonization, feminism, antiracism, and other movements that create and sustain radical, alternative ways of living and relating. [How

do and can] these radical movements prefigure new and old ways of living that are convivial and support thriving ecosystems and communities? How can place-based movements be radical, joyful, and responsible at the same time? How can permaculturalists and anarchists build networks of resistance and resilience, in ways that challenge colonialism, white supremacy, and patriarchy?[131]

Equally, Muslims and anarchists have much to learn from Indigenous peoples if we are to rediscover our indigeneity. As Anishinaabe-Métis-Norwegian scholar-activist Melissa K. Nelson writes in the introduction to *Original Instructions: Indigenous Teachings for a Sustainable Future*: "Our biological and psychological space is a communal ground, a commons ... we cannot be separated from these places. The bones and blood of our ancestors have become the soil, the soil grows our food, the food nourishes our bodies, and we become one, literally and metaphorically, with our homelands and territories."[132] Similarly, as Okanagan Jeannette C. Armstrong writes, the "indigeneity" she experiences emerges out of a palpable association with

> our *tmxwulaxw*, or land, gathering its bounty with my grandchildren and which forms the basis of my knowledge, my experience and therefore my identity and culture, as expressed through my Indigenous language. Through the words which produce the land's "images" in my mind, in my Indigenous *Nsyilxcen* language, I "re-construct" being a part of my "community" on my "land" in the land's images and dynamics. That "re-construction" includes the physical, psychological and philosophical dimensions of being.[133]

And by a similar token, James (Sákéj) Youngblood Henderson writes, "The land ... is not the ever-present 'Other' which supplies us with a sense of 'I'. It is rather a part of our being ... It is ourselves ... it [is] not a matter of being 'close to nature'," as a means to counter the 'domestication of human labor', 'fortress capitalism', and 'homostasis' amongst us as global communities and populations."[134]

Insurrections such as Tahrir cannot just serve as fleeting cathartic, joyful carnivalesque militant moments, otherwise they will remain lost opportunities. To the contrary, these historical instances must offer "concrete non-state political constructions, regardless of their eventual defeat."[135] As Mohammed Bamyeh writes of Tahrir's ongoing potential, but also demise:

> In these revolutionary experiments we encounter a rare combination of an anarchist method and a liberal intention: the revolutionary style is anarchist, in the sense that it requires little organization, leadership, or even coordination; tends to be suspicious of parties and hierarchies even after revolutionary success; and relies on spontaneity, minimal planning, local initiative, and individual will much more than on any other factors. On the other hand, the explicit goal of all Arab revolutions is the establishment of a liberal state – explicitly, a civic state – not an anarchist society.[136]

To ensure the permanence of our struggles we must connect with land, given what Frantz Fanon teaches of the ultimate lesson of insurrections: "You do not disorganize a society ... if you are not determined from the very start to smash every obstacle encountered ... [that is the] grandeur and weakness of spontaneity."[137] As Max Stirner further notes, while revolutions are "aimed at new arrangements," on the other hand, "insurrections lead us no longer to let ourselves be arranged, but to arrange ourselves, and sets no glittering hopes on 'institutions'."[138] By this logic, it is not a matter of partaking in another Zuccati Occupy sit-in and direct action battle, especially when we are confronted with "the state's surveillance of public places, its obsession with identification and information gathering, its management of crowds and movements of people, are measures designed to ensure everyone stays put, that everyone is counted, that nothing escapes its incorporation."[139] Rather, the idea is, as Alain Badiou puts it, learning to divest and "put the State at a distance" by reinvesting our resources and energies elsewhere.[140] After all, as noted in Chapter 3, our agency exists now and everywhere given how power does not function as only top down or bottom up, and this fact should enable us to engage in individual and communitarian acts of counter-conduct. As Michel Foucault states:

> [M]aybe this word "counter-conduct" enables us to avoid a certain substantification [or hero worship] allowed by the word "dissidence"... [B]y using the word counter-conduct, and so without having to give a sacred status to this or that person as a dissident, we can no doubt analyse the components in the way in which someone actually acts in the very general field of politics or in the very general field of power relations; it makes it possible to pick out the dimension or component of counter-conduct that may well be found in fact in delinquents, mad people and patients.[141]

All that remains left to say to authoritarians, capitalists, and all those adamant about maintaining segregated identitarian camps, is that what lies between us keen on creating different worlds and you, for now, are two Qurʾānic verses: "Unto us our works and unto you your works; let there be no dispute between you and us. God will bring us together and to God we shall return," therein God will decree as an Ultimate Judge the clear positions wherein we differed.[142]

As Patients We Come to Each Other's Aid

Many of the anti-authoritarian and anti-capitalist commitments I have discussed work against currently dominant interpretations of Islām. It is in constructing Anarcha-Islām that I am able to stand with an attitude of theological and epistemological certitude, becoming both anti-capitalist and anti-authoritarian, breaking through the walls that purportedly cordon Islām and anarchism from one another. Moreover, it is in constructing Anarcha-Islām, my clinic, that I remain a micro-fascist, yet one who despite their micro-fascisms is now becoming relatively de-Oedipalized. That is, I have no illusions of being completely free of the capitalist-state. I suggest only that I have begun to endlessly murder my micro-fascisms by rejecting the practices imposed upon me by the dominant order. Perhaps now that I have constructed Anarcha-Islām, and because of my willingness and openness to sharing values, resources, and spaces with Muslims, anarchists, and others in the newest social movements, we may collectively begin "building communities of resistance and reconstruction that are wider and more open to others," yet however that "remain non-integrative in their relation to others."[143]

Instead of the progressive-liberal and leftist embrace of empty Victorian Enlightenment platitudes of love and pathological rhetoric like there is "no place for hate in our society," we need to collectively understand that our struggles are about power and domination that relate to globally oppressive and engrained structural, systematic, and systemic forms of violence.[144] Whether in Tahrir or elsewhere, our transnational struggles are not simply about love/hate, because the same white supremacy that overtly and covertly permeates alt-right and progressive liberal-left movements and is responsible for the erasure of Black and Indigenous bodies in a post-9/11, post-Ferguson world, is no different than the white supremacy that has long silenced and rendered invisible Brown SWANA Muslims and non-Muslims in post-colonial nations. The fault of Egyptians during the Tahrir Uprisings, across their liberal, Islamist, and leftist spectrum was in themselves, when they did not consider that they represent an integral constituent part and problem of "the mass psychology of fascism."[145] This is not to claim that mass mobilizations are merely symbolic public displays of revolt, but rather it is to claim that there is nothing inherent and assured with mass protests either way, particularly, in the absence of the creation of decolonial alternatives and the willingness of a people to take up their own mantle of responsibilities. In this sense, there are no guarantees during insurrections, given that "protests can indeed register dissent of all forms – marches, blockades, civil disobedience, creative and artistic resistance, teach-ins, property destruction, kitchen table gatherings, walkouts etc. – but *all* the former *can* also be symbolic rituals or can [alternatively] profoundly transform social conditions."[146] Revolutions and insurrections are not just a matter of changing regimes, institutions, or those in power. As Allāh states in the Qur'ān, "Indeed, Allāh will not change the condition of a people until they change what is in themselves."[147]

5
Uprisings: On (Im)Possibilities and Militant Resistance

One never escapes the economy of war.

Jacques Derrida (1978, 148)[1]

The pacifists are a fine sight: neither victims nor torturers! Come now! If you are not a victim when the government you voted for and the army your young brothers [and sisters] served in commits genocide, without hesitation or remorse, then, you are undoubtedly a torturer. And if you choose to be a victim, risking one or two days in prison, you are simply trying to take the easy way out. But you can't; there is no way out. Get this into your head: If violence were only a thing of the future, if exploitation and oppression never existed on earth, perhaps displays of non-violence might relieve the conflict. But if the entire regime, even your nonviolent thoughts, is governed by a thousand-year-old oppression, your passiveness serves no other purpose but to put you on the side of the oppressors.

Jean-Paul Sartre (1961, lviii)[2]

Perhaps more than a few people think that we made the wrong choice; that an army cannot and should not endeavor toward peace. We made that choice for many reasons, it's true, but the primary one was and is because this is the way that we [as a rebel army] could ultimately disappear.

Subcomandante Insurgente Marcos (May 24, 2014)[3]

The Algerian fidaï, unlike the unbalanced anarchists made famous in literature, does not take dope. The fidaï does not need to be unaware of danger, to befog his consciousness, or to forget.

> The "terrorist", from the moment he undertakes an assignment, allows death to enter into his soul. He has a rendezvous with death. The fidaï, on the other hand, has a rendezvous with the life of the Revolution, and with his own life. The fidaï is not one of the sacrificed. To be sure, he does not shrink before the possibility of losing his life or the independence of his country, but at no moment does he choose death.
>
> Frantz Fanon (1994, 57)[4]

The Delusional Myth of Nonviolence

Cultures of whiteness and the so-called Euro-American "War on Terror" have mass manufactured an endless pipeline of Muslim violence. But terror was and is first associated with the exercise of state power, given the monopoly that modern-states possess over violence and its meanings. Euro-America, led by war criminals like George W. Bush, Tony Blair, Barack Hussein Obama, Hillary Clinton, Donald J. Trump, and innumerable others since modernity's advent, treat colonized and racialized people as less than animals. We are disappeared, tortured, hidden in prisons, and detention centers like Camp Bucca that helped birth reactionary neocolonized subjects for whom violence becomes the sole strategy, as propagated by the likes of Osama Bin Laden and Abu Bakr al-Baghdadi.

Muslims are consistently forced to witness Orientalist/Fundamentalist representations of themselves as either bandits or as a savage, nomadic race, while Muslim women are depicted as burqa-clad victims or shallow belly dancers serving evil, naive, and greedy sheikhs. Symbolically paramount is the image of the rifle in the hands of Muslim terrorists.[5] To argue that these depictions have no psycho-affective consequence on the colonized psyche or retaliatory responses ignores how in this instance the Egyptian state, Islamist-statist organizations like the Muslim Brotherhood, as well as endless non-statist *jihādi* narratives depict their nation, the Umma, and lands as a woman's body "whose rape was both the essence of violence and justification" for zealous hyper-masculinist vendettas of counterviolence against a crusading Euro-America.[6]

In her book *Terrorist Assemblages*, Jasbir Puar analyzed the case of Muhammad Atta, the 9/11 hijacker, who, as noted above, had written his MA thesis on the urban refurbishment of an Islamic quarter in the districts of dar al-Darb al-Ahmar, al-Husayniyya, and Suq al-Silah in Egypt, two years prior to 9/11.[7] Puar dissects and rejects the "negative identity hypothesis" that informs the dominant psychological profiles for terrorists and insinuates that Muslims, but in particular entitled men, are unable to assimilate themselves into the downwardly mobile economic rescaling of globalization.[8] She discusses the argument that misogynistic Muslim neoreactionary responses like Atta's are a by-product or proof of their internalized latent homosexuality or a consequence of an inherent malfunction of their personal deficiency of character, or even proof of a "sexual-orientation crisis" and a "failed masculinity."[9] Atta's trajectories are both repercussions of Muslim internalized shame (*'ār*), Third-World traumatization, and persisting political grievances as neocolonized subjects.

Puar notes that the narratives of new disciplines such as terrorism studies have ignored decades of feminist critiques that highlight agential power, subjectivity, and piety, and instead have adopted traditional Euro-American, Orientalist narratives of victimization and oppressor/oppressed binaries.[10] Terrorism studies scholars like Michael Kimmel and Lionel Tiger echo imperialist "Gay Internationalist" views, as opposed to attempting to situate "terrorism" within anti-colonial/anti-imperial political grievances to locate the justifications for non-statist, insurgent forms of resistance. For instance, Tiger and Barbara Ehrenreich both argue that Muslim terrorism is related to the prevalence of gender segregated spaces and polygamy, both of which serve as a condition and opportunity for erotic male-bonding between *jihādis* through shared terrorist commitments and the repressive self-denial of one's homosexual desire.[11]

In so doing, they argue that desperation associated with sexuality is what leads to terrorism, and in turn posit that the legalization of homosexuality in predominantly Muslim nations would delimit terror. In Kimmel's case, he perceives terror as a means of facilitating the restoration of a "failed masculinity" when faced with an emasculating globalization, as well as the forbiddance of homosexual identifications in Muslim societies.[12] Globalization's penetrating affect, Kimmel argues, magnifies humiliation and shame; but this rationale, as Puar notes, deletes all resistance and designates homosociality as engendered chiefly through the failure to secure a nomenclature heterosexuality.[13] As Puar writes, this overlooks the "possibility of same-sex liaisons, while also rendering an homosociality, indeed homosexuality, as mere defaults due to the apparent impossibility of fulfilling heterosexual relations."[14] In addition to essentializing the effects of cis-heteronormativity globally, this Orientalist view, as Puar notes, erases the homosocial character of societies such as Egypt's and the presence of "same-sex spaces, gender segregated as well as co-gendered arenas of domestic and public life in Muslim and Arab contexts."[15]

Atta's politically situated hyper-masculine-*jihādism* is a component of an inverted Orientalist repercussion, in the absence of decolonization. It is a consequence of an identity crises that is entwined with the neocolonized natives' desire to redeem their honor, that of Islām's, and ostensibly the Umma. In fact, the identity chasm emerges from the challenges of attempting to reconcile Euro-American and non-Euro-American institutional demands regarding Muslim identity and queer-feminist practices. They compose a search for social equity and justice in the face of generationally traumatic, emasculating, and egregiously continuing neocolonial and neoimperial encounters, as well as a hyper-sexual globalization that to the neocolonized native necessitates cleansing and purification (*taṭheer*). As Puar argues, suicide bombers symbolize queer assemblages that resist "queerness-as-sexual-identity."[16] They symbolize a palpable force within which exists the power to converge, implode, and rearrange time, space, and bodies against Euro-American exceptionalism and homonationalism, which are mutually constitutive and blend discourses of North American Manifest Destiny, racist foreign policy, and a Euro-American urge to document the irrational unknown (embodied in the terrorist) with the express goal of reconquering their territorialized bodies to render them manageable and knowable.[17]

At heart, the colonial/imperial violence we internalize and replicate is a sequel to our refusal to serve the instrumental dehumanizing dictums of capital and the delusional perception that Islām is reconcilable with the modern-state. Euro-American militarized humanitarian rescue discourses and neo-development projects cement the perception of our inferiority and render us as arithmetic statistics without names, narratives, or faces. To what end, then, will we continue to passively delude ourselves, as social movement participants, educators, knowledge keepers, and organizers – in succumbing to whitewashed liberal notions of nonviolence, civic disobedience, and what decolonial, insurrectionary revolt entails? Particularly, when we experience recurring lateral, systematic, and systemic incidents of racist, ableist, classist, sexist-gender-based violence every moment of every day.

Revolutions and decolonization inherently entail violence in the re-composition of society's forces and subjects who must confront their identity crises and the strategic contradictions and discursive limits of their identitarian trajectories. Illuminating how referring to Tahrir as "nonviolent" is an insult to the Egyptians martyred in the initial 18 days of the uprising, in 2011 the group *Comrades from Cairo* circulated an online letter addressed to the Occupy Wall Street Protestors in Zuccotti Park, New York, in which they stated,

> Those who said that the Egyptian revolution was peaceful did not see the horrors that police visited upon us, nor did they see the resistance and even force that revolutionaries used against the police to defend their tentative occupations and spaces ... Do not confuse the tactics that we used when we shouted "peaceful" with fetishizing nonviolence ... Had we laid down and allowed ourselves to be arrested, tortured and martyred to "make a point", we would be no less bloodied, beaten and dead.[18]

After all, during the first 18 days in Egypt, no less than 846 Egyptians died, with over 6000 injured, not including the disappearance of at least 1240 as well as unnamed countless more lives since. At present over 60,000 liberal, leftist, feminist, and Islamist political prisoners are incarcerated and subjected to an unprecedented number of summary trials, arbitrary military sentencing, detentions, prison terms, and bestial psychological and physical tortures.[19]

Capitalist-states recognize very well what the role of land is to liberation. In addition to radical Indigenous, Black, Arab, and Muslim scholarships discussed in previous chapters, others (like James Wertsch, Jennifer Gordon, Henri Lefebvre, Minet Schindehutte, Maurice Halbwachs, Gilles Deleuze, and Félix Guattari) have noted how symbolisms, public streets and architectural spaces, as well as images and monuments, are always subject to (counter) revolutionary acts of (de)territorializations and reterritorializations. No different from the Statue Wars over (neo)colonial symbols on Turtle Island, the Egyptian government, and its TV, Interior Ministry, education officials, and so-called economic experts, with the express purpose of creating historical amnesia, have now perversely convinced many Egyptians that the initial January 25 uprising – that united all factions in society under the false banner of nationalism – was led by the Muslim Brotherhood. This is not only taught to children in school, but Rabaa Square, the site of the massacre on August 14, 2013 – of over a thousand Muslim Brotherhood members opposing former and now dead president Mohamed Morsi's removal with a sit-in – has been renamed after Prosecutor General Hisham Barakat, who was assassinated by militant Muslims. At present, as Ahmed Elsayed writes, "the [Egyptian] military pursued *1984*'s Orwellian prophecy: 'he who controls the past controls the future' [such that] the walls of revolutionary graffiti were repainted, CCTV cameras were installed in central spaces, and governmental offices were relocated away from the heart" of Cairo's Tahrir to the new administrative capital.[20] In Egypt's case, the state's agents of repression are unconcerned with the "cultural capital," prestige, or prominence of these prisoners, their possession of dual passports, political affiliations, or even the international outrage that follows their arrests. The regime accuses all those who maintain, to one degree or another, a position of speaking truth to power of fomenting unrest, treason and breaking anti-protest laws, along with a host of other trumped-up charges.[21]

Those who fetishize nonviolence underestimate the challenges before us, when confronting geopolitical-corporate elites with arsenals of intercontinental ballistic missiles, smaller and smaller miniaturized undetectable nuclear warheads that could be attached to cruise missiles, underwater nuclear drones, supersonic arms, and laser weapons that we are told are strictly for defensive purposes. One need only confront the realities of companies such as Amazon and its collusion with the Department of Homeland Security agencies, the Pentagon, Immigration and Customs Enforcement (ICE) and Customs and Border Protection (CBP), in mass surveillance through facial recognition technologies against everyone in a post-Snowden National Security Age, and not just undocumented immigrants.

How can we not speak of the necessity for and the right of militant resistance, indeed, and if need be, an engagement in armed struggle, in this persistent and irresponsible, schizophrenic pressing moment in which our attentions are multiply divided, given the endless assaults and yet is the charade that is celebrity and armchair political "activism" completely disconnected from land-based struggles? Yet liberal-progressives tirelessly call for non-violent resistance, as one struggles to maintain any semblance of emancipatory vitality or hopefulness in it.

Generations have grown desensitized to the war we have been born into, as we have become numb to the circulation of infinite Fundamentalist/Orientalist images of ourselves, without reflecting on the violent effects of the internalization of these genocidal, homicidal, and suicidal spectacles.[22] We exchange these shocking displays online in our desperation, as if they will become beacons that are capable of spawning radical mobilizations to counter the nightmares we face, while privileged white allies write books that mine disenfranchised BIPOC's sacred knowledges and advocate for "joy." The truth is, in a deranged post-alternative truth world, there is an endless series of causes that one can engage in as one becomes a well-intentioned ally shopping around for solidarities. Though social media can connect us and alleviate the daily, solitary grind, it also sustains the depression, mental illness, and asymmetries of racial/sexual/gender/ableist/classist/ageist power emboldened by our "Oppression Olympics," while also propagating a false individualist and uncommitted sense of solidarity, as struggles become isolated, dispersed, and exoticized.

This is particularly the case in the absence of face-to-face encounters that ought to be grounded in an "ethics of care," and a genuine tender camaraderie.[23] One would have presumed that as disenfranchised peoples we would rally around one another instead of tearing each other apart in social movements that reproduce the micro-fascistic practices informed by Machiavellian and Manichean divide and conquer prejudices that we have internalized for generations. But what is it to no longer reproduce an individualistic life that is supported by temporary, uncommitted recurrences of solidarity?[24] How far are we willing to proceed with a distinct prefigurative strategic vision and what are willing to sacrifice of ourselves now in the name of our children and the liberation that we forsake? Or, are we destined to recurrently engage false choices that continuously entrap us in the status quo in this flagrant global epidemic of social injustice and chaos? What will it take for us to overcome our self-induced comas and amnesia to truly claim that we have lived life fully or are we destined to distance ourselves from the pain of others by claiming myopic "victories" as we march on? There is no erasing our culpability and abdicated responsibilities towards others. Our complicities cannot be hidden in our selective philanthropic endeavors and memorialization of atrocities in museums and exhibitions, in remembrance of the Other.[25] Contemporary conversations regarding social justice cannot be reduced to liberal discussions of love and hate that elide and neglect narratives and analyses that address power between our species and nonhuman life.

All these recurrences evoke in me the unabashed will to reclaim from Orientalists and Fundamentalists the concept of violence. I specifically examine it in the context of militancy and violence rather than its "greater" significant meaning (as in struggle with oneself, towards holistic knowledge and community etc.) in countering contemporary tyranny, white supremacy, and oppression as a means towards founding social justice for all. After all, no force, including that of my own wakeful Creator who gave me this right, could cut me off from either *jihād*'s appropriate usage or mobilization as a tactic of war, and its belonging to a wider strategy towards liberation. The dignified right to armed self-defense (whose abstract contours are abidingly laid naked here as "Rules of War") is a nonnegotiable pillar of Anarcha-Islām when facing the rancor of war machines whose wanton and senseless violence is informed by continuing centuries-old embezzlements and white-supremacist plunders wrought by colonial/imperial powers.

To rebel is to then understand and reflect on violence's necessary role, given these conditions. Having lived on front lines, including during the Tahrir Uprisings in 2011 and 2013, I argue that rebellion is not amateur mass protests and direct actions that are dogmatically and mistakenly adopted as the sole tactic for confrontation. I have grown sick of our confinement to combat zones, blockades, roadblocks, and protest politics in the absence of our acknowledgment of the battles that reside within ourselves. I have lived the thunderous taratantara of trumpets to the booming rataplan of beating drums that accompany red and black keffiyehs, ski masks, patches and balaclavas, as we are sheltered by the warmth of the sparks of our kindred spirits as the only glowing flare. All these acts, beyond symbolism, have been incapable of saving us from the thrust of the water cannons or the armored vehicles and barbed wire encircling us as the pincers form and the entrances to our city-squares are sealed.

As experientially educational as these situations are, still, to truly rebel is to be ill of the inescapable, dizzying, sick scent of expired tear gas, pressing against the pierced, gushing background whistles of riot, prior to the momentary lapse of pin drop silence, where we learn to face the propelled 40mm-Model 4431-CSI-canisters that spiral in the sky. I have grown ill of the melancholy of resistance and the short distance between ourselves and the for-hire goons that include corrupt government militias and *balṭagiya* (hatchet lawmen) as we attempt to maintain our turf and soil. I am tired of remembering that we should not touch our faces or pour water when the tear gas hits, and to instead try to use coke and milk.[26] I am sick of running against the wind and trying to keep calm, as I wait for the irritating and disabling burning pain and nausea to pass. I am exhausted by the thought that it is not going to be too long now, and that there is not much time to lose, as the 60-calliber Stinger rubber-bullets and empty sealed wads of gunpowder are being replaced with fresh cartridges of live ammo cocked by trigger-happy hands. *Watch out*, did you see those civilians standing beside the army and Ministry of Interior forces, they are undercover cops, not brainwashed supporters! I am tired of the riddled shells and punctured ricochet rounds of slugs, caps, and downtrodden bodies collapsing, falling, weightless, to a quaking ground, faster than shooting stars. I am exhausted by the image of the souls of our dead rising while biker rebels carry our fallen, whirling back and forth, when ambulances cannot reach the front lines, as our hearts and eyes are taken for targets, mutilated, and blinded. I am worn out by liquids, handkerchiefs, wet cloths, and rags, always being torn and passed around to deal with the parched thirst, fumes, and the ubiquitous miasma, as people cough, faint, and vomit. I am drained by the fact that most cannot afford masks, and the oxygen flow nourishing the capillaries to our lungs and trachea chokes us, as our cardiac muscles and mucus membranes grow constricted and we are suffocated. I am spent thinking of how our bodies are left clamoring and grasping for other bodies, as sirens that I can still hear scream, while we put up a fight alongside murals of our martyrs like Mina Daniel and Khaled Saeed, painted on grey walls that resemble prisons and jail cells.[27] We are always left teetering between being scattered again, gathering, and then reorienting. Our voices are all that is constantly defiant. Our bronchi are always left scouring for breath, in undeniable fear and nervousness, the only reminder, besides each other, strangers in this wilderness, that we are still alive and here.

What often accompany our disorganized protests are toxic dosages of trauma, factional sectarianism, and bad faith, given the bigotry and ideological stances that precede and inform our insurrection. This factionalism is only reified in our egoistic contentions and in light of the burnt personal-political bridges between us in the absence of an ethics from which we can disagree. Following protests we wound each other across our disjoined journeys, as we, fraught with activist burnout and fatigue, return to our affectless and disconsolate isolated corners as opposed to nursing each other and ourselves back to health. We lost the battle of direct action and, for now, even the war, as we live with the delirious aftershock of combat and anxiously await the ebb of another revolutionary rise as if the thrill of action is all that we have to offer each other. Addictive street actions and their exhilaration are all we depend on to restore us. We are left uncommunicative and exhausted, fatigued in our "paralyses," by our bruises and disfigurations, our hearts have been bled till we are left bereft of light, the adrenaline rush of our dependency on protest having come to an end. In the meanwhile, the bereavement, dreary solemnity, and joylessness settle in our disconsolate hurt at the realization of our own morbidity and that of others, as pieces of ourselves are now forever "lost."[28] Our martyrs' dust and their bright-lit fires are extinguished in the flames of war and yet are always what remain, as our dead return to the very earth from which they and we came forth. But beyond the resolute testimony of our resilient existence on our streets, "activism" is not a matter of regurgitated, procedural clashes of destructive and demoralizing skirmishes and showdowns to be re-enacted verbatim in battlefields, especially when each time they lead to no distinct consequence.

We must disrupt the disturbing myth that effective social change can only be achieved simultaneously and en masse, across an entire national or supranational space. As Richard J.F. Day notes, "We cannot wait for 'everyone' to choose to live in non-statist, non-capitalist relationships, or we will very likely wait forever. Nor can we force socialism on anyone, since that would violate our commitment to respecting the autonomy of individuals and groups."[29] Day's critique is one that directs us away from seeking to control centers of power, the hegemonic state, or the economy, but to instead build "affinity-based networks of radical activism."[30] The distinction between subscribing to a logic of hegemony versus affinity is that the latter non-reformist approach

> [d]oes not provide positive energy to existing structures and processes in the hope of their amelioration. Rather, it aims to reduce their efficacy and reach by withdrawing energy from them and rendering them redundant. Structural renewal therefore appears simultaneously as a negative force working against

> the colonization of everyday life by the state and corporations, and as a positive force acting to reverse this process via mutual aid. Just as the states and capitalism advance by percolating into everyday relations, structural renewal proceeds through its own dispersion of regularities, its own viral infections and subtle transformations. Landauer grasped the key insight of Foucault's governmentality thesis that we are not governed by "institutions" apart from ourselves, by a "state" set over against a "civil society". Rather we all govern each other via a complex web of capillary relations of power.[31]

Therefore, as Tahrir and protests in general prove, gathering hundreds of thousands, even millions, of marching dissenters on the street, and mobilizing variant segments of society under the umbrella of a temporary alliance, will not spontaneously usher in revolutionary change in the absence of strategic vision. Radical movements like the Zapatistas taught the need for what I refer to as the *biodiverse strategy of resistance*, which in Anarcha-Islām includes the construction of (1) alternative, feminist, socially just, decolonized education through Ijtihād, cultivating critical consciousness (*thaqāfat al-waʿy*), and knowledge (*al-intāg al-maʿrify*) and propaganda (in all its contemporary available forms be it through community radio or independent live broadcasting); (2) an ethics of conflict resolution and an ethics of hospitality, or what Islamically is referred to as *Uṣūl al-Ḍiyāfa.* (politics of friendship) that can inform our social interactions (*uṣūl al-muʿāmalāt*) and facilitate our re-knowing of one another towards the founding of sustainable horizontalist ways of learning, medicine, autonomous schools, and hospitals, in healing our relations to land and nonhuman life, and premised on collective redefinitions of what it is to live healthily; (3) and, finally, the means of self-defense that still must be anchored in ethico-political responsibilities to (non)human life, because as the Qur'ān, aḥādīth, and the Sunnah teach, self-defensive violence is grounded in specific rules of war and is not a strategy but rather a tactic, and the more people who are prepared to radically change themselves or are willing to partake in the individual/collective idea of a greater struggle (*al-jihād al-akbar*) against their micro-fascisms (*jihād al-nafs*), the less violence, armed conflict, and bloodshed will occur.[32]

More vital than insurrections is the breeding of revolutionary subjects willing to combat internalized discriminatory micro-fascistic tendencies such as cisheteropatriarchy, racism/ethnocentrism, sexism, biphobia, transphobia, ableism, individualism, authoritarianism, queerphobia, anti-Jewishness, and Islamophobia, as a central foundation to local, regional, and transnational face-to-face community building and affinity-based structures. After all, as Sun Tzu writes, in the *Art of War*: "If you neither know yourself or your enemy, you will succumb in every battle."[33] War ought to teach a rejuvenating spiritual and ethical-political "propaganda of the deed," a rebuttal of our constant fraying at the seams as we oscillate between victories and defeats.[34] For liberation to succeed in rebellion we must harmoniously synchronize our strategic decolonial anti-imperialist and anti-colonialist visions of tomorrow.

It is unfortunate that, in the absence of a decolonial strategy to illuminate identity categories' entwined relationship to modern-state and citizenship politics, progressive leftists and academics have reproduced anti-intersectional strategies based on "identity of interests or positions."[35] In contrasting response, as Richard Day, Sean Haberle, and I have argued elsewhere, anti-racist feminists such as Patricia Collins, bell hooks, Kimberle Crenshaw, and Sherene Razack have developed generalized anti-oppression frameworks of analysis "in the collective service of our joint, common, distinct, and colliding struggles."[36] As Harsha Walia writes,

> If Indigenous communities, homeless people, immigrants, LGBTs, seniors and others are all considered "special-interest groups" (despite the fact that they actually constitute an overwhelming demographic majority), then by default that suggests that, as Rinku Sen argues, straight white men are the sole standard of universalism. [However], addressing other systems of oppression, and the people those systems affect, isn't about elevating one group's suffering over that of white men. It's

about understanding how the mechanisms of control actually operate.[37]

This decolonial trajectory to accountable forms of solidarity has also been noted in "other traditions – from queer theory (Judith Butler, R. Hennesey, D. Morton, William J. Spurlin) to anarchism (Richard Day, David Graeber, Caitlin Hewitt-White Peggy Kornegger), to indigenous theory (Lee Maracle, Taiaiake Alfred), and in certain variants of Marxism (Sharmeen Khan, Leo Panitch)."[38]

In light of this, our movements, alliances, activist-scholarship and knowledge production ought to reflect an understanding that "technologies of power traverse each other, intersect, and the difference is more one of conjectural emphasis of one or the other – one might even say on particular relations of force."[39] In turn, it is pertinent that we recognize the fluid and dynamic nature of identity and tactically embrace a given set of identities when appropriate, while equally strategically valuing that our non-ideological subject-based dynamics positions shift from one moment to the next.[40] Transnational social movements must recognize that there are struggles within struggles. Activists such as Marragara Millan, Ashanti Alston, and Pauline Hwang have illuminated the multiple identities within both the Zapatista and anarchist movements, and Taiaiake Alfred, P. Monture-Angus, Andrea Smith, and Na'cha'uaht and Chiinuuks have long documented the diverse voices among the Indigenous activists in Canada. These communities "are not interested nor looking to that [colonizing] Other for recognition," but rather are "recognizing" each other and themselves and working together "in a constructive manner."[41] This accountable type of solidarity involves a commitment towards the cultivation of "responsibility for the freedom of others" as opposed to their ostracization, exclusion, and lack of incorporation.[42]

Violence, *Jihād*, and *Qitāl* in Islām: A Single Blunder Can Fuel a Great Fire

The distinction that I draw on and consider to be a founding pillar to Anarcha-Islām is Islām's conceptualization of armed, self-defensive violence as a tactic that is still bound by ethical and political principles upon which war is fought. At this juncture, it is mandatory to address the mistranslations and misinterpretations of *jihād*. Classic schema in Islām dictate at least two categories or general types of jihād-struggle that include what is regarded as the inner and greater struggle (*jihād al-nafs*) with oneself and alongside one's community in combating one's micro-fascisms, discussed in Chapters 2 and 3, and the second being jihād understood as Qitāl, the actual Qur'ānic term used for war, and militant armed combat. The word Qitāl is used in "171 verses in which the word qital appears in which 10 verses where the word ḥarb means war."[43] Jihād appears 41 times in the Qur'ān and "most occurrences are linguistically related to the exercise of effort, juhd … and the deployment of energy (on ten occasions), in relation tothe path of God (on 13 occasions), or in the context of combat."[44] If "holy war" were translated into Arabic it would be *al-ḥarb al-muqqaddasa*, a non-existent term in Islām. Rather, jihād, itself, linguistically and as a practice, is derived from the Arabic roots "juhd" or "jahd," denoting "to strive" or "struggle," etymologically interrelated to words such as: *mujāhadah*, which denotes "partaking in struggle, in contention," or "striving, and exerting oneself."[45] Jihād frequently appears in the Qur'ān through the idiomatic expression "striving in the way of God," or *al-jihād fī sabīl Allāh*, and is undoubtedly related to concepts and practices such as *Tahajjud* (referring to the solitary periodical worship of God at darkness and nightfall), as well as mujtahid-a and Ijtihād, which were discussed in Chapter 2. Holy war's origins, as an orientalist term, are, thus, a non-Islamic matter, given it is a Euro-Christian construct, invented prior to the advent of the Papalic legacies and incursive Crusades that emerged following holy war's sanctioning by Emperor Constantine in the fourth century. Unlike the case with Islām, "holy war" lacked clear divinely ordained and binding precedents, that could neither provide *jus ad bellum*, that is, the "condition in which war is waged," nor *jus in bello*, "the conduct upon which armed combat is fought." On the other hand, Islām laid forth rules of conduct in war and upon which war is fought, should all options, accords, and attempts at reconciliation with an enemy fail. From the beginning then, not all war or Qitāl is jihād and not all jihād is Qitāl (armed warfare). Thus, expending of resources, financial or immaterial, inciting controversial speeches and promoting knowledge and propaganda that shows interconnectedness between transnational social justice struggles, and even engaging in economic boycotts such as the Palestinian Boycott Divestment Sanctions (BDS) campaign, are forms of jihād. An action informed by divine intent and the circumstance of resistance is jihād. Other forms of jihād involve refusing to capitulate and compromise over strategic ethical-political commitments against an enemy's hegemonic dictums. Jihād is also partaking in steadfast resilience (*thabāt* or *al-ṣumūd*) and persistence (*al-baqā*) in active and not passive resistance against psychological warfare and in standing one's ground while defending land, be it in orchards, farms, mountains, deserts, or swamps. Jihād even includes those who do not personally partake in Qitāl, yet who economically, psychologically, politically, socially, support decolonial movements for sovereignty, be it by building tunnels or trenches, providing logistical support for the purchase of military arms, all can be regarded as *Mujāhideen* (participants in jihād). A mother who sees her child die in the name of liberation from aggression is no less of a participant in *jihād* than the child martyred. The difference between jihād and Qitāl is analogous to that between death and martyrdom (*Šahada*). Though in Islām, death is merely a transition from this world in which we are travelers to another world, Šahada is a specific type of death, in which a martyr (*Šahīd* (m)-*šahīda* (f)) transitions to the spirit world, while defending their land. Prophet Muḥammad further states, "[The] one who drowns is a martyr. One who burns to death is [a] martyr. The [one] who dies in a foreign land is a martyr. One who dies because of a snake bite is [a] martyr. One who dies because of a stomach problems is a martyr. One who dies because the roof of [their] house collapsed over [them] is a martyr. One who falls from the roof of [their] house and breaks [their] leg or neck and then dies, is a martyr. One who is buried under a rock and dies, is a martyr. A woman who guards her and her husband's honor, is like one who fights in Allāh's way, she shall get the reward of a martyr. One who is killed while defending [their] property is a martyr. One who is killed while defending [their] life is a martyr. One who is killed while defending their brother, is a martyr. One who is killed while defending [their] neighbor, is a martyr. One who bids to do good and forbids evil is a martyr."[46]

Jihād al-nafs is considered by all accounts as the "greater" form of jihād in contrast to the second type of jihād in the form of Qitāl although, crucially, they are not mutually exclusive. As Muslim scholars like Abu Nasr Abdallah B. Ali Al-Sarraj Al-Tusi and Hasan al-Basri, in particular, state, "Your enemy is not the one you are relieved from if you killed him. Rather, your true enemy is your own soul, between your two sides."[47] To individually and collectively engage in the greater jihād al-nafs is to found spiritual ethical-political social justice communities, and to abstain and ward off evils like arrogance (*takabur*), greed (*tamaʿ*), jealousy (*ḥasad*), lust or pleasure (*shahwah*), backbiting (*gheebah*), stinginess (*bokhl*), malice (*keena*), or any form of sedition (*fitna*), betrayal, killing, theft, and cheating in trade, as well as the gluttonous eating away at the rights of orphans, children, women, the elderly and poor on account of patriarchy, sexism, ageism, and classism, etc. Indeed, *jihād* can entail everything from confronting death at sea to becoming well accustomed to handling one's arms with dexterity in an inhospitable and hostile world drenched in perpetual turmoil. This way jihād is primarily contingent on the occasions and ethical-political contexts, and respective behaviors it is interrelated to.

Notable grammarian and Muslim scholar of the eleventh century, Al-Raghib al-Isfahani, in his text *al-Mufradat fi Gharib al-Qur'ān* (2010) interpreted jihād to be of three types: (a) Struggling against an apparent or visible enemy; (b) Struggling against the Devil; and (c) Struggling against the ego, or self.[48] An alternative reading of jihād, through seventh century jurist, and infamous "scholar of the heart" and *tazkiyah* ("purification of the soul"), Ibn al-Qayyim Al-Jawziyya, in his text *Al-Fawa'id* (or "Points of Benefit"), identifies "the believer to be in a perpetual state of jihād until he and/or she meets with the Creator, Allāh." To Al-Jawziyya, jihād possesses four stages: (a) First, to strive against one's ego "in learning guidance and the religion of truth, without which there will be no success"; (b) Second, striving against Satan "to act upon what has been learnt, since knowledge without action will not benefit, rather it will cause harm"; (c) Third, striving to encourage and invite others, particularly non-believers "towards it [i.e., Islām and social justice in general] and to teach those who do not know, otherwise one may be considered as amongst those who hide what Allāh has revealed of guidance and clear explanation"; and (d) Fourth, and finally, striving to be patient and persevering against hypocrites and those who knowingly "oppose this *da'wah* (call) to Allāh and those who seek to cause harm – patiently bearing all these hardships for the sake of Allāh."[49] As Tamim Al-Barghouti, writes:

> The concept of jihad has greatly transformed. Before the Crusades, jihad had two essential meanings. The first indicated the inner conflict between good and evil within the human soul – a good believer had to fight a jihad against his own desires; this was called *al-jihad al-akbar* (the greater jihad). The second notion referred to the expansionary wars fought by the early Umayyad Empire against the non-Muslim nations in Persia, Turkistan and North Africa. However, after Jerusalem's fall, jihad became the medieval Islamic equivalent of the modern concept of national liberation. It became a war of self-defense against foreign invaders. It is mainly the effect of the Crusades that the concept was so much romanticized and glorified beyond its original meaning.[50]

Even utilized within the context of war (*ḥarb*), the "smaller *jihād*" (*al-jihād al-asghar*) is also characterized and informed by circumstances, as can be seen across its distinct uses during the *Meccan* and the *Medinan* periods, in which Islām was revealed. The Meccan period commenced with the Prophet's first revelation through the archangel Gabriel on Mount Hira, and concluded approximately 13 years later, when the Medinan period began and concluded ten years later with the Prophet's death in 632 CE. During the Meccan period, when Muslims were a minority community, they were commanded to engage in "nonviolent" forms of resistance and jihād in struggling against a wealthy and politically influential elite polytheist class of Arabs in Mecca. Muslims were commanded to employ this approach of nonviolent jihād, such that they may learn to embody the primacy and superiority of the greater struggle of establishing and constructing themselves as a community first, while also determining what inalienable rights aggressors, despite their aggression, are afforded, given that these rights were granted by God. Early Muslims like Sumayya bint Khubbat, Bilal ibn Rabah al-Habashi, Umm Ubays, Al-Nahdiah, Lubaynah, Yasir ibn Amir, Khabbab ibn al-Aratt, Abu Fuhayra, Abu Fakih, Ammar ibn Yasir, and a myriad others were assaulted, cruelly tortured, murdered, enslaved, and exiled from their own families on account of embracing Islām; in instances, they were laid bare, nailed down, with their backs naked in the scorching heat of the Meccan desert with stones placed on their chests and breasts. A day came on which with the intensity of the cruelty and harshness of persecution rising, a group of Muslims approached the Prophet, who laid in the shade near the *Ka'bah*, the House of Abraham, and asked him: "Won't you invoke God for us, that God may help us?"[51] To which the Prophet affably, yet assertively, responded:

> Among the believers who came before you, many were thrown into ditches dug for them and were sawed in two from head to foot, and this did not turn them away from their religion; their flesh was torn apart from their bones and sinews with iron combs, and this did not turn them away from their religion. By God, this cause will certainly prevail, so it will be possible for the line traveler to go from Sanaa to Hadramout [regions in Yemen] without fearing anything but God, or the world for his sheep. But you are too impatient.[52]

As an immediate and initial response to Islām, two clans, *Makhzum* and *Banu Abd-Shams* of the polytheist Quraysh declared public boycotts against the clan of *Banu Hashim*, the clan to which the Prophet belonged, which also represented their commercial rival, in order to put pressure on the clan to withdraw its protection of Muḥammad and reduce Muslims to beggary; the boycott lasted between two to three years.[53] Quraysh's terms and conditions further included "that no one should marry their women nor give women for them to marry; and that no one should either buy from them or sell to them, and when they agreed on that they wrote it in a deed."[54] Hence, the Meccan period was informed by jihād, although Muslims were forbidden and given no permission to engage in Qitāl. In response to oppressions to which Muslims were exposed, the Prophet Muḥammad taught:

> Who amongst you sees something abominable [an evil and oppressive action] should modify it with the help of their hand (activism, organization, movement); and if there's not strength enough to do so, then they should do so with their tongue (by speaking out against it), and if they have not enough strength to do so, (even) then they should (abhor it) from their heart (by resenting what is evil or harmful), and that's the least of faith.[55]

This stance represents an exemplary spirit and practice of active and not passive nonviolent jihād, one that is hardly evoked or considered in relation to Islām's past and present history in which Muslims and non-Muslims regard the risk-free holding of placards for a cathartic few hours, having sought police permits, as resistance.

Prophet Muḥammad arrived to instruct Muslims, by example, to bear the responsibilities and the severe inconveniences associated with actively and uncomfortably combating oppressions. Quraysh offered Prophet Muḥammad wealth, further prestige, status, and even that he become their king, as means of dissuading, seducing and superficially luring him so that he may abandon his cause and mission of social justice, and yet Muḥammad and the early Muslims learned and embraced active patience (*ṣabr*) and strict engagement in intellectual combat (*ḥarb thaqāfiya*) through *jidāl* (disputation) as the Qur'ān notes in numerous verses like 29:46, and 16:125, in which the Creator states, "And argue with them in the best manner." To Quryash's seductive offers, Muḥammad's response remained:

> I am not possessed, nor do I seek among you honors or power. God has sent me to you as a messenger, He has revealed me a

> Book and has ordered me to bring you good news and warn you. I have conveyed to you my Lord's message and I have given you good advice. If you accept from me what I have brought, thus will cause you to succeed in this world and in the hereafter; but if you reject what I have brought, then I shall wait patiently until God judges between us.[56]

Early Muslims needed to be discomforted and unsettled to learn how to individually unsettle their polytheistic ways as well as collectively teach each other the means by which they can withstand, resist, and combat their vilification by re-envisioning their worldly conditions in conduct, in spirit, ethics, and politics. Nevertheless with time, it became impossible for Muḥammad and for Muslims to practice what was revealed, or what they were divinely commanded to live by in Mecca while living under persecution.[57] In turn, and as a young polity, Muslims were Qur'ānically told that God's earth is spacious and that there lie good tidings in migrating:

> Those who leave their homes in the cause of God, after suffering oppression, we will assuredly give a goodly home in this world; but truly the reward of the Hereafter will be greater, if they only realize. They are those who persevere in patience, and put their trust in their Lord.[58]

Upon the revelation of this verse, Muslims undertook preparations for the *Hijra* (migratory exile), during 614 and 616 CE, known as the first and second migrations, first to Abyssinia, and then to Medina. During the first Hijra, Muslims sought asylum with the Abyssinian Christian king Ashama ibn Abjar, Al-Najashi, otherwise referred to as King Negus, who later converted to Islām. The Quraysh proceeded to send emissaries to King Negus, to dissuade him from granting and offering Muslims asylum. The king's response is clearly evident, not solely in the King Negus' denial of the request, but rather too in his eventual conversion to Islām thereafter.

Meanwhile, while Muslims continued to migrate to Abyssinia and Medina, Muḥammad remained in Mecca, as opposed to saving himself first. Rather, he was adamant to assure the safe exile of his people first, as he awaited divine command to migrate himself with a handful of companions who were left behind. When he finally left, slipping away from an assassin's attack, the Meccans sent more of their most proficient assassins after him, with an assassin from each tribe to ensure that no single tribe would bare sole blame. Muḥammad and his companion Abū Bakr took refuge in a cave on an uncommon route South of Mecca, through *Jabal Thawr* (The Mount of the Bull), and Muslims are taught that it was during this time that God commanded two doves to soar down and lay eggs between a tree, and a spider to quickly weave a web across the mountain cave's mouth so that his pursuers would assume that there was no one within the cave.[59]

To whatever degree of truth and/or falsehood Muslims and non-Muslims regard this tale as folkloric myth, its oral history is still a critical part of Muslim lore, especially given what it reveals of courage, faith, steadfastness, and oppression. Whatever the details may be, a Qur'ānic verse affirmed the sentiments in the story's narrative:

> If ye help not (your Prophet), (it is no matter): for Allāh did indeed help him, when the Unbelievers drove him out: he had no more than one companion; they two were in the cave, and he said to his companion, "Have no fear, for Allāh is with us": then Allāh sent down His peace upon him, and strengthened him with forces which ye saw not, and humbled to the depths the word of the Unbelievers. But the word of Allāh is exalted to the heights: for Allāh is Exalted in might, Wise.[60]

Muslims during the Meccan period were therefore expressly forbidden from taking arms and engaging in Qitāl in retaliation to the vicious persecutions they faced.[61] It was the Muslim withstanding of persecution and oppression, and their adoption of a (non) violent position of jihād, prior and during the Hijra, that "drove the adherents of the Prophet in self-defense into a closer union."[62]

Becoming a community, a true Umma, without a single armed action in self-defense, is what permitted them the ability to

> stand forth with a more resolute aim and bolder front, for the severity of injustice of the Quraysh, overshooting the mark, aroused at once personal and family sympathies; unbelievers sought to avert of to mitigate the sufferings of the followers of the Prophet; and in so doing they were themselves sometimes gained over to his side.[63]

Muslims were commanded to first ensure that the truth does not die with those who place their lives at risk in battle during Qitāl. Thus, Allāh said in the Qur'ān: "And the believers should not all go out to fight. Of every troop of them, a party only should go forth, that they (who are left behind) may gain sound knowledge in religion, and that they may warn their folk when they return to them, so that they may beware."[64] The key here is that not *all* are to go to war because the "superior" worth of spiritual struggle over armed struggle is of immutable value in Islām. As the Qur'ān states, "Against your enemy, [first] make ready your strength to the utmost of your power."[65] The emphasis in the cited verses ought first to be resourceful preparation and on the spiritual and communitarian struggles above the immediate worldly reality of directly having to confront vicious oppression, in order to protect and preserve the legacy of what the community built and that, then, indeed, *later* is worthy of protecting. After all, it is the spiritual-social justice struggle that offers purpose and future upon which thereafter arrives the impetus, possibility, and usefulness to protect and arm. Therefore, though it is universally accepted that Islamic law sanctions armed struggle, such a sanction came with other priorities established first. This is the foundation of unarmed jihād and Qitāl. Muslims were expected to construct and honor covenants and treatises with the Quraysh, and build alliances with others in exile in Abyssinia, which included the *anṣār* (Medinan Muslims), as they collectively practiced patience and concretizes their unwavering faith in God's remembrance and deliverance. Even Prophet Muḥammad had to acquire the skill of patience, never retaliating, learning the criticality of humility, and first, building community, while praying:

> O al-Llah, to Thee I complain of my weakness, little resource, and lowliness before men. O Most Merciful, Thou art the Lord of the weak and Thou art my Lord. To whom wilt Thou confide me? To one afar who will misuse me? Or to an enemy to whom Thou hast given power over me? If Thou art not angry with me, I care not. Thy favor is more wide for me. I take refuge in the light of Thy countenance by which the darkness is illumined, and the things of this world and the next are rightly ordered, lest, Thy anger descend upon me or Thy wrath light upon me. It is for Thee to be satisfied until Thou art well pleased. There is no power and no might save in Thee.[66]

Today this is what must manifest between diasporic settler of color Muslims and Indigenous and Black peoples in settler-colonial U.S./Canada.

It was the early Muslims' withstanding of persecution and oppression, and their adoption of a nonviolent position of jihād, prior and during the Hijra, that fomented them into a community, a true Umma. It is in this context that Prophet Muḥammad said, "The best struggle (jihād) is to speak the truth before a tyrannical ruler."[67] Moreover, the Prophet also noted, "the best struggle [jihād] is to struggle against your soul and your passions in the way of God Most High."[68]

Thus, Muslims were required to first adamantly practice and master the finesse of "nonviolence." It is in this context that during the Medinan period that meticulous rules of war were determined, found, and grounded in political and ethical commitments, which would curtail Qitāl's excessive manipulation and address consequences of its abuse. Amongst these stringent rules is that war itself ought to be refrained from if opportune, for as Allāh states: "But turn away from them and say 'Peace!' for they shall soon come to know."[69] Acknowledging war as a form of tyranny, the Qur'ān also states, "War is allowed for those on whom war is imposed because it is a tyranny."[70] Therefore, unlike reductive views propagated by prevalent and prominent scholars of "terrorism studies," Qitāl is strictly for fighting unjust persecution and oppression and not out of a sense of vengeance, retribution, or pride.[71] This message is reiterated in multiple verses which affirm that violence is an appropriate response to tyranny and oppression, but scripture also crucially acknowledges that war, by its nature, is naturally despised, abhorred, and hateful to our species. The Qur'ān reveals that remaining oppressed is worse than using the legitimate right to defend through Qitāl, even if it means killing the propagator and incessant colonizer who refuses to stop committing the oppression and respecting the autonomy and right to self-determination of those oppressed. In turn, despite this permission, even during war, the Qur'ān maintains an emphasis on the continual need of seeking peace and honoring treaties:

> It is prohibited to fight those with whom you have a treaty or those who wish to make peace: Except those who join a group between whom and you there is a treaty (of peace) or those who approach you with hearts restraining them from fighting you as well as fighting their own people. If God had pleased, He could have given them power over you, and they would have fought you. Therefore if they withdraw from you and fight you not, and send you (guarantees of peace) then God has opened no way for you (to fight them).[72]

Upholding treaties and diplomatic accords in Islām is sacred, even if they are to the temporary detriment of Muslims. After all, as the Qur'ān explicitly states, "Had your Lord willed, all the people on earth would have believed. Do you want to force the people to become believers."[73] This stance is regardless of whom this "Other" is, as in whether they are a "polytheist," a "pagan," "idolaters," or other believers, for the Qur'ān asserts in, at least, three verses: "(The peace treaties are) not dissolved with those Pagans with whom you have entered in to accords, and who have not subsequently failed in their pledge, nor aided anyone against you. So fulfill your agreements with them to the end of their term."[74] The second Qur'ānic verse in which we find this injunction is:

"As long as the idolaters, with whom you have made treaties near the Sacred Mosque, keep the treaty, you should also honor the treaty with them."[75] The third Qur'ānic verse states: "If the enemy inclines towards peace, do thou (also) incline towards peace, and trust in Allāh: for He is the One that heareth and knoweth (all things). And if they seek to deceive you, then Allāh is All-Sufficient for you."[76] However, the Qur'ān continues, should they not desire it, there remains the pertinence of openly declaring war and "If thou fearest treachery from any group, throw back (their covenant) to them, (so as to be) on equal terms: for Allāh loveth not the treacherous."[77]

This attitude to treaties is clearly seen in the incident when many companions of the Prophet opposed the infamous *Treaty of Al-Ḥudaybiyah* which Prophet Muḥammad agreed to. The treaty states:

> In your name, O God! This is the treaty of peace between Muḥammad Ibn Abdullah and Suhayl ibn Amr. They have agreed to allow their arms to rest for ten years. During this time each party shall be secure, and neither shall injure the other; no secret damage shall be inflicted, but honesty and honour shall prevail between them. Whoever in Arabia wishes to enter into a treaty or covenant with Muḥammad can do so, and whoever wishes to enter into a treaty or covenant with the Quraysh can do so. And if a Qurayshite comes without the permission of his guardian to Muḥammad, s-he shall be delivered up to the Quraysh; but if, on the other hand, one of Muḥammad's people comes to the Quraysh, he shall not be delivered up to Muḥammad. This year, Muḥammad, with his companions, must withdraw from Mecca, but next year, he may come to Mecca and remain for three days, yet without their weapons except those of a traveller, the swords remaining in their sheaths.[78]

The treaty was controversial for several reasons, First, it clearly dictated that should a Muslim or non-Muslim from Quraysh in Mecca seek haven amongst free Muslims in Medina, they must be returned or "delivered" to Quraysh, whereas the reverse did not hold true. Second, Muslims were explicitly forbidden from performing pilgrimage that year and were to return the following year, as a condition of assuring a ten-year truce. Third, and finally, the original treaty between the Ambassador of the Quraysh, Suhayl ibn Amr, and Prophet Muḥammad, referred to Muḥammad as the Messenger of God, which was unacceptable to the Quraysh upon which the illiterate Muḥammad compromised and requested that his cousin, and son-in-law, ʿAlī ibn Abī Ṭālib, remove it. In response, ʿAlī stated "I will not be the person to rub it," after which Prophet Muhammed humbly erased the words himself.[79] Muslims were expected to "fulfill every promise" of the treaty.[80]

In 630 AD, the treaty was broken and breached by allies of Quraysh, namely the clan of *Banu Bakr*, who attacked the Bedouin tribe of Khuza'aa, allied with Muslims. Upon this, Prophet Muḥammad, yet again, offered the Quraysh three alternatives and did not zealously rush to abominable and admonished war, as he cited the clause in the treaty that stated that "an attack on an ally of the party, will be considered an attack on the party itself." The three options Muḥammad offered the Quraysh as a consequence of breaking the accord included that they could either: (1) Dissolve their treaty with Banu Bakr; or (2) Compensate Muslims; or alternatively (3) Dissolve the Treaty of Ḥudaybiyah. In turn, Quraysh responded to Muḥammad and chose the third alternative, which further reveals that they evidently always had the intent to pursue war. With the treaty broken and against an overwhelmingly prepared aggressive enemy, Muḥammad marched onto Mecca with a less resourced and severely outnumbered yet dedicated army of approximately 10,000 warriors which led to the Conquest of Mecca. Therefore, conditions of Qitāl established during the Medina period affirm that Muslims are bound through divine covenant to assist oppressed Muslims and non-Muslims, especially when they are victims of aggression and irrespective of what oppressions they face, except against those with whom they have treaties.

As the Qur'ān states:

> And why should ye not fight in the cause of Allāh and of those who, being weak, are ill-treated (and oppressed) – men, women,

> and children, whose cry is: "Our Lord! Rescue us from this town, whose people are oppressors; and raise for us from thee one who will protect; and raise for us from thee one who will help!"[81]

In another verse, God states, "To those against whom war is made, permission is given (to fight), because they are wronged; and verily, Allāh is most powerful for their aid."[82] This way, the Qur'ān affirms that Qitāl is permitted particularly against those who "have been expelled from their homes in defiance of right – (for no cause) except that they say, 'our Lord is Allāh'."[83] Islamic laws thus permit those oppressed to struggle with arms – Qitāl. Islām seeks to breed warriors who are capable and unwavering in their defense of divinely ordained rights and responsibilities in relation to social justice. Further to this, prisoners of war, by decree and Prophetic practice, ought to be treated with decency, with the objective of redressing grievances, not retributive revenge, and even pardoned. As the Qur'ān states: "You shall resort to pardon, advocate tolerance, and disregard the ignorant" and "Tell those who believe to forgive those who do not long for the days of (meeting) God. He will fully pay everyone for whatever they have earned."[84] The Qur'ān further states: "Allāh does not forbid you from those who do not fight you because of religion and do not expel you from your homes – from being righteous toward them and acting justly toward them. Indeed, Allāh loves those who act justly."[85] The Prophet prohibited Muslims from mutilating the corpses of the enemies, and ordered the return of corpses after battle.[86] After all, the dead deserve the protection of their sanctity as they ultimately belong to God and therefore ought to be regarded as sacred. Prophet Muḥammad warned, "Do not destroy the villages and towns, do not spoil the cultivated fields and gardens, and do not slaughter the cattle."[87] Furthermore Prophet Muḥammad taught, "Forbid your army from wreaking havoc for no army wreaks havoc, but that Allāh casts fear into their hearts; forbid your army from purloining the booty for surely no army defrauds but that Allāh will have them conquered by common foot-soldiers."[88]

Islamic rules of Qitāl include the absolute prohibition of harming, killing, or touching a hair on non-combatants. As Wahiduddin Khan states,

> There are certain verses in the Qur'ān which convey injunctions similar to the following: "Kill them wherever you find them." Referring to such verses, there are some who attempt to give the impression that Islam is a religion of war and violence. This is totally untrue. Such verses relate in a restricted sense, to those who have unilaterally attacked the Muslims. The above verse does not convey the general command of Islam.[89]

In fact, there are three verses that explicitly forbid committing violence against non-combatants. The first verse is: "Fight in the cause of Allāh, only those who fight you. Do not transgress the limits because God does not love the transgressors."[90] The second verse is:

"(Do not fight those) who join a group between whom and you there is a treaty or those who approach you with hearts restraining them from either fighting you or fighting their people … Therefore if they withdraw from the fight and instead offer for peace, then God has opened no way for you to war against them."[91]

The third verse is:

> Allāh does not forbid you to be kind and equitable to those who have neither made war on your religion nor driven you from your homes. Allāh loves the equitable. But He forbids you to make friends with those who have fought against you on account of your religion and driven you from your homes or abetted others to do so.[92]

The Qur'ān further teaches, "One ought not say a word of contempt to them, nor repel them, but address them in terms of honor. And out of kindness, lower to them the wing of humility, and say: 'My Lord! Bestow onto them Thy Mercy as they cherished me in childhood'."[93] This is stated while also appreciating the contemporary context of this zero hour in which anti-authoritarian and anti-patriarchal commitments ought to inform militant resistance. After all, revolutionaries ought to be already in a pre-existing struggle against misogyny and patriarchy that will undoubtedly be exacerbated with the traumas of Qitāl during war. As Friedrich Nietzsche states, "He who fights with monsters should be careful lest he thereby become a monster. And if thou gaze long into an abyss, the abyss will also gaze into thee."[94]

Islamic rules of combat also specify that there are to be no killing or abuse of wounded persons or those who are in or seeking sanctuary. Moreover, no killing or abuse of monks in monasteries or people seated in places and stations of worship. As the Qur'ān states, no one may "take life which Allāh has made sacred, except by way of justice and law: thus He commands you that you may learn wisdom."[95] This message is reiterated again in the following verse, "You shall not kill any person – for God has made life sacred except in the course of justice."[96] It is on account of this very directive, that the Qur'ān emphatically states, that it is ordained for Muslims as "for the Children of Israel that if any one slew a person – unless it be for murder or for spreading mischief in the land – it would be as if they slew the whole people: and if any one saved a life, it would be as if they saved the life of the whole people."[97] This is Qitāl, of which the Qur'ān states:

> Warfare is ordained for you, though it is hateful unto you; but it may happen that ye hate a thing which is good for you, and it may happen that ye love a thing which is bad for you. God knoweth, ye know not. / They question thee (O Muḥammad) with regard to warfare in the sacred month. Say: Warfare therein is a great (transgression), but to turn them from the way of God, and to disbelieve in God and in the Inviolable Place of Worship, and to expel God's people thence, is greater offence to God; for persecution is worse than killing. And they will not cease from fighting against you till they have made you renegades from your religion, if they can. And who so becometh a renegade and dieth in his disbelief: such are they whose works have fallen both in the world and the Hereafter. Such are the rightful owners of the Fire; they will abide therein.[98]

The divine acknowledgment and inherent recognition that by nature war is naturally despised, abhorred, and hateful to our species is absolutely critical to reiterate here. Nonetheless, if it is a choice between never-abating and continual domination and oppression, then the right to take arms is a purpose whose cause and limits ought to be clear. Thus, no prisoner should be put to "the sword." The Prophet prohibited the killing or abuse of the elderly, women, children as the most averse and wary of it, and anyone in captivity. Furthermore, the Prophet Muḥammad warned, "Do not destroy the villages and towns, do not spoil the cultivated fields and gardens, and do not slaughter the cattle."[99] The Qur'ān also affirms that war is permitted especially against those who

> have been expelled from their homes in defiance of right – (for no cause) except that they say, "our Lord is Allāh." And had not Allāh checked one set of people by means of another, there would surely have been pulled down monasteries, churches, synagogues, and mosques, in which the name of Allāh is commemorated in abundant measure. Allāh will certainly aid those who aid his (cause), for verily Allāh is full of Strength, Exalted in Might, (able to enforce God's Will).[100]

Expressly, Muslims are forbidden from Qitāl or physical fighting in the four Islamic months of Rajab, Zul'Qeda, Zul Haj and Muharram, as the Qur'ān commands: "They ask you concerning fighting in the Prohibited months. Say: Fighting therein is a grave offence."[101] One is only permitted to violate the sanctity of those months when an enemy initiates transgression first. It is strictly when an enemy violates those sacred months that Muslims are permitted to respond. As the Qur'ān states, "There is a law of equality. If anyone transgresses the prohibition against you, you can transgress likewise against your enemy."[102]

Finally, it is crucial to bear in mind: War-Qitāl is not concerned with weakness or strength in numbers, as this would contradict, at least, two Qur'ānic verses, if not the very archeology and genealogy of militaristic histories.[103] The first Qur'ānic verse being: "If there are twenty steadfast among you, they will defeat two hundred, and one hundred among you will defeat one-thousand of those who disbelieve, for they are a people who do not understand."[104] The second verse is: "How many a small party has defeated a larger party by God's leave! God is with the steadfast."[105]

Enough then, and let there be no apologists and apologies for its reference as *jihād*. As the Qur'ān states:

> Have you not seen [O Muḥammad!] those to whom it was said: "Withhold your hands [from fighting], keep up prayer, and pay the obligatory alms," when fighting was ordained for them. A party of them feared [other "enemy"] people as they ought to fear Allāh, or [even] with a greater fear, and said: "Our Lord! Why have You ordained fighting for us? If You have only granted us a delay to a near date?" Say [O Muḥammad!]: "The provision of this world is short, and the hereafter is better for s-he who acts dutifully toward Allāh; and you shall not be wronged in the very least.[106]

The Qur'ānic emphasis, as the verse demonstrates, is always on "the greater jihād," without fear or shyness of the right to self-defend, if jihād is indeed to be in the context of Qitāl.

This much I felt obliged to write, as a consequence of what was first proposed of (non)violence and the preliminary interrogations of the concepts of jihād, Qitāl, and Islām in these *confessions of an anti-militaristic militant jihādi.* I refrain from discussing the depths, intricacies, applications, and implications of Prophetic battles as that of: Badr, Uhud, Tabuk, and Al-Khandaq, and what they imply and can teach in the context of modern warfare. There persist a rich history and literature of jihād that could contribute to this conversation including discussions of *jihād* of the heart *(jihād al-qalb)*, *jihād* by the tongue *(jihād al-lisān)*, and *jihād* by the hand *(jihād bil-ayd)*. I also did not discuss the so-called sword verses (*ayat al-sayf*) (which make no reference to the word "sword" (*sayf*), as they do not alter the contours and parameters of Qitāl and jihād as established here. Moreover, ample and innumerable modern and medieval scholars have explicitly addressed and offered commentary on these Orientalized verse.[107] After all, commentary on these specific Qur'ānic verses clarify its intended meanings having noted "that not only is a Pagan seeking asylum during and in reference to that particular battle to be granted refuge, but rather also that they should be escorted to a secure place."[108] Furthermore, I did not discuss whether in the current predicament of Muslims whether jihād ought to be regarded as *farḍ kefāya* (a duty that if performed by some, the obligation falls from the rest) or *farḍ 'ayn* (a compulsory duty on every single Muslim to perform like praying and fasting) as such decisions require Shūrā, Ijmā', and Maṣlaḥa. Finally, I did not attempt to ignore or evade possibilities for a radical reconceptualization of terms conjured by (pre)modern Muslim jurists, although they are nonexistent in the Qur'ān and predominantly introduced to Islām by the Sunni Hanafi Fiqh tradition, that include: *ḍār al-Islām* (Abode of Peace), *ḍār al-Ṣulḥ* (Abode of Reconciliation), *ḍār al-Ahd or 'Muwāda'ah* (Abode of Treaty), *ḍār al-Ḥarb* (Abode of War), *ḍār Al-Kufr* (Abode of Unbelief), and even what Abdullah bin Bayyah refers to as *dār al-Muqām*, or *ḍār al-Muwāṭana'* (Abode of Citizenship).[109] After all, the composition of who is an ally, friend, foe, and enemy, at this juncture of the book ought be rather clear.

Indeed, there would be much to say about understanding Qur'ānic concepts such as *jizya* (a tribute paid) given how it exempts those able amongst Christians and Jews from physically fighting when an Umma they also collectively belong to is under assault and in which the former believers are under Muslim protection as so-called *dhimmīs*.[110] After all, Muslims possess responsibilities and obligations in safeguarding and protecting minorities, unless *dhimmīs* (those in their care) themselves choose to partake in defending the Muslim and non-Muslim community or collective Umma as well. In this case, the *jizya* is regarded as a minor Zakat for the Muslim "Other" to ostensibly die *in the place of* and *for* the non-Muslim "Other," towards the preservation of what both live for. I conclude with George Ishaq, a previously staunch leftist turned (neo)liberal and one of the founders of *Kefaya*, amongst the first movements in 2005 to openly oppose and criticize deposed (now dead) ex-president of Egypt, Muhammad Hosni El Sayed Mubarak, who stated to me in 2013: "For new grass to grow a lot of old grass dies. There's no revolution without victims. A revolution must have victims that sacrifice to life for the revolution to live."[111] As such, though unexpected incidents cannot be easily predicted in times of revolutionary action, there are inherent provisions and preparations that can be anticipated during the heated days of war.[112] Amongst these are a necessary accountability that revolutionaries who are assigned and choose to pick up arms have to the communities to which they belong, as part of the mutual answerability and procedural mechanisms devised within the movement.

From the Deception of "Nonviolence" to Red, Black, and Brown Power

Radical scholars and activists have long argued that violence is not a monolithic category but possesses distinct forms (symbolic, systemic, objective, subjective, revolutionary, violence that conserves laws, violence that founds laws). Indeed, revolutionary violence must be a component of a grander biodiverse strategy of resistance that recognizes how nonviolence aids and abates the modern-state.[113] Naive calls for nonviolent resistance tend to ignore what Slavoj Žižek refers to as daily violent traumas relating to two fundamental forms of violence, *Subjective* and *Objective. Subjective violence* is overt and perturbs the normal functioning of the peaceful state; it is a form of "violence perpetrated by an agent to whom the act can be rendered accountable."[114] In contrast, *objective violence* is invisible and is essential to the natural functioning of a peaceful state; it maintains the normalized apathetic and desensitized status quo. Indeed, Giorgio Agamben distinguishes between "violence that conserves law" (equivalent to the state's monopoly over legitimate violence) and "violence that founds the law" (the "original" violence necessary to create the state).[115] Similarly, Carl Schmitt discussed what he referred to as a "state of exception" in which the modern-state engages in the indefinite suspension of civil rights, as "emergency laws are enacted in the name of public welfare" through military-judicial-tribunals such as emergency laws are instituted, as the case in Egypt for over 65 years.[116]

In these conditions, Tahrir's violence challenges the romanticized possibility of pure nonviolent tactics on the road to freedom, as disseminated by Euro-American advocacy materials that teach the white-legitimized democratic means by which people should resist their own oppression and oppressors.[117] In this sense, violence and nonviolence cannot be treated as binaries. The interpretations of (non)violence and its relationship to resistance have become even more murky since the takeover of foreign, regional, and local security by profiteering privatized military-economic interests, such as the RAND Corporation and paramilitary-armed mercenary organizations such as Blackwater, renamed as Xe, founded by Education Secretary Betsy Devos' brother Erik Prince.[118] Neither space nor time are sufficient here to delve deeper into discussions of Sun Tzu, Mao, and Machiavelli's *Art of War* & *Guerrilla Warfare*, braiding them with a discussion of Ismā'īl ibn 'Umar ibn Kathīr's fourteenth century narration and commentary on the political and ethical practices in order to further dismantle binary notions of (non)violence, particularly in the hearts and minds of liberal-progressives.

However, we can see the lack of clear divisions between violence and nonviolence in Dr. Martin Luther King, who contradicted his nonviolent doctrine when he openly supported Israeli-Zionism and its violent and sadistically torturous settler-colonialism that continues to this day against Palestinians.[119] Similarly, Mahatma K. Gandhi's espousal of nonviolent visions elides and erases his engagement in racist and sexist violence.[120] Righteous moralists tend to selectively quote these two and neglect that prior to his assassination King became disillusioned with nonviolence. In the speech *When Peace Becomes Obnoxious*, he said,

> In a very profound passage which has been often misunderstood, Jesus utters this: He says, "Think not that I am come to bring peace. I come not to bring peace but a sword." Certainly, He is not saying that He comes not to bring peace in the higher sense. What He is saying is: "I come not to bring this peace of escapism, this peace that fails to confront the real issues of life, the peace that makes for stagnant complacency." Then He says, "I come to bring a sword not a physical sword. Whenever I come, a conflict is precipitated between the old and the new,

> between justice and injustice, between the forces of light and the forces of darkness. I come to declare war over injustice. I come to declare war on evil. Peace is not merely the absence of some negative force – war, tension, confusion, but it is the presence of some positive force – justice, goodwill, the power of the kingdom of God."[121]

Similarly, Gandhi states, "It is better to be violent, if there is violence in our hearts, than to put on the cloak of nonviolence to cover impotence." The fact is:

> The resistance in India was incredibly diverse, and Gandhi was a very important figure within that resistance, but the resistance was by no means pacifist in its entirety, that there were a number of armed guerrilla groups, a number of militant struggles, very important riots and other strong clashes which were a part of the struggle for Indian independence. So on the one hand Gandhi basically got negotiating power from the fact that there were other elements in the struggle which were more threatening to British dominance. So the British specifically chose to dialogue with Gandhi because he was for them the least threatening of the important elements of resistance and had those elements not existed they simply could've ignored Gandhi.[122]

Liberal understandings of nonviolence ignore George Jackson's words that "the concept of nonviolence ... [is] a false ideal ...when it presupposes the existence of compassion and a sense of justice on the part of one's adversary. When this adversary has everything to lose and nothing to gain by exercising justice and compassion, his reaction can only be negative."[123] Furthermore, pacifists tend to mistake nonviolence for "peace," despite incidents such as *Dharasana Satyagraha*, where Indians, under the leadership of Sarojini Naidu and Maulana Abdul Kalam Azad, protested British salt tax in May 1930, and in which participants were expected to remain entirely "passive" such that they were forbidden from even warding off the blows leveled against them by British colonial soldiers. This left by certain estimates 320 injured and two dead.[124]

Events such as this affirm that even in pacifism, violence already pre-exists, as Indian protestors knew full well that they marched to meet batons held in British hands and hence were aware that quite likely they would die in acts of violence. As per Jean-Paul Sartre's opening quote in this chapter and in stark contrast to the events of Dharasana Satyagraha, we find the limited extent that most contemporary "nonviolent" liberal-progressive Euro-American social movement participants are willing to go during protests, as they insist on upholding settler-colonial "rules of law" and condemn "rioting," despite that the latter represents the "language of the unheard."[125]

Accordingly, we ought to reserve the right to self-defense within ethical-political parameters. As Malcolm X said, "it's a crime for anyone being brutalized to continue to accept that brutality without doing something to defend himself."[126] As a tactic, violence cannot be romanticized. It is necessary to consider what constitutes "victory" and determine exactly what values and communities one is defending, as well as questions relating to the cost of violence on one's soul and the individual and collective responsibility for those engaging in militancy. As noted, victory in militant battle has little to do with the number of peoples with arms, but rather the ability to predict what tactics within a broader strategy of resistance are necessary in a given situation. If taken to an extreme, violence can only result in failure and transform us, in light of our never-abating micro-fascisms, into the same oppressors and colonizers we seek to dethrone. Certainly, the more masses that are out in the streets, the less likely that there will be blood shed during direct violent confrontations with obedient state-police and armed forces. Despite the growing militarization of police forces and their military grade body armor, drones, automatic rifles, tanks, planes and helicopters, it is less likely that a uniformed police or military officer will automatically fire when they see their sister, grandmother, daughter, aunt, brother, uncle, son, at the front lines, or simply en route to a grocery store, a clinic, or a hospital.[127] Such a sight might even perhaps awaken a poor disillusioned police and military officer's staunchly authoritarian consciousness, particularly if their subjectivity is that of a minority, as in being a person of color, queer, and/or woman, but that is never a guarantee. There are principles upon which war is fought, given its provisional purpose and what it bears in relationship to human and other-than-human life during its conduct.

As Arundhati Roy states:

> The thing that I'm thinking most about ... the question that occupies me a lot these days is what kind, what form, of resistance, is effective and acceptable to us because I see all over and all around us that obviously resistance, whether it is Palestine, or Iraq, or Kashmir or in the North-Eastern states of India, or now all over India, there is a kind of armed struggle rising up, being put down viciously by the state and at the same time non-violent resistance movements are given a lot of airtime, a lot of publicity, a lot of space, but it's also because it makes the state comfortable, it makes the uncomfortable comfortable. So between non-violent resistance and armed struggle where do we go, what is effective, what is the right thing to do, or do we need a bio-diversity of resistance, do we need all kinds of resistance? And do we need to stop this search for being pristine? Do we need to be able to accept that whatever form we choose, and all the various ways in which we decide to resist will not be pure. And we accept that impurity with some kind of generosity.[128]

The liberal understandings of nonviolence ignore the manner in which it serves to aid, abate, and protect the nation-state, as demonstrated by the fact that the CIA (Central Intelligence Agency) and Pentagon-funded organizations now contort and manipulate these ideals, promoting nonviolent training to effectively mediate and manage resistance with the explicit goal of quashing and taming rebellion.[129] Undoubtedly, it is these methods and attitudes, propagated by both whites and non-whites alike, that delimit the effectiveness of our strategic and tactical responses to colonialism/imperialism and capitalist-states. We underestimate the dominant order and the forces we confront when "nowadays the way that States rule is by accepting the inevitability of conflict and resistance and trying to manage it permanently."[130] As Peter Gelderloos notes,

> The State and the media train, especially more professionally minded activists within the resistance, to enforce this code of nonviolence so that they never incur that loss of popularity, or that bad press, and this creates a self-policing function and people who are the sort of politicians of the movement are more susceptible to it because they're thinking often in terms of their own careers.[131]

Again, terrorism and terrorists are not the root cause of violence, but rather they denote an internalized reaction to deep-seated injustices. *Jihādi* figures transcend divergent geographical and demographic, social-political-economic origins, and are interlinked by religion, historical and social justice grievances, contrary to their depiction as illiterate, petty thugs, and unreligious criminals, in addition to a host of other representations driven by a neurotic European Orientalist desire to rationalize their actions.[132] How dare we then homogenize and essentialize understandings of violence, when even the Napoleonic idea of conscription in creating France as a "nation of arms" is a model that serves as the foundation upon which every modern-state's military industrial complex was born.[133] This uniquely modern hierarchical-authoritarian schema was not just concerned with institutionalizing state-militaries, but also represented a way to technocratically discipline, control, and manage civilian populations (*'askarat al-mujtam'āt*), some in more overtly repressive ways than Euro-American "democratic" others.[134] In each case this means that entire generations of civilian populations were trained to unconsciously submit to orders, whether in schools, hospitals, factories, or the barracks, cultivating the desire within them for their own mass fascistic servitude and repression.[135]

As Gelderloos further argues:

> A lot of times people will justify non-violence making the very common sense, the very simple and ultimately false argument

> that violence is the government's strong suit and it makes no sense to fight the violence of the government with the violence of our own and what they're doing is conflating very, very, different activities.[136]

In taking this rhetorical stance, what advocates of nonviolence are suggesting, as Gelderloos rightly writes, is that:

> Somehow defending yourself against police violence or destroying commodities or taking over property, fighting to free prisoners, indigenous people fighting to take over stolen land, things of this nature, somehow has any similarities, with governments carpet bombing villages or using landmines or police torturing people or putting someone in prison, that just because by some linguistic coincidence these different things can be described as violence, that somehow there's not only similarities between them but that they're the same thing and that one is going to reproduce the other when in fact by fighting back people actually raise the stakes of repression and oppression for the State and actually make real short term differences and have a greater potentiality in ultimately destroying the state and capitalism and helping us create those worlds that we want. The Left to a large extent subconsciously has as its primary role to make resistance harmless.[137]

It is for these reasons that I emphasize Anarcha-Islām's stance regarding the right to self-defense, while maintaining, as highlighted numerous times, that great care ought to be taken to not reduce a strategy to a tactic, such that violence becomes the sole path and agenda.

To claim a purist nonviolent position is to be jaded by delusional fantasies of a post-racial America's psychosis regarding its weekly recurring horrors and the emotional roil of endemic oppression in travesties of mass shootings, whether in public cinemas, theaters, shopping malls or even schools. It is to be blind to the broader discussions between gun-violence and cisheteropatriarchy, white supremacy, a conjured War on Terror, sexism, toxic masculinity, imperialism/colonialism, and mental health, given the annual hundreds upon hundreds of homicides of prevalently Black and Latinx youth in cities such as Chicago, Illinois, as a consequence of gentrification and poverty-stricken gang-related violence in a fiercely hyper-masculine society that thrives on transnational military escapades and simulated violence in video games.[138] Nonviolence whitewashes police brutality, built on the legacy of slave-catchers, and erases the endless series of murders whether in cases such as Trayvon Martin in Sanford, Florida, or Oscar Grant's brutal assault in Oakland, California. Indeed, insisting on nonviolent stances erases and does injustice to the names and narrative of Sean Bell, John Crawford, Amadou Diallo, Tamir Rice, Eric Garner, Jonathan Ferrell, Kimani Gray, Kendrec McDade, Michael Brown in Ferguson, St. Louis, and Tarika Wilsons' in Lima, Ohio, as well as countless others who even in death are subjugated to attacks defaming their character in an effort to delegitimize the realities of what their martyrdom stand for. Indeed, here, the message is always clear: Think twice before wearing a hoodie. Pull up your trousers.[139] Do not aimlessly commute accompanied by more than two to three consorts. Swallow your pride and shut up when racially profiled and frisked by authorities because they are out there to keep you safe. Maintain and keep your unclutched hands where they can be visibly seen at all times. Do not disturb a non-existent peace, because no agitation and *anarchy* are permitted here! Moreover, if you happen to be a journalist reporting on these "random" incidents, leave your recording equipment behind, but be prepared for enforced emergency curfews and stay tuned to the announcement of your friendly local neighborhood no-fly zones. Finally, please be okay with the fact that unarmed crowds can be fired upon, by neighborhood friendly law enforcers and military personnel who signed up to holster their armed weapons. As Greg Howard writes in "America Is Not for Black People" (2014):

> If officers are soldiers, it follows that the neighborhoods they patrol are battlefields. And if they're working battlefields, it follows that the population is the enemy. And because of correlations rooted in historical injustice, between crime and income

> and income and race, the enemy population will consist largely of people of color, and especially of black men. Throughout the country, police officers are capturing, imprisoning, and killing black males at a ridiculous clip, waging a very literal war.[140]

This is the underlying premise of the American Dream, and its "Stand Your Ground laws," its "Common Ground Public Relations," as well as PR firms that are often called in by the nation-state to deal with the managing of official responses during times of heightened racial tensions and potential "Black Uprisings" such as Ferguson's.[141]

In the specific case of diasporic Muslims, the response to these facts is their continued self-delusion as they insist that prayers and patience will avail them, while falsely deferring to the Qur'ānic verse:

> Be sure We shall test you with something of fear and hunger, some loss in goods, lives, and the fruits of your toil. But give glad tidings to those who patiently persevere. Those who say, when afflicted with calamity, "To Allāh we belong, and to Him is our return" – They are those on whom descend blessings from their Lord, and mercy. They are the ones who receive guidance.[142]

However, this ahistorical cherry picking only results in our further complicit entrenchment in oppressions and the disconnection of our struggles from those of others. Instead, it is necessary to remember that Islām commands a constant commitment to human and nonhuman life, especially during violent insurrection and rebellion against injustice. We need to be able to envision the aftermath of violence, and not only in terms of our individual and collective healing. In other words, we must be capable of re-imagining a future, one that answers Elizabeth Grosz's question: What would "a newly considered humanities, one that seeks to know itself not in opposition to its others, the 'others' of the human, but in continuity with them … in which the other is always in some way associated with animality or the nonhuman" look like?[143]

Liberatory Victory

Victory in battle is no cause for boastfulness given what it bears in disdain and hubris that feeds into our vanity, and egotism. The only reason war is permitted is to selflessly protect and defend liberatory justice, mercy, and community. Prophet Muḥammad said: "Do not wish for an encounter with the enemy; Pray to Allāh to grant you security; but when you (have to) encounter them, exercise patience, and you should know that Paradise is under the shadow of the swords."[144] These are this Islamic interpretation and the Qur'ān's tenets of war that I take for Anarcha-Islām and which ought to put to rest cursory, uninformed discussions and decisions by the likes of controversial and conservative white convert Muslim scholar Hamza Yusuf along with other liberal-progressives who staunchly advocate for whitewashed notions of pacifism. Yusuf, who supports oppressive monarchic regimes in the Arabian Gulf Peninsula and does not believe in racial or social justice rights, shamefully joined the Trump Administration's "human rights" council. Moreover, in the name of quelling "anarchy," preserving order, and minimizing rebellion, Yusuf condemned the revolutionary aspirations associated with the "Arab Spring" as well as Black Lives Matter, ignoring a rich tradition in which rebellion is permitted against tyrants. But as Usaama Al-Azami notes in his article, "The Question of Rebellion in the Islamic Tradition, "Yusuf hardly engages the "variety of responses to how one should oppose such governments, ranging from the more quietist – opposing them only in one's heart – to the more activist – opposing them through armed rebellion."[145]

Yusuf conveniently ignores an entire corpus on this subject that includes ʿAbdullah al-Dumayji, Abū Ḥanīfa (d. 150/767), Ibn Mālik (d. 179/795), al-Shāfiʿī (d. 204/820), Aḥmad ibn Ḥanbal (d. 241/855), Abū Bakr ʿAbdallāh ibn al-ʿArabī (d. 543/1148), Abū Bakr ibn al-Jaṣṣāṣ (d. 370/981), Ibn ʿAqil (d. 513/1119), Ibn al-Jawzī (d. 597/1201), Ibn Rajab al-Hanbali, Fakhr al-Dīn al-Rāzī (d. 606/1210), Ibn Ḥajar al-ʿAsqalānī, and even Muhammad al-Ghazzali and "his teacher Juwaynī" and even Yusuf al-Qaradawi (b. 1345/1926), Abdullah Bin Bayyah (b. 1353f./1935).[146]

As Al-Azami writes, even "the majority of later scholars, including masters such as al-Ghazzali (d. 505/1111), Ibn Rajab al-Hanbali (d. 795/1393), and Ibn Ḥajar al-ʿAsqalānī (d. 852/1449) appear to have fallen somewhere between these two poles, advocating rebellion only in limited circumstances, and mostly advising a vocally critical posture towards tyranny. Of course, some early scholars, such as the sanctified member of the Prophetic Household, Sayyiduna Husayn (d. 61/680), had engaged in armed opposition to the tyranny of the Umayyads resulting in his martyrdom. Similarly, the Companion ʿAbd Allāh ibn al-Zubayr ibn al-ʿAwwām (d. 73/692), grandson of Abū Bakr (d. 13/634), and son of al-Zubayr ibn al-ʿAwwām (d. 36/656), two of the ten Companions Promised Paradise, had established a caliphate based in Makkah that militarily tried to unseat the Umayyad caliphal counter-claimant."[147]

Let this be a cautionary tale to The Foe then in and regarding what arrives next.

6
Conclusion: There Are Only Middles, No Beginnings and No Ends. Between BLM, NoDaPL-INM, and Tahrir

The impossibility of "fellow feeling" is itself the confirmation of injury. The call of such pain, as a pain that cannot be shared through empathy, is a call not just for an attentive hearing, but for a different kind of inhabitance. It is a call for action, and a demand for collective politics, as a politics based not on the possibility that we might be reconciled, but on learning to live with the impossibility of reconciliation, or learning that we live with and beside each other, and yet we are not as one.

Sara Ahmed (2014, 39)[1]

Imagine government officials, church officials, nuns, priests and teachers from a particular residential school in a circle with the people that had survived their sexual, physical, emotional and spiritual abuse. This is a fundamentally different power relationship between perpetrators of violence and survivors of that violence, where the abusers must face the full impact of their actions. Reconciliation then becomes a process embodied by both the survivor and the perpetrator. And part of that restoration means that the community maintains the authority to make that individual accountable for future wrongs … Restorative models work in Nishnaabeg communities because ethically taking responsibility for one's actions is paramount in the healing or restoration process; as well, the purpose of these models in the long term is the rehabilitation and restoration of all those individuals back into mino bimaadiziwim.

Leanne Simpson (2011, 24)[2]

> America is false to the past, false to the present, and solemnly binds herself to be false to the future ... A horrible reptile is coiled up in ... [her] nation's bosom; the venomous creature is nursing at the tender breast of ... [her] youthful republic.
>
> Frederick Douglass (1852)[3]

The War on Terror, the lengthiest war in American history, has been a war on and within Islām. It has resulted in modern contradictions and a neoliberal identity crisis. A majority of Arabs, North Africans, and Muslims whether in Egypt or as newcomer diasporas unwittingly uphold settler-colonial identities that are anchored in militarized homonationalism and pinkwashing, as well as neo-developmentalist civic and human rights paradigms. Because mainstream Muslims refuse to address festering anti-blackness, queerphobia, cisheteropatriarchy, sexism, racial capitalism, and religious dissent within Muslim communities, persecution and inferiority complexes have been internalized. This has contributed to the transnational rise of benevolent ostracized ex-Muslim council organizations such as Ex-Muslims of North America and Britain. These groups promote Euro-American Christian secularism, and have arguably been indoctrinated and terrorized to resent, if not purge, their cultures' political-spiritual traditions. It is understandable that these self-Orientalizing ex-Muslims abandon an Islām that has been "disfigured." However, it is equally damaging that these ex-Muslims strictly equate Islām with Muslim-militancy, Arab supremacy, and slavery. They regurgitate Fundamentalist/Orientalist discourses that breed and nurture a culture of Islamophobia, spearheaded by evangelical liberal and conservative voices such as Pamela Gellar, Ann Coulter, Bill Maher, Steve Bannon, Newt Gingrich, and John Bolton, as well as movements like Brigitte Gabriel's ACT for America.[4] ACT for America, designated by the Southern Poverty Law Center (SPLC) as an extremist group, regularly calls for nationwide marches against *sharī'a*.[5]

This book deploys Islamic methodologies and transnational social movement theories to reveal emergent insights that will allow scholars/activists in settler- and franchise-colonial societies to grapple with the strategic limits of identity politics and with non-Euro-American understandings of agency centered on social justice as a spiritual act. By centering a social movement perspective, the book exposes numerous impediments to social movement mobilization amongst Muslims and leftists in relation to the Umma that include the perpetuation of internalized discriminations and oppressions.

Dominant identitarian scholars normalize post-colonial conditions and often advocate for a multicultural, colorblind politics of recognition. They do not, however, problematize the persisting neocolonial/neoimperial effects of capitalist-state frameworks that regulate and organize the desire for liberation in settler- and franchise-colonial societies. On the other hand, this book offers sustainable decolonial alternatives through a *biodiverse strategy of resistance*, relative to human and nonhuman life, towards envisioning another world of decolonial possibilities. Anarcha-Islām suggests that a radical decolonial anti-authoritarian and anti-materialist, feminist, and Qur'ānic re-interpretation of Islām configured around past and contemporary Muslim identity is needed as a foundation for a social justice Islām and a Qur'ān of the oppressed. Such a re-interpretation would facilitate a transnational ethic of accountable local, regional, and transnational solidarities that address the mutually constitutive systems of franchise and settler coloniality.

The first step in this journey is to elucidate the circulatory relationship between settler- and franchise-colonial conditions that frame and situate Islām and Muslims. This book argues that global Orientalism and Euro-American support for repressive, (neo)colonial regimes in franchise-colonial nations, which in turn have spawned Muslim SWANA diasporas, positions Muslims as outsiders both within and outside of Empire. At the same time, Euro-American imperial othering of Muslims is nourished by the forms of white-supremacist othering that precede or intersect it, such as the settler-colonial othering of Indigenous people and anti-Black racism. Without decolonization, attempts to build a social justice Islām, empty of Qur'ānic engagement, is one that risks its own liberal-progressive depoliticization. It could become a Euro-American or "West-oxified" individualistic Islām that validates progressive-liberal colorblind multiculturalism and dismisses the link between ongoing colonialism, Muslim history, and racism.[6] Moreover, a liberal-progressive Islām that does not center on decolonization is likely to retain racisms and sexisms across both franchise- and settler-capitalist nation-state paradigms, given how the U.S./Canadian empire relies on obscuring globally projected Orientalisms (creating, for instance, diasporic queer-feminist Muslim migration).[7] To free ourselves, Muslims and, generally, BIPOC must contend against the "successes" of our own incorporation into capitalist-states, which are founded on "the cultivation of subjects of liberal multiculturalism that have played off each other to cohere a pernicious binary that has emerged – not recently, but during the last 40 years of the post-civil rights era – in U.S. legislative, activist, and scholarly realms: the homosexual other is white, the racial other is straight."[8] Muslims need to unwaveringly critique the state and develop alternative forms of governance. We need to focus on sexual ethics and gender egalitarianism, as opposed to Euro-American sexual identitarian frameworks and strive towards a pluriversal vision of the Umma and an ethico-political relationship to land.

In this book critical race and anti-racist feminist scholarship were used to examine how POC have embraced their racial/ethnic construction as white, and adopted an anti-Black sentiment.[9] As colonized peoples, Muslims have developed what Frantz Fanon refers to as a pathological dependency complex.[10] The internalization of violent injury that is a product of colonialism represents a form of Fanonian psycho-affectivity.[11] This has been translated into neoreactionary calls to violence and oppression by those colonized directed at others who are also colonized, including members of our own community, as in the case of ISIS' neosectarian murders of Muslims of the same supposed sect, particularly Sunnīs. The ongoing neocolonial trauma has left many Muslims with a deep sense of shame that drives them to engage in violent neoreactionary struggles to suppress and sanitize their histories, or to over-embellish the Orientalist/Occidentalist decadence of their Abbassid and Ottoman medieval past.[12] Continuing shame leads neoliberal SWANA dictators and Islamists to explain that the immoralities of the present are a strict result of Euro-America's neoliberal hyper-sexual influence. This is then used to justify the repressive policing of gender for instance, or leads SWANA liberals and leftists to embody an Islamophobic sentiment as part of the full-scale adoption of Euro-American discourses.

I began the book by discussing the destructive legacy of liberalism and how minority Muslims in general and progressive and conservative Muslims in particular are suspended between dichotomous representations of terrorism and oppression. I argued that despite these paradigms, there are Muslim anarchists who seek to transcend identitarian and non-identitarian debates on Islām. These Muslims espouse anarchistic, anti-imperialist, anti-colonial, anti-cisheteropatriarchal politics to expand the understanding of Muslim and global liberation. These individuals understand the strategic limits of identity politics, and seek to transcend it by "transversing the gaps, puncturing the holds [of representations] ... opening up the new world order to a quite different and new world of the multiple."[13]

Muslim anarchists offer a horizon through which all minorities can transcend these dichotomous representations, despite their isolation and ostracization from purportedly leftist circles since 9/11. Muslim anarchists are not paralyzed and complacent, nor have they internalized Islamophobia, as other SWANA Muslims have, despite the damaging representations they are exposed to. Instead, they understand their standing(s) and positioning(s) as spiritually inclined ethico-political subjects and choose to never become "subjects of the signifier [subjects of Euro-American representations, and] ... [of] Knowledge, Power, Money."[14] Liberalism's destructive legacy has had radiating effects on social movements that have led to the emergence of progressive Muslim-Zionist perspectives that are supportive of progressive Muslim and Muslim feminist friendly causes. Examples of liberal Muslim friendly interfaith initiatives that uphold Zionism include the Muslim Leadership Initiative (MLI) and Muslim Jewish Advisory Council (MJAC), which have organized trips to Israel in the name of American peace and diversity. This, of course, only serves to normalize the colonization of Indigenous peoples in the U.S. as well as Israeli settler-colonialism and occupation – hence forsaking Palestine. Zionist Muslims across the U.S./Canada and Europe, some of whom identify as queer, include Irshad Manji, Raheem Kassim, Fareed Zakaria, Zuhdi Jasser, Tarek Fatah, Qanta Ahmed, Raheel Raza, and Asra Nomani.[15] All of them share a conviction of Israel's right to exist. The crisis of Muslim theological interpretation that advocates for secularism is rooted in liberalism, which in itself holds blatantly contradictory positions. This is exemplified by anti-Zionist and Washington Women's March activists like Palestinian-American Linda Sarsour, who ebulliently supports imperialist socialists like Bernie Sanders, who opposes the Palestinian Boycott, Divestment and Sanctions Campaign (BDS) against Israel, believes in closed American borders, is inadequate at best on issues of racial-gender-queer justice, and supported the 1995 Embassy Act and Trump's recent declaration of Jerusalem as Israel's capital.

Not only do Muslim anarchists insist on the congruence of their interpretations of anarchism and Islām, they have re-interpreted both to acknowledge the similarities and differences in their racialized geopolitical and geographic positionings. Based on that choice, these Muslim anarchists are engaging in molecular revolutions that allow them to re-interpret their spiritualities and to create new aesthetic, cultural, and ethico-political alternatives. Rejecting the perception of themselves as victims, Muslim anarchists have creatively envisioned and pragmatically embodied a distinct vision of Islām in non-Euro-American and Euro-American societies. This has come at the cost of their ostracization from the broader settler Muslim and anarchist communities in Euro-America, and from the majority of social movements in predominantly Muslim societies such as Egypt. This ostracization and the absence of community is the price paid for their allegiance to ethico-political commitments. As the Qur'ān notes: "Truly God alters not what is in a people until they alter what is in themselves."[16]

Emerging from Anarcha-Islām is a new framework for identifying the theoretical and methodological positionings necessary for discussing Muslim subjectivities in Islām in the present day. I develop a decolonial, anti-racist, anti-authoritarian, anti-materialist and queer-feminist methodology I called *Anarchic Ijtihād.* This critique challenges the tendency of diasporic Muslims to uncritically applaud and ignore settler-colonialism and take post-colonialism and decolonization for granted. Hence, they "mask the national, class, regional, religious based identities that are being continually recast through the miasma of oppositionality."[17] Anarchic Ijtihād is also based on the understanding that a Euro-American instrumentalist notion of desire is attached to liberation. Anarchic Ijtihād is used to construct a non-authoritarian and non-capitalist *Anarcha-Islām*. It is a critique of Euro-American social movement theory's racial, (trans)national, and neoimperial/neocolonial formation, which functions across settler/franchise-colonial societies.[18] This anti-authoritarianism inherent to Islām is especially relevant to diasporic Muslims. There is a need for decolonized and reindigenized understandings of Umma, as a global polity of Muslims and non-Muslims, premised on the Medina Charter established by the Prophet Muḥammad, and whose boundaries are premised solely on the existence of identifiable non-statist spiritual-ethico-political and socially just commitments between communities and in relation to land.

Anarchic Ijtihād is necessary not only because of Islām's unique geopolitical figuration, but also because Arab and Muslim conceptualizations of what constitutes Muslim governance are being challenged by both colonized subjectivities and non-statist Islamist movements such as ISIS and secular-nationalist Egyptian military dictatorships such as that of Abdel-Fattah al-Sisi all who seek to manipulate Islām for their own agendas.

I lamented the general absence of *thaqāfa* (a critical cultural consciousness and intellect) and *Ijtihād* (the use of independent reasoning in the critical exegesis or *tafsīr* of the Qur'ān, Sunnah (the Prophetic practice), and aḥādīth – the Oral Tradition – and Islamic texts and legal sources, which are needed at a time when Muslims are abandoning Islām in an age of Islamisms. I also discussed the issues of internalized shame, sexism, cisheteropatriarchy, racism, and Islamophobia in Muslim circles. I illuminated how these internalized discriminations have led to the perpetuating internalized reproduction of micro-fascistic practices that have stunted the liberatory possibilities of an Orientalized Arab Spring/Islamist Winter.

Every oppression we have internalized is intimately entwined with a plethora of other oppressions and social justice concerns, and in the absence of their overcoming we will forever remain incapable of achieving true liberation. For diasporic Muslims in Turtle Island as well as a majority of Muslims in Egypt, this entails a discussion of how we interpret our double-conscious identities.[19] As Muslims we need to ethically-politically associate our identities with a communal sense of responsibility towards the Other. Collectively, leftists and Muslims need to re-establish boundaries between the realms of the private (*khuṣūṣiyāt*) and public (*ʿumūmiyāt*) that have eroded if not withered away globally. That is, if we truly seek to found a non-racialized, global, Muslim Umma that embodies the spirit of the Medina Charter, and hence includes non-Muslims and orbits around decolonial tenets of social justice. A decolonized Umma is critical given how the Qur'ān speaks in the language of differing spiritualities (*rūḥāniyya*) and faiths (*īmān*), and not in the exclusionary context of addressing only Muslims. The Qur'ān's message is universal. After all, as the Qur'ān emphasizes: "There is no Coercion in Religion," and acknowledges: "And had thy Lord willed, all those who are on the earth would have believed all together. Wouldst thou compel people till they become believers?"[20] There is no concept of favoritism in Islām. In the Creator's sight the "best" are the tribes and nations that maintain social justice, egalitarian relations, and ethical and political conduct towards others and nonhuman life. The Qur'ān states: "Not all people are alike" and

> For each among you We have appointed a law and a way. And had God willed, They would have made you one community [Umma], but [God willed otherwise], that God might try you in that which God has given you. So vie with one another in good deeds. Unto God shall be your return all together, and They will inform you of that wherein you differ.[21]

The vision of a decolonized Umma, especially from a decolonial Islamic anarchistic perspective, corresponds with that of Joseph

Bauerkemper and Heidi Kiiwetinepinesiik Stark who use "the phrase 'Indigenous transnationalism'" to describe "the linkages, cross-references, and movement of ideas, practices, and obligations between indigenous nations."[22]

There is a monumental difference between *iṣlāḥ* (liberal-progressive reform) and *al-tajdīd al-thawry* (revolutionary renewal) in the context of Tahrir's January 2011 Uprising, the (counter) revolutionary outcomes of Mohammad Mahmoud Street, and the June 2013 revolt that ousted the Muslim Brotherhood, which can debunk the illusion of choice between military dictatorships based on neoconservative statist-Islamist rule or blind emulation of liberal democracies in Euro-America.

This book seeks to affirm genuine solidarity; similarly, the so-called Euro-American Left needs to reconceptualize its relation to BIPOC beyond a politics of guilt, rights, and pity. We need to learn to locate the oppressor within us and to un-learn abuse through decolonization. Muslim anarchists expose the problematics associated with the Euro-American Orientalized fetishization of nonviolence, with geopolitical Euro-American complicity, and responsibility in settler-colonial societies. Anarchic Ijtihād attempts to redress the fetish of reformist resistance by emphasizing how "complicity has indeed led to a reification of the polarity of the two terms."[23]

Euro-America has succeeded in geopolitically infantilizing Muslims as opposed to radicalizing them. Euro-America has built a manufacturing plant of neoreactionary Wahhābi-terrorists. Muslims are now fated to forever perceive "life and death through a looking glass, darkly," as their identities are fragmented along the dividing "wall that separates childhood from adulthood, innocence from guilt."[24] As Robert Fisk put it (in a piece titled "Isis Has Not Radicalised Young Muslims, It Has Infantilised Them – and That Is Why It Is so Powerful and Dangerous"), there exist innumerable accounts of internally conflicted parents, who in this new age of ISIS and al-Qaeda, have become child-man murderers instead of being "driven to remorse by the birth of their own children."[25] One need solely observe the disfigured hardening of Muslim hyper-masculinity (*murū'a* or *muruwwa*) in videotapes of children who have been transformed into "television terrorists" as they are recorded smiling while hacking away at prisoners' necks and limbs with a finely sharpened knife.[26] In this war to defeat ISIS, al-Qaeda, and others, the open Israeli treatment of wounded neo-Fundamentalist Muslim militants, strictly to return them to their battlefields in Iraq and Syria, is hardly analyzed or discussed. Premised on an analysis of over 40,000 war-items, arms-monitoring group Conflict Armament Research (CAR) determined that the majority of ISIS' weapons exceed those that were gained by warfront capture or as a consequence of the shifting of proxy alliances within the Syrian opposition, whether in terms of proliferated quantity and quality of arms.[27] Rather, the majority of combat munitions can directly be traced to Saudi Arabia, Israel, and the U.S., the last denoting the largest arms-dealer and ordinance manufacturer in the globe.[28]

The destructive legacy of liberalism is its offer of a shiny, whitewashed veneer of inclusion and pluralism, anchored in Euro-American exceptionalism and progress. In his article "On the Beach – The Beckoning of Nuclear War," John Pilger states that those who refer to themselves as liberals or "tendentiously 'the resistance' and 'the left' are eager participants in this manipulation, and its brainwashing, which today revert[s] to one name: an odious human being named, Donald J. Trump, the ultimate gift, as Luciana Bohne memorably wrote, for 'liberal brains pickled in the formaldehyde of identity politics'."[29] The obsession with "Trump – the man – not Trump as a symptom and caricature of an enduring system – beckons great danger" in a time in which the "glimpse of sanity, or simple pragmatism, is an anathema to 'national security' managers who guard a system based on war, surveillance, armaments, threats."[30] The Jerusalem Bill that was unanimously passed by a bipartisan vote in the U.S. Congress demonstrates that there is no fundamental difference on many issues between Social Democrats like Bernie Sanders and Republicans like Trump. The terms "left" and "right" are meaningless in a world where politics operates on a circular continuum and when liberal Democrats, and not conservatives, have provoked the majority of America's modern wars. Pilger reminds us that Obama not only oversaw

American's longest war, but an unprecedented campaign of extrajudicial murders by drones. It was Obama whose intervention during the "Arab Spring/Islamist Winter" triggered the flow of migrants into Europe, including the unprecedented Arab and North African Eastern Christian exodus from the so-called Middle East to Euro-America and Israel.[31]

A majority of Canadian/American mainstream Muslims adamantly maintain their settler-colonial, Euro-American identities, without acknowledging the contradictions with their Islamic theological social justice commitments. This exists despite innumerable clichéd depictions of sexually repressed Muslims' torturous suffering in Abu Ghraib and Guantanamo Bay (GITMO). This should not be surprising given the numerous instances in which even Muslim American conscripts in the U.S. military are subject to ongoing abuse. For example, Marine training recruits Ameer Bourmeche and Rekan Hawez recently accused Gunnery Sergeant Joseph Felix of torture.[32] Felix ordered Bourmeche and Hawez into industrial clothes dryers, which he then turned on, as he verbally addressed them as ISIS and terrorists.[33] Felix was found guilty of "'maltreatment' in his physical, mental, and verbal abuse of three American Muslims."[34] Since Felix's sentencing, the family of another Muslim American soldier, who fell 12m to his death, filed a $100 million civil lawsuit against the U.S. military.[35] This ostracization of diasporic Muslims who are tolerated, and not accepted, in Euro-America is also evident in how the FBI has a pattern of fabricating terror cases against Muslims.[36]

In this context, diasporic SWANA Muslims in Euro-America can no longer afford to neglect their responsibilities and duties to Indigenous peoples, or give in to fears and claim that we do "not know" and are not responsible for their genocidal plights. The Qur'ān states that a Muslim's responsibility is to pursue social justice. This is regarded as a personal obligation (*farḍ ʿayn*) as well as a collective duty (*farḍ kifāya*) to liberate and alleviate hardships (*rafʿ al-ḥaraj*) for all who are disenfranchised, "through enjoining what is right and forbid what is wrong."[37] After all, how can we, as complicit participants in upholding settler-colonialism in the Americas, otherwise claim to struggle for Palestine whose liberation ought to serve as the ethical-political compass that drives our activist mobilizations in relation to Indigenous peoples in Turtle Island. Newcomer Muslims cannot plead ignorance and elide Indigenous people's plight as wards of a settler-state, which as settlers-of-color we choose to sustain, as opposed to educating ourselves about and learning from their dignified resistance, whose lead we ought to follow.

In light of the fact that non-Indigenous Muslim POC in the diasporas participate in settler-colonialism, it must be understood that in Islām, "the Arabic term for migration is *hijra*, whose active participle is *muhajir* (migrant)."[38] Islām bears two interrelated "terms to hijra, *ghurba* (estranged) and *gharib* (stranger). The difference between *hijra* and *ghurba* is that *hijra* involves permanent relocation, whereas *ghurba* can be either permanent or temporary."[39] The early history of Islām is one of physical and spiritual migration. As noted in Chapter 5, Muslims during Islām's early period migrated twice due to persecution by members of their own families, including the polytheist elite Arab tribes of Quraysh. The first *hijra* was to Abyssinia (modern day Ethiopia), and the second *hijra* was to Medina.

Echoing the spirit of the Two Row Wampum or *Guswhenta* and *Kaswhenta* treaty, which emphasizes the embracing of a mutual responsibility and a positive desire to live an interdependent peaceful co-existence, the Muslim objective of migration during the *hijra* was to construct mutual reciprocal treaties and build alliances while in exile in Abyssinia and Medina between the *anṣār* (Medinian locals who support the migrants) and *muhājireen* (migrants).[40] Both the *anṣār* and *muhājireen* were required to learn to exercise patience, nourish their faith in God's deliverance, and partake in *al-jihād al-akbar* (the struggle against authoritarian, utilitarian-materialist, and patriarchal tendencies in one's self and one's community). The Qur'ān addresses migration and treaties, particularly with regards to those who are oppressed, in many verses, and states,

> Truly those who believe, and migrate, and strive with their wealth and themselves in the way of God, and those who shel-

> tered and helped – they are protectors of one another. As for those who believe and did not migrate, you owe them no protection until they migrate. But if they ask your help for the sake of religion, then help is a duty upon you, except against a people with whom you have a covenant.[41]

According to these verses, Allāh recognizes racial/ethnic and tribal differences, but also that every member of our species possesses a rightful liberty to ethically seek their *rizq* (secure provisions) beyond these tribal boundaries. Arguably, from an Islamic anarchistic perspective, striving for the "cause of God" in these verses implies adhering to ethical-political commitments to the people and land that Muslims migrate to, and appreciating pre-existing communities and nations. This is the opposite of the contemporary non-binding apologies by settlers and nation-states that are often issued "to salve the blemishes on the face of the U.S. liberal state" and often represents a justification for and serves as an alibi for the continued futurity of the settler-state.[42]

By reneging on our Islamic politico-spiritual responsibilities and migrants' role in decolonization, we become Zionists on stolen land and we expose our hypocritical fantasies of "freeing" Palestine. Supporting Indigenous causes is distinct from our obligations to Palestine, despite the Qur'ānic significance that *al-quds* (Jerusalem) bears in theological practice because it was the *Qiblah* (the first direction Muslims prayed to) prior to our realignment to Mecca's *Ka'bah* (House of Abraham). Honoring Palestine by recognizing our settler-colonial collusion as exiles in North America is vital because, in the absence of our commitment to cardinal Islamic commandments, we are no longer Muslim. In the Qur'ān, Allāh emphasizes the dual themes of "knowing the other" and "mutual aid against social injustices" – "we have made you unto different Shu'ūb (large tribes) and Qa'bā'il (smaller tribes) such that you may get to know one another" and "O you who believe! Be steadfast maintainers of justice, witnesses for God, though it be against yourselves, or your parents and kinsfolk, and whether it be someone rich or poor, for God is nearer unto both. So follow not your caprice, that you may act justly."[43]

Euro-American-arrivant Muslims must understand that Indigenous peoples in Canada continue to be exposed to mock commissions and unheeded calls for national inquiries, despite the false apologies such as the one for the many missing and murdered Indigenous women and girls.[44] In the U.S./Canada, Indigenous peoples have been forced to adopt Euro-American Christianity and banned from partaking in ceremonial potlatches (a communitarian act of sharing food and wealth, that non-native colonists and missionaries perceived to be excessive and wasteful). Indigenous peoples struggle with high infant mortality and suicide rates (among the highest in the world), as well as shorter life expectancies and chronic impoverishment. Indigenous peoples in Canada endured a residential school system that involved approximately 150,000 Indigenous children, of whom at least 4000 died between the 1870s and 1996.[45] Indigenous peoples have undergone forced sterilization and "nutritional" and medical experiments as "test subjects." Indigenous children were abducted and removed from their birth-families and communities during the Sixties Scoop, and exposed to physical and sexual abuse; this persists today under child and social welfare systems and policies. They were dispossessed of their ancestral languages, spirituality, traditions, and heritage thereby severing their lineages and links to the land.

By seeking assimilation, arrivant SWANA Muslims contribute to what continues to be an unacknowledged genocide that is prolonged by the rejection of Indigenous rights to sovereignty and self-determination, beyond liberal reconciliatory efforts that merely constitute new forms of neocolonization.[46] The "greatness" of settler-colonial societies is founded on the continuing legacy of Indian reservation systems, colonial band councils, and, in Canada, on 1896 Indian Acts. By deploying blood-quantum logics, these Acts disrupted matrilineal kinship structures. All of this paved the way for the prevalent depraved epistemic and systematic racist construction of Indigenous peoples, in the settler psyches, as "dependent," "filthy," "lazy," and "living off of taxpayer monies."[47]

Our radical interventions, as arrivants, ought to confront these grave injustices (*maẓālim*), particularly given the intricate and interconnected racial links between their manifested application in Palestine and Turtle Island.[48] Palestine will not be free unless Black peoples in the U.S. are freed, and Indigenous land is repatriated and rematriated.[49]

By a similar token, it is critical to note diasporas seeking migration to Euro-America or who fetishize Israel as a "democratic nation," that the U.S. and Canada historically engaged in anti-Jewish acts during the Holocaust and their sole objective is to strategically maintain Israel's settler-colonial existence. This is because Israel assures and secures the U.S./Canada's own neo-imperial/neocolonial socio-political and economic interests. Similarly, Palestinians cannot forget the discriminatory humiliation they suffer at the hands of their Arab and Muslim neighbors, "not least of which is the Saudi clan of 20,000 princes and princesses," as well as Egyptian military regimes that are supported by a tawdry pillaging and ignorant intellectual class of thieves and for-hire propagandists, and who are one of the two principal jailers of Gazan Palestinians, "the largest concentration camp in the world."[50]

The age of Trump openly demonstrates how white supremacy and racist alt-right platforms can be simultaneously anti-Jewish and supportive of Zionism.[51] The U.S. and Canada's historical anti-Jewishness is part of a common history of the enslavement of Blacks, 1923 Chinese Exclusion Act, Tuskegee Trials, as well as a re-enactment of Japanese internment camps.[52] The protectorate contract between Zionist-Israel and an evangelical Euro-American Christianity is a utilitarian and strategic relationship of mutual conveniences. The goal of such an alignment is to usher in the Second Coming and the return of the Jewish Messiah, through an alliance between white supremacy and Zionism. Israel rests on the white-supremacist and Zionist-European control over meanings of Jewishness, far remote from other non-white and non-Zionist anarchistic horizons of Jewishness.[53]

In the absence of land-based alternatives to capitalist-states, actions such as Women's Marches, candle-light vigils, and the removal of statues of white racists are only symbolic. They are nothing but tokenized Tahrir-moments that essentialize women,

Black, and queer experiences based on assimilationist identity politics. They also lionize peaceful resistance and nonviolence, and empower settler-states and colonialism/imperialism. This fetishization of nonviolence persists in social movements despite critiques that show how nonviolence ultimately serves to pacify resistance, which is the reason that the Qurʾān permits in exceptional circumstances self-defense as an ethical-political tactic.[54] To preach nonviolence is to ignore America's psychosis regarding its ongoing genocidal past, homicidal present, and suicidal future.[55] Nonviolence ignores the daily violence that is visited on Black people who are routinely killed and, in death, subject to innuendos and slander.

We must connect the fires of our interrelated struggles. We must engage in decolonized education and construct liberatory spiritual frameworks to combat cisheteropatriarchy and establish gender-egalitarian spaces. Mobilizing Black, Brown, and Red peoples and allies in movements such as Black Lives Matter (BLM), No Dakota Pipeline Access (NoDaPL), and Tahrir, across and beyond tactically useful but strategically limited racial/ethnic, sexual, and gender-based identity politics is defeatist. We must situate our alliances within our entwined and fraught histories of struggles, responsibilities, solidarities, and accountabilities to each other by recognizing how U.S. internal settler-colonization is tied to imperialist military adventurism; the struggle for Black Lives and abolition must also mean aborting the United States Africa Command (AFRICOM) and not just the "progressive" demand to relabel ten local U.S. army bases named after confederate generals.[56] Mass mobilizations do not constitute a movement, as the experiences of Tahrir and the Orientalized Arab Spring/Islamist Winter have proven, in the absence of recognizing, as noted in Chapter 2, that there are Black, Brown, and Red skinned peoples with white masks. BIPOC must transcend their desire to assimilate into a white multicultural sphere and venture towards their collective construction of a pluriversal world, premised on the knowing and acceptance of each other as opposed to the mere toleration of each another. This anti-racist, feminist, anti-oppressive, anti-authoritarian, anti-material, and decolonial socially just pluriverse ought to be built on foundations that do not sterilize or appropriate spiritualties and cultures for ulterior neocolonialist ends. Nor should they be designed to reinforce the cisheteropatriarchal and xenophobic understandings of nation in our species' yearning for communitarian belongings. Liberation demands that social movements be vigilant in relation to all we have internalized of Machiavellian, Manichean, divide-and-conquer misconceptions and prejudices, on which tyranny, oppression, and white domination thrive. Founding this pluriversal world necessitates a *biodiverse strategy of resistance.*

Frantz Fanon states: "Decolonization does not take place unnoticed"; it is an ever-constant struggle.[57] Decolonization demands unsettling and dismantling our romanticized, pure, and superior sense of our own identities, histories, and indeed ourselves, with humility. Our liberation rests on the decolonial relations we establish in relation to each other, without harkening to whitewashed notions of our return to innocence and living off the land like anti-war hippies. Resurgence, political alliances, and decolonial coalition building demand constant self-reflection, face-to-face community building, and a distinction between morals and ethics. For example, morals such as the overarching principle "Thou shalt not kill" do not mean enslaved people do not have the ethical right to resist threats to their values, lands, and lives. However, as ethics are always dynamic, they are inextricably linked to intent and context. Liberation demands the development of an ethics of communal care, an ethics of conflict resolution or, as discussed in Chapter 3, what in Islām is referred to as *Uṣūl al-Ikhtilāf*, for mitigating our ethico-political differences, especially in light of the authoritarian egoistic tendencies that hinder local, regional, and transnational solidarities. Some traditions have already developed the non-statist ethical approaches necessary for mitigating disagreements in a community's social affairs (*mu'āmalāt*), be it composed of Muslims, non-Muslims, or both.[58] The Indigenous communities in Chiapas, Mexico, refer to this process as *positive conflict resolution.*[59]

In addition to an ethics of conflict resolution, liberation requires an ethics of hospitality, Islamically referred to as *Uṣūl al-Ḍiyāfa* (ethics of hospitality), to facilitate our re-knowing of one another as fragmented nations. The ethical-political practice I advocate for between Muslims and non-Muslims is one that builds on what Leela Gandhi, following Jacques Derrida, Jean Luc Nancy, and Maurice Blanchot, refers to as a *politics of friendship*.[60] *Uṣūl al-Ḍiyāfa* are the incentives that accompany a politics of friendship. Friendship is predicated on a paradoxical stance of unconditional hospitality that is at the same time conditional on the sharing of similar ethical-political, social justice commitments. This is similar to Richard Day's comment on the "need to guide our relations with other communities according to the interlocking ethico-political commitments of *groundless solidarity* and *infinite responsibility*" towards constructing "the coming communities."[61] In this sense, social movement actors should examine themselves to understand their positionality, identity, and subjectivity in relation to themselves and each other. These practices can facilitate the development of decolonial conceptualizations that enable healing and the renegotiating of socio-historical misconceptions, such that we may cultivate an ethics of humility and a politics of forgiveness that recognize the infinite responsibilities and compassionate accountability we must shoulder in relation to each other.[62]

This book seeks to stimulate the conversation and transcend the identitarian and non-identitarian debates regarding Islām and anarchism by examining their effects as signifiers. I strove to expose and trouble social movement trajectories that are entangled in dichotomous understandings of Islām and anarchism. The embodied collective experiences of Black, Indigenous, and people of colour, particularly those of children and women, can represent lived alternatives to cisheteronormative constructions of gender, political systems, and rules of dissent. These constructs refuse to replicate racial capitalism and cisheteropatriarchy in conformity with white Christian forms of monogamous lifelong marriage and Euro-American sexual prescriptions that introduce rigid colonial gender binaries in policy and practices within franchise- and settler-colonial societies. The Euro-American nation-state has always had a strong interest in assimilating racially gendered/sexualized bodies into Euro-American gender roles, and infusing our families with heteropatriarchy to ensure management and control. The result is the near erasure of queer genders and sexual practices in pre-colonial histories, as well as the confinement of women to the domestic spheres, and the ongoing criminalization of same-sex practitioners and women of color in urban, peripheral rural, and reserve spaces. Colonialism and imperialism have resulted in the confinement of men of color to the roles of patriarchal husbands and fathers, as men remain at the top of the pyramid, while women are placed in the middle, and nonconforming genders are at the bottom, if not completely disappeared through individual and systemic violence.

Self-determination, at a personal level, means the ability to choose how to identify one's experience, sovereignty over one's body, and respect for the decisions a person makes over their own lives. This is tied to our communities and process-centered modes of living that generate profoundly different grounded normative conceptualizations of nationhood and governmentality. Indeed, ones that are not based on enclosure, authoritarian power, and hierarchy, but rather are anchored in ways of knowing that come from land through practices relating to our modes of intelligence and hence that include water, air, fire, (sub)soils, plants, animals, and the spiritual world – a peopled cosmos of symbiotically mutually influencing powers. We must undertake a decolonial struggle until, in the Creator's good time, a reindigenized pluriversal Umma emerges to found a new world. Indeed, this world is drenched in seas of beautiful madness that are misunderstood yet worth dying for. Not the madness of asylums but the madness in each of us – a madness hidden – that starves and liberates – a madness of our own inner unsettling and undoing, indeed our own becoming. Affirm your nonbeing then, and *become* …

… There is no other way out.

Notes

Websites last accessed January, 2022.

1. Introduction: Panegyric Desert of the Present

1. Gilles Deleuze, quoted in Gilles Deleuze and Michel Foucault, *Intellectuals and Power* (1972), www.atlasofplaces.com/essays/intellectuals-and-power/.
2. J.A. Massad, *Islam in Liberalism* (Chicago: University of Chicago Press, 2015).
3. Salman Sayyid, *Recalling the Caliphate: Decolonization and World Order* (London: Hurst & Company, 2015), 7; also see Mehraj Bhat's article "Being a Muslim in the Modern World," https://medium.com/@bhat.mehraj7/being-a-muslim-in-the-modern-world-cd62d9e3960f.
4. W.E.B. Du Bois, *The Souls of Black Folks* (New York: Dover Publications, 1903), 2–3.
5. S.K. Hassan and Azeezah Kanji, "The Problem with Liberal Opposition to Islamophobia," *Roar Magazine*, 2017.
6. Ibid.
7. J.A. Byrd, *The Transit of Empire: Indigenous Critiques of Colonialism* (Minneapolis: University of Minnesota Press, 2011).
8. Madeline Farber, "Orlando Shooter's Employer Admits 'Clerical Error'," *Fortune* (2016). Mateen declared that the Pulse shooting was in specific retaliation to ISIS commander Abu Wahib's assassination in what represents one in over 28,353 coalition airstrikes and 102,082 bombs and missiles dropped by an over 60 nation coalition in Iraq, Syria, and Libya, excluding Yemen and Afghanistan, since Barack Hussein Obama, referred to ISIS as a Junior Varsity (JV) team in 2014. For a decade, Mateen's father was a secret FBI informant. Mateen was an employee of the world's grandest global security, paramilitary, and mercenary firm G4S that falsified thousands of psychological tests and forms in relation to Mateen and others, which it later attributed to a "clerical error" (ibid.). As a British corporation, G4S employs 610,000 ex-soldiers and operates in 110 countries, serving as an extension of America's military industrial complex. In fact, G4S has been endowed with nearly $830 million worth of federal, state, and local lucrative contracts, through the Department of Homeland Security, established by George H.W. Bush. G4S, like the controversial Blackwater – that was renamed Xe in 2009 and later Academi in 2011, and was formerly owned

by Trump's Education Secretary Betsy Devos' brother, Erik Prince – had been accused of extrajudicial murders and the mismanagement of two-dozen juvenile administrative detention centers for children aged between 12 and 17 and in other cases supervises facilities, as in Manus Island, Papa New Guinea, that house asylum Syrian, Iraqi, Sudanese, Iranian, Sri Lankan, Rohingya Muslims from Myanmar and Afghani seekers and refugees. G4S's international invisible army monitor and surveil airports, water and power plants, nuclear facilities, immigration, transportation, as well as gated communities, and offer clandestine support to militias in war-ravaged Third-World countries, as well as act as guardians to self-titled royal family members of oil and natural gas-Persian-Gulf nations. Furthermore, G4S, like Blackwater, provides security services, CCTV cameras, and screening equipment to Israel's Zionist courts and prisons, like Ofer and Ktzi'ot in the Negev Desert, that regularly incarcerate without trial, under suspended habeas corpus rights, occupied Palestinian political prisoners, youth and women, and subjects them to carefully chosen special means of psychological, mental, emotional, and physical torture like beating, slapping, screaming and forcing Palestinians to squat against a wall with their hands handcuffed for extended durations of time, in a vain attempt to break their defiant spirits.

9. Qwo-Li Driskill, Chris Finley, Brian Joseph Gilley, and Scott Lauria Morgensen, *Queer Indigenous Studies: Critical Interventions in Theory, Politics, and Literature* (Tucson: University of Arizona Press, 2011); David L. Eng, Judith Halberstam, and José Esteban Muñoz, "Introduction: What's Queer about Queer Studies Now?" *Social Text* 23, no. 3–4 (84–85) (2005); José Esteban Muñoz, *Disidentifications: Queers of Color and the Performance of Politics*, vol. 2 (Minneapolis: University of Minnesota Press, 1999); Roderick A. Ferguson, *Aberrations in Black: Toward a Queer of Color Critique* (Minneapolis: University of Minnesota Press, 2004); Martin F. Manalansan, "Queer Intersections: Sexuality and Gender in Migration Studies," *International Migration Review* 40, no. 1 (2006); Yasmin Nair, "Against Equality, against Marriage: An Introduction," in *Against Equality: Queer Critiques of Gay Marriage*, ed. Ryan Conrad (Oakland: AK Press, 2010), 1–9; Dean Spade and Craig Willse, *Marriage Will Never Set Us Free* (Manchester: Subversion Press, 2015).
10. Jasbir K. Puar, *Terrorist Assemblages: Homonationalism in Queer Times* (Durham, NC: Duke University Press, 2007), 58.
11. Shireen Hamza, "Hammams Then & Now: Changing Sites of Healing, Gathering, and Vulnerability," *The Revealer* (2018); Farīd al-Dīn 'Aṭṭār, *The Conference of the Birds*, trans. Dick Davis (London: Penguin, 1984); Elyse Semerdjian, "Naked Anxiety: Bathhouses, Nudity, and the Dhimmī Woman in 18th-Century Aleppo," *International Journal of Middle East Studies* 45, no. 4 (2013), 651–76; Srinivas Aravamudan, "Lady Mary

Wortley Montagu in the Hammam: Masquerade, Womanliness, and Levantinization," *ELH* 62, no. 1 (1995), 69–104; May Telmissany, Mayy Talmisānī, and Eve Gandossi, *The Last Hammams of Cairo: A Disappearing Bathhouse Culture* (Cairo: American University in Cairo Press, 2009); Shivananda Khan and Arif Jafar, "A Glimpse of the Beloved: Faith, Cultures and Sexualities – a Pilot Study on the Impact of Islamic Belief, Traditions and Customs on Muslim Males Who Have Sex with Males" (Naz Foundation International, 2004). Naguib Mahfouz in the novel *Children of Gebelawi* (Norwell: Anchor, 1996) illustrates the non-monolithic nature of gender in Islām through the concept of *fata* (meaning youth) and *futuwwa* (which refers to masculine traditions of medieval Muslim chivalry). One can also find classical texts such as that "of Salma and Suvad; the Book of Sawab and Surur (of Justice and Happiness); the Book of al-Dahma and Nisma (of the Dark One and the Gift from God)." There is also a new generation of Arab writers challenging non-binaric Arab and Muslim gender and sexual boundaries. As Joobin Bekhard's BBC article "The Ancient 'Arabic Karma Sutra'" (2017) notes, Leïla Marouane's *The Sexual Life of an Islamist in Paris* trans. from the French by Alison Anderson (New York: Europa Editions, 2010), "for instance, tells of the humorous misadventures of an Algerian virgin and his interrupted sexual encounters." Bekhard also points to how Ammar Abdulhamid's *Menstruation* (Saqi Books, 2001) "relates the story of the son of an imam with a unique olfactory talent who becomes embroiled in a racy affair with a married woman." Bekhard also indicates that "In 2005, *The Almond*, penned under the pseudonym 'Nedjma', was published and [...] was referred to at the time as the 'first erotic account written by an Arab woman.' And, while not necessarily falling under the umbrella of erotica, one can nonetheless point to classics replete with risqué moments like Tayeb Salih's *Season of Migration to the North* (1966), Turki al-Hamad's Hisham al-Abir trilogy of novels (banned in his native Saudi Arabia), and the autobiographical writings of Morocco's Mohamed Choukri, brimming with detailed passages about prostitutes and venereal diseases." Finally, Tantawi fails to acknowledge the vast complicated judicial legacy in addressing concerns relating to gender and sexual ethics in Islamic legal histories that have been betrothed to but neglected by Muslims, whether through Ali ibn Ahmad ibn Abi Talib (598–661 CE), Abu Muhammad 'Ali ibn Ahmad ibn Sa'id Ibn Hazim (994–1062 CE), Ibn Yusuf al-Juwayni (1028–85), Abu Hamid al-Ghazali (1058–1111 CE), Fakhr as-Din ar-Razi (1149–1209 CE), Najm ad-Din at-Tufi (1316 CE), Ibn Qayyim al-Jawziyyah (1229–1350 CE), Abu Ishaq ash-Shatibi (1388 CE), Jalal ad-Din al-Asyuti (1445–1505 CE), Muhammad 'Abduh (184–1905 CE), and Rashid Rida (1865–1935 CE). For Bekhard's BBC article: www.bbc.com/culture/article/20170725-the-ancient-arabic-kama-sutra.

12. Muslim anarchist and Islamic anarchist discourses, through what I refer to as *Anarcha-Islām* (an anarchistic, Qur'ānic non-authoritarian, non-capitalist, feminist, and social just interpretation of Islām, and Islamic interpretation of anarchism), explicitly argue that capitalist nation-states that are inherently cisheteropatrairchal, theologically, ethico-politically, contradict Qur'ānic Islamic communal non-authoritarian and non-capitalist governance concepts such as *Shūrā* (mutual consultation), *Ijmā* (mutual consensus), *Maṣlaḥa* (public welfare), *Muḍārabah/Mushārakah* (productive partnerships), and pluralistic, as opposed to singular, conceptualizations of *Khulafā* (caretakers), such that governance and leadership is embodied, acted, if not *remade* every day, vis-à-vis egalitarian practices related to deep reciprocity (*tabādul al-ḍiyāfa*), intimate practices (*hamīma* or *ulfa*). Moreover, Islamic anarchist discourses tend to argue for a global interdependence that spirals across and through space-time, and emergent from and responsive to networks of (non)human relationships. Also see my article "The Revolutionary Wonderings of Queer-Feminist Egyptians and Muslims" (forthcoming, *Feral Feminisms*, 2022).
13. Lisa Lowe, *The Intimacies of Four Continents* (Durham, NC: Duke University Press, 2015), 7.
14. Mark Rifkin, "Native Nationality and the Contemporary Queer: Tradition, Sexuality, and History in Drowning in Fire," *The American Indian Quarterly* 32, no. 4 (2008), 443–70; *When Did Indians Become Straight?: Kinship, the History of Sexuality, and Native Sovereignty* (New York: Oxford University Press, 2011); Joanne Barker, *Native Acts: Law, Recognition, and Cultural Authenticity* (Durham, NC: Duke University Press, 2011).
15. The legacy of Euro-American scientific racism through Tuskegee trials, eugenics, phrenology, forced sterilizations and more, against BIPOC, the disabled, and poor is well documented in the name of "objectivity." Margaret Kovach, *Indigenous Methodologies* (Toronto: University of Toronto Press, 2009); Linda Tuhiwai Smith, *Decolonizing Methodologies: Research and Indigenous Peoples* (London: Zed Books, 2013); Julian Carter and Vernon A. Rosario, *Science and Homosexualities* (London: Routledge, 1997).
16. C. Schmitt, *Political Theology: Four Chapters on the Concept of Sovereignty* (Chicago: University of Chicago Press, 1985), 36. Also see Saul Newman, *Max Stirner*, ed. Saul Newman (New York: Palgrave Macmilan, 2011), 6–7.
17. Cornel West, George J. Sefa Sei, bell hooks, Lata Mani, and Leela Fernandes have equally noted this vitality of the sacred. J.M. Alexander, *Pedagogies of Crossing: Meditations on Feminism, Sexual Politics, Memory, and the Sacred* (Durham, NC: Duke University Press, 2005), 15. Also see Natalie Avalos' "Taking a Critical Indigenous and Ethnic Studies Approach to Decolonizing Religious Studies," in *Contending Modernities*,

2020, https://contendingmodernities.nd.edu/decoloniality/critical-indigenous-approach/.

18. Michel Foucault, "A quoi rêvent les Iraniens," *Le Nouvel Observateur*, October 16, 1978, no. 726: 48–9. Translation from Didier Eribon's *Michel Foucault*, trans. Betsy Wing. Cambridge, MA: Harvard University Press, 1991: 285; J. Afary and K.B. Anderson, *Foucault, Gender, and the Iranian Revolution: The Seductions of Islamism* (Chicago: University of Chicago Press, 2005).
19. Zaheer Kazmi, "The Limits of Muslim Liberalism," *Los Angeles Review of Books* (2014).
20. Ibid.
21. General examples of liberal Euro-American Muslims include: former Omani Ambassador to the United States, Sadek Jawad Sulaiman, Tariq Ramadan (grandson of the Muslim Brotherhood's founder, Sheikh Hassan Al-Banna), Washington Women's March organizer Linda Sarsour, Dalia Mogahed, Suhaib Webb, Mehdi Hasan, Reza Aslan, Khaled Beydoun, Zahra Billio, as well as "Rachid Ghannouchi … Bassam Tibi, Abdolkarim Soroush, Farid Esack, Asef Bayat, Omid Safi, and Abdullahi An-Na'im, Hamza Yusuf in the United States and Tim Winter in the United Kingdom, as well as 'de-radicalized' think-tankers such as Ed Husain and Maajid Nawaz, and a host of younger-generation Muslim academics and civil society advocates" (Kazmi, "The Limits of Muslim Liberalism"). Other contemorary liberal Muslim scholars include: Abdullah Ahmad An-Naim, Abdolkarim Souroush, Mahmoud Mohamed Taha, Muhammad Said al-Ashmawy, Fazlur Rahman, Muhammad Shahrur, Asghar Ali Engineer, Chandra Muzaffer, Subhi Mahmasani, Khaled Abou El-Fadl, and ample others.
22. M. Abdou, *Anarca-Islam*, Master's Thesis, Queen's University (2009); Muhammad Abduh, *The Theology of Unity*, trans. Ishaq Musa'ad and Kenneth Cragg (Petaling Jaya: (Islamic Book Trust, 2004); Muḥammad Abduh, Mustafā 'Abd-ar-Rāziq, and Bernard Michel, *Rissalat Al Tawhid* (Paris: Geuthner, 1965); Nikki R. Keddie, *An Islamic Response to Imperialism: Political and Religious Writings of Jamāl Ad-Dīn 'al-Afghānī* (University of California Press, Berkeley and Los Angeles, 1968); Habib Ali al-Jifri, *The Concept of Faith in Islam* (Amman: Royal Islamic Strategic Studies Centre, 2000).
23. Homonationalization shows that homosexual integration into a nation does not necessarily undermine society's heterosexual structure, and more critically patriarchy. In fact, it supports and conceals the sexist, classist, racist, and colonial/imperial citizenship axes and politics that structure the latter, while simultaneously rendering queer and religious as contradictory terms. Queer Muslims are only permitted to exist in the Orientalist fantasy of perversely sexualized terrorist corporeality that are already queer and improperly so because their queerness is

perceived as contradictory to Islām. Neoliberal understandings of queerness cast spiritual and religious queers as subjugated, sexually repressed (and repressive, rather than productive), as well as void of agency (reinscribing its own transgressiveness by comparison). Neoliberal queerness transforms non-heteronormative gender/sexual practices into a rationale for complicity with other identity norms, while concealing these violent complicities because religious and racial communities are always regarded as being "more homophobic than white mainstream communities are racist." Ongoing settler-colonization and global imperialism is sustained by both homonationalism (which domesticates and neutralizes queer communities to white settler-state authority) and cisheteropatriarchy (which preserves Victorian notions of nuclear family units, privatized routes of inheritance, and the individualist and commoditized ownership of land and nonhuman life). Pinkwashing is the particular manifestation of homonationalism in occupied Palestine. Puar, *Terrorist Assemblages*, 15.

24. The Red Nation, *The Red Deal: Indigenous Action to Save Our Earth*, http://therednation.org/wp-content/uploads/2020/04/Red-Deal_Part-I_End-The-Occupation-1.pdf.
25. Ibid., 67; Youssef M. Choueiri, "The Middle East: Colonialism, Islam and the Nation State," *Journal of Contemporary History* 37, no. 4 (2002), 649–63; "Arab Nationalism," in *The Routledge Handbook of Muslim-Jewish Relations*, ed. Josef Meri (New York: Routledge, 2016), 317–30.
26. www.gold.ac.uk/calendar/?id=12284. Other scholars like Ella Shohat and Ramón Grosfoguel.
27. See https://nikolehannahjones.com. Besides eliding Indigenous peoples and settler-colonialism, what Hannah-Jones' 1619 project also elides is that a third to a fifth of transatlantic slaves were Muslims from the Iberian peninsula, and hence the confluence of race and religion.
28. Ella Shohat, "Rethinking Jews and Muslims: Quincentennial Reflections," *Middle East Report* (Middle East Research and Information Project), Special Issue entitled "1492 + 500," vol. 178 (September–October, 1992), 25–9; Chan-Malik, Sylvia, *The Immanent Frame: Secularism, Religion, and the Public Sphere* (May 15, 2020), https://tif.ssrc.org/2020/05/15/race-chan-malik/.
29. Ella Shohat, *Staging the Quincentenary: The Middle East & The Americas*, Third Text, 6:21, 97.
30. Massad, *Islam in Liberalism*, 68.
31. Frantz Fanon, *Black Skin, White Masks*, trans. Richard Philcox (New York: Grove Press, 1967). First published 1952. Internalizing beliefs about European superiority and cultural hegemony, beyond colonial military, political, and economic domination, stripped Arabs and Muslims of their self-definition and self-determination.

32. Alice Speri, *Fear of a Black Homeland: The Strange Tale of the FBI's Fictional "Black* Identity *Extremism*," The Intercept, 2019; Alleen Brown, Will Parrish, and Alice Speri, *Leaked Documents Reveal Counterterrorism Tactics Used Standing Rock to Defeat Pipeline Insurgency*, The Intercept, 2017.
33. I read the Sunnah and *aḥādīth* that informs it as including the role of women scholars as *muḥaddithāt* (narrators) in Islām. See Mohammad Akram Nadwi, "Al-Muhaddithat: The Women Scholars in Islam" (London and Oxford: Interface Publications, 2007); Asma Barlas, "12 Women's Readings of the Qur'an," in *The Cambridge Companion to the Qur'*ān, ed. Jane McAuliffe (Cambridge: Cambridge University Presss, 2006), 255; Carolyn Rouse, *Engaged Surrender: African American Women and Islam* (Berkeley: University of California Press, 2004); S.D. Shaikh, "Transforming Feminisms: Islam, Women, and Gender Justice," in *Progressive Muslims: On Justice, Gender And Pluralism*, ed. Omid Safi (Oxford: Oneworld Publications, 2003), 147–62; O. Abou-Bakr, "To Be or Not to Be … a Muslim Feminist in the Arab (Islamic) Spring," *AMEWS E-Bulletin* 1, no.1–2 (2013), 1–2.
34. T. Al-Barghouti, *The Umma and the Dawla: The Nation State and the Arab Middle East* (London: Pluto Press, 2008), 66.
35. Ibid., 66.
36. Ibid.
37. Ibid., 43.
38. Ibid., 43.
39. Harsha Walia, *Undoing Border Imperialism* (Oakland, AK Press, 2013).
40. Numerous contemporary scholars rightly argue that zealot Muslim sectarianism in the contemporary is an exacerbated product of European colonial modernity, unlike during the early period of the Umma in which differences greatly enriched Muslims and non-Muslims alike notwithstanding strife that, also, nurtured maturity and growth.
41. Patricia Crone's "Ninth-Century Muslim Anarchists," *Past and Present*, no. 167 (May, 2000), 3–28. Published by Oxford University Press on behalf of The Past and Present Society, www.jstor.org/stable/651252?seq=1.
42. Ibid.
43. Ibid.
44. Tamim Al-Barghouti, "Kharijites: Early Muslim Rebels Espoused Democratic Principles," the *Daily Star*, www.dailystar.com.lb/Culture/Art/2004/Mar-15/91278-kharijites-early-muslim-rebels-espoused-democratic-principles.ashx
45. As the Qur'ān states, "Call to the way of your Lord with wisdom and goodly exhortation, and have disputations with them in the best manner; surely your Lord best knows those who go astray from His path, and He knows best those who follow the right way" (16:125). (This is a simplified citation to: Qur'ān, Chapter 16: Chapter of "The Bees," Verse: 125 and this format will be used henceforth.)

46. According to Arab and Islamic lexicons and etymologies, and as Khaled Adham notes, *thaqāfa* "comes from the verb *thaqaf* … which had two meanings for early Arabs. The first is the ability to understand complex matters, to be astute, shrewd, skillful, or clever. To say a person is a *muthaqaf* in something is to indicate that the person fathomed this thing, apprehended it, mastered it, or got to the bottom of the issue. The second meaning implied the act of refining, correcting, straightening, or sharpening the head of an arrow, spear, or sword. In both usages, *thaqaf* was a qualitative verb that depicted an event; it had an immaterial connotation. It did not refer to culture in the sense it is used today. In the present day, thaqāfa, the noun derived from the verb thaqaf, is popularly used to refer to the ideational, intellectual, intangible aspects of society's achievements in art and literature. As in English, thaqāfa refers to a general state of mind. It also carries the idea of perfection, as in "high-culture" ("Making or Shaking the State," *Cairo Cosmopolitan: Politics, Culture, and Urban Space in the New Globalized Middle East* (Cairo: American University in Cairo Press, 2006), 50.
47. Jason Michael Adams in his article "Postanarchism in a Nutsehll" (The Anarchist Library, 2003), https://theanarchistlibrary.org/library/jason-adams-postanarchism-in-a-nutshell.
48. Mikhail Bakunin, "God and the State," trans. Benjamin Tucker (New York: Mother Earth, 1916; Emma Goldman, "2012," in *Anarchism and Other Essays* (New York: Mother Earth Publishing, 1910) and *The Tragedy of Woman's Emancipation* (New York: Mother Earth Publishing, 1910); Pëtr Kropotkin, "Are Prisons Necessary?" in *Russian and French Prisons (1887)* (Montana: Kessinger Publishing, 2010); Peter Kropotkin, *Kropotkin: "The Conquest of Bread" and Other Writings* (New York: Cambridge University Press, 1995); *Mutual Aid: A Factor of Evolution* (Massachusetts: Courier Corporation, 2012); Petr Alekseevich Kropotkin, *Anarchist Communism, Its Basis and Principles* (London: "Freedom" Office, 1887); Gustav Landauer, *Revolution and Other Writings: A Political Reader* (Oakland: PM Press, 2010); Pierre-Joseph Proudhon, "What Is Property," trans. Benjamin Tucker (New York, Humboldt, 1840).
49. Adams writes of how he employs the terms "Western" and "non-Western" as follows: "By employing the label 'Western' I am not referring to the *actual* history of anarchism but rather to the way in which anarchism has been *constructed* through the multiple lenses of Marxism, capitalism, Eurocentrism and colonialism to be understood as such. This distorted, decontextualized and ahistoric anarchism with which we have now become familiar was constructed primarily by academics writing within the context of the core countries of the West: England, Germany, France, Italy, Spain, Canada, United States, Australia and New Zealand. Since there was virtually no real subversion of the Eurocentric understanding of anarchism until the 1990s, the vast

majority of literature available that purports to deliver an 'overview' of anarchism is written in such a way that one is led to believe that anarchism has existed solely within this context, and rarely, if ever, outside of it. Therefore, the anarchism that becomes widely known is that which has come to be identified with the West, despite its origins in the East; Kropotkin, Bakunin, Godwin, Stirner, and Goldman in first wave anarchism: Meltzer, Chomsky, Zerzan, and Bookchin in second and third wave anarchism. Rarely are such seminal first wave figures as Shifu, Atabekian, Magon, Shuzo, or Glasse even mentioned; a similar fate is meted out for such second and third wave figures such as Narayan, Mbah, and Fernandez – all of non-Western origin." See www.geocities.com/ringfingers/nonwesternweb.html.

50. Ashanti Alston, "Towards a Vibrant and Broad African-Based Anarchism" (Anarchist Library, 2003), https://theanarchistlibrary.org/library/ashanti-alston-towards-a-vibrant-broad-african-based-anarchism; Frank Fernández, *Cuban Anarchism: The History of a Movement* (See Sharp Press, 2014); Landauer, *Revolution and Other Writings*; Sam Mbah and Chaz Bufe, *African Anarchism*, trans. Charles Bufe (Tuscon: See Sharp Press, 2014); John Zerzan, *Elements of Refusal* (Seattle: Left Bank Books, 1988); T. Alfred, *Wasase: Indigenous Pathways of Action and Freedom* (Toronto: University of Toronto Press, 2005); Fiscella, "Imagining an Islamic Anarchism: A New Field of Study Is Ploughed," in *Religious Anarchism: New Perspectives*, ed. Alexandre J.M.E. Christoyannopoulos (London: Cambridge Scholars Publishing, 2009), 280–317; I. Khuri-Makdisi, *The Eastern Mediterranean and the Making of Global Radicalism, 1860–1914* (Berkeley, University of California Press, 2010).

51. The particularity of uniquely molding anarchism is accomplished by these individuals and communities, while generally attempting to preserve anarchism's anti-authoritarian and anti-capitalist tenants, in so far as the two commitments are understood to be the foundations upon which classical anarchism was grounded. J. Heckert, "Sexuality as State-Form," in *Post-Anarchism: A Reader*, ed. D. Rousselle and S. Evren (Ann Arbor and London: Pluto Press, 2011), 195–207; A. Alston, "North American First Peoples: Slipping up into Market Citizenship?" *Citizenship Studies* 8, no. 4 (2004), 349–65; Lorenzo Kom'boa Ervin, "Black Capitalism" (Anarchist Library, 2001), https://theanarchistlibrary.org/library/lorenzo-kom-boa-ervin-black-capitalism; S. Jeppesen, "Queer Anarchist Autonomous Zones and Publics: Direct Action Vomiting against Homonormative Consumerism," *Sexualities* 13, no. 4 (2010), 463–78; Allan Antliff, *Only a Beginning; an Anarchist Anthology* (Vancouver: Arsenal Pulp Press, 2004); Daniel Colson, *A Little Philosophical Lexicon of Anarchism from Proudhon to Deleuze* trans. Jesse Cohn, (London: Minor Compositions, 2018); S. Newman, *From Bakunin to Lacan: Anti-Authoritarianism and the Dislocation of Power*, (Minneapolis: Lexington

Books, 2001); Kolářová, Marta. "Sexuality Issues in the Czech Anarchist Movement," in *Anarchism & Sexuality: Ethics, Relationships and Power*, ed. J. Hecker and R. Cleminson (London: Routledge, 2011), 185–99; Arif Dirlik, *Anarchism in the Chinese* Revolution (Berkeley and Los Angeles: University of California Press, 1991).

52. In the future, and upon discovering the "new" commitments, these commitments are to be included, at minimum, with the two commitments that will have been pre-established for Anarcha-Islām in this book.
53. Mohammed A. Bamyeh, "Anarchist Philosophy, Civic Traditions and the Culture of Arab Revolutions 1," *Middle East Journal of Culture and Communication* 5, no. 1 (2012), 32–41; Harold Barclay, "Islam, Muslim Societies and Anarchy," *Anarchist Studies* 10, no. 2 (2002), 105–18; Patricia Crone and Martin Hinds, *God's Caliph: Religious Authority in the First Centuries of Islam*, vol. 37 (Cambridge: Cambridge University Press, 2003); Heba Raouf Ezzat, interview by Rosemary Bechler (Open Democracy, 2005), www.opendemocracy.net/en/article_2497jsp/; H.R. Ezzat, "The Umma: From Global Civil Society to Global Public Sphere," in *Bottom-up Politics*, ed. D. Kostovicova and M. Glasius (New York: Springer, 2011), 40–9; Anthony Gorman, "Anarchists in Education: The Free Popular University in Egypt (1901)," *Middle Eastern Studies* 41, no. 3 (2005), 303–20; Ahmet T. Karamustafa, *God's Unruly Friends: Dervish Groups in the Islamic Later Middle Period, 1200–1550* (Salt Lake City: University of Utah Press, 1994).
54. Part and parcel of thaqāfa include(s): "different bodies of philosophical, theological, jurisprudential, medical, literary, and scientific works, as well as to culinary, sexual, social, economic, religious, ritualistic, scholarly, agricultural, and urban practices engaged in by Muslims from the seventh to the nineteenth century and beyond, as well as much, much more." See Joseph Massad's interview with Jadaliyya, titled "New Texts Out Now: Joseph A. Massad, Islam in Liberalism," www.jadaliyya.com/Details/31871. Moreover, for an expanded discussion of the concept of *turāth*, see Joseph Massad's *Desiring Arabs* (Chicago: University of Chicago Press, 2008). For further discussions on amorphous Orientalist discussions of Islām and its Euro-American ambiguous reference see Joseph Massad, "Psychoanalysis, Islam, and the Other of Liberalism," *Psychoanalysis and History* 11, no. 2 (2009), 71.
55. Mohamed Jean Veneuse, *Transnational Decolonization Is the Solution, Not Movements Such as Bernie Sanders' and the Women's March*, https://theanarchistlibrary.org/library/mohamed-jean-veneuse-transnational-decolonization-is-the-solution-not-movements-as-bernie-sande.
56. Afary and Anderson, *Foucault, Gender, and the Iranian Revolution*, 38–40.
57. A. Al-Azmeh, *Islams and Modernities* (London: Verso, 1993), 1.

58. Asef Bayat, "A New Arab Street in Post-Islamist Times," *Foreign Policy* (2011), https://foreignpolicy.com/2011/01/26/a-new-arab-street-in-post-islamist-times/.
59. Olivier Roy, *Globalized Islam: The Search for a New Umma* (New York: Columbia University Press, 2006), 10.
60. Allāh, Qur'ān, 15:9, emphasis added.
61. Taha Jabir Al'Alwani, *The Ethics of Disagreements in Islam* (Herndon, VA: International Institute for Islamic Thought, 1993), 2; J.P. Piscatori, *Islam in a World of Nation-States* (Cambridge: Cambridge University Press, 1986), 105; Larbi Sidiki, *The Search for Arab Democracy: Discourses and Counter-Discourses* (New York: Columbia University Press, 2004).
62. Piscatori, *Islam in a World of Nation-States*, 106.
63. Fazlur Rahman, *Islam & Modernity: Transformation of an Intellectual Tradition* (Chicago: University of Chicago Press, 1982), 140.
64. Guy Burak, "The Second Formation of Islamic Law: The Post-Mongol Context of the Ottoman Adoption of a School of Law," *Comparative Studies in Society and History* 55 no. 3 (2013), 579–602; Khaled Fahmy, *In Quest of Justice: Islamic Law and Forensic Medicine in Modern Egypt* (Oakland: University of California Press, 2018); Rudolph Peters, *Shari'a, Justice and Legal Order: Egyptian and Islamic Law: Selected Essays*, Studies in Islamic Law and Society, vol. 51 (Leiden; Boston: Brill, 2020); Liat Kozma, *Policing Egyptian Women: Sex, Law and Medicine in Egypt 1850–1882* (New York: Syracuse University Press, 2011).
65. Muñoz, *Disidentifications*; M. Cobb, D.L. Eng, J. Halberstam, and J.E. Muñoz, "Introduction: What's Queer about Queer Studies Now?" *Social Text* 23, no. 3–4 (84–85) (2005).
66. Gayatri Chakravorty Spivak, "The Politics of Translation," *Outside the Teaching Machine* (New York: Routledge, 1993). As Spivak writes, "If you are making anything else accessible [when translating], through a language quickly learned with an idea that you transfer content, then you are betraying the text and showing rather dubious politics" (191).
67. Gayatari Spivak, quoted in Massad, *Colonial Effects: The Making of National Identity in Jordan* (New York: Columbia University Press, 2012), 121; *Islam in Liberalism*, 244.
68. Massad, *Islam in Liberalism*, 241.
69. Some of the scholarship addressing these material and symbolic relations include: Steven Salaita, *The Holy Land in Transit: Colonialism and the Quest for Canaan* (New York: Syracuse University Press, 2006); *Inter/Nationalism: Decolonizing Native America and Palestine* (Minneapolis: University of Minnesota Press, 2016); David Lloyd, "Settler Colonialism and the State of Exception: The Example of Palestine/Israel," *Settler Colonial Studies* 2, no. 1 (2012), 59–80; Omar Jabary Salamanca, Mezna Qato, Kareem Rabie and Sobhi Samour, "Past Is Present: Settler Colonialism in Palestine, " *Settler Colonial Studies* 2 no. 1 (2012), 1–8;

Collected Edition, "Settler-Colonialism," *Settler Colonial Studies* vols 1–8 (2011–18); Mike Krebs and Dana M. Olwan, "'From Jerusalem to the Grand River, Our Struggles Are One': Challenging Canadian and Israeli Settler Colonialism," *Settler Colonial Studies* 2, no. 2 (2012), 138–64; Dana M. Olwan, "On Assumptive Solidarities in Comparative Settler Colonialisms," *Feral Feminisms* 4 (2015), 89–102.

70. Taiaiake Alfred and Jeff Corntassel, "Being Indigenous: Resurgences against Contemporary Colonialism," *Government and Opposition* 40, no. 4 (2005), 597–614; Adam J. Barker, "'A Direct Act of Resurgence, a Direct Act of Sovereignty': Reflections on Idle No More, Indigenous Activism, and Canadian Settler Colonialism," *Globalizations* 12, no. 1 (2015), 43–65; Jeff Corntassel, "Re-envisioning Resurgence: Indigenous Pathways to Decolonization and Sustainable Self-Determination," *Decolonization: Indigeneity, Education & Society* 1, no. 1 (2012), 86–101; Leanne Simpson, *Lighting the Eighth Fire: The Liberation, Resurgence, and Protection of Indigenous Nations* (Winnipeg: Arbeiter Ring Pubishers, 2008); Angela Cavender Wilson and Michael Yellow Bird, *For Indigenous Eyes Only: A Decolonization Handbook* (Santa Fe: School of American Research, 2005).

71. Steven Salaita, *Arab American Literary Fictions, Cultures, and Politics* (New York: Springer, 2006); *Inter/Nationalism*.

72. See Prado's website for details on his scholarship, and works here: http://abdennurprado.wordpress.com; for Yakub Islam, www.tasneemproject.info/manarchist.htm; for information on the nineteenth century anarchist Josset and Rafanelli, who was a contemporary of Emma Goldman, see Fiscella, "Imagining an Islamic Anarchism: A New Field of Study is Ploughed," in *Religious Anarchism: New Perspectives*, ed. Alexandre J.M.E. Christoyannopoulos (Cambridge: Cambridge Scholars Publishing, 2009), 280–317; also see Leda Rafanelli, *I Belong Only to Myself: The Life and Writings of Leda Rafanelli*, ed. Andrea Pakieser (Oakland, AK Press, 2014); also see Bas Moreel, *Religious Anarchism and Criticism of Religion*, www.geocitiescom/christianarchy/basmoreel7htm.

73. Other examples of Muslim anarchist participation in new social movements include the Bay Area's Intifada: http://bayareaintifada.wordpress.com. Of course, there are ample other "Muslim anarchists" from Doaa Eladl, a 34-year-old Egyptian woman and cartoonist whose works appeared in prominent newspapers such as *Al-Masry Al-Yuom*. For information on Eladl, see "Meet the 'Muslim Anarchist' Whose Cartoons Are Driving Fundamentalists in Egypt Crazy": http://news.infoshop.org/article.php?story=20130331140548132. Please also see anarchist websites/blogs based in the Middle East and anarchist organizations in predominantly Muslim countries at the end of this note. Furthermore, a quick search on Muslim anarchists reveals others such as Davi Barker, a self-described Muslim agorist and voluntary

anarchist (see www.muslimagorist.com) to self-titled Salafi Muslim anarchist websites such as: https://themuslimanarchist.wordpress.com/about/. Accessing these sites, and especially the correspondences, over the course of a decade, be it with participants and organizers in the Global North and South, demonstrates not only a keen interest but also a desire, particularly on behalf of Muslims, to reconcile these identities. A pamphlet/zine titled "Varieties of Islamic Anarchism" (www.alpineanarchist.org/about/Islamic_Anarchism_Zine.pdf) written by Anthony Fiscella, neither a self-identifying Muslim nor anarchist, was even composed and circulated widely over the course of the years. It provides a wonderful summary of the different scholarships surrounding the topic. Other examples include websites such as Al-Rua'a/Visions: www.ru-a.org/2009/11/rua-program-english.html. And we should not forget scholars such as Heba Raouf Ezzat, Mohammed Bamyeh, and Ilham Khuri Makdisi or even Zaheer Kazmi who have written or touched on the topic, particularly in so far as anarchism's relation to Muslims and Arabs.

Anarchist Websites/Blogs Based in the Middle East:

https://tahriricn.wordpress.com (Tahrir ICN Anarchist news in Muslim regions)

www.organizedrage.com/2012/05/turkish-muslim-anti-capitalists.html (New Turks)

www.anarkismo.net/article/19880 (Interview with Malaysian anarchists)

http://anarchiststudies.org/2013/07/19/ (Palestinian Anarchists in Conversation)

http://anarchisminarabic.blogspot.se (Anarchist ideas in Arabic)

http://tarekshalaby.com (Revolutionary socialist/horizontalist Tarek Shalaby's blog)

http://she2i2.blogspot.se (Jano Charbel's anarchist blog from Cairo)

www.ahewar.org/m.asp?i=1385 (Syrian anarchist blog in Arabic)

http://libcom.org/library/anarchism-indonesia (Interview with Indonesian anarchist)

http://nefac.net/node/2541 (Interview with Nidal Tahrir from Black Flag in Egypt)

http://nefac.net/node/1731 (Interview with an Iranian anarchist)

Anarchist Organizations in Predominantly Muslim Countries:

www.cgtandalucia.org/Norte-de-Africa (North African syndicalists – in Spanish)

www.anarkismo.net/article/19666 (Egypt's Libertarian Socialist Movement)

www.struggle.ws/africa/aware.html (Anarchist Awareness League in Nigeria)

www.anarkismo.net/article/22396 (Interview w/ Kurdish Anarchist Forum)
www.antikapitalistmuslumanlar.org ("Anti-Capitalist Muslim Youth" in Turkish)
http://anarchism-jordan.blogspot.se (the Jordanian anarchists)
http://flag.blackened.net/revolt/inter/albadil.html (Anarchists in Lebanon)
http://negasi-negasi.blogspot.se or http://membakarsenja.noblogs.org (Indonesian anarchists).

74. Fiscella, "Imagining an Islamic Anarchism."
75. Richard Day, *Gramsci Is Dead: Anarchist Currents in the Newest Social Movements* (London: Pluto Press, 2005), 9; Richard Day, "Can There Be a Postcolonial Multiculturalism? A Response to Lan Angus," *International Journal of Canadian Studies/Revue internationale d'*études canadiennes, no. 26 (2002), 127–32.
76. Day, *Gramsci Is Dead*, 9.
77. *Ikhtilāf* is "the Arabic term ... [meaning] taking a different position or course from that of another person either in opinion, utterance, or action" (Al'Alwani, *The Ethics of Disagreements in Islam* (Herndon, VA : International Institute for Islamic Thought, 1993), 11. Ikhtilāf is from "the related word *khilaf* ... from the same root ... sometimes used synonymously with [Ikhtilāf] ... mean[ing] difference, disagreement, or even conflict broader in meaning and implication than the concept of direct opposition ... because two opposites are necessarily different from each other whereas two things, ideas, or persons that differ are not necessarily opposed to or in conflict with each other" (p. 11).
78. Edward S. Herman and Noam Chomsky, *Manufacturing Consent: The Political Economy of the Mass Media* (London: Vintage, 1988), 306.
79. Ali al-Arian, *Insiders, Outsiders, and the Ice Cream Politics of American Muslims* (Medium, 2019), https://medium.com/@alialarian/insiders-outsiders-and-the-ice-cream-politics-of-muslim-americans-6e46707a80c9.
80. As I noted elsewhere, the irony of movements as the Women's March is that their "resistance" manifests on stolen land as they are surrounded by anti-Black trigger-happy catching cops. They are premised "on bleached notions of non-violence, gay marriage, [homonationalist] coming out narratives, pride, and shame." See Mohamed Abdou, "Let Empire Collapse: Why We Need a Decolonial Revolution," *Roar Magazine* (November 2, 2020), https://roarmag.org/essays/let-empire-collapse-why-we-need-a-decolonial-revolution/.
81. G. Deleuze and F. Guattari, *A Thousand Plateaus: Capitalism and* Schizophrenia, trans. Brian Massumi (Minneapolis: University of Minnesota Press, 1988), 205.
82. Ibid., 224.
83. Qur'ān, 2:26.

84. Newman, *From Bakunin to Lacan*, 6.
85. Al-Barghouti, *The Umma and the Dawla*.
86. G. Agamben, *State of Exception* (Chicago: University of Chicago Press, 2005), 2, 52–5.
87. Frantz Fanon, "Concerning Violence," in *The Wretched of the Earth*, trans. Constance Farrington (New York: Grove/Atlantic, 1961), 94.

2. Authoritarianism, Capitalism, and Capitalist Nation-States: Anarcha-Islām's Playground and Ethical-Political Consciousness

1. bell hooks, "bell hooks and John Perry Barlow Talk 'Prana in Cyberspace'," in *Lion's Roar: Buddhist Wisdom for Our Time* (2018), www.lionsroar.com/bell-hooks-talks-to-john-perry-barlow/.
2. E. Tuck and K.W. Yang. "Decolonization Is Not a Metaphor." *Decolonization: Indigeneity, Education & Society* 1 no. 1 (2012), 1–40.
3. G. Deleuze and F. Guattari, *A Thousand Plateaus: Capitalism and Schizophrenia* (London: Bloomsbury Publishing, 1988), 214–15.
4. Ibid., 214–15.
5. Mohamed Abdou, "Let Empire Collapse: Why We Need a Decolonial Revolution," *ROAR Magazine* (November 2, 2020), https://roarmag.org/essays/let-empire-collapse-why-we-need-a-decolonial-revolution/.
6. Ibid.
7. Ibid.
8. Ibid.
9. Ibid.
10. Richard J.F. Day, *Gramsci Is Dead: Anarchist Currents in the Newest Social Movements* (London: Pluto Press, 2005).
11. Ibid., 14.
12. Ibid., 127.
13. Philip J. Deloria, *Playing Indian* (New Haven, Yale University Press, 1988); Robert Allen Warrior, *Tribal Secrets: Recovering American Indian Intellectual Traditions* (Minneapolis: University of Minnesota Press, 1995).
14. Ben Pitcher and Henriette Gunkel, "Q&A with Jasbir Puar [Interview]," *Dark Matter: In the Ruins of Imperial Culture* (2008). In the interview, Puar also notes how "Surveillance technologies and related bioinformatic economies – DNA encoding and species preservation, stem-cell research, digitization, biometrics, life logging capacity, GPS, whose role includes increasing the contact zones and points of interface between bodies and their beyond – force all sorts of questions about bodies and their materialities."

15. Regarding this idea of spatial-temporal evictions, see Juliana Hu Pegues, *Space-Time Colonialism: Alaska's Indigenous and Asian Entanglements* (Chapel Hill: University of North Carolina Press, 2021).
16. Jeannette C. Armstrong, *Slash* (Penticton, BC: Theytus Books, 1988); Robert Lovelace, "Decolonization: The Fundamental Struggle for Liberation," *Rabble* (2013); Jodi A. Byrd and Michael Rothberg, "Between Subalternity and Indigeneity: Critical Categories for Postcolonial Studies," *Interventions* 13, no. 1 (2011), 1–12.
17. Danielle Sandhu, *Theorizing Brown Identity* (Toronto: University of Toronto Press, 2014), 18.
18. Scott Lauria Morgensen, "White Settlers and Indigenous Solidarity: Confronting White Supremacy, Answering Decolonial Alliances," in *Decolonization: Indigeneity, Education & Society* 26 (2014), https://decolonization.wordpress.com/2014/05/26/white-settlers-and-indigenous-solidarity-confronting-white-supremacy-answering-decolonial-alliances/.
19. Tuck and Yang, "Decolonization Is Not a Metaphor," 25.
20. Regarding the necessity for decolonizing leftist, humanist, feminist, and anti-racist research frameworks, also see Linda Tuhiwai Smith, *Decolonizing Methodologies: Research and Indigenous Peoples* (London: Zed Books, 2013).
21. When deployed in the U.S./Canadian context, I use the term "Indigenous" to refer to the descendants of those who traditionally occupied the territory now known as U.S./Canada before the arrival of European settlers and powers. At a more general level, I use the term "native" in an international context to refer to those in Euro-American and non-Euro-American societies that have also suffered the weight of European colonialism and whose claims to specific territories have been historically defined by particular geographic terrains.
22. Audre Lorde, "The Master's Tools Will Never Dismantle the Master's House," in *Sister Outsider: Essays and Speeches by Audre Lorde* (Berkeley: The Crossing Press Feminist Series, 1984), 110–13.
23. bell hooks, "Theory as Liberatory Practice," *Yale Journal of Feminism* 4 (1991), 1; Michel Foucault and Gilles Deleuze, "Intellectuals and Power," *Language, Counter-Memory, Practice: Selected Essays and Interviews* (New York: Cornell University Press, 1977), 205–9.
24. Asef Bayat, "The Coming of a Post-Islamist Society," *Critique: Critical Middle Eastern Studies* 5 no. 45–6.
25. I use the term "Islamist" as opposed to "Islamic" to define these movements given that an "Islamic" characterization is contingent on movements abiding by particular ethico-political commitment identified here. See Dokhanchi, M. (2020). "Post-Islamism Redefined: Towards a politics of post-Islamism" in *Journal of the Contemporary Study of Islam*, *1*(1), 28–54.

26. J.L. Esposito, *What Everyone Needs to Know about Islam* (New York: Oxford University Press, 2002), 159.
27. Taha Jabir Al'Alwani, *The Ethics of Disagreement in Islam* (Herndon, VA: International Institute of Islamic Thought (IIIT), 2015), 25; Taha Jabir Al'Alwani, *Ijtihād*, vol. 4 (Herndon, VA: International Institute of Islamic Thought (IIIT), 1993); J.P. Piscatori, *Islam in a World of Nation-States* (Cambridge: Cambridge University Press), 1; Tariq Ramadan, *Radical Reform* (Oxford: Oxford University Press, 2008); Wael B. Hallaq, "Was the Gate of Ijtihād Closed?" *International Journal of Middle East Studies* 16, no. 1 (1984), 3–41; "From Fatwās to Furū: Growth and Change in Islamic Substantive Law," *Islamic Law and Society* 1, no. 1 (1994), 29–65; *The Origins and Evolution of Islamic Law*, vol. 1 (Cambridge University Press, 2005); Khaled Abou El Fadl, *Reasoning with God: Reclaiming Shari 'Ah in the Modern Age* (Lanham: Rowman & Littlefield, 2014); Zakia Salime, "Mobilizing Muslim Women: Multiple Voices, the Sharia, and the State," *Comparative Studies of South Asia, Africa and the Middle East* 28, no. 1 (2008), 200–11.
28. Piscatori, *Islam in a World of Nation-States*, 1, 3; Al-Alwani, *Ijtihād*, 4; Al'Alwani, *The Ethics of Disagreement in Islam*; Ramadan, *Radical Reform.*
29. Piscatori, *Islam in a World of Nation-States*, 1, 5–17; H. Corbin, *History of Islamic Philosophy* (New York: Routledge, 2014).
30. M. Alipour, "Islamic Shari'a Law, Neotraditionalist Muslim Scholars and Transgender Sex-Reassignment Surgery: A Case Study of Ayatollah Khomeini's and Sheikh Al-Tantawi's Fatwas," *International Journal of Transgenderism* 18, no. 1 (2017), 91–103.
31. Ibid.; Hallaq, "From Fatwās to Furū"; *The Impossible State: Islam, Politics, and Modernity's Moral Predicament* (New York: Columbia University Press, 2014).
32. Eugene B. Young, *The Deleuze and Guattari Dictionary* (Edinburgh: A&C Black, 2013), 111; Deleuze and Guattari, *A Thousand Plateaus*; Spinoza, *Ethics*, ed. James Gutmann (New York: Hafner Publishing Company, 1949). On the one hand, morality involves "universalized imperatives (*kulliyyat*)" that are often grounded in a transcendental ideal (that is, an inaccessible) law that people may blindly follow, and on the other hand, "*ethics* involves *capacity* or power" (ibid., 111). Ethics is not centrally concerned with "essences, [as] it doesn't believe in essences, [given] it speaks to us only of power (puissance]" (ibid., 111). In other words, as Khaled Abou El Fadl notes, *fiqh* (ethical jurisprudence) relates to "not what the thing is, but what it is capable of supporting and capable of doing" and hence is concerned with the multiplicity of derivative particulars *(juz'iyyat*; singular *juz'i*) that acts as an integrated foundation for the universal ("The Epistemology of the Truth in Modern Islam," *Philosophy and Social Criticism* 41, no. 4–5 (2015), 473–86). Strictly focusing on moralistic approaches limits "the evolution of consciousness"

that exists because of the "reality of an ever creative and creating God" (ibid., 478). The constant flow between what is referred to as "*mawjudat* (existence) and *mukhluqat* (creation)" creates "contingencies and new realities that challenge the human consciousness … so that the equations that were sufficient to achieve wisdom [*hikma*] in one age become radically inadequate in a different age" (ibid., 479).

33. Qur'ān, 2:173.
34. Qur'ān, 2:286.
35. Abou El Fadl, "The Epistemology of the Truth in Modern Islam." Abou Fadl notes, if "the equations of *hikma* [wisdom] for one age" are "inadequate for another, you can then say this applies ten-fold or even a hundred-fold to" *maʿrifa* (ibid., 479).
36. Ibid.
37. Ibid.
38. Muhammad M. Khan, *Ṣaḥīḥ al-Bukhārī: The Translation of the Meanings of Sahih al-Bukhari: Arabic-English* (Riyadh-Saudi Arabia: Dar-us-Salam Publications, 1997), Book 1, Hadith Number: 4090.
39. Queer Muslim critique is first based on the understanding that a Euro-American modernist and instrumentalist notion of desire is attached to the word queer. Queer Muslims' lives and desires in Islam cannot be explained in this Eurocentric way. Second, queer Muslim critique is a subject and subject-less-based critique of queer theory's racial, (trans) national, and neoimperial/neocolonial formation that functions across both settler and franchise-colonial societies, given the way Islam and queerness act as global signifiers. Queer Muslim critique builds on and is an extension of a *Anarchic Ijtihād*.
40. On the concept of "Ghayb," see Kecia Ali and Oliver Leaman, *Islam: The Key Concepts* (London: Routledge, 2007); Alalwani, *The Ethics of Disagreement in Islam*; Louay Fatoohi, "The Concept of 'Ghayb' (Unseen) in the Qur'an," *Qur'anic Studies: Writings about the Qur'an, Islam, and Religion* (2010, www.quranicstudies.com/quran/the-concept-of-ghayb-unseen-in-the-quraṇ/. The Islamic concept of *al-ghayb* implies having faith in the unseen, hidden, invisible, and unknown and not just in what is seen prior to believing He neglects that *širk* (associating any entity with the Creator, including the worship of wealth, children, a country, nation, or authority figure) is a far graver sin than being gay, which is forgivable, even if one were to concede it a sin, because the former violates the creed of *Tawḥīd* (monthesitic unity).
41. Al-Alwani, *Ijtihad*, 27.
42. Ibid., 82.
43. Ibid., 82.
44. Peter Lamborn Wilson in a 2009 interview with Sean Haberle and myself as part of the Affinity project. See https://theanarchistlibrary.org/library/affinity-project-interview-with-peter-lamborn-wilson.

45. Larbi Sadiki, *The Search for Arab Democracy: Discourses and Counter-Discourses* (New York: Columbia University Press, 2004), 320–32.
46. The first and most important work to be written in this field is the *Kitāb al-bayān wa al-tabyīn* by al-Jāḥiẓ (ninth century). As Ibn Khaldūn later wrote in his Muqaddima, scholars classified the following works as the foundation of everything to do with this field of study, including literary theory, linguistic theories, literary criticism, grammar, philology: (1) *Kitāb al-bayān wa al-tabyīn* by al-Jāḥiẓ; (2) *Adab al-kātib* by Ibn Qutayba (a student of al-Jāḥiẓ); (3) *Kitāb al-kāmil* by al-Mubarrad (a student of al-Jāḥiẓ); (4) *Kitāb al-nawādir* by Abū ʿAlī al-Qālī. He wrote: "all other works after and apart from these four are secondary sources which draw upon them." There is consensus that *al-Jāḥiẓ's Kitāb al-bayān* is the first and most important and detailed work to be written on this subject. Though unfortunately unavailable in English also *Jalāl al-Dīn al-Suyūṭī's Kitāb al-Muzhir fi ʿulūm al-lugha* (the Luminous Work Concerning the Sciences of language). Also Imam al-Ghazali's: (1) Al-maqāṣid al-asnā (in so far as the chapter on ism (noun) and musammā (referent)). The former book was translated into English and published by Islamic Texts Society under the title: *Al-Ghazali on the Ninety-nine Beautiful Names of God: Al-Maqsad al-Asna fi Sharh Asma' Allah al-Husna*; (2) Al-Mustaṣfā (Professor Ebrahim Moosa is a specialist on this text). The chapter on the theological debates relating to "noun" and "referent" in Ibn Ḥazm's Kitāb *al-faṣl fi al-milal wa-al-ahwā' wa-al-niḥal*. Almost all key classical works of *uṣūl al-fiqh* have chapters dealing specifically with words and meanings. The following studies are also brilliant: *The Arabic Lexicographical Tradition: From the Second/Eighth to the Twelfth/18th Century*, by Ramzi Baalbaki; *The Arabic Linguistic Tradition*, by Georges Bohas, Jean-Patrick Guillaume, Djamel Eddine Kouloughli.
47. Allāh, Qur'ān, 15:9.
48. Allāh, Qur'ān, 56:77–80.
49. Michel Foucault, in Janet Afary and Kevin B. Anderson, *Foucault and the Iranian Revolution: Gender and the Seductions of Islamism* (Chicago: University of Chicago Press, 2005), 125; Foucault, in *Iraniha Che Roya'I dar Sar Darand?* Persian edition of the fall 1978 articles on Iran, trans. Hussein Ma'sumi Hamadani (Tehran: Hermes Press, 1998).
50. Tom Nairn, *The Break-up of Britain: Crisis and Neo-Nationalism* (Altona, Victoria: Common Ground, 2003), 347; B. Anderson, *Imagined Communities: Reflections on the Origin and Spread of Nationalism* (London: Verso, 2008); Anderson, Sharma, and Wright, "'We Are All Foreigners:' No Borders as a Practical Political Project," in *Citizenship, Migrant Activism and the Politics of Movement*, ed. P. Nyers and K. Rygiel, K. (New York: Routledge, 2012), 73–91; Eric Hobsbawm and Terence Ranger (eds), *The Invention of Tradition* (Cambridge: Cambridge University Press,

2012); Eric J. Hobsbawm, *Nations and Nationalism since 1780: Programme, Myth, Reality* (Cambridge: Cambridge University Press, 2012).

51. Ernest Gellner, *Thought and Change* (London: Weidenfeld and Nicholson, 1964); *Nations and Nationalism* (Ithaca: Cornell University Press, 1983), 169; *Nation and Nationalism, New Perspectives on the Past* (Oxford: Basil Blackwell, 1983); *Muslim Society* (Cambridge: Cambridge University Press, 1983).
52. Khaled Fahmy, *All the Pasha's Men: Mehmed Ali, His Army and the Making of Modern Egypt*, vol. 8 (Cambridge University Press, 1997); Timothy Mitchell, *Colonising Egypt: With a New Preface* (University of California Press, 1991).
53. Fahmy, *All the Pasha's Men: Mehmed Ali, His Army and the Making of Modern Egypt*, vol. 8 (Cambridge: Cambridge University Press, 1997); Mitchell, *Colonising Egypt*.
54. Al-Barghouti, *The Umma and the Dawla: The Nation State and the Arab Middle East* (London: Pluto Press, 2008); Abd al-Aziz, "Al-Judhur Al-Tarikhiyya Li-L-Shuubiyya" (Beirut, n.d.); Abd al-Aziz Duri, *Early Islamic Institutions: Administration and Taxation from the Caliphate to the Umayyads and Abassids* (New York: IB Tauris, 2011); *The Historical Formation of the Arab Nation* (New York: Routledge, 2012); *The Rise of Historical Writing among the Arabs*, vol. 1103 (Princeton: Princeton University Press, 2014); Hassan A. El-Najjar, *The Gulf War, Overreaction & Excessiveness* (Dalton, GA: Amazone Press, 2001); Muhammed Ahmed Khalaf-Allah, al-Qawmiyyah al-ʿArabiyyah w'al-Islām (Beirut: Center for Arab Unity Studies, 1981).
55. Qwo-Li Driskill, *Queer Indigenous Studies: Critical Interventions in Theory, Politics, and Literature* (Tuscon: University of Arizona Press, 2011); Lee Maracle, *I Am Woman: A Native Perspective on Sociology and Feminism* (London: Global Professional Publishing, 1996); Leanne Betasamosake Simpson, *As We Have Always Done: Indigenous Freedom through Radical Resistance* (Minneapolis: University of Minnesota Press, 2017).
56. Wolfe, in Glen Sean Coulthard, *Red Skin, White Masks: Rejecting the Colonial Politics of Recognition* (Minneapolis: University of Minnesota Press, 2014), 6–7.
57. Lorenzo Veracini, *Settler Colonialism: A Theoretical Overview* (New York: Springer, 2010).
58. Mark Rifkin, "Native Nationality and the Contemporary Queer: Tradition, Sexuality, and History in Drowning in Fire," *The American Indian Quarterly* 32, no. 4 (2008), 443–70; *When Did Indians Become Straight?: Kinship, the History of Sexuality, and Native Sovereignty* (New York: Oxford University Press, 2011); Joanne Barker, *Native Acts: Law, Recognition, and Cultural Authenticity* (Durham, NC: Duke University Press, 2011).

59. Bani Amor, "The Fragility of the Western Traveler Time to (Un)Pack the Colonial Baggage," *Bitchmedia* (2017); Mary Fillmore, "Women and Tourism: Invisible Hosts," *Invisible Guest* (1994).
60. M. Cobb, David L. Eng, Judith Halberstam, and José Esteban Muñoz, "Introduction: What's Queer about Queer Studies Now?" *Social Text* 23, no. 3–4 (84–85) (2005), 15.
61. Ibid., 4.
62. David L. Eng, *The Feeling of Kinship: Queer Liberalism and the Racialization of Intimacy* (Durham, NC: Duke University Press, 2010), 95.
63. See also Roderick A. Ferguson, *Aberrations in Black: Toward a Queer of Color Critique* (Minneapolis: University of Minnesota Press, 2004). Ferguson illuminated how non-white understandings of queer freedom did not necessarily suppress racial differences, as much as it coincides with the erasure and lack of intersectional exploration of race and racial differences as relevant in relation to gender, queer, and imperial/colonial national identities despite the perceived minuscule accomplishments of the civil rights movements of the 1950s, 1960s, and 1970s.
64. G. Gopinath, *Impossible Desires: Queer Diasporas and South Asian Public Cultures* (Durham, NC: Duke University Press, 2005), 3.
65. José Esteban Muñoz, *Disidentifications: Queers of Color and the Performance of Politics*, vol. 2 (Minneapolis: University of Minnesota Press, 1999); Michel Pêcheux, *Language, Semantics and Ideology* (New York: Springer, 1975); "The Subject-Form of Discourse in the Subjective Appropriation of Scientific Knowledges and Political Practice," in *Language, Semantics and Ideology*, ed. Edward L. Keenan (New York: Springer, 1982), 155–70.
66. Muñoz, *Disidentifications*, 161.
67. Ibid., 12.
68. Hiram Perez, "You Can Have My Brown Body and Eat It, Too!" *Social Text* 84 (2005), 171. These interdisciplinary and intersectional approaches are critical, as the neoliberal globalization of Euro-American queerness, intertwined with notions of the nuclear family, private property, and capitalist economics, has hindered, and in some cases opposed, the development of anti-racist, post-colonial, anti-imperialist, anti-colonial, and Third-World feminist agendas concerned with transnational solidarity and combating cisheteropatriarchy.
69. George Lipsitz, *The Possessive Investment in Whiteness: How White People Profit from Identity Politics* (Philadelphia: Temple University Press, 2006), vii.
70. Day, *Gramsci Is Dead*, 14–22.
71. Ibid., 5–8.
72. Examples of Black Marxism include Cedric Robinson's *Black Marxism: The Making of the Black Radical Tradition* (Chapel Hill: University of North Carolina Press, 2000) and Walter Rodney's *Decolonial Marxism: Essays from the Pan-African Revolution* (New York: Verso, 2020) . Alternatively, I

find more affinity with Black anarchist traditions and writings such as that of Ashanti Alston, Lorenzo Kom'Boa Ervin, Marquie Bey, Kuwasi Balagoon, Greg Jackson, and William C. Anderson. For writings by the latter, see https://theanarchistlibrary.org/category/topic/black-anarchism.

73. T. May, *The Political Philosophy of Poststructuralist Anarchism* (Pennsylvania: Penn State Press 1994), 10–11.
74. Ibid., 10–11.
75. Ibid., 11.
76. Tuck and Yang, "Decolonization Is Not a Metaphor," 4; Anderson, *Imagined Communities*; Partha Chatterjee, "Secularism and Toleration," *Economic and Political Weekly* 29 no. 28 (1994), 1768–77; Hobsbawm, *Nations and Nationalism since 1780*.
77. Tuck and Yang, "Decolonization Is Not a Metaphor," 26; See also A.J. Barker, "What Does 'Decolonize Oakland' Mean? What Can 'Decolonize Oakland' Mean," *Tequila Sovereign* (October 30, 2011).
78. Tuck and Yang, "Decolonization Is Not a Metaphor," 18. Tuck and Yang note, "There are important parallels between Occupy/Decolonize and the French/Haitian Revolutions of 1789–1799 and 1791–1804, respectively" given that "Haiti has the dubious distinction of being 'the poorest country in the Western hemisphere'." Central Intelligence Agency, *The World Factbook* (Haiti, May 12, 2012), www.cia.gov/library/publications/the-world-factbook/geos/ha.html; yet, it was the richest of France's colonies until the Haitian Revolution, the only slave revolution to ever found a state" (ibid., 26).
79. T. Alfred, *Wasase: Indigenous Pathways of Action and Freedom* (Toronto: University of Toronto Press, 2005); Coulthard, *Red Skin, White Masks*; G. Esteva, "Gustavo Esteva: Recovering Hope – the Zapatista Example," *Upside Down World* (2013), https://upsidedownworld.org/news-briefs/news-briefs-news-briefs/gustavo-esteva-recovering-hope-the-zapatista-example/; S. Marcos, "The Fourth World War Has Begun," in *The Zapatista Reader*, ed. Tom Hayden (New York: Thunder's Mouth Press/Nation Book, 2002), 270–83.
80. Abdou, "Let Empire Collapse."
81. Ibid.
82. Ibid.
83. Ibid.
84. Ibid.
85. Ibid.
86. G. Deleuze and F. Guattari, *Anti-Oedipus: Capitalism and Schizophrenia*, trans. Robert Hurley, Mark Seem, and Helen R. Lane (Minneapolis: University of Minnesota Press, 1983), 251–65; G. Deleuze, *Negotiations, 1972–1990* (New York: Columbia University Press, 1995).

87. Saul Newman, *From Bakunin to Lacan: Anti-Authoritarianism and the Dislocation of Power* (Minneapolis: Lexington Books, 2001), 99.
88. R. Perez, *On an (Archy) and Schizoanalysis* (Brooklyn, NY: Autonomedia, 1990), 27.
89. Pierre Clastres, *Society against the State* (Cambridge, MA: MIT Press, 1974); H. Barclay, "Islam, Muslim Societies and Anarchy," *Anarchist Studies* 10, no. 2 (2017), 105–18.
90. Richard J.D. Day, *Multiculturalism and the History of Canadian Diversity* (Toronto: University of Toronto Press, 2000), 42.
91. Deleuze and Guattari, *A Thousand Plateaus*, 437.
92. Ibid., 177.
93. Saul Newman, *The Politics of Postanarchism* (Edinburgh: Edinburgh University Press, 2010).
94. S. Uzelman, "Media Commons and the Sad Decline of Vancouver Indymedia." *The Communication Review* 14, no. 4 (2011), 21; Deleuze and Guattari, *A Thousand Plateaus.*
95. Uzelman, "Media Commons," 22.
96. Ibid., 22.
97. Ibid., 22; Michel Foucault, "Subjectivity and Truth," in *Michel Foucault, Ethics, Subjectivity and Truth*, ed. Paul Rabinow, trans. Robert Hurley and Others (New York: New Press, 1997), 299.
98. Uzelman, "Media Commons," 22; Michel Foucault, "The Ethic of Care for the Self as a Practice of Freedom," in *The Final Foucault*, ed. J. Bernauer and D. Rasmussen (Cambridge: MIT Press, 1988), 114, 123.
99. Uzelman, "Media Commons," 22.
100. Ibid., 23; Foucault, "The Subject and Power," in *Power: Essential Works of Foucault 1954–1984*, ed. J.D. Faubion (London: Penguin Books, 2002).
101. Day, *Gramsci Is Dead*, 169; Uzelman, "Media Commons," 23.
102. Uzelman, "Media Commons," 16–17.
103. Ibid., 24; Simons, J. *Foucault and the Political*, (New York, London: Routledge, 1995).
104. In this sense, revolutions entail moving beyond restorative justice models that reify the state's role and reforming laws. Instead, revolutions entail that we reconceive our relationships to land, life, and one another (Uzelman, "Media Commons," 24; Simons, *Foucault and the Political.* On abolition and the impossibility of police reform, see Mariame Kaba's *We Do This 'Til We Free Us: Abolitionist Oranizing and Transformative Justice* (Chicago: Haymarket Books, 2021). Also see Ruth Gilmore Wilson's *Change Everything: Racial Capitalism and the Case For Abolition* (Chicago: Haymarket Books, 2022).
105. As Jasbir K. Puar points out in *Terrorist Assemblages: Homonationalism in Queer Times* (Durham, NC: Duke University Press, 2007), "In control societies, surveillance imprints its presence far beyond an egregious intrusion of privacy or intimacy, as has been theorized in the case of

panoptic disciplinary sites" (164). In other words, "to imply that only the privacy and intimacy of the bodies are violated through such intimate bodily practice of surveillance belies a liberal fantasy about bodily integrity, a projection of wholeness that many are not accorded, a privileged marker of liberal subjecthood as well as marker of privileged liberal subjecthood" (165).

106. Michel Foucault, *Discipline and Punish: The Birth of the Prison*, trans. Alan Dheridan (New York: Vintage, 1979), 169. As Manuel De Landa further notes, this entailed the conscription of "soldiers as not only counselors of state, but also junior officers, not only the men of the courts, but also the men of the camps" (Manuel De Landa, "Economics, Computers and the War Machine," *Infowar*, 1999). With each iteration of these disciplinary logics and the schematic enforcement of controlling penal codes, the Romanic reference that accompanied each formation bared with it a technocratic and bureaucratic "double index: citizens and legionnaires, law and maneuvers" towards "the individual and collective coercion of bodies" (ibid.).
107. Deleuze and Guattari, *A Thousand Plateaus*, 228.
108. L. Call, *Postmodern Anarchism* (Minneapolis: Lexington Books, 2003), 51.
109. Deleuze and Guattari, *A Thousand Plateaus*; Wilhelm Reich and Vincent R. Carfagno, *The Mass Psychology of Fascism* (New York: Farrar, Straus & Giroux, 1970).
110. Deleuze and Guattari, *A Thousand Plateaus*, 205; Wilhelm Reich, *The Mass Psychology of Fascism* (New York: Farrar, Straus & Giroux, 1970).
111. F. Guattari, *The Three Ecologies*, trans. Ian Pindar and Paul Sutton (London and New Brunswick: The Athlone Press, 2000), 50. Capitalistic subjectivity, like Guattari writes, "no matter in what dimension or by what means it is engendered, is manufactured to protect existence against any event intrusive enough to disturb and disrupt opinion."
112. Karl Marx, 1818–1883, *Das Kapital, A Critique of Political Economy.* (Chicago: H. Regnery, 1959), 1055.
113. Deleuze and Guattari, *A Thousand Plateaus*, 436.
114. Newman, *The Politics of Postanarchism*, 6; Coulthard, *Red Skin, White Masks*; Fanon, *Black Skin, White Masks*, trans. Richard Philcox (New York: Grove Press, 1967); Charles Taylor, "The Politics of Recognition," in *Multiculturalism and the Politics of Recognition*, ed. A. Gutmann (Princeton: Princeton University Press, 1992), 25–74.
115. Saidiya V. Hartman, *On Working with Archives: An Interview with Writer Saidiya Hartman*, https://thecreativeindependent.com/people/saidiya-hartman-on-working-with-archives/
116. Mohamed Abdou, *Anarcha-Islam*, Master's Thesis, Queen's University (2009); Patricia Crone, "Ninth-Century Muslim Anarchists," *Past & Present*, no. 167 (2000), 3–28; Anthony Fiscella, "Imagining an Islamic Anarchism: A New Field of Study Is Ploughed," in *Religious*

Anarchism: New Perspectives, ed. Alexandre J.M.E. Christoyannopoulos (London: Cambridge Scholars Publishing, 2009), 280–317. This thesis distinguishes between anti-authoritarianism and non-authoritarianism. The former represents a polemical/rhetorical stance, whereas the latter denotes the extraction of decolonial, ontological, and epistemological concepts and practices from one's cultural and spiritual paradigm(s) of reference.

117. Steven Salaita, *Arab American Literary Fictions, Cultures, and Politics* (New York: Springer, 2006); *Inter/Nationalism: Decolonizing Native America and Palestine* (Minneapolis: University of Minnesota Press, 2016).

3. Anarcha-Islām: An Anti- and Non-Authoritarianism Islām

1. Félix Guattari, *Chaosophy*, ed.Sylvère Lotringer (New York: Semiotext(E), 1995), 51.
2. Aimé Césaire, *Discourse on Colonialism* (New York: Monthly Review Press, 1972), 27.
3. Abul Alā Al-Mawdūdī , "Jihad in Islam (Lahore)" (Islamic Publications, n.d.), lecture delivered at Lahore in 1939.
4. I distinguish between being anti-authoritarian/capitalist and non-authoritarian/capitalist given that the former constitutes a rhetorical move that does not imply an engagement with the decolonial act of decolonizing one's tradition(s) to actually extract the non-authoritarian/non-capitalist concepts/practices that inform new ontological and epistemological foundations.
5. Habib Ali al-Jifri, *The Concept of Faith in Islam* (Amman: Royal Islamic Strategic Studies Centre, 2000); Yusuf Al-Qaradawi, T*he Lawful and the Prohibited in Islam*, trans. Kamal el-Helbawy, M. Moinuddin Siddiqui, and Syed Shukry (London: Shorouk International, 1985); Abdelwahab Bouhdiba, *Sexuality in Islam* (London: Routledge, 2013); Tariq Ramadan, *Islam, the West and the Challenges of Modernity* (Leicester: The Islamic Foundation, 2001); George Tarabishi, *Sharq Wa Gharb Rujulah Wa Unathah* (Beirut: Dar al-Taliaah, 1988); Mubeen Vaid, "Can Islam Accommodate Homosexual Acts," MuslimMatters (2015); Muhammad Zafeeruddin, *Islam on Homo-Sexuality: The First Authentic Book on the Evils of Homosexuality* (Karachi: Darul Ishaat, 1996).
6. J.M. Adams, *Nonwestern Anarchisms: Rethinking the Global Context* (South Africa: Zabalaza Books, 2003); M. Bamyeh, "Anarchist, Liberal and Authoritarian Enlightenments: Notes from the Arab Spring," *Jadaliyya* (July 30, 2011); "Anarchist Philosophy, Civic Traditions and the Culture of Arab Revolutions 1," *Middle East Journal of Culture and Communication* 5, no. 1 (2012), 32–41; H.R. Ezzat, "The Umma: From Global Civil Society to Global Public Sphere," in *Bottom-Up Politics*,

ed. D. Kostovicova, D. and M. Glasius, (New York: Springer, 2011), 40–9; Adam Lewis, *Decolonizing Anarchism: Expanding Anarcha-Indigenism in Theory and Practice*, MA Thesis. Queen's University (2012); S. Mbah and C. Bufe, *African Anarchism* (New York: Sharp Press, 2014); M. Ramnath, *Decolonizing Anarchism: An Antiauthoritarian History of India's Liberation Struggle* (Oakland: AK Press, 2012), 3.

7. Ramnath, *Decolonizing Anarchism*, 3.
8. Budour Youssef Hassan, "The Colour Brown: Decolonizing Anarchism and Challenging White Hegemony" (2013), https://budourhassan.wordpress.com/2013/07/24/the-colour-brown-de-colonising-anarchism-and-challenging-white-hegemony/.
9. Yasser Abdullah, "Tārīkh al-Haraka al-Anārkiyyah Fī Miṣr" trans. Mohamed Abdou, Public lecture on "The History of the Anarchist Movement in Egypt," www.youtube.com/watch?v=XUF-rRiBLig (2013); I. Khuri-Makdisi, *The Eastern Mediterranean and the Making of Global Radicalism, 1860–1914* (Berkeley: University of California Press, 2010).
10. Akin Sefer, *Ilham Khuri-Makdisi. The Eastern Mediterranean and the Making of Global Radicalism, 1860–1914* (Berkeley: University of California Press, 2010), xi; Khuri-Makdisi, *The Eastern Mediterranean*.
11. Ibid.
12. Ibid.
13. Ibid.
14. Milad Dokhanchi, "Post-Islamism Redefined: Towards a Politics of Post-Islamism," *Journal of the Contemporary Study of Islam* 1, no. 1, 28–54.
15. Ibid.
16. Ibid.
17. Ibid.
18. Ibid.
19. Heba Raouf Ezzat, interview by Rosemary Bechler (2005).
20. Ibid.
21. Lewis, *Decolonizing Anarchism*.
22. Ashanti Alston, "Beyonvd Nationalism But Not without It," *Libcom* (2011), https://libcom.org/library/beyond-nationalism-not-without-it; interview by D. José Antonio Gutiérrez (2009).
23. The link is to an article submitted by Chris R. and purportedly written by Muslim syndicalists in Spain titled "Islam and Anarchy Join Together" on Brain-Fear and PJPs' misconception: http://news.infoshop.org/article.php?story=03/06/06/7983966 (the website is no longer available).
24. Ibid.
25. The link here is to the article titled "Anarchist Orientalism and the British Muslim Community" by Adam K (2007): http://news.infoshop.org/article.php?story=02-05-19-2887013.

26. J. Massad, "Psychoanalysis, Islam, and the Other of Liberalism," *Psychoanalysis and History* 11, no. 2 (2009), 43.
27. Andrew Flood, "The Trouble with Islam" (2002), http://struggle.ws/wsm/rbr/rbr7/islam.html.
28. Please see various examples of religious anarchisms, ranging from Christian, to Buddhist, to Daoist, and Muslim in *Religious Anarchism: New Perspectives*, ed. Alexandre J. M. E. Christoyannopoulos (Cambridge: Cambridge Scholars Publishing, 2009). The text includes writings by the likes of Richard A. Davis, Bojan Aleksov, John A. Rapp, Michael T. Van Dyk, and André de Raaij. See the link here for further details: www.c-s-p.org/Flyers/978-1-4438-1132-3-sample.pdf.
29. Flood, "The Trouble with Islam."
30. Foucault, in Janet Afary and Kevin B. Anderson, *Foucault and the Iranian Revolution: Gender and the Seductions of Islamism* (Chicago: University of Chicago Press, 2010), 259.
31. For instance, this is slightly misguided in Islām's case, even during the period when "perhaps the single most damaging blow to Islamic knowledge came in the tenth century under the Abbassids when the 'Gate of Ijithad'... was declared closed," thus leading to a more concretized institutionalization of Islām (J.L. Esposito, *Islam and Politics* (Syracuse: Syracuse University Press, 1984), 19.
32. L. Gandhi, *Affective Communities: Anticolonial Thought, Fin-De-Siècle Radicalism, and the Politics of Friendship* (Durham, NC: Duke University Press, 2006), 188.
33. Ibid.
34. Ibid., 188.
35. John S. Howard, "Subjectivity and Space: Deleuze and Guattari's Bwo in the New World Order," in *Deleuze and Guattari: New Mappings in Politics, Philosophy, and Culture*, ed. E. Kaufman (Minneapolis: University of Minnesota Press, 1998)), 112–26.
36. Adam Lewis' thesis can be found here: http://qspace.library.queensu.ca/bitstream/1974/7563/1/Lewis_Adam_G_201209_MA.pdf. Ashanti's quote is an excerpt taken from an interview titled *Building a Non-Eurocentric Anarchism in Our Communities: Dialogue with Ashanti Alston*. Ashanti's interview can be found here: www.anarkismo.net/article/13583. The Arabic version of Raouf-Ezzat's article can be found here:

    www.heba-ezzat.com/2001/07/29/الترجمة-ظلمتها-التى-الفلسفة-الفوضوية/

    A wide variety of Bamyeh's works and articles can be found here: www.jadaliyya.com/pages/contributors/4687. Milad Dokhanchi is, of course, a well-known filmmaker, especially in relation to two documentaries he directed. One is titled, *Revolution in Motion: Featuring Mahmoud Ahmadinejad* (2009) and the second is titled *Multiculturalism Unveiled (Is Canada Really Multicultural)* (2012). An excerpt of the first documentary can be found here: www.youtube.com/watch?v=n0I6W6wOtuw. The second documentary can be found here: http://vimeo.com/51260894. For reviews of Ilham Khuri-Makidsi's work, from which text has been cited, see Akin Sefer's review: www.newperspectivesonturkey.net/Content/Npt/Issue_7/Review_13/203-205_44_NPT_Spring.pdf. Also see Thomas Philipps' review: www.h-net.org/reviews/showrev.php?id=31749.

37. M. Rodinson, *Islam And Capitalism*, trans. Brian Pearce (New York: Pantheon, 1973), 226.
38. John Esposito and John Obert Voll, *Islam and Democracy* (New York: Oxford University Press, 1996), 26.
39. Qur'ān, 2:26.
40. Saul Newman, *From Bakunin to Lacan : Anti-authoritarianism and the Dislocation of Power* (Lanham: Lexington Books, 2001), 6.
41. Hasan Azad, "Do Muslims Belong in the West? An Interview with Talal Asad," *Jadaliyya* (February 3, 2015), www.jadaliyya.com/Details/31747.
42. Tamim Al-Barghouti, *The Umma and the Dawla: The Nation State and the Arab Middle East* (London: Pluto Press, 2008).
43. Qur'ān, 5:2.
44. Qur'ān, 2:62. Also see "Indeed, the believers, Jews, Sabians and Christians – whoever truly believes in God and the Last Day and does good, there will be no fear for them, nor will they grieve" (5:69) and "Indeed, the believers, Jews, Sabians, Christians, Magi, and the polytheists – God will judge between them all on Judgment Day. Surely God is a Witness over all things" (22:17).
45. M. Abdou, *Anarca-Islam*, Master's Thesis, Queen's University (2009); Muhammad Abduh, *The Theology of Unity*, trans. Ishaq Musa'ad and Kenneth Cragg (Petaling Jaya: Islamic Book Trust, 2004); Muḥammad Abduh, Mustafā 'Abd-ar-Rāziq, and Bernard Michel, *Rissalat Al Tawhid* (Paris: P. Geuthner, 1965); Jamal al-Din Al-Afghani, "An Islamic Response to Imperialism," in *Islam in Transition*, trans. and ed. Nikki R. Keddie (Berkeley: University of California Press, 1983), 17–19; al-Jifri, *The Concept of Faith in Islam*.
46. Joanne Barker, "Recognition," *American Studies* 46, no. 3/4 (2005), 133–61; J. Corntassel, "Re-envisioning Resurgence: Indigenous Pathways to Decolonization and Sustainable Self-Determination," *Decolonization: Indigeneity, Education & Society* 1, no. 1 (2012), 86–101; G. Coulthard, "Beyond Recognition: Indigenous Self-Determination as Prefigurative Practice," in *Lighting the Eighth Fire: The Liberation, Resurgence, and Protection of Indigenous Nations*, ed. Leanne Simpson (Winnipeg: Arbeiter Ring Publishing, 2008), 187–203; Qwo-Li Driskill, Chris Finley, Brian Joseph Gilley, Scott Lauria Morgensen, *Queer Indigenous Studies: Critical Interventions in Theory, Politics, and Literature* (Tuscon: University of Arizona Press, 2011); Leanne Betasamosake Simpson, *As We Have Always Done:*

Indigenous Freedom through Radical Resistance (Minneapolis: University of Minnesota Press, 2017).

47. Ramadan, *Islam, the West and the Challenges of Modernity*, 81; Mohammed Arkoun, *Rethinking Islam: Common Questions, Uncommon Answers* (Boulder: Westview Press, 1994); F. Esack, *Qurán, Liberation and Pluralism: An Islamic Perspective of Interreligious Solidarity against Oppression* (London: Oneworld Publications, 1997); J.P. Piscatori, *Islam in a World of Nation-States* (Cambridge: Cambridge University Press Cambridge, 1986), 1.
48. Allāh, Qur'ān, 42:36–38.
49. Esposito and Voll, *Islam and Democracy*, 28.
50. Muhammad, in *Ramadan, Islam, the West and the Challenges of Modernity*, 83.
51. "Is there not in Hell an abode for the proud?" (Surah az-Zumar 39:60). "It shall be said: Enter the gates of hell to abide therein; so evil is the abode of the proud" (Surah az-Zumar 39:72). In Surah Ghafir (Verse 35) Almighty remarks, "Thus does Allāh set a seal over the heart of every proud, haughty one" (Surah Ghafir 40: 35). In another verse, though there exist innumerable more, the Qur'ān states, "The Messiah does by no means disdains that he should be a servant of Allāh, nor do the angels who are near to Him, and whoever disdains His service and is proud, He will gather them all together to Himself. Then as for those who believe and do good, He will pay them fully their rewards and give them more out of His grace, and as for those who disdain and are proud, He will chastise them with a painful chastisement" (Surat an-Nisā' 4:172–173).
52. Félix Guattari and Antonio Negri, *Communists Like Us: New Spaces of Liberty, New Lines of Alliance* (Los Angeles: Semiotext (E), 1990), 116.
53. Ibid.
54. Muhammad Baqir al-Majlisi, "Bihar Al-Anwar. 110 Volumes," in *The Encyclopedic Compendium of Shi 'ite Traditions on the Qa'irn and the Mahdi from the Beginning to the Seventeenth Century* (Beirut: al-Wafa', 1983), Vol. 19, Hadith No. 31, 182.
55. Félix Guattari, *The Three Ecologies* (New York: Bloomsbury Publishing, 2005), 138.
56. Ibid.
57. Without a similar courtesy however bestowed, or extended, during a matter's pertinence to what there is collective contention over. Due, in other words, to the matter's pertinence as a necessity with respect to the community's existence as a cohesive, healthy, egalitarian community.
58. Allāh, Qur'ān, 49:12.
59. Guattari, *The Three Ecologies*.
60. T.J. Al'Alwani, *The Ethics of Disagreement in Islam* (Herndon, VA: International Institute of Islamic Thought (IIIT), 2015), 24.
61. Allāh, Qur'ān, 5:48.

62. Guattari, *The Three Ecologies*; Jacques Rancière, "The Cause of the Other," *Parallax* 4, no. 2 (1998), 25–33.
63. Al'Alwani, *The Ethics of Disagreement in Islam*, 75.
64. Mohamed Abdou, "On the Ethics of Disagreements (*Uṣūl al-Ikhtilaf*) and the Ethics of Hospitality (*Uṣūl al-Dhiyafa*) between Spiritual and Non-Spiritual Leftists in the Newest Social Movements," *Political Theology* (2021).
65. T.J. Al-Alwani, *Ijtihad* (Herndon, VA: International Institute of Islamic Thought (IIIT), 1993), 11.
66. Tariq Ramadan, *To Be a European Muslim* (Leicester: The Islamic Foundation, 1998), 80.
67. The ethical and political practice I advocate for between Muslims, anarchists, and other activists is one that builds on what Leela Gandhi, following Jacques Derrida, Jean Luc Nancy, and Maurice Blanchot, refers to as a *politics of friendship* in her text – *Affective Communities*. *Uṣūl lil-Ḍiyāfa* are the incentives that accompany a politics of friendships. A friendship, which one would hope for, is predicated on a paradoxical stance of unconditional hospitality conditional on the sharing of similar ethical and political commitments. This represents a similar call to what Richard J.F. Day says when he writes – in line with other scholars – of the "need to guide our relations with other communities according to the interlocking ethico-political commitments of *groundless solidarity* and *infinite responsibility*" towards constructing "the coming communities" (J.F. Day, *Gramsci Is Dead: Anarchist Currents in the Newest Social Movements* (London: Pluto Press, 2005), 18, 186–202. See also R. Braidotti, "The Politics of Ontological Difference," in *Between Feminism and Psychoanalysis*, ed. Teresa Brennan (London: Routledge, 2002) 89–105; D. Haraway, "A Cyborg Manifesto: Science, Technology, and SocialistFeminism in the Late Twentieth Century," in *Simians, Cyborgs and Women: The Reinvention of Nature* (New York: Routledge, 1991), 149–81; Diane Elam, *Feminism and Deconstruction* (New York: Routledge, 1994); L. Feinberg, *Trans Liberation: Beyond Pink or Blue* (Boston: Beacon Press, 1998); G. Agamben, *The Coming Community* (Minneapolis: University of Minnesota Press, 1993).
68. Tariq Ramadan, *To Be a European Muslim: A Study of Islamic Sources in the European Context* (Leicester: Islamic Foundation, 1999), 81.
69. Provided hopefully the community's interests are not deemed "bad" interests. Because "bad" interests can exist regardless of the type of collectivity given that there is "rural [*micro*] *fascism* and city or neighborhood *fascism*, *fascism* of the Left and *fascism* of the Right, *fascism* of the couple, family, school and office" (Lewis Call, *Postmodern* Anarchism (Lanham: Lexington Books, 2003), 52.
70. Ramadan, *Islam, the West and the Challenges of Modernity*, 148.
71. Esposito and Voll, *Islam and Democracy*, 25.
72. Qur'ān, 20:111.

73. Qur'ān, 4:29.
74. Qur'ān, 7:74.
75. Esack, *Qurán, Liberation and Pluralism*, 175.
76. Ibid., 158.
77. Qur'ān, 42:6. Allāh says to the Prophet: "For those who take as *awl'yâ'* [guardians] others besides Him [even then] Allâh is *hafîz* [protector] over them and you [O Muḥammad] are not a *wakîl* [a disposer of their affairs or have say] over them" (ibid.).
78. Ramadan, *Islam, the West and the Challenges of Modernity*, 148.
79. Al-Barghouti, *The Umma and the Dawla*, 69; also see Qur'ān, 9:47–49.
80. Al-Barghouti, *The Umma and the Dawla*, 43.
81. Muhammad Abdul Rauf, *The Islamic Doctrine of Economics and Contemporary Economic Thought: Highlight of a Conference on a Theological Inquiry into Capitalism and Socialism* (Washington: American Enterprise Institute Press, 1979), 13.
82. Rodinson, *Islam and Capitalism*, 226.
83. Esposito and Voll, *Islam and Dgemocracy*, 26.
84. Walaa M. Sabry and Adarsh Vohra, "Role of Islam in the Management of Psychiatric Disorders," *Indian Journal of Psychiatry* 55, Suppl. 2 (2013), 212.
85. Joseph Massad, "The Destructive Legacy of Arab Liberals," *The Electronic Intifada* (2015).
86. An example of this is how accusations of sexual deviancy have become a political weapon of choice by both Islamist and ethnonationalist military forces, and between rival political opponents. Following the June 2013 uprising that unseated Morsi and drove the criminalized Muslim Brotherhood underground, there were a series of arrests for homosexual conduct surrounding a teacher in the Cairo suburb of Helwan. In this instance, the Egyptian press claimed that "the lead defendant [was] a terrorist who recruited men to Islamism by sleeping with them." Prosecutors in the Helwan case added that the defendant flashed "the Brotherhood's four-fingered salute during sex," a hand-gesture that first appeared in late August 2013 in the wake of Morsi's overthrow. Since the Muslim Brotherhood's ouster, Egyptian state media representatives such as Amr Adib and Lamis Elhadidy have openly called for the use of rape as a weapon of war, in particular, against Muslim Brotherhood members and secular dissidents in prisons, in addition to the large-scale massacres of unarmed protesters, mass death sentences, draconian legislation, and arrests that have occurred since Tahrir's 2011 Uprising. Quotes are from Scott Long's article, "Egyptian Activists to Netanyahu's Pr Men: Our Lives Are Not Propaganda," *A Paper-Bird: Sex, Rights & the World* (2014). I discuss this point further relative to two historical-archival case studies, The Queen Boat and the transgnder case of Sally Abd'Allah, in my PhD. See www.academia.

edu/38647128/Ph_D_Thesis_Islam_and_Queer_Muslims_Identity_and_Sexuality_in_the_Contemporary_CH2. Also see my al-Raida article, "Gender-Based Sexual-Harassment & the Racialized-Feminized Queering of Tahrir Square: The Radical-Abolitionist Case of Queer-Feminist Egyptians in Egypt" here: www.alraidajournal.com/index.php/ALRJ/article/view/1857/1909.

87. This can be seen in Tantawi's long-standing perspective on the necessity of banning the niqab and his toleration of interest/usury (*ribā*), which in the case of the latter Islam and Qur'ān strictly forbid.
88. Hamza Hendawi, "Egypt's President Alarmed by 40 Per Cent Divorce Rate, Suggests Delegalizing Verbal Divorce," *Toronto Star* (2017); Unknown, "Egypt's Poverty Level Hit 27.8% in 2015: Capmas," *Egypt Independent* (2016). Approximately "40 per cent of Egypt's 900,000 annual marriages end in divorce after five years" – one divorce occurs almost every three minutes. Moreover, approximately 61 percent of the Egyptian population are under the age of 30, of which 40 percent are between the ages of 10 and 29. Amongst the youth, 26 percent are unemployed and 51 percent live in poverty.
89. The quote is part of the Sunnah: www.geocities.com/islamicwayz/20_of__40_hadith_on_the_superior.htm.
90. Arkoun, *Rethinking Islam*, 106.
91. Esposito and Voll, *Islam and Democracy*, 26.
92. Ramadan, *Islam, the West and the Challenges of Modernity*, 148.
93. Ibid.
94. This includes bills like 501C that permit designated "social welfare" organizations to contribute to electoral campaigns. See Brendan James' article "Princeton Study: U.S. No Longer An Actual Democracy" (2014) here: http://talkingpointsmemo.com/livewire/princeton-experts-say-us-no-longer-democracy. Also see Sahil Kapur's article "Supreme Court Deals Another Blow to Campaign Finance Limits" (2014), http://talkingpointsmemo.com/dc/supreme-court-campaign-contribution-limits-mccutcheon-fec-2; Jamilah King, "Ferguson Hires All-White Pr Firm to Help Deal with Black Uprising: The City's Leaders Just Don't Get It" (2014), www.colorlines.com/articles/ferguson-hires-all-white-pr-firm-help-deal-black-uprising.
95. Esposito, 1996, 25–6.
96. Musnad Imam Ahmad, Mishkat, Chapter Al-Anzar Wal Tahzir, Verse 273.
97. Esposito, and Voll, *Islam and Democracy*, 26.
98. Ibid.
99. Amina Wadud, "Towards a Qur'ānic Hermeneutics of Social Justice: Race, Class and Gender," *Journal of Law and Religion* 12, no. 1 (1995), 37–50; Asma Barlas, *"Believing Women" in Islam: Unreading Patriarchal Interpretations of the Qur'ān* (Austin: University of Texas Press, 2002);

Kecia Ali, *Sexual Ethics and Islam: Feminist Reflections on Qur'ān, Hadith and Jurisprudence* (Oxford: Oneworld Publications, 2015).

100. Esposito and Voll, *Islam and Democracy*, 26.
101. Ibid.
102. Ibid., 27.
103. Ibid.
104. Al-Barghouti, *The Umma and the Dawla*, 38.
105. Ibid.
106. Ibid. Also see *Lisan al-Arab*, 5:25.
107. Ibid.
108. Ibid. Also see *Lisan al-Arab*, 5: 24–6.
109. Ibid., 42.
110. M.K. Masud, "The Doctrine of Siyasa in Islamic Law," *Recht Van De Islam* 18 (2001), 14; Yamal al-Din Muhammad Ibn Manzur, *Lisan Al-Arab* (Al Dar al-Misriyya Li-l-ta'lif wa-l-tarhim, 1975), 1405, vol. 6:108.
111. Ibid.
112. Masud, "The Doctrine of Siyasa in Islamic Law," 4.
113. Ibid., 8; Buṭrus Al-Bustānī, *Muḥīṭ Al-Muḥīṭ: Qāmūs Muṭauwal Li-'L-Luġa Al-'arabīya* (Bayrūt: Maktabat Lubnān, 1998); Abu Yala Al-Farra and Abu Ya'la al-Hanbali, "Al-Ahkam Al-Sultaniyya" (Egypt: Mustafa Babi al-Halabi, 1966); Abu Hamid Al-Ghazali, A*l-Tibr Al-Masbuk Fi Nasihat Al-Muluk*, trans. and ed. Frank Bagley as the Book of Counsel for Kings (Oxford: Oxford University Press, 1964); Taqī al-Dīn Aḥmad Al-Maqrīzī, "Al-'Abbâs Ahmad B. Alî," *Kitâb al-Mawâ'iz wa al-I'tibâr bi Dhikr al-Khitat wa al-Âthâr* (London: Al-Furqan Islamic Heritage Foundation, Centre for the Study of Islamic Manuscripts, 2013); Taqī al-Dīn Aḥmad Al-Maqrīzī, *Ighāthat Al-Umma Bi-Kashf Al-Ghumma*, ed. Muḥammad Muṣṭafā Ziyāda and Jamāl al-Dīn al-Shayyāl (Cairo: Lajnat al-Ta'līf wa-al-Tarjama wa-al-Nashr, 1940); Taqī al-Dīn Aḥmad al-Maqrīzī, Muḥammad Muṣṭafā Ziyāda, and Sa'īd 'Abd al-Fattāḥ 'Ašūr, *Kitāb Al-Sulūk Li-Ma'rifat Duwal Al-Mulūk* (Cairo: Association of Authorship, Translation &Publication Press, 1939); Muhammad Al-Mawardi, *The Ordinances of Government: A Translation of Al-Ahkam Al-Sultaniyya Wa Wilayat Al-Diniyya*, trans. Wafaa H. Wabha (Reading, U.: Center for Muslim Contribution to Civilization-Garnet, 1996); Niẓām al-Mulk, *The Book of Government: Or, Rules for Kings: The Siyāsat-Nāma or Siyar Al-Mulūk* (New Haven: Yale University Press, 1960); Shams al-Din Al-Sarakhsi, *Al-Mabsat*, 30 Vols (Cairo, Matba 'at al-Sa 'adah), 1324; Shams al-Din Muhammad ibn AbiTalib al-Dimashqi, *Al-Siydsaft 'Ilm Al-Firasa* (Cairo: Association of Authorship, Translation & Publication Press, 1914); Frank Ronald Charles Bagley, *Ghazālīs' Book of Counsel for Kings: (Nasīhat Al-Mulūk)* (London: Oxford University Press, 1964); Farabi, *Al-Siyasah Al-Madaniyah* (Bayrūt: al-Maṭba'ah

al-Kāthūlīkīyah, 1964); Qutayba Ibn, *Ta'rīḫ al-ḫulafā' al-rāšidūn wa-dawlat banī Umayya al-ma'rūf bi-al-Imāma wa-al-siyāsa* (Cairo: al-Maktaba al-tiğāriyya al-kubrā bi-Miṣr, 1904); Abū ăl-Wafā' 'Alī Ibn 'Aqīl, *Kitab Al-Funan*, ed. George Makdisi (Beirut: Dar el-Machreq Editeurs, 1986).

114. Masud, "The Doctrine of Siyasa in Islamic Law," 4.
115. Ibid., 8.
116. Ibid.; "Religion and State Are Twin Brothers: Classical Muslim Political Theory," *Islam and Civilisational Renewal (ICR)* 9, no. 1 (2018), 9–26.
117. Masud, "The Doctrine of Siyasa in Islamic Law."
118. Ibid., 8–9.
119. Ibn 'Aqil, *Kitab Al-Funan*, 10–11; Masud, "The Doctrine of Siyasa in Islamic Law," 9; George Makdisi, *Ibn 'Aqil: Religion and Culture in Classical Islam* (Edinburgh: Edinburgh University Press, 1997).
120. Masud, "The Doctrine of Siyasa in Islamic Law," 9; Ibn 'Aqil, *Kitab Al-Funan*; Makdisi, *Ibn 'Aqil.*
121. Masud, "The Doctrine of Siyasa in Islamic Law," 9; Ibn 'Aqil, *Kitab Al-Funan*, vol. 1, 279.
122. Ibid.; Ibn al-Qayyi al-Jawziyya, *Al Turuq Al-Hukmiyya Fil-Siyasat Al-Shariiya* (Methods of Judgment in a Shariah-Oriented Policy) (Cairo: al-Muassasa al-Arabiyya lil-Tabaa, 1961), vol. 4, 362; Ibn Qayyim al-Jawziyya, Shams al-Din Muhammad ibn Abi, and Bakr al-Zarl al-Dimashqi, "Ahkâm Ahl Al-Dhimma, Ed," *Subhî al-Sâlih* (2 vols, Beirut, 1381/1961), I (1980).
123. Masud, "The Doctrine of Siyasa in Islamic Law," 9.
124. Ibn Tiqtiqa in ibid.; Sherman A. Jackson, "In Defense of Two-Tiered Orthodoxy: A Study of Shihab Al-Din Al-Qarafi's '*Kitab Al-Ihkam Fi Tamyiz Al-Fatawaan Al-Ahkam Wa Tasarrufat Al-Qadi Wa Al-Imam*," Dissertations available from Pro*Quest* (1991).
125. Masud, "The Doctrine of Siyasa in Islamic Law," 11; Ibn Taymiyya, "Al-Siyasa Al-Shar'iyya," trans. H. Laoust, Le traité de droit public d'Ibn Taimiya (Beirut: Institut Français de Damas, 1948), 184.
126. Masud, "The Doctrine of Siyasa in Islamic Law," 12; Ibn Taymiyya, "Al-Siyasa Al-Shar'iyya," trans. H. Laoust, Le traité de droit public d'Ibn Taimiya (Beirut: Institut Français de Damas, 1948), 184. Fazular Rahman, working with Ibn Taymiyyah's understanding of it, identifies "Shari'a from the root Shar'" as meaning "'the path or the road leading to the water', i.e. a way to the very source of life. The verb *shari'a* means literally 'to chalk out or mark out a clear road to water'. In its religious usage, from the earliest period, it has meant 'the highway of good life', i.e. religious values, expressed functionally and in concrete terms, to direct a [hu]man's life. It differs from the term 'Sunna' in that the subject of the Sunna 'leads the way' by actual example and, therefore, his action as such is of the same kind as those who follow him in accepting the example, whereas the subject of Shar' shows or ordains the way

and is, therefore, none else than God, the source of religious values" (Fazular Rahman, *Islam*, Chicago: University of Chicago Press, 1979), 100. Nonetheless, this interpretive reading of it must comprehend the paramount distinction between ethics and morals, the need for the decolonization of the judiciary, as Sharia's fundamental anchoring in social justice, and non-monolithic nature, befitting of the argument of this text, if not the myriad comprehension of Uṣūl Al-Fiqh. Please see Abdullahi Ali Ibrahim's *Manichaean Delirium: Decolonizing the Judiciary and Islamic Renewal in the Sudan, 1898–1985* (Brill: Islam in Africa, vol. 7, 2008).

127. al-Jawziyya, *Al Turuq Al-Hukmiyya Fil-Siyasat Al-Shariiya*, 5; al-Jawziyya, ibn Abi, and al-Dimashqi, "Ahkâm Ahl Al-Dhimma, Ed"; Ibn Nujaym, *Zayn Al-Din (Nd), Al-Bahr Al-Raiq Sharh Kanz Al-Daqaiq* (Beirut: Dar al-Marifa); Masud, "The Doctrine of Siyasa in Islamic Law," 11–12.
128. Masud, "The Doctrine of Siyasa in Islamic Law," 13.
129. Ibid., 12; al-Maqrīzī, Ziyāda, and 'Abd al-Fattāḥ 'Ašūr, *Kitāb Al-Sulūk Li-Ma'rifat Duwal Al-Mulūk*, vol. 2, 220; al-Maqrīzī, "Kitāb Al-Mawā'iẓ Wa Al-I'tibār Bi-Dhikr Al-Khiṭaṭ Wa *Al-Āthār*."
130. Masud, "The Doctrine of Siyasa in Islamic Law," 12; al-Maqrīzī, Ziyāda, and 'Abd al-Fattāḥ 'Ašūr, *Kitāb Al-Sulūk Li-Ma'rifat Duwal Al-Mulūk*; al-Maqrīzī, "Kitāb Al-Mawā'iẓ Wa Al-I'tibār Bi-Dhikr Al-Khiṭaṭ Wa Al-Āthār."
131. al-Maqrīzī, Ziyāda, and 'Abd al-Fattāḥ 'Ašūr, *Kitāb Al-Sulūk Li-Ma'rifat Duwal Al-Mulūk*, vol. 2, 220; al-Maqrīzī, "Kitāb Al-Mawā'iẓ Wa Al-I'tibār Bi-Dhikr Al-Khiṭaṭ Wa Al-Āthār"; Masud, "The Doctrine of Siyasa in Islamic Law," 14.
132. Rifā'ah Rāfi' aṭ-Ṭahṭāwī, in Masud, "The Doctrine of Siyasa in Islamic Law," 21; Rifaa Badawi Rafi al-Tahtawi, "Fatherland and Patriotism," in *Islam in Transition: Muslim Perspectives*, ed. John J. Donohue and John L. Esposito (Oxford: Oxford University Press, 1982).
133. Masud, "The Doctrine of Siyasa in Islamic Law," 21.
134. Ibid., 21–2; Abu 'Abd al-Fattah 'Ali ibn Hajj, *Al-Irshiid Wa'l-Nusub Fl Bayan Ahkam Al-Ridda Wa'l-Sulh* (Algiers: al-Jabha al-Islamiyya li'lInqadh, 1995).
135. Masud, "The Doctrine of Siyasa in Islamic Law," 22.
136. Ibid., 22; ibn Hajj, *Al-Irshiid Wa'l-Nusub Fl Bayan Ahkam Al-Ridda Wa'l-Sulh*.
137. Masud, "The Doctrine of Siyasa in Islamic Law," 22; ibn Hajj, *Al-Irshiid Wa'l-Nusub Fl Bayan Ahkam Al-Ridda Wa'l-Sulh*.
138. While I take seriously and am cognizant of the politics of citation relating to scholars like Tariq Ramadan, Seyyed Hossein Nasr, and others like Farid Esack that have been recently accused of gender-sexual violence, harassment, abuse, and even rape, this manuscript was drafted over 12 years ago. I note this not to elide their re-citing with an "easy

justification and excuse," but rather because their prominent views are already widespread and have been reproduced in a myriad of discourses and by innumerable other scholars and activists on contextual points in this book's arguments. I stand by and believe those who were abused.

139. T. Ramadan, *The Arab Awakening: Islam and the New Middle East* (London: Penguin, 2012), 82–6.
140. Ibid., 90.
141. Ibid.
142. Coulthard, "Beyond Recognition"; G. Coulthard and L.B. Simpson, "Grounded Normativity/Place-Based Solidarity," *American Quarterly* 68, no. 2 (2016), 249–55; G. Coulthard, *Red Skin, White Masks: Rejecting the Colonial Politics of Recognition* (Minneapolis: University of Minnesota Press, 2014); R. Day, "Can There Be a Postcolonial Multiculturalism? A Response to Lan Angus," *International Journal of Canadian Studies/ Revue Internationale D'études Canadiennes* 26 (2002), 127–32; Frantz Fanon, *The Wretched of the Earth*, trans. Constance Farrington (New York: Grove Press, 1963); *Toward the African Revolution: Political Essays*, trans. Richard Philcox (New York: Grove Press, 1969); B. Lawrence and E. Dua, "Decolonizing Antiracism," *Social Justice* 32, no. 4 (2005), 120–43; Lovelace, "Decolonization: The Fundamental Struggle for Liberation," *Rabble* (2013); "Connecting Palestinian and Indigenous Peoples' Struggles for Freedom" (2015), http://rabble.ca/news/2015/02/connecting-palestinian-and-indigenous-peoples-struggles-freedom; "The Philosophy of Indigeneity Knowledge, Identity and the Inclusion of Aboriginal Peoples in the Academy" (The Equity and Women's Concerns Committee of the Department of Philosophy, Queen's University, 2016); C. Taylor, *Multiculturalism: Examining the Politics of Recognition*, ed. Amy Gutmann (Princeton: Princeton University Press, 1994); Driskill et al., *Queer Indigenous Studies*.
143. Coulthard, "Beyond Recognition"; Coulthard and Simpson, "Grounded Normativity/Place-Based Solidarity"; Coulthard, *Red Skin, White Masks*; Day, "Can There Be a Postcolonial Multiculturalism?"; Fanon, *The Wretched of the Earth*; *Toward the African Revolution*; Lawrence and Dua, "Decolonizing Antiracism"; Lovelace, "Decolonization"; "Connecting Palestinian and Indigenous Peoples' Struggles for Freedom"; "The Philosophy of Indigeneity Knowledge; Taylor, *Multiculturalism*.
144. Isabel Altamirano-Jiménez, "Nunavut: Whose Homeland, Whose Voices?" *Canadian Woman Studies* 26, no. 3/4 (2008), 128; "Neoliberalism, Racialised Gender and Indigeneity," in *Indigenous Identity and Resistance: Researching the Diversity of Knowledge*, ed. B. Hokowhitu, N. Kermoal, I. Altamirano-Jiménez, and P. Rewi (Dunedin, New Zealand: Otago University Press, 2010), 193–206; Winona LaDuke, *All Our Relations: Native Struggles for Life and Land* (Cambridge, MA: South End Press, 1999); L. Simpson, *Mohawk Interruptus: Political Life across the Borders of*

Settler States (Durham, NC: Duke University Press, 2014); *Lighting the Eighth Fire: The Liberation, Resurgence, and Protection of Indigenous Nations* (Winnipeg: Arbeiter Ring Publishers, 2008); *As We Have Always Done*; A. Smith, "Heteropatriarchy and the Three Pillars of White Supremacy," in *Color of Violence: The Incite Anthology*, ed. INCITE! Women of Color Against Violence (Durham, NC: Duke University Press, 2006), 66–73; "Unmasking the State: Racial/Gender Terror and Hate Crimes," *Australian Feminist Law Journal* 26, no. 1 (2007), 47–57; "Queer Theory and Native Studies: The Heteronormativity of Settler Colonialismr," *GLQ: A Journal of Lesbian and Gay Studies* 16, no. 1–2 (2010), 41–68.

145. Esposito, and Voll, *Islam and Democracy*, 25.
146. Allāh, Qur'ān, 18:110.
147. For further emphasis, see reference to Ali Abdel Razeq (1925), "Al-Islam wa Usul al-Hukum – Islam and the Principles of Governance," in Ulil Abshar-Abdalla, *Muhammad: Prophet and Politician* (May 9, 2004), http://74.125.95.132/search?q=cache:3yd4xlk72wYJ:islamlib.com/en/article/muhammad-prophet-and-politician/+ali+abdel+%22islam+and+principles+of+governance%22&hl=en&ct=clnk&cd=1&gl=ca. Furthermore, see Yunan Labib Rizk, "Cabinet Toppled by a Book," *Al-Ahram Weekly Online* 522 (February 22–28, 2001), http://weekly.ahram.org.eg/2001/522/chrncls.htm.
148. Allāh, Qur'ān, 42:6.
149. Allāh, Qur'ān, 2:256.
150. Allāh, Qur'ān, 2:135–139.
151. J. Massad, *Islam in Liberalism* (Chicago: University of Chicago Press, 2015); A. Wadud, *Qur'ān and Woman: Rereading the Sacred Text from a Woman's Perspective* (Oxford: Oxford University Press, 1999); Carolyn Rouse, *Engaged Surrender: African American Women and Islam* (Berkeley: University of California Press, 2004).
152. For as it is, numerically Muslims resemble "grains of salt within a sea" but are as "the foam of the waves" as narrated above in the Sunnah.
153. Saul Newman, *From Bakunin to Lacan: Anti-Authoritarianism and the Dislocation of Power* (Minneapolis: Lexington Books, 2001), 6.
154. See variant examples of religious anarchisms, ranging from Christian, to Buddhist, to Daoist, and Muslim in *Religious Anarchism: New Perspectives*. An example of Jewish anarchism includes the work of Orthodox Jewish anarchist Dan "Mobius" Sieradski. An interview with Sieradski is available at: www.kriskrug.com/2005/04/28/422/
155. However, there is a cost to the anti-religious anarchists *perception* that the metaphysical slaughtering of God is an anti-authoritarian "solution" to every type of authority. For with the presumed metaphysical "Death of God" there arrive infinite demagogues, mini-gods, vying and squabbling over the displaced dead God's space and power. In other words, to presume that upon God's metaphysical death, God's space

and power will remain void and unoccupied is absurd, given that God's space does not disappear with the "Death of God." Rather, God's space and power, upon God's death merely becomes a battleground.

156. 'Abd al 'Aziz al-Duri, *Al-Judhur Al-Tarikhiyya Li'l Qawmiyya al-'Arabiyya*, (Beirut, 1960), 31–40; Al-Barghouti, *The Umma and the Dawla*. George Antonious, *The Arab Awakening: The Story of the Arab National Movement* (Beirut: Librairie Du Liban, 1969); Said Bensaid, "Al-Watan and Al-Umma in Contemporary Arab Use," in *The Foundations of the Arab State*, ed. Ghassan Salame (London: Routledge, 1987), 152–9; Hassan El-Najjar, *The Gulf War, Overreaction & Excessiveness* (Dalton, GA: Amazone Press, 2001); Fred Halliday, *Islam and the Myth of Confrontation: Religion and Politics in the Middle East* (New York: IB Tauris, 2003); Sayed Khatab, *The Power of Sovereignty: The Political and Ideological Philosophy of Sayyid Qutb* (New York: Routledge, 2006).
157. Al-Barghouti, *The Umma and the Dawla*, 179; Rashid Khalidi, "Arab Nationalism: Historical Problems in the Literature," *The American Historical Review* 96 no. 5 (1991), 1363–73; Youssef Choueiri, *Arab Nationalism: A History* (Oxford and Malden: Blackwell Publishers, 2000).
158. Al-Barghouti, *The Umma and the Dawla*, 179. In the 1880s, "Salim Al-Bustani [son of Butrus Al-Bustani, a central figure within the Arab Renaissance] defined nationalism as … solidarity resulting from the interaction among people who have the same religion, language, and territory." Adding to Al-Bustani's definition in 1871, Abd al-Hamid Al-Zahrawi, a foremost proponent of Arab nationalism, "history, traditions, and common interests." El-Najjar, *The Gulf War*; al-Duri, "Al-Judhur Al-Tarikhiyya Li-L-Shuubiyya," al-Qawmiyyah al-ʿArabiyyah w'al-Islām.
159. Allāh, Qur'ān, 49:13.
160. Muhammed, in D.A. Turner, *This Is Not a Peace Pipe: Towards a Critical Indigenous Philosophy* (Toronto: University of Toronto Press, 2006), 35–6.
161. Marshall G.S. Hodgson, *The Venture of Islam, Volume 2: The Expansion of Islam in the Middle Periods* (Chicago: University of Chicago Press, 1977); *The Venture of Islam, Volume 1: The Classical Age of Islam* (Chicago: University of Chicago Press, 2009); Peter Mandaville, "Islam and International Relations in the Middle East: From Umma to Nation State," in *International Relations of the Middle East*, ed. Louise Fawcett (New York: Oxford University Press, 2009), 170–87; *Global Political Islam* (New York: Routledge, 2010); *Transnational Muslim Politics: Reimagining the Umma* (New York: Routledge, 2003); Massad, *Islam in Liberalism*; Piscatori, *Islam in a World of Nation-States*, 1.
162. Al-Barghouti, *The Umma and the Dawla*, 61.
163. Anver Emon, "Reflections on the 'Constitution of Medina': An Essay on Methodology and Idealogy in Islamic Legal History," in *UCLA Journal of Islamic and Near Eastern Law* 103 (2001), 106.

164. Tamim Al-Barghouti, *The Umma and the Dawla*, 61.
165. Munis, in Anver Emon, "Reflections on the 'Constitution of Medina'", 122.
166. 49:13.
167. Al-Barghouti, *The Umma and the Dawla*, 37.
168. Ibid., 39.
169. Al-Barghouti, *The Umma and the Dawla*, 39.
170. Qur'ān, 16:120.
171. Al-Barghouti, *The Umma and the Dawla*, 61; Ibn Hashim, 2:109–12.
172. Ibid. The treaty stated: "In The name of God the all Mighty the all Merciful: This is the writing of Muḥammad the Prophet, between the Believers and Muslims from Quraysh and [those from] Yathrib, and whoever followed them, joined them and fought along their side: That of all they are one Umma *(Ummatun Wahidatun min duni'l-nas)*. The pious believers are against whoever commits a crime amongst them, or seeks to do injustice, sin, aggression, or corruption among believers, even if [s]he was one of their sons. No believer is to kill another believer in revenge for an infidel, and no believer should help an infidel against a believer, and that the trust of God is one ... Believers are one another's allies vis-a-vis the rest of the world, and whoever follows us of the Jews would be helped and supported and they are not to be oppressed. The peace of the believers is one; no believer is to make without the consent of other believers when at war, unless they agree on that fairly. And believers should take revenge for one another for their blood shed in the way of God. And whoever kills a believer and is proven to have done so in purpose and in aggression should be killed in return unless the victim's relatives agree to a settlement ... No believer, of who have what is in this document and who believed in God and in the Last Day, can help a criminal nor protect him [and/or her] and whoever does that will endure God's curse and wrath in the Day of Resurrection ... And whatever you disagree upon, you refer it to God and the almighty [the Qur'ān] and to Mohammad ... And the Jews of *Bani'awf* are an Umma with the believers [could also be translated as form an Umma alongside the believers]. Jews have their *din* [religion-tradition-faith] and to the Muslims their *din* ... except for those who commit an aggression or a sin, for they should not endanger but themselves and their households ... and to the Jews of *Bani Najjar* the same rights of the Jews of *Bani'awf* ... And the friends and allies of the Jews are like the Jews regarding rights, and that no one of them is to leave without the permission of Mohammad, and whoever cheats or deceives, would only endanger himself [and/or herself] and his [and/or her] family, except in case of aggression [in case all out war between the Jews and the Prophet] and that Jews and Muslims are allies against whoever fights against the peoples of this document, and that they will defend Yathrib [Medina],

And that Mohammad is the Messenger of God" (Ibn Hashim, 2:109–12, in Al-Barghouti, *The Umma and the Dawla*, 61). See also Marshall Hodgson, *The Venture of Islam, Volume 2* or alternatively: http://en.wikisource.org/wiki/Medina_Charter.

173. Qur'ān, 60:8.
174. Qur'ān, 109:6 and 18:29.
175. Qur'ān, 88: 21–22.
176. Al-Barghouti, *The Umma and the Dawla.*
177. Ibid., 56. It is in this sense that debates such as that between decolonial theorists like Ramon Grosfoguel, as to whether "the Ottoman state was not an empire, but rather a sultanate," or others like Walter Mignolo and Salman Sayyid who argue "that the Ottoman state was indeed an imperial configuration" operate from a faulty premise given what they take as given in the notion of the "state" as well as their attachment to the concept of the so-called "Caliphate" as opposed to the Umma, where sovereignty truly lies. While I concede that pre-modern Muslims developed an empire, with imperialist dimensions, this book decolonially contests the idea of "rulership" following the Prophet's death to begin with.
178. Al-Barghouti, *The Umma and the Dawla*, 37.
179. Ibid., 57.
180. Ibid., 57.
181. Ibid., 58; Hodgson, *The Venture of Islam, Volume 2*; Piscatori, *Islam in a World of Nation-States.*
182. See Osman Rifat Ibrahim's article on Al-jazeera, titled "Why Abu Bakr Al-Baghdadi Is an Impostor" (2014): www.aljazeera.com/indepth/opinion/2014/07/baghdadi-impostor-20147991513785260.html
183. Al-Barghouti, *The Umma and the Dawla*, 58.
184. Abdul Rahman Ibn Khaldoun (1332–1406) was a fourteenth century Muslim historian and sociologist, born in Seville in Muslim Spain. He is best known for his text *Al-Muqaddimah* and his theory on "'assabiyya" as a form of tribal solidarity that describes the rise and fall of princedoms. Regarding it, he states "that such an ethic developed because of the nomadic forms of production and social organization, and that it enabled nomads to invade settled societies, at which point they gradually turn into settled communities themselves, allowing tribal bounds to loosen, forming a specialized economy, where defence is delegated to mercenary forces, thus making them vulnerable to fresh nomadic invasions" (Al-Barghouti, *The Umma and the Dawla*, 62). Arab nationalists saw "in Ibn Khaldun's ideas a non-religious, pre-colonial expression of Arabism" (ibid., 72). Islamists, on the other hand, "accepted this congruence, only to emphasize that, like Ibn Khaldoun's Assabiyya, Arab nationalism was but a sheer emotional force that holds no moral content" seeing as "it refers to a group's coherence,

but not to its purpose and direction, neither does it suggest anything about its form of government" (ibid., 73). Being an Arab Muslim, Ibn Khaldoun's theories were "of exceptional value to Arab nationalist theorists," given his interpretation of history didn't refer to a divine order, which gave him the appearance of "a secular Arab scientist from the middle ages who recognized tribal (Arab nationalists read that as ethnic) solidarity as the basis of political association" and that ultimately led, as Al-Barghouti argues, to misinterpretations of his work by Arab nationalists (ibid., 151). The attempt thus "to assimilate with the colonial master resulted in deforming both the colonially imported culture and the native one" where, unsurprisingly, a colonial hybrid, here the concept of Arab Qawmiyyah, "lacked the consistency of both its parents, European nationalism and Khaldounian Assabiyya" (ibid., 180).

185. Al-Barghouti, *The Umma and the Dawla*, 62.
186. Ibid., 66.
187. Ibid., 57.
188. Ibid., 67; Choueiri, *Arab Nationalism*.
189. Al-Barghouti, *The Umma and the Dawla*, 76.
190. Ibid., 88.
191. Ibid., 88.
192. John L Esposito, *Islam: The Straight Path*, vol. 4 (New York: Oxford University Press, 1998), 33–5; Al-Barghouti, *The Umma and the Dawla*; M. Bamyeh, *Anarchy as Order: The History and Future of Civic Humanity* (Lanham: Rowman & Littlefield, 2009); Hodgson, *The Venture of Islam, Volume 2*; *The Venture of Islam, Volume 1: The Classical Age of Islam*; Mandaville, "Islam and International Relations in the Middle East"; Mandaville, *Transnational Muslim Politics*; Piscatori, *Islam in a World of Nation-States*, 1; A. Hourani, *Islam in European Thought* (Cambridge: Cambridge University Press, 1992); *A History of Arab Peoples* (Cambridge, MA : Belknap Press of Harvard University Press, 1991); E. Said, *Covering Islam: How the Media and the Experts Determine How We See the Rest of the World* (New York: Random House, 2008); Karen Armstrong, *Muhammad Prophet for Our Time* (New York: HarperOne, 2006); *Fields of Blood : Religion and the History of Violence.* (New York ; Toronto :Alfred A. Knopf, a division of Random House LLC, 2014); Hugh N. Kennedy, *The Great Arab Conquests: How the Spread of Islam Changed the World We Live In* (Philadelphia: Da Capo, 2007); Youssef Aboul-Enein, *Islamic Rulings on Warfare* (Carlisle, PA: Strategic Studies Institute, US Army War College, 2004); Ira Lapidus, *A History of Islamic Societies* (New York : Cambridge University Press, 2014); Thomas Arnold, *The Spread of Islam in the World* (Delhi: Goodword Books, 2008).
193. Esposito, *Islam: The Straight Path*, 33–5; Al-Barghouti, *The Umma and the Dawla*; Bamyeh, *Anarchy as Order*; Hodgson, *The Venture of Islam, Volume*

2; *The Venture of Islam, Volume 1*; Mandaville, "Islam and International Relations in the Middle East"; Mandaville, *Transnational Muslim Politic*; Piscatori, *Islam in a World of Nation-States*, 1.

194. Esposito, *Islam: The Straight Path*, 33–5.
195. Ibid.
196. Ibid.
197. Ibid.
198. Peter R. Demant, *Islam vs. Islamism: The Dilemma of the Muslim World*, Forward by Asghar Ali Engineer (Westport: Praeger, 2006), 29–31; Al-Duri, 1981: 31–40; Khalidi; "Arab Nationalism"; Al-Barghouti, *The Umma and the Dawla*; Choueiri, *Arab Nationalism*; Bensaid, "Al-Watan and Al-Umma in Contemporary Arab Use"; Khatab, *The Power of Sovereignty*; Dawisha, 2003; Halliday, *Islam and the Myth of Confrontation*.
199. *Islam vs. Islamism*, 29–31; Gilles Kepel, *The War For Muslim Minds* (Cambridge, MA: Harvard University Press, 2004); Piscatori, *Islam in a World of Nation-States*.
200. Al-Barghouti, *The Umma and the Dawla*, 178.
201. Ibid., *Islam vs. Islamism*, 29–31; Al-Duri, 1981, 31–40; Khalidi, "Arab Nationalism"; Choueiri, *Arab Nationalism*; Bensaid, "Al-Watan and Al-Umma in Contemporary Arab Use"; Khatab, *The Power of Sovereignty*; Adeed Dawisha, *Arab Nationalism in the Twentieth Century: From Triumph to Despair* (Princeton: Princeton University Press, 2016); Halliday, *Islam and the Myth of Confrontation*).
202. Tamim Al-Barghouti, "History Repeats Itself," in *The Daily Star*, Beirut (July 23, 2003).
203. Ibid.
204. This analysis is irrespective of the Chicago and Freiburg or Frankfurt schools of thought that have theorized what neoliberalism "is." T. Lemke, "'The Birth of Bio-politics': Michel Foucault's Lecture at the Collège De France on Neo-liberal Governmentality," *Economy and Society* 30, no. 2 (2001), 19–207; Michel Foucault, "The Birth of Biopolitics," in Michel Foucault, *Ethics: Subjectivity and Truth*, ed. Paul Rabinow (New York: The New Press, 1997), 73–9; Colin Gordon, "Governmental Rationality: An Introduction," in *The Foucault Effect: Studies in Governmentality*, ed. Graham Burchell, Colin Gordon, and Peter Miller (Hemel Hempstead: Harvester Wheatsheaf, 1991), 43; J. Donzelot, "The Mobilization of Society," in *The Foucault Effect: Studies in Governmentality*, ed. Graham Burchell, Colin Gordon, and Peter Miller (Chicago: University of Chicago Press, 1991), 169–79.
205. Foucault, in Lemke, "'The Birth of Bio-politics", 8; Foucault, Lecture, March 21, 1979. See also Donzelot, *The Foucault Effect*.
206. Gustavo Esteva, "Recovering Hope: The Zapatista Example," *Upside Down World* (2013).
207. Driskill et al., *Queer Indigenous Studies*.

208. Eve Tuck and K. Wayne Yang, "Decolonization Is Not a Metaphor," *Decolonization: Indigeneity, Education & Society* 1, no. 1 (2012), 12.
209. Isabel Altamirano-Jiménez, *Indigenous Encounters with Neoliberalism: Place, Women, and the Environment in Canada and Mexico* (Vancouver: UBC Press, 2013), 57.
210. As evidenced by the anti-colonial and anti-imperial Third-World nationalist independence movements of the 1950s, 1960s, and 1970s, which at best embodied a Eurocentric, structuralist, Marxist-Leninist, socialist trajectory, and hence merely emulated, appealed to, and adopted white superior, civilizational, Euro-American paradigms.
211. R. Dhamoon, "A Feminist Approach to Decolonizing Anti-Racism: Rethinking Transnationalism, Intersectionality, and Settler Colonialism," *Feral Feminisms* 4 (2015), 33.
212. Tuck and Yang, "Decolonization Is Not a Metaphor," 4.
213. Sandy Grande, "Whitestream Feminism and the Colonialist Project: Toward a Theory of Indigenista," in *Red Pedagogy: Native American Social and Political Thought* (Lanham: Rowman & Littlefield, 2004), 27.
214. Jodi A. Byrd and Michael Rothberg, "Between Subalternity and Indigeneity: Critical Categories for Postcolonial Studies," *Interventions* 13, no. 1 (2011), 3.
215. Tuck and Yang, "Decolonization Is Not a Metaphor," 12.
216. Ibid., 19.
217. Ibid., 219.
218. Ibid., 18. Tuck and Yang note, "There are important parallels between Occupy/Decolonize and the French/Haitian Revolutions of 1789–1799 and 1791–1804, respectively" given that "Haiti has the dubious distinction of being 'the poorest country in the Western hemisphere' (Central Intelligence Agency, 2012); yet, it was the richest of France's colonies until the Haitian Revolution, the only slave revolution to ever found a state" (ibid., 26).
219. Anti-colonial critiques, in the absence of an analysis of the entwined circulatory relationship between settler- and franchise-colonial societies, are always doomed to reproduce colonialist horizons.
220. Dhamoon, "A Feminist Approach to Decolonizing Anti-Racism," 31; Patrick Wolfe, "Settler Colonialism and the Elimination of the Native," *Journal of Genocide Research* 8, no. 4 (2006), 387–409.
221. Wolfe, "Settler Colonialism and the Elimination of the Native," 388.
222. Dhamoon, "A Feminist Approach to Decolonizing Anti-Racism," 32.
223. Tuck and Yang, "Decolonization Is Not a Metaphor," 10; Philip Joseph Deloria, *Playing Indian* (New Haven: Yale University Press, 1998); Tallbear, in Francie Latour, "The Myth of Native American Blood," *Boston. com* (2012); Mary Louise Fellows and Sherene Razack, "The Race to Innocence: Confronting Hierarchical Relations among Women," *Journal of Gender Race & Justice* 1 (1997), 335.

224. Tuck and Yang, "Decolonization Is Not a Metaphor," 10.
225. Simpson, *Mohawk Interruptus*.
226. J.A. Byrd, *The Transit of Empire: Indigenous Critiques of Colonialism* (Minneapolis: University of Minnesota Press, 2011), xiii.
227. A.L. Brandzel, *Against Citizenship: The Violence of the Normative* (Chicago: University of Chicago Press, 2016), 102.
228. Coulthard, *Red Skin, White Masks*, 60.
229. Achille Mbembe, Necropolitics (London: Allen Lane, 2003), 25.
230. Ibid., 26.
231. Ibid., 26.
232. Brandzel, *Against Citizenship*, 129. S. Audra and S. Andrea, *Theorizing Native Studies* (Durham, NC: Duke University Press), 11.
233. Tuck ana Yang, *Decolonization Is Not A Metaphor*, 1.
234. Ibid.; see also Brandzel, *Against Citizenship*. As Byrd argues, in reference to radical and non-statist conceptualizations of Indigenous decolonization, intellectual and emotional headaches are a necessary component of decolonization.
235. Manu Vimalassery, Juliana Hu Pegues, and Alyosha Goldstein, "Introduction: On Colonial Unknowing," *Theory & Event* 19, no. 4 (2016), 7; Sara Ahmed, *Queer Phenomenology: Orientations, Objects, Others* (Durham, NC: Duke University Press, 2006).
236. Tuck and Yang, "Decolonization Is Not a Metaphor," 18.
237. Brandzel, *Against Citizenship*, 128–9.
238. Linda Tuhiwai Smith, *Decolonizing Methodologies: Research and Indigenous Peoples* (London: Zed Books, 2013); Lawrence and Dua, "Decolonizing Antiracism."
239. Lawrence and Dua, "Decolonizing Antiracism."
240. Bonita Lawrence and Zainab Amadahy, "Indigenous Peoples and Black People in Canada: Settlers or Allies?" in *Breaching the Colonial Contract: Anti-Colonialism in the US and Canada*, ed. Arlo Kempf (New York: Springer, 2010), 107.
241. Byrd, *The Transit of Empire*, xxxviii–xxxix.
242. Ibid., xix; Edward Kamau Brathwaite, *The Arrivants: A New World Trilogy – Rights of Passage/Islands/Masks* (Oxford: Oxford Unviersity Press, 1988); Kamau Brathwaite, *Roots* (Michigan: University of Michigan Press, 1993).
243. Byrd, *The Transit of Empire*, 229.
244. Ibid., 222.
245. See also, for example, the work of Shona N. Jackson, Achille Mbembe, Stephanie Smallwood, Eve Tuck, Wayne Yang, M. Jacqui Alexander, Saidiya Hartman, Kyle T. Mays, Bonita Lawrence, Zainab Amadahy, Frank Wilderson III, Jared Sexton, Tiffany Lethabo King, Alaina E. Roberts, Melissa Phung, and Omise'eke Natasha Tinsley. Shona N. Jackson, for example, discusses "practices of belonging and becoming

that have provided a new material, symbolic, and discursive relationship to the land for blacks, Indo-Guyanese, *and* Indigenous Peoples." Shona N. Jackson, *Creole Indigeneity: Between Myth and Nation in the Caribbean* (Minneapolis: University of Minnesota Press, 2012), 64.

246. Saidiya Hartman, *On Working with Archives: An Interview with Writer Saidiya Hartman*, https://thecreativeindependent.com/people/saidiya-hartman-on-working-with-archives/; Katherine McKittrick, *Demonic Grounds: Black Women and the Cartographies of Struggle* (Minneapolis: University of Minnesota Press, 2006). More recently, there have been a series of blog posts concerning anti-blackness and settler-colonialism hosted by the journal *Decolonization: Indigeneity, Education, and Society*, https://decolonization.wordpress.com/tag/antiblackness/.

247. Amadahy and Lawrence, "Indigenous Peoples and Black People in Canada"; also see Charles S. Aiken, "A New Type of Black Ghetto in the Plantation South," *Annals of the Association of American Geographers* 80, no. 2 (1990), 223–46. As Tuck and Yang note, "Black and Native people alike were induced to raid and enslave Native tribes, as a bargain for their own freedom or to defer their own enslavibility by the British, French, and then American settlers" ("Decolonization Is Not a Metaphor," 33). As they note, "The rising number of impoverished, all black townships is the result of mechanization of agriculture and a fundamental settler covenant that keeps black people landless" and "when black labor is unlabored, the Black person underneath is the excess" (ibid., 33–4; also see Aiken, "A New Type of Black Ghetto"). As Dennis Childs writes, "the slave ship and the plantation" and not Bentham's panopticon as presented by Foucault, "operated as spatial, racial, and economic templates for subsequent models of coerced labor and human warehousing – as America's original prison industrial complex" ("You Ain't Seen Nothin' Yet": Beloved, the American Chain Gang, and the Middle Passage Remix," *American Quarterly* 61, no. 2, 2009), 288). Moreover, Childs states, "despite the rise of publicly traded prisons, farms are not fundamentally capitalist ventures; at their core, they are colonial contract institutions much like Spanish Missions, Indian Boarding Schools, and ghetto school systems" (ibid., 235). In other words, "the labor to cage black bodies is paid for by the state and then land is granted, worked by convict labor, to generate additional profits for the prison proprietors" but "it is the management of excess presence on the land, not the forced labor, that is the main object of slavery under settler colonialism" (ibid., 235). Also see Iyko Day, "Being or Nothingness: Indigeneity, Antiblackness, and Settler Colonial Critique," *Critical Ethnic Studies* 1, no. 2 (2015), 102–21.

248. Afua Cooper, "The Invisible History of the Slave Trade, " in *The Toronto Star* (March 25, 2007), www.thestar.com/opinion/2007/03/25/the_invisible_history_of_the_slave_trade.html; also see "Acts of Resistance:

Black Men and Women Engage Slavery in Upper Canada, 1793–1803," *Ontario History* 99, no. 1 (2007), 5–17; R. Bruce Shepard, *Deemed Unsuitable: Blacks from Oklahoma Move to the Canadian Prairies in Search of Equality in the Early 20th Century, Only to Find Racism in Their New Home* (Los Angeles: Umbrella Press, 1997). This point is critical given the "ongoing legacy of enslavement, exclusion and exploitation of Black and African migrants" and the exploitation and oppression of "diasporic African peoples in Canada" (Farrah-Marie Miranda, "Anti-Blackness and Undoing the Territory of Migrant Justice," *Decolonization: Indigeneity, Education & Society* (2015), https://decolonization.wordpress.com/2015/12/02/antiblackness-and-undoing-the-territory-of-migrant-justice/).

249. Irrespective of the origins of individuals along the landscape in which blackness functions, all are subject to militarized policing that within itself is akin to slave catchers who chased runaways and prevented slave revolts. Police are involved in the monitoring, surveilling, stop-and-frisking, and assassination of Black bodies, wherein all Maritimers of African descent, Caribbeans, and from regions such as Central and South America and even Somalis and Middle-Easterners are homogeneously cast as simply Black. Nonetheless, it is this reading of blackness that also confirms America's riddled founding on anti-Muslim sentiment since inception.
250. Beydoun, "The Colour of Slavery," *Al-Jazeera* (2013).
251. Kecia Ali, "The Truth about Islam and Sex Slavery History Is More Complicated Than You Think," *Huffington Post* (2015).
252. Ibid.
253. Mahmood Mamdani, "Introduction: Trans-African Slaveries Thinking Historically," *Comparative Studies of South Asia, Africa and the Middle East* 38 no. 2 (2018), 185–210; Samar Attar, *Debunking the Myths of Colonization: The Arabs and Europe* (Lanham: University Press of America, 2010); Aziz Al-Azmeh, "Nationalism and the Arabs," *Arab Studies Quarterly* 17, no. 1–2 (1995), 1–17 (1995); Antonious, *The Arab Awakening*; Youssef M. Choueiri, "Arab Nationalism: Arabness, Arab Jews and the Arab Spring," in *The Routledge Handbook of Muslim-Jewish Relations*, ed. J. Meri (London and New York: Routledge, 2016), 317–30; Patricia Crone, "Imperial Trauma: The Case of the Arabs," *Common Knowledge* 12, no. 1 (2006), 107–16; Abd al-Aziz Duri, *The Historical Formation of the Arab Nation (Rle: The Arab Nation)* (New York: Routledge, 2012); Farabi, *Al-Siyasah Al-Madaniyah*; Khalidi, "Arab Nationalism; Abd al-Wahhab Khallaf, *Masadir Al-Tashrial-Islami Fi Ma La Nass Fihi* (Cairo: Mahad al-Dirasat al-Arabiyyah al-Alamiyyah, 1954); Yamal al-Din Muhammad Ibn Manzur, *Lisan Al-Arab*; Bassam Tibi and Peter Sluglett, *Arab Nationalism: A Critical Enquiry* (New York: Springer, 1990); Choueiri, *Arab Nationalism*; Hourani, *Islam in European Thought*; *A History of the Arab Peoples: Updated Edition* (London: Faber & Faber, 2013); Karen

Armstrong, *Islam: A Short History* (New York: Modern Library, 2007). Dumbing down the conversation to Arab supremacy as equivalent to the Middle Passage is demeaning to our mutually constitutive histories when the "Congo, for example, was one of the largest slave holding nations – *prior* to European colonialism or even European contact. [The] Congo conquered other African nations and tribes and peoples and enslaved innumerable numbers of black Africans [and] later, they had engagement with Europe and began to trade with Portugal." Valerie Complex, Son of Baldwin, Isabelle Masado, and Law Ware, "Wakanda Future Do You Imagine? A Critical Examination of the Aesthetics, Culture, Politics, and Symbolism of the Blockbuster Film 'Black Panther'," *Medium* (2018).

254. Abdullah bin Hamid Ali, "Beyond Racism: The Challenge of Turning the Islamic Ideal into Reality," *Renovatio: The Journal of Zaytuna College* (2017).
255. Lee, in Rod Dreher, "Georgetown Prof Defends Islamic Slavery," *The American Conservative* (2017); Leena Habiballa, "Too Black to Be Arab, Too Arab to Be Black," *Media Diversified* (2016), https://mediadiversified.org/2016/01/16/too-black-to-be-arab/; Idil Akinci "The Multiple Roots of Emiratiness: The Cosmopolitan History of Emirati Society," *Open Democracy* (2018), www.opendemocracy.net/en/beyond-trafficking-and-slavery/the-multiple-roots-of-emiratiness/; Ana Lucia Araujo, *Reparations for Slavery and the Slave Trade: A Transnational and Comparative History* (New York: Bloomsbury Publishing, 2017).
256. Admirably, groups such as *Believers Bail Out* (BBO) inspired by Su'ad Abdul-Khabeer, Maytha Alhassan, and Kecia Ali are "community-led effort[s] to bail out Muslims in pretrial incarceration and ICE custody." See https://believersbailout.org/about/.
257. Similarly, the case with non-Black Muslim ignorance regarding towering Black Muslim figures such as Sundiata Keita, Usman Dan Fodio, Mansa Musa.
258. Tuck and Yang, "Decolonization Is Not a Metaphor," 3.
259. Vimalassery, Pegues, and Goldstein, "Introduction: On Colonial Unknowing," 1.
260. T. Alfred, *Peace Power Righteousness: An Indigenous Manifesto* (Don Mills, Ontario: Oxford University Press, 1999); Corntassel, "Re-envisioning Resurgence.
261. Tavia Nyong'o, "Queer Africa and the Fantasy of Virtual Participation," *WSQ: Women's Studies Quarterly* 40, no. 1 (2012), 40–63; *Black Queer Studies: A Critical Anthology*, ed. E. Patrick Johnson and Mae G. Henderson (Durham, NC: Duke University Press, 2005); M. Cobb, David L. Eng, Judith Halberstam, and José Esteban Muñoz, "Introduction: What's Queer about Queer Studies Now?" *Social Text* 23, no. 3–4 (84–85) (2005); Gayatri Gopinath, *Impossible Desires: Queer Diasporas and South Asian Public*

Cultures (Durham, NC: Duke University Press, 2005); Joon Oluchi Lee, "The Joy of the Castrated Boy," *Social Text* 23, no. 3–4 (84–85) (2005), 35–56; Judith Halberstam, *In a Queer Time and Place: Transgender Bodies, Subcultural Lives* (New York: SUNY Press, 2005).

262. Homi K. Bhabha, *The Postcolonial and the Postmodern: The Question of Agency* (NewYork and London: Routledge,1994); Crenshaw, "Mapping the Margins: Intersectionality, Identity Politics, and Violence against Women of Color (1994)," in *Violence against Women: Classic Papers*, ed. R.K. Bergen, J.L. Edleson, and C.M. Renzetti (Auckland: Pearson Education New Zealand, 2005), 282–313; Leela Gandhi, *Postcolonial Theory: A Critical Introduction* (New York: Columbia University Press, 1998); T. Minh-ha Trinh, "Not You/Like You: Post-colonial Women and the Interlocking Questions of Identity and Difference," *Inscriptions* 3 (1988), 71–7; Rauna Kuokkanen, "Sámi Women, Autonomy, and Decolonization in the Age of Globalization," *Rethinking Nordic Colonialism. A Postcolonial Exhibition Project in Five Acts. Act* 4 (2006), 2.
263. Brandzel, *Against Citizenship*, 113; also see Byrd, *The Transit of Empire*; Danielle Sandhu, *Theorizing Brown Identity* (Toronto: University of Toronto Press, 2014), 18.
264. Sandhu, *Theorizing Brown Identity*, 18.
265. Vimalassery, Pegues, and Goldstein, "Introduction: On Colonial Unknowing," 7; Ahmed, *Queer Phenomenology*. The concept of arrivant can help us move beyond clear divisions and "between social location and claim to place." Particularly given that Byrd notes that there are "moments where the representational logics of colonial discourses break down" such that we may be able to engage "multiple colonial experiences grounded not only in race but gender, indigeneity, conquest, and sexuality as well" (*The Transit of Empire*, 53).
266. Vimalassery, Pegues, and Goldstein, "Introduction: On Colonial Unknowing," 7. See also Miranda, "Anti-Blackness and Undoing the Territory of Migrant Justice"; Shepard, *Deemed Unsuitable*.
267. Ahmed, *Queer Phenomenology*.
268. Ibid., 40.
269. Vimalassery, Pegues, and Goldstein, "Introduction: On Colonial Unknowing," 8.
270. Ibid.
271. Tuck and Yang, "Decolonization Is Not a Metaphor," 31; Albert Memmi, *The Colonizer and the Colonized*, trans. Howard Greenfeld (Boston: Beacon, 1991).
272. Ibid.
273. Nandita Sharma and Cynthia Wright, "Decolonizing Resistance, Challenging Colonial States," *Social Justice* 35, no. 3 (113) (2008), 122–3; Dhamoon, "A Feminist Approach to Decolonizing Anti-Racism," 22.
274. Dhamoon, "A Feminist Approach to Decolonizing Anti-Racism," 22.

275. Ibid., 23.
276. Ibid., 24.
277. Beenash Jafri, "Privilege Vs. Complicity: People of Colour and Settler Colonialism," *Equity Matters* 21 (2012); also Dhamoon, "A Feminist Approach to Decolonizing Anti-Racism," 25.
278. Byrd and Rothberg, "Between Subalternity and Indigeneity," 3.
279. Ibid., 4; see also Gaurav Desai, "Between Indigeneity and Diaspora: Questions from a Scholar Tourist," *Interventions* 13, no. 1 (2011), 53–66; Gaurav Gajanan Desai and Supriya Nair, *Postcolonialisms: An Anthology of Cultural Theory and Criticism* (New Brunswick: Rutgers University Press, 2005).
280. Byrd and Rothberg, "Between Subalternity and Indigeneity," 3.
281. Ibid., 4. As Byrd and Rothberg argue, the "question of fit suggests that at stake in exploring the resonance between the categories 'subaltern' and 'indigenous' is a matter of urgent translation – translation in all its senses, linguistic, cultural, and spatial. Indeed, the question of translation goes beyond the question of how to relate two autonomously developing intellectual traditions to each other (indigenous studies and subaltern/postcolonial studies)" (ibid., 4).
282. Ibid., 8; Desai, "Between Indigeneity and Diaspora."
283. Byrd and Rothberg, "Between Subalternity and Indigeneity," 8; Desai, "Between Indigeneity and Diaspora."
284. Byrd and Rothberg, "Between Subalternity and Indigeneity," 9.
285. Ibid., 8–9.
286. Jeannette Armstrong, *First Nations on Ancestral Connection* (Stone Circle Press, n.d.). Here, indigeneity is conceived "beyond race, ethnicity or political definitions, [and hence] indigeneity can become a social ethic. In this way, the re-indigenized person or community is a perfectly integrated part of nature rather than separate from it."
287. Robert Lovelace, "The Last Fire in Ghostland – Keynote Address," paper presented at the The Association for Literature, Environment, and Culture in Canada/L'Association pour la littérature, l'environnement et la culture au Canada (ALECC), Queen's University, Kingston, Ontario (2016); "The Philosophy of Indigeneity Knowledge: 'Indigenous – Meaning What?'" paper presented at the Notes for Panel presentation at Congress of the Humanities and Social Sciences, Ottawa, Ontario (2015).
288. Ibid.
289. "Asserting Our Savage Nature," paper presented at the 15th Annual Symposium on Indigenous Research, Queen's University (2013). Lovelace notes, "The root of the word indigenous is gignère. While it has Latin roots in English it has even deeper beginnings throughout the Mediterranean world" ("The Philosophy of Indigeneity Knowledge"). Lovelace further states, "in Modern English you can recognize the

word in such forms as Genesis, Genealogy, Genuine, and of course Genecology and genitals. [In the] 1640s, from Late Latin *indigenus* 'born in a country, native', from Latin *indigena* 'sprung from the land', as a noun, 'a native', literally 'in-born', or 'born in (a place)', from Old Latin *indu* 'in, within" (earlier *endo*) + **gene-*, root of *gignere* (perf. *genui*) 'beget', from PIE **gen-* 'produce'" (ibid.). Through reindigenization, our species can transcend the transgressive colonial/imperial boundaries that splinter humanity; we can move beyond rights-based discourses of reconciliation and the same old exploitive arrogance towards the earth.

290. Lovelace, "The Philosophy of Indigeneity Knowledge."
291. Z. Amadahy, "Interview with Zainab Amadahy,"*Feral Feminisms* 4 (2015), 38–43; Zainab Amadahy in Conversation with *Feral Feminisms*' Guest Editors.
292. Ibid.
293. Ibid.
294. Dhamoon, "A Feminist Approach to Decolonizing Anti-Racism," 24. The re-interpretation of indigeneity is to construct new coordinates for collective and global mobilization by troubling the politics of decolonizing solidarity as the in vogue intellectual flavor of the moment. There is no crystal ball that we can defer to unequivocally to be assured of what we will become by engaging decolonization either.
295. Zainab Amadahy in Conversation with *Feral Feminisms*' Guest Editors"; Jeannette C. Armstrong, *Slash* (Penticton, BC: Theytus Books, 1988); Lovelace, "Decolonization."

4. Anarcha-Islām: An Anti- and Non-Capitalist Islām

1. Antonin Artaud, "To Have Done with the Judgment of God," in *Antonin Artaud: Selected Writings*, ed. Susan Sontag, Helen Weaver, and Don Eric Levine (New York: Farrar, Straus and Giroux,1976), 556.
2. Félix Guattari and Antonio Negri, *Communists Like Us: New Spaces of Liberty, New Lines of Alliance*, trans. Michael Ryan, (New York: Semiotext(E), 1990), 17.
3. Z. Ahmad, *Islam, Poverty and Income Distribution: A Discussion of the Distinctive Islamic Approach to Eradication of Poverty and Achievement of an Equitable Distribution of Income and Wealth* (Markfield, U.K.: Islamic Foundation, 1991), 33.
4. Ibid., 33.
5. J.L. Esposito, *What Everyone Needs to Know about Islam* (New York: Oxford University Press, 2002), 163.
6. Tariq Ramadan, *Western Muslims and the Future of Islam* (Oxford: Oxford University Press, 2003), 89.
7. Ahmad, *Islam, Poverty and Income Distribution*, 46.

8. It is the role of *property* to *drag*. For it is reported in the Sunnah, through "Abu Huraryrah that the Prophet [peace be upon him] said: 'The poor will enter paradise five hundred years ahead of the rich'." Safdar Hasan Siddiqi and Muhammad ibn Abd Allāh, *Muhammad (Peace be Upon Him) Messenger of Allah, on Social Behaviour* (Lahore: Ferozsons, 1984), 91. That is, while the latter remain behind accounting for accrued and hoarded wealth, how they received it and how they expended it, the former will not be answerable for any such thing; in this sense, property drags.
9. Foucault, in T. Lemke, "'The Birth of Bio-politics': Michel Foucault's Lecture at the Collège De France on Neo-liberal Governmentality," *Economy and Society* 30, no. 2 (2001), 199.
10. As Allāh says in the Qur'ān, "Sees thou not that to Allāh bow down in worship all things that are in the heavens and earth, the sun, the moon, the stars; the hills, the trees, the animals; and a great number among humankind" (22:18). And from which all have been from water, when Allāh says, " We made from water every living thing" (21:30) while continuing in another verse saying, "And God has created every animal from water of them there are some that creep on their bellies; some that walk on two legs; and some that walk on four … It is he who has created humans from water" (24:45). This is a demonstration of not only the oneness of the Divine, to whom all belongs all, constructed of the same element that we are, but rather the recognition of the symbiotic communal responsibilities each carries in relation to the other.
11. Qur'ān, 2: 267 & 74.
12. Siddiqi and Abd Allāh, *Muhammad (Peace be Upon Him)*, 91; N.H. Ammar, "Islam and Deep Ecology," in *Deep Ecology and World Religions: New Essays on Sacred Ground*, ed. David Landis Barnhill and Roger S. Gottleib (New York: SUNY Press, 2001), 193–212.
13. John Thomas Cummings, Hossein Askari, and Ahmad Mustafa, "Islam and Modern Economic Change," in *Islam and Development* (New York: Syracuse University Press, 1980), 37.
14. Ibid.
15. Ibid.
16. Muhammad, in Ammar, "Islam and Deep Ecology," 204.
17. Allāh, Qur'ān, 54:28.
18. There are four other Qur'ānic verses that confirm this aspect of God as Absolute owner of property. The emphasis in each of the four verses below is on the constantly returned keyword "We." The Qur'ān confirms: "And the earth We have spread out (like a carpet); set thereon mountains firm and immovable; and produced therein all things in due balance. And We have provided therein means as subsistence, for you and for those whose subsistence ye are not responsible. And there is not a thing but its (sources and) treasures (inexhaustible) are with Us; but We only send down thereof in due and ascertainable measures. And We

send the fecundating winds, then cause the rain to descend from the sky, therewith providing you with water (in abundance), through ye are not the guardian of its stores, so intend not corruption of the earth" and "Do not kill a soul which Allāh has made sacred" (Qur'ān, 15:19–22; 6:151).

19. Cummings, Askari, and Mustafa, "Islam and Modern Economic Change," 36.
20. Akhtar A. Awan, *Equality, Efficiency, and Property Ownership in the Islamic Economic System* (Lanham: University Press of America, 1983).
21. Ibid., 30.
22. Ibid., 31.
23. Ibid.
24. Ibid.
25. Cummings, Askari, and Mustafa, "Islam and Modern Economic Change," 44.
26. Ahmad, *Islam, Poverty and Income Distribution*, 37.
27. John L. Esposito and Hossein Askari, *Islam and Development: Religion and Sociopolitical Change* (New York: Syracuse University Press, 1980), 42.
28. F. Guattari and A. Negri, *Communists Like Us: New Spaces of Liberty, New Lines of Alliance* (Los Angeles: Semiotext(E), 1990), 17.
29. The standard story told by economists is that money was invented to replace the barter system but rather than "the standard story" and in line with Graeber, I believe "first there's barter, then money, then finally credit comes out of that – if anything its precisely the other way around. Credit and debt comes first, then coinage emerges thousands of years later and then, when you do find 'I'll give you twenty chickens for that cow' type of barter systems, it's usually when there used to be cash markets, but for some reason – as in Russia, for example, in 1998 – the currency collapses or disappears" (2011). From an interview with David Graeber titled *What Is Debt?* www.nakedcapitalism.com/2011/08/what-is-debt-%E2%80%93-an-interview-with-economic-anthropologist-david-graeber.html.
30. David Graeber, *Debt: The First 5000 Years* (London: Penguin, 2012), 280.
31. As Graeber argues, "In Islamic society, the merchant" was "not just a respected figure, but a kind of paragon: like a warrior, a man of honour able to pursue far-flung adventures; unlike him, able to do so in a fashion damaging to no one" (ibid., 277). Our lady Khadija bint Khuwaylid, the Prophet's first spouse, and who proposed to Muḥammad, marrying him at 40, while he was approximately 25, had been one of the most successful merchants of Arabia. However, it ought to be noted that despite having profound respect for Graeber's work and scholarship, I do take issue with a comment he made, in which he stated, "In discussing topics ranging from the origins of free market capitalism (Islam) to the virtues of anarchism … free market ideology – does anyone know where it first

comes from? It comes from medieval Islam, and specifically, Shari'a. Because Shari'a provided this commercial law that is independent from the state" (ibid.). I take issue with two matters, given both: (a) Graeber's misuse of "Shari'a" in light of how it is defined and what is argued in this book; and (b) Graeber's premise that "Islam is responsible for free market ideology," with much bearing of the distinction between "free markets" and "capitalism" given what I state of Islām's commitment to anti-capitalism and extensive espousal of non-capitalist concepts and practices whether relating to debt cancelation or non-Euro-American understandings of property as discussed in this book chapter. David Graeber's comments were made *in conversation with Rebecca Solnit* on May 1, 2012 and the full transcript can be found here: www.guernicamag.com/interviews/beholden/

32. For further detail, see Abdul-Hamid Ahmad Abu-Sulayman, "The Theory of Economics of Islam: The Economics of Tawhid and Brotherhood; Philosophy, Concepts and Suggestions," in *Contemporary Aspects of Economic Thinking in Islam* (Plainfield: American Trust Foundations), and the proceedings of the Third East Coast regional Conference of the Muslims Students Association of the USA and Canada, American Trust Publications (April 1968).
33. Cummings, Askari, and Mustafa, "Islam and Modern Economic Change," 41.
34. Ahmad, *Islam, Poverty and Income Distribution*, 33.
35. Ibid., 33.
36. Masudul Alam Choudhury, *Money in Islam* (London: Routledge, 1997), 110.
37. Ibid.
38. Ibid.
39. Muḍārabah/Mushārakah seeks to minimize the production of what a community is not in need of by transforming the threshold of production or consumption into the exchange limit, in which exchange is of interest to a consumer and a producer. As Deleuze and Guattari note: The exchange limit is "one of temporal succession[s] because … [it] preserves itself [from iṣrāf] by switching territories [of that which is produced and consumed by way of a joint consensual collaborative operation between both parties, [consumer and producer,] at the conclusion of each period (*itinerancy*, *itineration*) … [and it is] this *iteration* [that] will govern the apparent exchange" (G. Deleuze and F. Guattari, *A Thousand Plateaus: Capitalism and Schizophrenia* (London: Bloomsbury Publishing, 1988), 440. Capitalism, in contrast, thrives on stockpiling, as its cardinal law and concern is that of "the simultaneous exploitation of different territories; or, when the exploitation is successive, the succession of operation periods bares [exploitation] on one and the same territory" till "the force of serial iteration is superseded by … global comparison";

that is, capitalism functions by over-producing, under-producing, intentionally, serially, locally, or globally, the consequence of which are exploitative assemblages, markets, in the absence of consensual collaborations between consumers and producers (ibid.,: 440).

40. Deleuze and Guattari, *A Thousand Plateaus*, 440.
41. Choudhury, *Money in Islam*, 110.
42. Muhammad Taqi Usmani, "An Introduction to Islamic Finance – Idaratual Maarif Karachi," *Pakistan-1999* (1998); Muhammad Imran Ashraf Usmani and Zeenat Zubairi, I*slamic Banking* (Karachi: Darul-Ishaat Urdu Bazar, 2002); ibid.
43. Ibid.
44. Ibid.
45. Ibid.
46. Ibid.
47. Ibid.
48. Ibid.
49. Ibid.
50. Ibid.
51. Usmani, "An Introduction to Islamic Finance"; Masudul Alam Choudhury and Mostaque Hussain, "A Paradigm of Islamic Money and Banking," *International Journal of Social Economics* 32, no. 3 (2005), 203–17; Sohail H. Hashmi, "Islamic Ethics in International Society," in *Islamic Political Ethics: Civil Society, Pluralism, and Conflict*, ed. S.H. Hashmi and J. Miles (Princeton: Princeton University Press, 2002), 148–72; Muhammad Rauf, *The Islamic Doctrine of Economics and Contemporary Economic Thought: Highlight of a Conference on a Theological Inquiry into Capitalism and Socialism* (Washington: American Enterprise Institute for Public Policy Research, 1979); Ramla Sadiq and Afia Mushtaq, "The Role of Islamic Finance in Sustainable Development," *Journal of Islamic Thought and Civilization* 5, no. 1 (2015), 46–65; Usmani and Zubairi, *Islamic Banking*; Ibrahim Warde, *Islamic Finance in the Global Economy* (Edinburgh: Edinburgh University Press, 2000); Rodney Wilson, *Economics, Ethics and Religion: Jewish, Christian and Muslim Economic Thought* (New York: Springer, 1997); Rodney Wilson, "Parallels between Islamic and Ethical Banking," Center for Middle-Eastern and Islamic Studies (University of Durham, 1997, www.islamonline.net/english/Contemporary/2004/02/Article01.shtml).
52. Usmani, "An Introduction to Islamic Finance."
53. Ibid.
54. Ibid.
55. Ibid.
56. Ibid.
57. Ibid.
58. Ibid.

59. Allāh, Qur'ān, 3:130; 4:61; 30:39; 2:275–280.
60. Ibid., 2:275.
61. Diederik Van Schaik, "Islamic Banking," *The Arab Bank Review* 3, no. 1 (2001), 45–52; Sadiq and Mushtaq, "The Role of Islamic Finance in Sustainable Development"; Warde, *Islamic Finance in the Global Economy*; Wilson, "Parallels between Islamic and Ethical Banking."
62. Van Schaik, "Islamic Banking"; Usmani and Zubairi, *Islamic Banking*; Wilson, "Parallels between Islamic and Ethical Banking." *Ribā al-faḍl* is also known as *Ribā al-buyuʿ*. See www.islamic-banking.com/glossary_R.aspx. Please also refer to Fazalur Rahman's *Riba & Interest* (1964) which can be found and downloaded at: http://fazlur-rahman.livejournal.com/2102.html.
63. Ibid.
64. Ibid. *Usury* of debt was an established practice amongst Arabs during the pre-Islamic period. The increment was known as *Ribā al-nasiah*. Interest in all conventional banking transactions come under the scope of *Ribā al-nasiah*. Also known as *Ribā al-diyūn*.
65. Esposito, *What Everyone Needs to Know about Islam*, 163.
66. Ahmad, *Islam, Poverty and Income Distribution*, 36.
67. Allāh, Qur'ān, 2:280.
68. Graeber, *Debt: The First 5000 Years.*
69. It is worthwhile noting as well the existence of other varying forms of Zakāt that are also considered to be rights. For example, *Infāq* and *Iṭʿām*. Infāq of Ṣadaqah denotes the act of the voluntary spending of charity and although it is not obligatory, it is directed to the welfare of those in more need, and is encouraged as a practice amongst the community. Of course there remains then Iṭʿām. Iṭʿām is the act of leaping beyond worldly glory, to hosting and being able to do so without cost, calculation, or rationalization, and therefore co-existing and voluntarily feeding guests, foreigners, brothers and sisters in need of sustenance (Ahmad, *Islam, Poverty and Income Distribution*, 42).
70. Allāh, Qur'ān, 9:60.
71. Cummings, Askari, and Mustafa, "Islam and Modern Economic Change," 26–7. Unlike examples like Arab and Muslim sheikhs, or even George Soros and Bill Gates who are praised and elevated in lavish esteem, rank and prestige, and who made their privileged fortunes through ruthless financial speculation before deciding to become global philanthropists and at least in Gate's case, at the price of quashing out competition and creating a "virtual monopoly." The fact is that for these people to learn to *give* they had to hypocritically first learn to steal and *take*.
72. Allāh, Qur'ān, 2:264.
73. Ramadan, *Western Muslims and the Future of Islam*, 193.
74. Ibid., 182.

75. Ibid., 89.
76. Ali Budak, *Fasting in Islam & the Month of Ramadan: A Comprehensive Guide*, trans. and ed. Süleyman BaUsaran (Somerset, NJ: The Light, 2005), 93–6.
77. Esposito, *What Everyone Needs to Know about Islam*, 167–8.
78. Graeber, *Debt: The First 5000 Years*, 275.
79. Aidit Ghazali, *Development: An Islamic Perspective* (Malaysia: Pelanduk Publications, 1990; K.A. Nizami, *Shah Wali-Allah ke Siyasi Maktubat (the Political Letters of al-Dihlawi)*, ed. and trans. K.A. Nizami (Aligarh, Delhi: Nadwatul Musannifin, 1955).
80. Ghazali, *Development*, 49–50. To Ghazali and Nizami, "those who need special attention and kind treatment in order to win their hearts" included three main categories: "a) Muslims who are wavering, including the newly-converted Muslim, b) Muslims living in border areas who need stronger support for defence, and c) Non-Muslims who agree not to fight against Muslims and/or otherwise become helpful to the Muslims and/or the 'Islamic state'" (ibid.).
81. Graeber, *Debt: The First 5000 Years*, 280.
82. Ibid., 280.
83. Van Schaik, "Islamic Banking"; Usmani and Zubairi, *Islamic Banking*; Wilson, "Parallels between Islamic and Ethical Banking."
84. Ibid.
85. Ibid.
86. Ibid.
87. Ibid.
88. Ibid.
89. Ibid.
90. Ibid. Dr. Nimrad Raphaeili has an important discussion here: http://islamizationwatch.blogspot.ca/2009/10/islamic-banking-financial-smoke-and.html.
91. Ibid.
92. Graeber, *Debt: The First 5000 Years*, 276.
93. Van Schaik, "Islamic Banking"; Usmani and Zubairi, *Islamic Banking*; Wilson, "Parallels between Islamic and Ethical Banking."
94. Ibid.
95. Ibid.
96. Ibid
97. Ibid.
98. Ibid.
99. Ibid.
100. Ibid.
101. Ibid.
102. Ibid.
103. Choudhury, *Money in Islam*, 178.

104. Cummings, Askari, and Mustafa, "Islam and Modern Economic Change," 35. Decolonizing inheritance laws from a queer-feminist is a pursuit I draw on in my forthcoming publication on *Islam and Queer-Feminist Muslims: Identity, Gender, Politics, Religion and Sexuality in the Contemporary World*, based on my already completed PhD work that is too extensive to include and do justice to here.
105. Cummings, Askari, and Mustafa, "Islam and Modern Economic Change," 35.
106. Allāh, Qur'ān, 3:180; 02:1–3.
107. David Graeber and Thomas Piketty, "Soak the Rich: A Conversation on Capital, Debt and the Future," *Baffler* (July 2014), https://thebaffler.com/odds-and-ends/soak-the-rich; David Harvey, "David Harvey Reviews Piketty's Capital in the 21st Century," *The Socialist Worker* (May 17, 2014), https://socialistworker.org/blog/critical-reading/2014/05/18/david-harvey-reviews-thomas-pi; Thomas Coutrot, Patrick Saurin, and Eric Toussaint, "Cancelling Debt or Taxing Capital: Why Should We Choose?" in *Committee for the Abolition of Illegitimate Debt* (November 2, 2013), www.cadtm.org/Cancelling-debt-or-taxing-capital.
108. Jasbir K. Puar, *The Right to Maim: Debility, Capacity, Disability* (Durham, NC: Duke University, 2017). Puar discusses the purposeful police and army tactic of maiming of Black and Palestinian protestors; this is a similar approach to that carried out by Egyptian security forces during the Tahrir Uprisings and following on demonstrations.
109. P. Amar, *The Security Archipelago: Human-Security States, Sexuality Politics, and the End of Neoliberalism* (Durham, NC: Duke University Press), 135; Jarett Kobek, *Atta & the Whtman of Tikrit* (New York: Semiotext(E), 2011); Muhammad El-Amir Atta, *Khareg Bab-En-Nasr: Ein Gefahrdeter Altstadtteil in Aleppo: Stadtteilentwicklung in Einer Islamisch-Orientalischen Stadt*, MA Thesis, Technical University of Hamburg-Harburg, 1999). Atta mirrors prophet Muḥammad's statements in the oral tradition regarding a sign of the end times, in which humanity will witness and "see the barefoot, naked, indigent shepherds compete in building tall structures," akin to Saudi Arabia's unholy destruction of Islamic heritage sites and the construction of *Burj al Mamlakah*, known as Mile-High Tower, that overshadows the *Ka'bah* (House of Ibrahim). The prophetic quote is from *Sharh Sahih al-Bukhari*, 183, 1409 H, Umm-Al Qura University, Markaz Ihya' at-Turath al-Islam, 183.
110. Amar, *The Security Archipelago*, 135.
111. Ibid.
112. See Jerome Taylor's article titled "Mecca for the Rich: Islam's Holiest Site 'Turning into Vegas'" (2011) here: www.independent.co.uk/news/world/Middle East/mecca-for-the-rich-islams-holiest-site-turning-into-vegas-2360114.html. Furthermore, see Andrew Johnson's "Saudis Risk New Muslim Division with Proposal to Move Mohamed's Tomb (2014),

www.independent.co.uk/news/world/Middle East/saudis-risk-new-muslim-division-with-proposal-to-move-mohameds-tomb-9705120.htmlIbid; Carla Power, "Saudi Arabia Bulldozes over Its Heritage" (2014), http://time.com/3584585/saudi-arabia-bulldozes-over-its-heritage/; Lorena Muñoz-Alonso, "Saudi Arabia Destroyed 98 Percent of Its Cultural Heritage" (2014), https://news.artnet.com/art-world/saudi-arabia-destroyed-98-percent-of-its-cultural-heritage-174029.

113. Taylor, "Mecca for the Rich."
114. Ibid.
115. Gustavo Esteva, "Recovering Hope – the Zapatista Example," *Upside Down World*, (January 20, 2013). Esteva's excerpt can be found here: http://upsidedownworld.org/main/news-briefs-archives-68/4068-gustavo-esteva-recovering-hope-the-zapatista-example.
116. Esteva, "Recovering Hope"; John Holloway, *Change the World without Taking Power: The Meaning of Revolution Today* (London:, Pluto Press, 2010); Leandro Vergara-Camus, *Land and Freedom: The MST, the Zapatistas and Peasant Alternatives to Neoliberalism* (London: Zed Books, 2014).
117. Ibid.
118. As Heckert writes, Colin Ward "wrote directly about key concerns of the Transition movement – the importance of allotments (*The Allotment: Its Landscape and Culture* [1988]), critiques of industrial agriculture, the unequal distribution of land and the need for sustainable housing (*Cotters and Squatters: The Hidden History of Housing* [2004]), car culture (*Freedom to Go: After the Motor Age* [1991]), and the uses and abuses of natural resources (*Reflected in Water: A Crisis of Social Responsibility* [1997]) as well as documenting rarely told British histories of self-organized non-profit communal spaces (*Goodnight Campers! The History of British Holiday Camps* [1986] and *Arcadia for All* [2003], both co-written with Prof. Dennis Hardy). Ward was also editor of BEE (*Bulletin of Environmental Education*) from 1971 to 1979. J. Heckert, "Anarchist Roots & Routes," *European Journal of Ecopsychology* 1, no. 30 (2010), 19.
119. Heckert, "Anarchist Roots & Routes," 19–22.
120. Ibid., 19–22.
121. Kropotkin, in ibid., 21; T. Roszack, *The Voice of the Earth: An Exploration of Ecopsychology* (Newburyport: Red Wheel/Weiser, 2001), 229.
122. Heckert, "Anarchist Roots & Routes," 22; J. Aylward, "The Contributions of Paul Goodman to the Clinical, Social, and Political Implications of Boundary Disturbances," *Gestalt Review* 3, no. 2 (1999), 112; A. Fisher, *Radical Ecopsychology: Psychology in the Service of Life* (New York: State University of New York Press, 2002), 182.
123. Goodman and Roszak, in Heckert, "Anarchist Roots & Routes," 22; Roszack, *The Voice of the Earth*, 229.
124. Heckert, "Anarchist Roots & Routes," 23–4.

125. S. Newman, *The Politics of Postanarchism* (Edinburgh: Edinburgh University Press, 2010), 7.
126. See Richard J.F. Day's *Gramsci Is Dead: Anarchist Currents in the Newest Social Movements* (London: Pluto Press, 2005).
127. Heckert, "Anarchist Roots & Routes," 25.
128. Ibid., 28–9.
129. Ibid., 29.
130. Nicholas Montgomery, *Molarization and Singularization: Social Movements, Transformation and Hegemony*, MA Thesis, University of Victoria (2010), 165. See Nicholas' blog titled *Cultivating Alternatives: Decomposing the Dominant Order; Cultivating Alternatives to the Exploitation of Land and People*, available here: http://cultivatingalternatives.com.
131. Nick Montgomery, "Cultivating Alternatives to Empire," *Cultivating Alternatives* (2014), https://cultivatingalternatives.com.
132. K. Nelson, *Original Instructions: Indigenous Teachings for a Sustainable Future* (New York: Simon & Schuster, 2008), 1008.
133. Jeannette C. Armstrong, "International Expert Group Meeting Indigenous Peoples: Development with Culture and Identity Articles 3 and 32 of the United Nations Declaration on the Rights of Indigenous Peoples" (2010), 3, www.un.org/esa/socdev/unpfii/documents/jeanette-armstrong.pdf; also see *Constructing Indigeneity: Syilx Okanagan Oraliture and tmixwcentrism*, Inaugural Doctoral Dissertation (2009), https://d-nb.info/1027188737/34; Winona LaDuke, *All Our Relations: Native Struggles for Land and Life* (Cambridge, MA: South End Press, 1999); Robin Wall Kimmerer, *Braiding Sweetgrass: Indigenous Wisdom, Scientific Knowledge, and the Teachings of Plants* (Minneapolis: Milkweed Editions, 2013).
134. James (Sákéj) Youngblood Henderson, "Míkmaw Tenure in Atlantic Canada," *Dalhousie Law Journal* 18 no.1 (1995), 216–24; James Sakej Youngblood Henderson, Marjorie L. Benson, and Isobel M. Findlay. *Aboriginal Tenure in the Constitution of Canada* (Scarborough, Ontario; Carswell Thompson Professional Publishing, 2000), 409; Eve Tuck and Sefanit Habtom, "Unforgetting Place in Urban Education through Creative Participatory Visual Methods," *Educational Theory* 69 no. 2 (2019), 241–56; Eve Tuck, Marcia McKenzie, and Kate McCoy, "Land Education: Indigenous, Post-colonial, and Decolonizing Perspectives on Place," *Environmental Education Research* 20, no. 1 (2014), 1–23; Dolores Calderon, "Speaking Back to Manifest Destinies: A Land Education-Based Approach to Critical Curriculum Inquiry," *Environmental Education Research* 20, no. 1 (2014), 24–36; Megan Bang, Lawrence Curley, Adam Kessel, Ananda Marin, Eli S. Suzukovich III, and George Strack, "Muskrat Theories, Tobacco in the Streets, and Living Chicago as Indigenous Land," *Environmental Education Research* 20, no. 1 (2014), 37–55.
135. Newman, *The Politics of Postanarchism*, 5.

136. Mohammed Bamyeh, "Anarchist, Liberal, and Enlightenment Authoritarian Notes from the Arab Spring," *Jadaliyya* (July 30, 2011), www.jadaliyya.com/Details/24260.
137. Frantz Fanon, " On Violence," in *The Wretched of the Earth*, trans. Constance Farrington (New York: Grove Press, 1963), 3.
138. Stirner, in S. Newman, *From Bakunin to Lacan: Anti-Authoritarianism and the Dislocation of Power* (Minneapolis: Lexington Books), 66.
139. Newman, *The Politics of Postanarchism*, 3.
140. A. Badiou, *Being and Event*, trans. Oliver Feltham (London: Continuum Press, 2006), 264.
141. Michel Foucault, *Lectures at the College de France, 1977–1978*, trans. Graham Burchell, ed. Michel Senellart (New York: Palgrave Macmillan, 2007), 201–2; Arshin Adib-Moghaddam, *On the Arab Revolts and the Iranian Revolution: Power and Resistance Today* (London and New York: Bloomsbury Publishing, 2013).
142. Allāh, Qur'ān, 42:15; 2:139.
143. Day, *Gramsci Is Dead*, 176.
144. H. Walia, "Decolonizing Together: Moving Beyond a Politics of Solidarity toward a Practice of Decolonization," *Briarpatch Magazine* (January 1, 2012), https://briarpatchmagazine.com/articles/view/decolonizing-together; *Undoing Border Imperialism*, vol. 6 (Oakland: AK Press, 2013).
145. M. Abdou, *Anarca-Islam*, Master's Thesis, Queen's University (2009); G. Deleuze and F. Guattari, *Anti-Oedipus: Capitalism and Schizophrenia*, trans. Robert Hurley, Mark Seem, and Helen R. Lane (Minneapolis: University of Minnesota Press, 1983); *A Thousand Plateaus*; Wilhelm Reich and Vincent R. Carfagno, *The Mass Psychology of Fascism* (New York: Farrar, Straus & Giroux, 1970).
146. Harsha Walia, "Letter to Occupy Together Movement," *Rabble.ca: News for the Rest of Us* (October 1 2011), https://rabble.ca/human-rights/acknowledgement-occupations-occupied-land-essential/.
147. Allāh, Qur'ān, 13:11.

5. Uprisings: On (Im)Possibilities and Militant Resistance

1. Jacques Derrida, *Writing & Difference*, trans. Alan Bass (Chicago: University of Chicago Press, 1978), 148.
2. "Preface," in Frantz Fanon, *The Wretched of the Earth*, trans. Constance Farrington (New York: Grove Press, 1963).
3. Subcomandante Insurgente Marcos, "Marcos Is Gone! Between the Light and the Shadow," *Between Light and Shadow* (May 24, 2014, Mexico City), https://schoolsforchiapas.org/marcos-gone-light-shadow/.
4. Frantz Fanon, *A Dying Colonialism* (New York: Grove Atlantic, 1994), 57. Referring to the Arabic *fedayi* meaning "those who sacrifice themselves."

5. Faisal Devji, *The Terrorist in Search of Humanity: Militant Islam and Global Politics* (New York: Columbia University Press, 2008); Diego Gambetta and Steffen Hertog, *Engineers of Jihad: The Curious Connection between Violent Extremism and Education* (Princeton: Princeton University Press, 2017); Jack G. Shaheen, "Reel Bad Arabs: How Hollywood Vilifies a People," *The Annals of the American Academy of Political and Social Science* 588 (2003), 171–93. Jihādi figures transcend divergent geographical and demographic, social-political-economic origins, and are interlinked by religion, historical and social justice grievances, contrary to their depiction as illiterate, petty, thugs and unreligious criminals, in addition to a host of other depictions driven by a neurotic European Orientalist desire to rationalize their actions.
6. P. Amar, *The Security Archipelago: Human-Security States, Sexuality Politics, and the End of Neoliberalism* (Durham, NC: Duke University Press), 116. Also see Jasbir K. Puar, *Terrorist Assemblages: Homonationalism in Queer Times* (Durham, NC: Duke University Press, 2007), 59.
7. In his discussion of Atta, Amar assumes that neoliberal colonialism in settler- and franchise-colonial societies has ended, contrary to what anti-racist feminist, Indigenous, and social movement theorists and sociologists have argued. See Amar, *The Security Archipelago*, 87.
8. Puar, *Terrorist Assemblages*, 59.
9. Ibid.
10. Ibid., 59.
11. Ibid., 57–9; see also Lionel Tiger, "Rogue Males," *Guardian* (October 2, 2001), 8; Barbara Ehrenreich, "A Mystery of Misogyny," *The Progressive* (December 1, 2001).
12. Michael Kimmel, "Gender, Class, and Terrorism," *The Chronicle of Higher Education* (February 8, 2002).
13. Puar, *Terrorist Assemblages*, 58.
14. Ibid., 57.
15. Ibid., 58.
16. Ibid., 205.
17. Ibid.
18. *Comrades from Cairo*, "To the Occupy Movement – the Occupiers of Tahrir Square are with You," *Guardian* (2011), www.theguardian.com/commentisfree/2011/oct/25/occupy-movement-tahrir-square-cairo.
19. Ibid.
20. Ibid.
21. See the following articles on the overwhelming arrest of dissenters these past few years, but particularly since June 30, 2013, and the ousting of the Muslim Brotherhood: Scott Long's "Yara Sallam in Jail, and the Moral Bankruptcy of the United States," http://paper-bird.net/2014/06/23/yara-sallam-in-jail-and-the-moral-bankruptcy-of-the-united-states/; "Comrade Mahienour's Sentence Sparks Solidarity

Action from Brazil to Austria" that highlights the numerous activists, from the April 6 movement onwards such as "Ahmed Douma, Louay al-Qahwagi, Amru Hadhaq and our colleagues Alaa Abdel-Fattah and Mohamed Hosni who were sentenced on the same charge in the 'Shūrā Council' case to El-Sisi's prisons, as well as dozens of other young activists detained and dragged before the judges on charges of breaking this law" (2014), http://global.revsoc.me/2014/05/comrade-mahienours-sentence-sparks-solidarity-action-from-brazil-to-austria/. Also see the recent article on Michel Georgy, "Leading Anti-Mubarak Activist Sentenced to 15 Years" (2014), www.reuters.com/article/2014/06/11/us-egypt-activist-idUSKBN0EM0MV20140611. Also see the article on Egypt's secret prisons and industrial complex by Patrick Kingsley, "Egypt's Secret Prison: 'Disappeared' Face Torture in Azouli Military Jail (*Guardian* interviews with former detainees reveal up to 400 Egyptians being held without judicial oversight amid wider crackdown on human rights) (2014), www.theguardian.com/world/2014/jun/22/disappeared-egyptians-torture-secret-military-prison; and also Paul Amar, "Turning the Gendered Politics of the Security State Inside Out?" *International Feminist Journal of Politics* 13, no. 3 (2011), 299–328. Finally, there is Amar's *The Security Archipelago*, www.dukeupress.edu/Assets/PubMaterials/978-0-8223-5398-0_601.pdf.

22. Spectacles like Precise kill-lists and NATO airstrikes in the name of "democracy," "freedom" and "human rights," classified death squad operations and the depleted uranium of our children, the rampant sexual and gender-based abuses by the Red Cross, UNICEF, and CARE aid-agencies who exchange aid for sex in impoverished nations, targeted assassinations, black sites, cyber-attacks, prodigious security, and biological, nuclear, and chemical warheads in a world fraught with foreign renditions and immure incarcerations by dubious machines of "peace" that benefit from enmity and conflict, born as they are of it.
23. It is unfortunate that, of all the matters we discuss as social movement participants and scholars, we seldom talk about love and death despite their pivotal roles in our lives and the communities we wish to found and construct, in spite of their relation and subjugation to variant orders of country, family, society, mind, concept, perception, sensation, affect, heart, soul, science, law, justice, right and wrong, religion, verbs, and language (Antonin Artaud, *Antonin Artaud: Selected Writings* (New York: Farrar, Straus and Giroux, 1976). Love also relates to these concerns on paradoxical conditional yet unconditional hospitality (as in *Uṣūl al-Ikhtilāf* and *Uṣūl al-Ḍiyāfa* in Chapter Four, particularly in the endnotes). Indeed, love relates to the question of "Who/& What" (of whether ones loves "someone" or the "something of the someone" as in the attributes, that within themselves are subject to changes and fluxes). Love also relates to questions of envy and jealousy, and what we covet of related commitments

as the foundation upon which relationships (including those that are romantic) ought be built. Love and death are not premised on conceiving "the Other" as a separate entity or even as an event, because their existence, in essence, seeks union with all, be it in relation to self, a lover, or community. Love always sprouts from middles. Indeed, love and death are liberations that arrive from the darkness of non-being, from a chasm that is without a past or future that can destroy all future plotting. Also see John Portevi's essay titled "Love" (2002), www.protevi.com/john/Love.pdf; José Ortega y Gasset, 1883–1955, *On Love: Aspects of a Single Theme* (New York: Meridian Books, 1957); Alain Badiou, Nicolas Truong, and Peter R. Bush, *In Praise of Love* (New York: The New Press, 2012); Leanne Betasamosake Simpson, *Islands of Decolonial Love: Stories & Songs* (Winnipeg: Arbeiter Ring Publishing, 2013); Gwendolywn (Mitikomis) Benaway, "Decolonial Love: A How to Guide" (2013, 2018), http://workingitouttogether.com/content/decolonial-love-a-how-to-guide/; Dalia Gabriel, "Decolonising Desire: The Politics of Love" (2017), www.versobooks.com/blogs/3094-decolonising-desire-the-politics-of-love.

24. See the article titled "Accomplices Not Allies: Abolishing the Ally Industrial Complex" (2014), www.indigenousaction.org/accomplices-not-allies-abolishing-the-ally-industrial-complex/.
25. *Time magazine*'s June 2006 cover story, as Žižek writes, was titled "The Deadliest War in the World" focusing on the "around 4 million people" dead in the DRC (Democratic Republic of Congo), regarding which there was "none of the usual humanitarian uproar followed … as if some kind of filtering mechanism blocked this news from achieving its full impact in our symbolic space," Slavoj Žižek, *Violence: Six Sideways Reflections* (New York: Picador Press, 2008), 3. See also S. Critchley, *The Faith of the Faithless: Experiments in Political Theology* (New York: Verso Books, 2012). As Žižek writes, there need be no "further proof that the humanitarian sense of urgency is mediated, indeed overdetermined, by clear political considerations" (Žižek, *Violence*; see also Critchley, *The Faith of the Faithless*).
26. Briefly, it refers to "security police in civilian clothes ('baltagiya')" (Amar, *The Security Archipelago*). See the Wikipedia entry on *Baltagiya* here: http://en.wikipedia.org/wiki/Baltagiya. Also see the article by Paul Amar titled "Turning the Gendered Politics of the Security State Inside Out?" (2011), www.global.ucsb.edu/sites/secure.lsit.ucsb.edu.gisp.cms/files/sitefiles/people/amar/Amar_article_IFJP_SecurityStateSexHarassmentEgypt_Aug2011.pdf.
27. I consciously chose Khaled Saeed and Mina Daniel as examples relating to the idea of "martyrdom" which, as stated, I take rather seriously given not only the discourses being discussed, but rather too because "martyrdom" has somewhat become a fetishized occupation particularly for Arabs and Muslims in this era of a "War on Terror." Nowadays,

some have suggested celebrating Tunisian "*Mohamed Bouazizi International Day*" who self-immolated himself and "sparked" the uprisings in Tunis. I oppose this suggestion and state this without meaning to demean Bouazizi's audacity and courage or downgrading the subsequent events of an Orientally dubbed "the Arab Spring/Islamist Winter." I oppose because I am unwilling to fetishize individuals like Bouazizi, and the innumerable martyrs since while equally reductively reducing without "adequate" account or analysis other antecedent events that led to the culmination of a so-called "Bouazizi moment"; one that is now taken generally as "the significant spark" that lit these uprisings, and the breaking point that led to their explosion. Bouazizi's life is no more worthy of being celebrated than those who perished before, during, and since.

28. David Graeber, *Direct Action: An Ethnography* (New York: AK Press, 2009); Ann Hansen, *Direct Action: Memoirs of an Urban Guerrilla* (Toronot: Between the lines, 2001).
29. R. Day, *Gramsci Is Dead: Anarchist Currents in the Newest Social Movements* (London: Pluto Press, 2005), 126.
30. Ibid., 5.
31. Ibid., 124.
32. Qur'ān, 2: 217; 4:90; & 8:72. On the specific Islamic rules of war, see Nawal H. Amar, "Restorative Justice in Islam: Theory and Practice," in *The Spiritual Roots of Restorative Justice*, ed. Michael L. Hadley (New York: State University of New York Press, 2001), 161–80); "Islam and Deep Ecology," *Deep Ecology and World Religions: New Essays on Sacred Ground* (2001); Heba Raouf Ezzat and Mary Kaldor, "'Not Even a Tree': Delegitimising Violence and the Prospects for Pre-emptive Civility," *Global Civil Society* 7 (2006), 36–7; Al-Hafiz Basheer Ahmad Masri, *Animal Welfare in Islam* (Leicestershire: Kube Publishing, 2016); Zaid Shakir, "Jihad Is Not Perpetual Warfare," *Seasons* 1, no. 4 (2003), 53–64; Karen Armstrong, *Holy War: The Crusades and Their Impact on Today's World* (New York: Anchor, 2001); *Fields of Blood: Religion and the History of Violence* (New York and Toronto: Random House, 2015); "The Myth of Religious Violence," *Guardian* (2014). In Islām, war is not to be fought out of vengeance or for domination. The Qur'ān states: "Fight them on until there is no more persecution, and the religion becomes God's. But if they cease, let there be no hostility except to those who practice oppression" (2:193).
33. Sun-Tzu and Samuel B. Griffith, *The Art of War* (Oxford: Clarendon Press, 1964), 18.
34. Johann Most, "Action as Propaganda (1885)," in the *Anarchist Library*, https://theanarchistlibrary.org/library/johann-most-action-as-propaganda; M. Bakunin, *God and the State*, trans. Benjamin Tucker (New York: Mother Earth, 1916); S. Newman, *From Bakunin to Lacan: Anti-Authoritarianism and the Dislocation of Power* (Minneapolis:

Lexington Books, 2001); Mikhail A. Bakunin and Marshall Shatz *Statism and Anarchy* (Cambridge: Cambridge University Press, 1990); Murray Bookchin, *Post-Scarcity Anarchism* (Berkeley: Ramparts Press, 1971); Alexandre J.M.E. Christoyannopoulos, *Religious Anarchism: New Perspectives* (Cambridge: Cambridge Scholars Publishing, 2009); Süreyyya Evren, "Postanarchism and the 3rd World (2006)," in *the Anarchist Library*, https://tvheanarchistlibrary.org/library/sureyyya-evren-postanarchism-and-the-3rd-world; F. Fernández, *Cuban Anarchism: The History of a Movement*, trans. Charles Bufe (Tuscon: See Sharp Press, 2014); E. Goldman, H. Havel, and Paul Avrich Collection, *Anarchism and Other Essays* (New York: Mother Earth Publishing Association, 1917); A.G. Lewis, *Decolonizing Anarchism: Expanding Anarcha-Indigenism in Theory and Practice*, MA Thesis. Queen's University (2012); S. Mbah and C. Bufe, *African Anarchism* (New York: See Sharp Press, 2014); M. Ramnath, *Decolonizing Anarchism: An Anti-authoritarian History of India's Liberation Struggle* (Oakland: AK Press, 2012), 3; Budour Hassan, "The Colour Brown: Decolonizing Anarchism and Challenging White Hegemony" (2013) in her blog *Random Shelling*, https://budourhassan.wordpress.com/2013/07/24/the-colour-brown-de-colonising-anarchism-and-challenging-white-hegemony/.

35. Mohamed Abdou, Richard J.F. Day, and Sean Haberle, "Towards a Grassroots Multiculturalism? A Genealogical Analysis of Solidarity Practices in Canadian Activism Today," *Racism and Justice: Critical Dialogues on the Politics of Identity, Inequality, and Change*, ed. S. Hier, P. Bolaria, B. Singh, and D. Lett (Halifax: Fernwood, 2009), 214.
36. Ibid., 212.
37. Harsha Walia, "Letter to the Occupy Together Movement," *Rabble*, 2011. See also Rinku Sen, "Race and Occupy Wall Street," *Nation* (2011); Rinku Sen and Fekkak Mamdouh, *The Accidental American: Immigration and Citizenship in the Age of Globalization* (Oakland: Berrett-Koehler Publishers, 2008).
38. Ibid.
39. Ibid.
40. Ibid.; Teo Ballvé, "Territory by Dispossession: Decentralization, Statehood, and the Narco Land Grab in Colombia," presentation at the *International Conference on Global Land Grabbing*. April 6–8, 2011.
41. Abdou, Day, and Haberle, "Towards a Grassroots Multiculturalism? 212–14.
42. Ibid.; see also Emmanuel Levinas, *Totality and Infinity*, trans. A. Lingis (Pittsburgh: Duquesne University Press, 1969), 136.
43. Ali Mostfa, "Violence and Jihad in Islam: From the War of Words to the Clashes of Definitions," *Religions* 12, no. 966 (2021), 13, www.google.com/url?sa=t&rct=j&q=&esrc=s&source=web&cd=&ved=2ahUKEwiryeudydv1AhUdDmMBHV0KClAQFnoECAMQAw&url=https%3A%2F%2Fwww.mdpi.com%2F2077-1444%2F12%2F11%2F

966%2Fpdf&usg=AOvVaw2lad87rhnm48O1tAdlgR9J; Muhammad Farooq Khan, *Islam and the Modern World: A Discussion on Some Important Contentious Issues* (Pakistan: Awareness for Moderation, 1995); Nichola Khan, "Time and Fantasy in Narratives of Jihad: The Case of the Islami Jamiat-I-Tuleba in Karachi," *Human Affairs* 20, no. 3 (2010), 241–8.

44. Mostfa, "Violence and Jihad in Islam, 14.
45. As Tanveer Hussain (2014) writes on the topic of Jihad: "The Arabic word '*Jihad*' or '*jihaad(un)*' (also spelt as '*Jihaad*') is a noun. The meanings of every Arabic noun depend mainly upon two factors: a) What is the Arabic root of the noun word, and the signification or meaning of that root; and b) What is the form or measure (or *baab*, as they call it in Arabic) of that noun word?" Given, that is, "The Arabic root of the word '*Jihad*' is '*jahd(un)*' or '*juhd(un)*', with the following meanings: Power; Influence; Energy; Ability; Labour; Toil; Exertion; Effort; Endeavour; Diligence; Painstaking, or extraordinary painstaking; The utmost of one's power or force or ability or energy or effort or endeavour; Hard earning; Fruit of labour; Solemnity; Earnestness" (Tanveer, 2014). After all, as Hussain writes, "The word '*juhd*' (meaning 'fruit of labour') appears in the Qur'ān, Sura 9 Verse 79. The word '*jahd*' (meaning 'solemn' or 'earnest') appears in the Qur'ān, Sura 5 verse 53, Sura 6 verse 109, Sura 16 verse 38, Sura 24 verse 53, and Sura 35 verse 42" (2014). While, that is, "the noun '*jihad(un)*' is according to the form or measure '*fiaal(un)*'. This form or measure adds two important significations to the meanings of the root of the word, when the noun denotes an act that affects an object: a) A sense of intention, effort, attempt or striving (to do or exert what the root of the word implies); and b) A sense of reciprocity, i.e. another does to one what one does to another." Therefore, as Hussain continues: "The sense of reciprocity is often implied whenever the word '*Jihad*' affects another object. Whenever there is '*Jihad*' against an object (be it another human being or one's own evil inclinations), the other object strives to exert its utmost influence or power against you and you, in return, strive to exert your utmost influence or power against that object. As soon as the other object ceases to strive hard against you, you can no longer be in '*Jihad*' with that object." See Tanveer Hussain's commentary online here: http://quranicteachings.org/jihad/.
46. Hamid Ibrahim Ahmad and Muhammad Hussain Al-Aqbi, *Despair Ye Not of Allah's Mercy*, trans. Z. Bainter (Karachi: Darul Ishaat, 2010), 66.
47. Tahdhīb al-Āthār Musnad 'Umar 2/812.
48. Allāh, Qur'ān, 22:78.
49. Ibn Qayyim al-Jawziyya, "Al-Fawa'id," 9–11.
50. See Tamim Al-Barghouti's article titled "The Crusades: The Fall of Jerusalem: How the Concept of Jihad Has Changed" (2003) available here: www.countercurrents.org/pa-barghouti050803.htm

51. T. Ramadan, *The Messenger: The Meanings of the Life of Muhammad* (London: Allen Lane, 2007), 53–4.
52. Ibid., 54.
53. Francis E. Peters, *Muhammad and the Origins of Islam* (New York: SUNY Press, 1994), 54.
54. Ibid., 54.
55. An-Nawawi, Yahya bin Sharaf. *Al-arbaʿīn al-nawawiyyah (Forty Hadith)*, (Jeddah, Saudi Arabia: Abul-Qasim Publishing House, 1999), Ḥadīth No. 34: 79. Retrieved from https://d1.islamhouse.com/data/en/ih_books/single2/en-hadith-nawawy-sahih.pdf; Tariq Ramadan, In the Footsteps of the Prophet: Lessons from the Life of Muhammad (Oxford: Oxford Unviresity Press, 2009); "Religious Allegiance and Shared Citizenship," in Belonging? Diversity, Recognition, and Shared Citizenship in Canada, ed. K. Banting, T.J. Courchene, and L. Seidle (Montreal: Institute for Research on Public Policy, 2007), 451–64; "Plotting the Future of Islamic Studies: Teaching and Research in the Current Political Climate," Academic Matters 9 (2007), 6–8; "What the West Can Learn from Islam," The Chronicle of Higher Education (February 16, 2007), www.chronicle.com/article/what-the-west-can-learn-from-islam/.
56. Ramadan, *In the Footsteps of the Prophet*," 45.
57. Armstrong, *Holy War*; *Fields of Blood.*
58. Allāh, Qur'ān, 16:41–42.
59. M.G. Hodgson, *The Venture of Islam, Volume 2: The Expansion of Islam in the Middle Periods* (Chicago: University of Chicago Press, 1974), 451; *The Venture of Islam, Volume 1: The Classical Age of Islam* (Chicago: University of Chicago Press, 1974); Ismāʿīl ibn ʿUmar ibn Kathīr, *The Life of the Prophet Muhammad: A Translation of Al-Sira Al-Nabawiyya*, trans. Trevor Le Gassick (Reading: Garnet Publishing Company, 1998); Ian Richard Netton, *Islam, Christianity and the Mystic Journey: A Comparative Exploration* (Edinburgh: Edinburgh University Press, 2011), 57.
60. Allāh, Qur'ān, 9:40.
61. Khan, *Islam and the Modern World*, www.javedahmadghamidi.com/books/islam-and-the-modern-world
62. S.W. Muir, *The Life of Mahomet, Vol. I–IV* (London: Smith Elder and Co., 1861), 63.
63. Ibid., 63; Khan, *Islam and the Modern World.*
64. Allāh, Qur'ān, 9:122.
65. Allāh, Qur'ān, 8:60.
66. I. Ishaq, *Muhammad. The Life of Muhammad*, trans. A. Guillaume (Oxford: Oxford University Press, 1955), Sira 280, 193; Armstrong, *Holy War*, 137; *Islam: A Short History*.
67. Al-Nasa'i, al-Sunan,Kitab al-Ba'yah,with similar hadith in Ibn Majah's Sunan, Kitab al-Fitan and in the Sunan of AbuDawud, Kitab al-Mulahim.

68. A Nawawi, *Riyadh-Us-Saleheen* (Riyadh: International Islamic Publishing House, 1983), Volume 1, Hadith 195.
69. Allāh, Qur'ān, 43:89.
70. Allāh, Qur'ān, 22:39.
71. Gambetta and Hertog, *Engineers of Jihad*; M.S. Kimmel, "Globalization and Its Mal(e)Contents: The Gendered Moral and Political Economy of Terrorism," *International Sociology* 18, no. 3 (2003), 603–20; Nancy Ehrenreich, "Disguising Empire: Racialized Masculinity and the Civilizing of Iraq," *Cleveland State Law Rev*iew 52 (2004), 131–8; Anna M. Agathangelou and Lily H.M. Ling, "Power, Borders, Security, Wealth: Lessons of Violence and Desire from September 11," *International Studies Quarterly* 48, no. 3 (2004), 517–38.
72. Allāh, Qur'ān, 4:90.
73. Allāh, Qur'ān, 10:99.
74. Allāh, Qur'ān, 9:4.
75. Allāh, Qur'ān, 9:7.
76. Allāh, Qur'ān, 8:61–62.
77. Allāh, Qur'ān, 8:58.
78. Safiyu al-Rahman al al-Mubarakfuri, *Rahīq Al-Makhtūm*, Cet. I (Beirut: Dār al-Fikr, 2008); Armstrong, *Holy War*; "We Cannot Afford to Maintain These Ancient Prejudices against Islam," *IslamCity* (September 19, 2006), www.islamicity.org/2978/we-cannot-afford-to-maintain-these-ancient-prejudices-against-islam/; "Violent Islamic Radicals Know They Are Heretical," *Guardian* (July 8, 2006), www.theguardian.com/commentisfree/2006/jul/08/comment.religion; *The Battle for God: A History of Fundamentalism* (New York: Ballantine Books, 2011); "The Myth of Religious Violence," *Guardian* (September 25, 2014), www.theguardian.com/world/2014/sep/25/-sp-karen-armstrong-religious-violence-myth-secular; *Fields of Blood.*
79. Al-Qushairî, "Sahih Muslim," Volume 3, Book 49, 862 & Volume 3, Book 50, 74; M.M. Khan, *Sahih Al-Bukhari: Arabic-English* (Lahore: Taleem-Ul-Quran Trust, 1971), Book 19, Hadith 4404.
80. Ibid., 3:50:891.
81. Allāh, Qur'ān, 4:75.
82. Allāh, Qur'ān, 22:39.
83. Allāh, Qur'ān, 22:40.
84. Allāh, Qur'ān, 7:199 & 45:14.
85. Allāh, Qur'ān, 60:8.
86. Sohail H. Hashmi, "Interpreting the Islamic Ethics of War and Peace," in *The Ethics of War and Peace: Religious and Secular Perspectives*, ed. Terry Nardin (Princeton: Princeton University Press, 1998), 195–216; Heba Aly, "Islamic Law and the Rules of War," *The New Humanitarian* (April 24, 2014), www.thenewhumanitarian.org/2014/04/24/islamic-law-and-rules-war/. Also see Ahmed Al-Dawoody, "Islamic Law and International

Humanitarian Law: An Introduction to the Main Principles," *International Review of the Red Cross* 99, no. 3 (2017), 995–1018; "Conflict in Syria," https://library.icrc.org/library/docs/DOC/irrc-906-al-dawoody.pdf; *The Islamic Law of War: Justifications and Regulations* (London: Palgrave Macmillan, 2011);JJila Hussain, *Islam: It's Law and Society* (Alexandria, Australia: Federation Press, 2004).04).

87. Ibid.
88. IBP USA, *Islamic International Law and Jihad (War) Law Handbook* (Washington, International Business Publications, 2017), 51; also see Hussain, I*slam: It's Law and Society*, 61.
89. Allāh, Qur'ān, 2:191.Wahiduddin Khan, *The True Jihad: The Concept of Peace, Tolerance and Nonviolence in Islam* (New Delhi: Goodword Books, 2002), 42–3.
90. Allāh, Qur'ān, 2:190.
91. Allāh, Qur'ān, 4:90.
92. Allāh, Qur'ān, 4:8–9.
93. Allāh, Qur'ān, 17:23–24.
94. Friedrich Wilhelm Nietzsche, 1844–1900. *Beyond Good and Evil: Prelude to a Philosophy of the Future* (2009), E-Book, trans. Helen Zimmern, www.gutenberg.org/files/4363/4363-h/4363-h.htm.
95. Allāh, Qur'ān, 6:151. As Taiaiake Alfred and Jeff Corntassel write, "the imperative of the *warrior* is to awaken and enliven the truth and to get people to invest belief and energy into that truth. The battle is a spiritual and physical one fought against the political manipulation of the people's own innate fears and the embedding of complacency, that metastasizing weakness, into their psyches" ("Being Indigenous: Resurgences against Contemporary Colonialism," *Government and Opposition* 40, no. 4 (2005), 603). As Alfred and Corntassel write, "Fanon pointed out that the most important strength of Indigenous resistance, unity, is also constantly under attack as colonial powers erase community histories and senses of place to replace them with doctrines of individualism and predatory capitalism: 'In the colonial context . . . the natives fight among themselves. They tend to use each other as a screen, and each hides from his neighbor the national enemy'" (603; see also F. Fanon, *The Wretched of the Earth*, trans. Constance Farrington (New York: Grove Press, 1963), 306–7). Taiaiake Alfred and Jeff Corntassel's writing can be found at: http://web.uvic.ca/igov/uploads/pdf/Being%20 Indigenous%20GOOP.pdf. For further reading and scholarship on warriors and warrior societies, see Taiaiake Alfred and Lana Lowe's "Warrior Societies in Contemporary Indigenous Communities," www.attorneygeneral.jus.gov.on.ca/inquiries/ipperwash/policy_part/research/pdf/Alfred_and_Lowe.pdf.
96. Allāh, Qur'ān,17:33.
97. Allāh, Qur'ān, 5:32.

98. Allāh, Qur'ān, 2:217.
99. Allāh, Qur'ān, 2:217.
100. Allāh, Qur'ān, 22:40. An example of Muslim women who fought in war is Nusaybah bint Ka'ab who partook in the battles of Hunain, Yamamah and the Treaty of Ḥudaybiyah.
101. Allāh, Qur'ān, 2:217.
102. Allāh, Qur'ān, 2:194.
103. Deleuze and Guattari, *Anti-Oedipus: Capitalism and Schizophrenia*, trans. Robert Hurley, Mark Seem, and Helen R. Lane (Minneapolis: University of Minnesota Press, 1983); *A Thousand Plateaus: Capitalism and Schizophrenia* (London: Bloomsbury Academic, 1988).
104. Allāh, Qur'ān, 8:65.
105. Allāh, Qur'ān, 2:249.
106. Allāh, Qur'ān, 4:77.
107. The particular verse(s) being referred to is the following: "But when the forbidden months are past, then fight and slay the Pagans wherever ye find them, and seize them, beleaguer them, and lie in wait for them in every stratagem (of war); but if they repent, and establish regular prayers and practise regular charity, then open the way for them: for Allāh is Oft-forgiving, Most Merciful" (9:5). As numerous scholars have discussed, the verse must be read in the context of the Chapter itself, and therefore from the first verse, which describes a treaty between Muslims and the Mushrikeen (pagans or polytheists) of Mecca, and which the latter had violated. The chapter begins with "A (declaration) of immunity from Allāh and the Messenger, to those of the Pagans with whom ye have contracted mutual alliances: Go ye, then, for four months, backwards and forwards, (as ye will), throughout the land, but know ye that ye cannot frustrate Allāh (by your falsehood) but that Allāh will cover with shame those who reject Them; If one amongst the Pagans ask thee for asylum, grant it to him, so that he may hear the word of Allāh; and then escort him to where he can be secure. That is because they are men without knowledge."
108. See the transcript from *Rethinking Reform* (2010) and Hamza Yusuf's reference to his teacher, sheikh Abdullah bin Bayyah on "'dar al-harb', 'dar al-islam' and 'dar al-ahad', or 'muwada'ah'" here: http://sheikhhamza.com/transcript/Rethinking-Reform. For Yusuf Al-Qaradawi's commentary on these terms, see Ahmed Khalil's article titled "Dar Al-Islam And Dar Al-Harb: Its Definition and Significance" (2002), http://en.islamway.net/article/8211/dar-al-islam-and-dar-al-harb-its-definition-and-significance. See also Patricia Crone, "Imperial Trauma: The Case of the Arabs," *Common Knowledge* 12, no. 1 (2006), 456; "Post-Colonialism in Tenth-Century Islam," *Der Islam* 83, no. 1 (2006), 2–38; *Medieval Islamic Political Thought* (Edinburgh: Edinburgh University Press, 2014); Kecia Ali and Oliver Leaman, *Islam: The Key*

Concepts (London: Routledge, 2007), 69; al-Jawziyya, ibn Abi, and al-Dimashqi, "Ahkâm Ahl Al-Dhimma, Ed.," *Subhî Al-Sâlih* (Beirut, 1381/1961), I: 23–4; P. Crone and M. Hinds, *God's Caliph: Religious Authority in the First Centuries of Islam* (Cambridge: Cambridge University Press, 2003), 37; Seyyed Hossein Nasr and Oliver Leaman, *History of Islamic Philosophy* (New York: Routledge, 2013); Ibn Hishām, 'Abd al-Malik, *Al-Sīra Al-Nabawiyya* (London: Oxford University Press, 1955); Margaret Pettygrove, "Conceptions of War in Islamic Legal Theory and Practice," *Macalester Islam Journal* 2, no. 3 (2007), 34–42; Khaled Abou El Fadl, "Islamic Law and Muslim Minorities: The Juristic Discourse on Muslim Minorities from the Second/Eighth to the Eleventh/Seventeenth Centuries," *Islamic Law and Society* 1, no. 2 (1994), 141–87; "Legal Debates on Muslim Minorities: Between Rejection and Accommodation," *The Journal of Religious Ethics* (1994), 127–62; Saba Mahmood, Interview by Nathan Schneider (2011); Masthurhah Ismail et al., "The Views of Ibn Qayyim Al-Jawziyyah on the Religious Rights of Non-Muslims in Ahkam Ahl Al-Dhimmah," paper presented at the Proceedings of the Colloquium on Administrative Science and Technology, 2015); Elyse Semerdjian, "Naked Anxiety: Bathhouses, Nudity, and the Dhimmī Woman in 18th-Century Aleppo," *International Journal of Middle East Studies* 45, no. 4 (2013), 651–76.

109. Yusuf Al-Qaradawi, *Islamic Awakening: Between Rejection and Extremism* (International Institute of Islamic Thought (IIIT), 2006); *The Lawful and the Prohibited in Islam* (Herndon: The Other Press, 2013).

110. By evoking the term Umma I am not interested in romanticizing pre-modern Muslim terms such as *jizya*, *mawāli*, and *dhimmīs* used to denote non-Muslims living within Muslim territories, who were afforded legal protection under property laws, contracts, and obligations as well as being subject to particular restrictions. The term *dhimmī* literally translates to "protected person." It was obligatory for *dhimmīs* to pay a *jizya* tax, which complemented the Zakat (the right of the poor over the wealthy) paid by the Muslim subjects and it was the duty of Muslims to protect them. See Hodgson, *The Venture of Islam, Volume 1*; Ibn Qayyim al-Jawziyya, Shams al-Din Muhammad ibn Abi, and Bakr al-Zarl al-Dimashqi, "Ahkâm Ahl Al-Dhimma, Ed.," *Subhî al-Sâlih* (2 vols, Beirut, 1381/1961), I (1980); Ismail et al., "The Views of Ibn Qayyim Al-Jawziyyah on the Religious Rights of Non-Muslims in Ahkam Ahl Al-Dhimmah"; El Fadl, "Islamic Law and Muslim Minorities; "Legal Debates on Muslim Minorities.

111. In the words of George Ishaq, a self-identifying liberal, the Kefaya movement "started in Ramadan 2003. We were at a gathering of *Iftar* (i.e. breaking fast) during Ramadan at engineer Ibrahim Umaras'. And there were about 35 public figures of which were Abdul-Wahab El-Miseeree, Abdul-Monim Futooh, Abu-Ela Maadee, Ameen Iskander,

Hamdeen Sabaahee, Ahmad Bahaa Shabaan, Dr. Sayyid Abdul Sataar, Mohammad Saeed Idris. In this gathering there was supposed to be presidential and parliamentary elections in 2005 and we said we're not going to wait till 2005 and begin to think what we're going to do, we need to think now. So we formed a council of 6 individuals that were chosen by the 35 people who were present, and some of them were: Sayyid Abdel-Satar of the Muslim brotherhood, our brother Ameen Iskandar, a *Qawmee* (i.e. for an 'Arab people-hood') and Nasserite, Mohammed Saeed Idris, also, for 'Arab people-hood', Ahmad Pasha Shabaan, a Communist, and myself, George Ishak. And we agreed the 6 of us to write a mission statement to state what this group wants to do. And a famous lawyer joined us, whose name is Ahmad Bahaa. And so we began to write this mission statement and we met for 8 months, across the political spectrum, until we completed a mission statement that was called '*Lil'Kadaa Alaa El-Haymana Al-Amrikiya Wal-Arbada Al-Israeliya*" (i.e. To End American hegemony and Israeli unilateral whim) which required we call for democracy and begin a democratic process or program, the same requests that were submitted on January 25th were the same that were proposed in this mission statement or document. This included a new constitution, free elections, judicial monitoring of elections, and all the requests that were made, and we started to do the first protest on December 12th, 2004 in front of '*Dar El-Kadaa El-Aly*' (i.e. the Supreme Court'), then the protests started to continue throughout all of Egypt. We opened 23 spaces or 'centers' for Kefaya with 23 coordinators and organizers for the movement. We did all our protests at the same time in Cairo and all the districts and this had tremendous effect on the regime. And in my estimation Kefaya did 3 important things: it broke the mental or intellectual barrier of fear of Egyptians, it established the right to protest, and it gave people the right to criticize the president of the republic. This in summary is what happened with regards to Kefaya. And then of course supporting judges, and supporting any demands of the workers, or farmers, or issues of equality, or issues of citizenship, our protest of the sectarian divisions that were present and that the regime had a hand in and would organize, with Kefaya doing all this." The excerpt is from an interview I conducted with Ishak under the auspices of the Affinity Project in 2012. For a further profile of the movement, see http://en.wikipedia.org/wiki/Kefaya.

112. Mohamed Abdou, interview with Alaa Abd El-Fattah (2013). Goodman and Abdel Kouddous, "Exclusive: Egyptian Activist Alaa Abd El-Fattah on Prison & Regime's 'War on a Whole Generation'," *Democracy Now* (March 31, 2014), www.democracynow.org/2014/3/31/exclusive_egyptian_activist_alaa_abdel_fattah.
113. G. Agamben, *State of Exception* (Chicago: University of Chicago Press, 2005), 2, 5–5; Peter Gelderloos, *How Nonviolence Protects the State*

(Cambridge, MA: South End Press, 2007). For nuanced discussions of the false binary of violence/nonviolence, see the writings of Chairman Mao, Machiavelli, Carl Von Clausewitz, Antoine-Henri Jomini, Walter Benjamin, Rosa Luxemburg, and David Henry Thoreau. See especially Max Stirner, *Stirner: The Ego and Its Own* (Cambridge: Cambridge University Press, 1995); Saul Newman *Max Stirner*. (Basingstoke: Palgrave Macmillan, 2011); G. Sorel, *Sorel: Reflections on Violence* (Cambridge: Cambridge University Press, 1999); W. Benjamin, *Critique of Violence, Selected Writings; Volume 1; 1913–1926*, ed. Marcus Bullock and Michael W. Jennings (London: The Belknap Press of Harvard University Press, 1996); Rosa Luxemburg, *The Essential Rosa Luxemburg: Reform or Revolution and the Mass Strike* (Chicago: Haymarket Books, 2007); Dwight D. Eisenhower, "The Military Industrial Complex," *American Journal of Economics and Sociology* 46, no. 2 (1987), 150; Henry David Thoreau, *Civil Disobedience* (Peterborough: Broadview Press, 2016); Sami Khatib, "Towards a Politics of 'Pure Means': Walter Benjamin and the Question of Violence," *Conflicto armado, justicia y memoria* (2015).

114. Žižek, *Violence*, 2. As Peter Gelderloos notes, "violence is inherent in social revolution and the oppressive status quo that precedes it" (*How Nonviolence Protects the State*, 81).
115. Giorgio Agamben, Lorenzo Fabbri, and Elisabeth Fay, "On The Limits of Violence," *Diacritics* 39, no. 4, Contemporary Italian Thought (2) (Winter 2009), 103–11.
116. Carl Schmitt, *Politische Theologie: Vier Kapitel Zur Lehre Von Der Souveränität* (Berlin: Duncker & Humblot, 1922).
117. Gene Sharp, *The Politics of Nonviolent Action* (New York: Porter Sargent, 1973).
118. Please refer to Jeremy Scahill's reporting and article titled "Blackwater's Black Ops: Internal Documents Reveal the Firm's Clandestine Work for Multinationals and Governments" (2010), www.thenation.com/article/154739/blackwaters-black-ops. Moreover, on Blackwater's purported purchase by Monsanto (a multinational agrochemical and agricultural bio-technological corporation) and relationship with Chevron, see http://politicalblindspot.com/yes-monsanto-actually-did-buy-the-blackwater-mercenary-group/. Also see www.thenation.com/node/153/blackwater.
119. See the video *Standing Up for Israel: Martin Luther King Jr*, www.youtube.com/watch?v=kcCOT9JhEH0. Also see Fadi Kiblawi and Will Youman's article "Israel's Apologists and the Martin Luther King Jr. Hoax," https://electronicintifada.net/content/israels-apologists-and-martin-luther-king-jr-hoax/4955.
120. See the NPR article "Gandhi Is Deeply Revered, But His Attitudes on Race and Sex Are Under Scrutiny" (2019), www.npr.org/2019/10/02/766083651/gandhi-is-deeply-revered-but-his-attitudes-

on-race-and-sex-are-under-scrutiny; see also Mayukh Sen's article, "Gandhi Was a Racist Who Forced Young Girls to Sleep in Bed with Him" (2015), www.vice.com/en/article/ezj3km/gandhi-was-a-racist-who-forced-young-girls-to-sleep-in-bed-with-him

121. See https://kinginstitute.stanford.edu/.../when-peace-becomes.
122. Gelderloos, *How Nonviolence Protects the State.* Examples of obscured BIPOC militant views on violence given Gandhi's fetishization include figures like Wounded Knee's Russell Charles Means, Dennis Banks and imprisoned Leonard Peltier, as well as the Black Panthers, movements such as the Weather Underground, even ANTIFA, as well as the anti-colonialist Sikh anarchist Bhagat Singh. In this sense, while BLM is not a homogeneous movement as some of its liberal-progressive elements are interested in reactionary police reform while decolonial others are keen on outright abolition, it is the latter that I side with. To "be decolonial" means developing alternatives like the Black Panthers did with their Free Breakfast Programs and armed separatist visions as opposed to a mere strategic confinement to street protests.
123. George Jackson, *Soledad Brother: The Prison Letters of George Jackson* (Chicago: Chicago Review Press, 1994), 97, https://libcom.org/files/soledad-brother-the-prison-letters-of-george-jackson.pdf.
124. Webb Miller and Roy Wilson Howard, *I Found No Peace: The Journal of a Foreign Correspondent* (New York: Simon & Schuster, 1936), 193–9; Jackson, *Soledad Brother.*
125. Dr. Martin Luther King Jr.'s "A Riot Is the Language of the Unheard" (1966), www.youtube.com/watch?v=_K0BWXjJv5s
126. Malcolm X, *Malcolm X Speaks: Selected Speeches and Statements* (New York: Grove Press, 1965); "The House Negro and the Field Negro" (January 23, 1963) from transcribed text, https://ccnmtl.columbia.edu/projects/mmt/mxp/speeches/mxt17.html.
127. Greg Howard, "America Is Not for Black People" (2014), https://theconcourse.deadspin.com/america-is-not-for-black-people-1620169913. The transfer of military-grade equipment to local and state police occurs through the 1997 National Defense Authorization Act, specifically through the 1033 or LESO Program.
128. Arundhati Roy, in "Copyleft Video: Arundhati Roy," *Dropping Knowledge,* www.droppingknwoeldge.org/bin/media/show/66.page; also in John Martin Collins, *Global Palestine* (London: Hurst Publishers, 2011), 146; *War Talk* (Boston: South End Press, 2003); *Walking with the Comrades* (London: Penguin, 2011).
129. Gelderloos, *How Nonviolence Protects the State.*
130. Gelderloos, in "Interrogating Non-Violence," *Scottish Left Review* (n.d.), www.scottishleftreview.scot/interrogating-non-violence/; also see "How Nonviolence Protects the State" in the *Anarchist Library,* https://theanarchistlibrary.org/library/peter-gelderloos-how-nonviolence-

protects-the-state; Peter Gelerloos Interview, "How Nonviolence Protects the State," www.youtube.com/watch?v=w23hDyLqqR4.

131. Gelderloos, "How Nonviolence Protects the State"; Peter Gelerloos Interview, "How Nonviolence Protects the State."
132. Devji, *The Terrorist in Search of Humanity*; Gambetta and Hertog, *Engineers of Jihad*.
133. Fahmy, *All the Pasha's Men: Mehmed Ali, His Army and the Making of Modern Egypt*, vol. 8 (Cambridge: Cambridge University Press, 1997); "The Anatomy of Justice: Forensic Medicine and Criminal Law in Nineteenth-Century Egypt," *Islamic Law and Society* 6, no. 2 (1999): 224–71.
134. Fahmy, *All the Pasha's Men*; Timothy Mitchell, *Colonising Egypt: With a New Preface* (Berkeley: University of California Press, 1991).
135. Michel Foucault, *Discipline and Punish: The Birth of the Prison*, trans. Alan Dheridan (New York: Vintage, 1979).
136. Gelderloos, "How Nonviolence Protects the State"; Peter Gelerloos Interview, "How Nonviolence Protects the State"; *The Failure of Nonviolence: From the Arab Spring to Occupy* (Seattle: Left Bank Books, 2013); "Reflections for the US Occupy Movement" in *Counter Punch* (October 14, 2011), www.counterpunch.org/2011/10/14/reflections-for-the-us-occupy-movement/.
137. Ibid.
138. See the following few and minor statistics of violence in Chicago: Hidden Documentary on ABC news: *Chicago's Gang Violence: By the Numbers*(2011–12),http://abcnews.go.com/Nightline/fullpage/chicago-gang-violence-numbers-17509042; *Crime in Chicago*, http://en.wikipedia.org/wiki/Crime_in_Chicago#Violent_crime; *By the Numbers: Chicago-area Gangs* (2013), www.cbsnews.com/news/by-the-numbers-chicago-area-gangs/.
139. See Howard, "America Is Not for Black People"; Nyle Fort's article "White Supremacy Is the Real Culprit," in Ferguson, *The Excuses Just Prove It* (2014), www.theguardian.com/commentisfree/2014/aug/20/white-supremacy-ferguson-black-excuses; Kazembe Balagun and Hank William's article "Openings and Possibilities: The Meaning of Obama" (2008), www.leftturn.org/openings-and-possibilities-meaning-obama; Terry Davis' article "A First-Hand Account of the Jena 6 Case by Terry Davis, Investigator for Mychal Bell" (2007), http://publici.ucimc.org/?p=1204; Aura Bogado's article "9 Things about Ferguson That Will Make You Go Hmmm" (2014), http://colorlines.com/archives/2014/08/9_things_about_ferguson_that_will_make_go_hmmm.html; Rebecca Rose's article Ferguson "Disgrace: Police Fire on Unarmed Crowds, Attack News Trucks" (2014), http://jezebel.com/ferguson-disgrace-police-fire-on-unarmed-crowds-attac-

1621352164?utm_campaign=socialflow_jezebel_facebook&utm_source=jezebel_facebook&utm_medium=socialflow.

140. Howard, "America Is Not for Black People."
141. See Jamilah King's article "Ferguson Hires All-White PR Firm to Help Deal with Black Uprising" (2014), http://colorlines.com/archives/2014/.
142. Allāh, Qur'ān, 2: 155–157.
143. Grosz, *Becoming Undone: Darwinian Reflections on Life, Politics, and Art* (Durham, NC: Duke University Press, 2011), 13. See also *Time Travels: Feminism, Nature, Power* (Durham, NC: Duke University Press, 2005); Grosz, *Volatile Bodies: Toward a Corporeal Feminism* (Bloomington: Indiana University Press, 1994).
144. Al-Qushairî, "Sahih Muslim," Book 19, Hadith 4314.
145. Usaama Al-Azami notes in his article, "*The Question of Rebellion in the Islamic Tradition*," *MuslimMatters*, https://muslimmatters.org/2019/09/15/shaykh-hamza-yusuf-and-the-question-of-rebellion-in-the-islamic-tradition/?fbclid=IwAR1v8ptyu_1NTBbAHN3-ULeVrc4TVChcu8133FQv27JGv2u1PbZzbsdLNu4.
146. Ibid.
147. Ibid.

6. Conclusion: There Are Only Middles, No Beginnings and No Ends. Between BLM, NoDaPL-INM, and Tahrir

1. Sara Ahmed, *The Cultural Politics of Emotion* (Edinburgh: Edinburgh Unviersity Press, 2014), 39.
2. *Dancing on Our Turtle's Back: Stories of Nishnaabeg Re-creation, Resurgence, and a New Emergence* (Winnipeg: Arbeiter Ring Publishing, 2011).
3. Frederick Douglass, "What to the Slave Is the Fourth of July?" (Rochester, NY, July 5, 1852). Extract from Oration in *My Bondage and My Freedom* (London: Partridge and Oakey).
4. *ACT for America* represents the largest U.S. grassroots anti-Muslim institution, with over a 1000 chapters and close to 750,000 members.
5. SPLCenter, "Act for America."
6. In Persian, the term is "gharbzadegi" and it was "coined by the Iranian secular intellectual Jalal al-e Ahmad to describe the fascination with and dependence upon the West to the detriment of traditional, historical, and cultural ties to Islam" and Muslim societies. Quote from the Oxford Reference found here: www.oxfordreference.com/view/10.1093/oi/authority.20110803121918757. Also see Ali Mirsepassi, *Transnationalism in Iranian Political Thought: The Life and Times of Ahmed Fardid* (Cambridge: Cambridge University Press, 2007), 147.
7. Amy L. Brandzel, *Against Citizenship: The Violence of the Normative* (Chicago: University of Chicago Press, 2016); Audra Simpson, "On the Logic

of Discernment," *American Quarterly* 59, no. 2 (2007), 479–91; Leanne Simpson, *Lighting the Eighth Fire: The Liberation, Resurgence, and Protection of Indigenous Nations* (Winnipeg: Arbeiter Ring Publishers, 2008).

8. Ben Pitcher and Henriette Gunkel, "Q&A with Jasbir Puar [Interview]," *Dark Matter: In the Ruins of Imperial Culture*, 2008).
9. Stuart Hall's work on "moral panic" as well as Fanon's "phobogenic objectification" are useful in understanding this phenomena. Stuart Hall and Tony Jefferson, *Resistance through Rituals: Youth Subcultures in Post-War Britain*, vol. 7 (New York: Psychology Press, 1993).
10. Frantz Fanon, *Black Skin, White Masks* (New York: Grove Press, 1986), 83.
11. Ibid.
12. Sherene Razack, Sunera Thobani, and Malinda Smith, *States of Race: Critical Race Feminism for the 21st Century* (Toronto: Between the Lines, 2010). Shame has led to a cyclical transnational dynamic in which the Egyptian nation-state engages in the militarized policing of desire and ethnicity/race to safeguard the honor of the effeminate nation and the bodies of Arab and Muslim women from an Occidentalist, foreign, corrupting Euro-American queer influence. In response, Euro-America intervenes with humanitarian and post-development projects to save Arab Muslim women and queers from Brown Arab and Muslim men.
13. John S. Howard, "Subjectivity and Space: Deleuze and Guattari's BwO in the New World Order," in *Deleuze and Guattari: New Mappings in Politics, Philosophy, and Culture*, ed. E. Kaufman (Minneapolis: University of Minnesota Press, 1998), 123–4.
14. Félix Guattari, *Molecular Revolution: Psychiatry and Politics* (New York: Penguin Group, 1984), 143.
15. A number of the aforementioned liberal and queer friendly Muslim Zionists like Nomani do not hide their infatuation with and belief in Trump's America. Others like Jasser and Ahmed even support his travel ban and reify terms such as the "Islamic state" as well as defer to non-existing terms in Islam as "anal jihad." Anal *jihād* originally emerged when an "Egyptian cleric Mazher Shahin gave an address on the Egyptian Al-Tahrir TV channel, in which he lambasted the Muslim Brotherhood, claiming that it permitted homosexuality among its members." The cleric states, "anal jihād" is proof that the Muslim Brotherhood are "a bunch of hopeless and desperate peddlers, who have reached a state of foolishness, stupidity, filth, and so on – to the highest imaginable degree" (Unknown, "Egyptian Propaganda: Fatwa Permits 'Anal Jihad' for Muslim Brotherhood Members," Middle-East Media Research Institute, 2014). The above incident is similar to the purported existence of a fatwa that bans Muslim women from buying bananas and cucumbers because they provoke "illicit thoughts" that is indicative of the paranoia and hysteria in Egypt

(Asra Q. Nomani, "The Fatwa against Women Touching Bananas and Other Stupid Islamic Orders," *The Daily Beast* (2012).

16. Qur'ān, 13:11.
17. "Q&A with Jasbir Puar," *Dark Matter: In the Ruins of Imperial Culture* (May 2, 2008), http://www.darkmatter101.org/site/2008/05/02/qa-with-jasbir-puar/.
18. Mohamed Abdou, *Anarcha-Islam*, Master's Thesis, Queen's University (2009); Mohamed Jean Veneuse, "Be Condemned to a Clinic: The Birth of the Anarcha-Islamic Clinic," in *Religious Anarchism: New Perspectives*, ed.Alexandre J.M.E. Christoyannopoulos (Cambridge: Cambridge Scholars Publishing, 2009), Chapter 11. As scholars such as Wael Hallaq and I have argued in *Anarcha-Islam*, there is no such thing as an Islamic State.
19. In Egypt, two Egyptian singers, Shaimaa Ahmed and Layla Amer, were sentenced to prison and fined for obscene sexually suggestive overtones in their music videos. The former Ahmed was "jailed for two years after appearing in her underwear while suggestively eating a banana." Unknown, "Egypt Singer Jailed for 'Inciting Debauchery' in Music Video," *BBC News* (2017). See also Unknown, "Claim Filed against Yet Another Female Singer for 'Sexual Gesturing'," *Egypt Independent* (2017).
20. Qur'ān, 2: 256 & 10:99.
21. Qur'ān, 4: 113; & 5: 48.
22. Joseph Bauerkemper and Heidi Kiiwetinepinesiik Stark, "The Trans/National Terrain of Anishinaabe Law and Diplomacy," *Journal of Transnational American Studies* 4, no. 1 (2012), 8; see also R. Dhamoon, "A Feminist Approach to Decolonizing Anti-Racism: Rethinking Transnationalism, Intersectionality, and Settler Colonialism," *Ferral Feminisms* 4 (2015), 28. Dhamoon writes, "for Bauerkemper and Stark, Anishinaabe nationhood is intrinsically transnational because cultural practices of diplomacy, intellectual traditions, kinship networks, stories, and customs are rooted in intranational alliances among Anishinaabe peoples and international treaties with other Indigenous nations as well as colonial states. This form of lateral transnationalism both challenges the inevitability of settler nation-states and also locates nationhood as a potential site of liberation."
23. "Q&A with Jasbir Puar."
24. Robert Fisk, "Isis Has Not Radicalised Young Muslims, It Has Infantilised Them – and That Is Why It Is So Powerful and Dangerous," *Independent* (2016).
25. Ibid.
26. Ibid. An example of this hardening of Muslim masculinity is Australian ISIS fighter Khaled Sharroud's adolescent seven-year-old that without hesitation famously gripped a severed human head, by his hands, drained of life and blood. As Fisk notes, it is Euro-American ambivalence to

internalized violences that they have incepted within Muslims that led "a French judge" in 2016 to express his surprise at the juvenile nature of *jihādist* behavior when during a courtroom break a suspected youth requested that their mother cook and bring him "food he like to eat [as was the case] when he was schoolchild" (ibid.).

27. Unknown, "Isil Weapons Traced to US and Saudi Arabia," *Al-Jazeera* (2017).
28. Ibid.
29. John Pilger, "On the Beach – the Beckoning of Nuclear War," *Dissident Voices* (2017).
30. Ibid.
31. Ibid.
32. Unknown, "US Marine Trainer Guilty of Abusing Muslim Recruits," *Al-Jazeera* (2017).
33. Ibid.
34. Ibid.
35. Ibid.
36. Glenn Greenwald, "Why Does the FBI Have to Manufacture Its Own Plots If Terrorism and Isis Are Such Grave Threats?" *The Intercept* (2015).
37. Qur'ān, 3:110.
38. Zeki Saritoprak, "The Qur'anic Perspective on Immigrants: Prophet Muhammad's Migration and Its Implications in Our Modern Society," *The Journal of Scriptural Reasoning* 10, no. 1 (August 2011).
39. Ibid. Moreover, "the Qur'an speaks of the migrant experiences of many prophets such as Adam, Eve, Abraham, Lot, Jonah, Jacob, Moses and Muhammad. Islam regards Adam and Eve's migration from paradise a temporary relocation, meaning that all human beings as immigrants" (ibid.). According to Islam, "the entire earth is God's holy land, and there is no sanctity associated with the place of one's birth. Muslims who migrated from Mecca were financially weak because they had to abandon all their possessions behind, and Muslim citizens in Medina prior to the arrival of Meccan immigrants, were referred to as *anṣār* (supporters) who embraced their kin, and they shared with the newly arriving *muhajireen* (migrants)," all their wealth, land, inheritance, communal bonds, and possessions, in effect becoming brothers and sisters to one another, and the former were subject to immense praise in the Qur'ān (ibid.).
40. Taiaiake Alfred, "Idle No More and Indigenous Nationhood," in *The Winter We Danced: Voices from the Past, the Future, and the Idle No More Movement*, ed. The Kino-nda-niimi Collective (Winnipeg: Arbeiter Ring Publishing, 2014), 347–9. The Two-Row Wampum emphasized that both settlers and Indigenous peoples paddle their own canoes as they

journey together down the same river, with neither party interfering with the other.

41. Qur'ān, 8:72. See also 4:97, 4: 99–100, 9: 20–22, & 16: 41–42.
42. Brandzel, *Against Citizenship*, 116–17.
43. Qur'ān, 49:13 & 4:135.
44. Antonio Hrynchuk, Craig Silliphant, and Tate,Angie. "Stolen Sisters" (Documentary by Fahrenheit Films, 2007); Amnesty International, "Canada: Stolen Sisters – a Human Rights Response to Discrimination and Violence against Indigenous Women in Canada" (2004), www.amnesty.org/en/documents/amr20/003/2004/en/; Mary Agnes Welch, *New Database Lists 824 Murdered, Missing Native Women in Canada* in Warrior Publications (Winnipeg Free Press, 2014), https://warriorpublications.wordpress.com/2014/01/24/updates-on-missing murdered-indigenous-women-in-canada/; Robert Lovelace, "Violence against Aboriginal Women and the Right to Self-Defence," *Rabble* (December 20, 2022), https://rabble.ca/indigenous/right-self-defense/; Unknown, "#Bbctrending: Why Are First Nations Women Being Killed?" *BBC News* (2014).
45. Robert Lovelace, "Decolonization: The Fundamental Struggle for Liberation," *Rabble* (2013); Unknown, "Aboriginal Children Used in Medical Tests, Commissioner Says," *CBC News* (2013).
46. V. Watts-Powless, "Indians, Animals, Dirt: Place-Thought and Agency Amidst Indigenous Cosmologies," paper presented at the Keynote presentation at "Learning How to Inherit in Colonized and Ecologically Challenged Lifeworlds" symposium, University of Victoria, Canada, September, 2014).
47. Philip Joseph Deloria, *Playing Indian* (New Haven: Yale University Press, 1998); Jennifer Denetdale, "Chairmen, Presidents, and Princesses: The Navajo Nation, Gender, and the Politics of Tradition," *Wicazo Sa Review* 21, no. 1 (2006), 9–28; B. Lawrence, *"Real" Indians and Others: Mixed-Blood Urban Native Peoples and Indigenous Nationhood* (Lincoln: University Of Nebraska Press, 2004); Lovelace, "Violence against Aboriginal Women"; "Decolonization"; Lee Maracle, *I Am Woman: A Native Perspective on Sociology and Feminism* (London: Global Professional Publishing, 1996); Ben Powless, "Idling No More," *Alternatives Journal* 39, no. 6 (2013), 59; Andrea Smith, *Conquest: Sexual Violence and American Indian Genocide* (Durham, NC: Duke University Press, 2015).
48. Michael Connors Jackman and Nishant Upadhyay, "Pinkwatching Israel, Whitewashing Canada: Queer (Settler) Politics and Indigenous Colonization in Canada," *WSQ: Women's Studies Quarterly* 42, no. 3 (2014), 195–210; M. Krebs and D.M. Olwan, "'From Jerusalem to the Grand River, Our Struggles Are One': Challenging Canadian and Israeli Settler Colonialism," *Settler Colonial Studies* 2, no. 2 (2012),138–64; David Lloyd, "Settler Colonialism and the State of Exception:

The Example of Palestine/Israel," *Settler Colonial Studies* 2, no. 1 (2012), 59–80; Steven Salaita, *Inter/Nationalism: Decolonizing Native America and Palestine* (Minneapolis: University of Minnesota Press, 2016); Omar Jabary Salamanca et al., "Past Is Present: Settler Colonialism in Palestine," *Settler Colonial Studies* 2, no. 1 (2012), 1–8.

49. Richard C. Powless, "A Short Note to Correct Canadian Misconceptions about Indians Living Off 'Taxpayers Monies'," *White Spotted Horse* (2014).
50. Joseph Massad, "Egypt's Propagandists and the Gaza Massacre," *The Electronic Intifada* (2014).
51. Ali Abunimah, "The Zionist-White Supremacist Alliance in Trump's White House," *The Electronic Intifada* (2017).
52. Irving Abella and Harold Martin Troper, *None Is Too Many: Canada and the Jews of Europe, 1933–1948* (Toronto: University of Toronto Press, 2012); Alan Davies, "How Silent Were the Churches? Canadian Protestantism and the Jewish Plight during the Nazi Era: Notes on Method," *The Reference Librarian* 29, no. 61–62 (1998), 83–8; Unknown, "Voyage of the St. Louis," www.ushmm.org/wlc/en/article.php?ModuleId=10005267; "U.S. Policy during the Holocaust: The Tragedy of S.S. St. Louis (May 13–June 20, 1939)," www.jewishvirtuallibrary.org/the-tragedy-of-s-s-st-louis. Regarding permitting Jewish immigrants during the Nazi era, anti-Semitic Canadian Director of Immigration Frederick Charles Blair, who was a part of Prime Minister William Lyon Mackenzie King's Administration, stated that: "None were considered too many" (ibid.). Blair even compared "Jews clamoring to get into the country (i.e. Canada) to hogs at feeding time" and issued repugnant statements like: "Why don't you people learn to live with your neighbors wherever you are? Why are you hated?" (ibid.).
53. Lisa Bhungalia, "Parting Ways by Judith Butler – Reviewed by Lisa Bhungalia," *Society & Space* (2014),
54. Such as were Trayvon Martin, Oscar Grant, Sandra Bland, Sean Bell, John Crawford, Amadou Diallo, Eric Garner, Jonathan Ferrell, Kimani Gray, Kendrec McDade, Michael Brown, and Tarika Wilson. These lives and names should be read out loud and honored by action and not just be part of reactionary-based politics. Violence is a tactic and not a strategy. The term for war in Islam is not *jihād* but rather *Qitāl*. Muslims in the early period of their migration to Medina were first required to adamantly practice and master the finesse of "nonviolence" and understand what it is to build community and change themselves as they became "anew." During the early period, Muslims were forbidden from defending themselves and experienced expulsion from their families and abodes, the seizure of their property, and were subject to persecution, torture and murder, coercion, embargoes and pressure to abandon their faith in God and Prophet Muḥammad. Indeed, critical

became the spiritual, communitarian, and educative component of the first polity's struggle that even upon the revelation of their permission to fight and the right to engage in defensive armed conflict, Muslims were commanded to first ensure that the truth does not die with those who place their lives at risk in battle. Furthermore, even during war Muslims were expected to mercifully respect the dignity and sanctity of nonhuman life, as well as to safeguard "prisoners of war and exchanges," and honor the sacredness of public and private property and "houses of worship." See the Qur'ānic verses 9:122, 43:89, 22:39, 6:15, 17:33, 5:32, & 2:217.

55. To claim a purist nonviolent position is to ignore Nelson Mandela's legacy as a leader and his willingness to use violence, as he stated during the Rivonia Trial in which he claimed that he did not plan violence, "[i]n a spirit of recklessness, nor because I have any love of violence, [but rather] I planned it as a result of a calm and sober assessment of the political situation that had arisen after many years of tyranny, exploitation, and oppression of my people by the Whites" (Nelson Mandela, "Full Text: Mandela's Rivonia Trial Speech," *News24* ([1964]/2011).
56. Tom Gross, "Ayatollah Compares Ferguson, Gaza," www.tomgrossmedia.com/mideastdispatches/archives/2015_01.html. In response to Donald Trump's support of civil unrest and protests in Iran, Ayatollah Ali Khamenei tweeted on Black Lives Matter, and wrote, "If #Jesus were among us today he wouldn't spare a second to fight the arrogants & support the oppressed. #Ferguson #Gaza" and also "The U.S. gov. commits oppression inside the U.S., too. U.S. police murder black women, men, & children for no justifiable reason, and the murderers are acquitted in U.S. courts. This is their judicial system! And they slam other countries' and our country's judicial system. #BLM" (ibid.). Frankly both leaders are attempting to manipulate social justice for their ends.
57. Frantz Fanon, Jean-Paul Sartre, and Constance Farrington, *The Wretched of the Earth*, vol. 36 (New York: Grove Press, 1963), 36.
58. Mohamed Abdou, "On the Ethics of Disagreements (*Uṣūl al-Ikhtilaf*) and the Ethics of Hospitality (*Uṣūl al-Dhiyafa*) between Spiritual and Non-Spiritual Leftists in the Newest Social Movements," *Political Theology*.
59. For example, see the organization CORECO Mission Statement, "N.D.," http://coreco.org.mx/wordpress/?page_id=333. The Commission of Assistance towards Community Unity and Reconciliation (CORECO) trains people in positive conflict resolution from a perspective that is "outside" the paradigm of the nation-state. The purpose of CORECO is not, as Columbian philosopher Estanislao Zuleta argues, "the eradication of conflict and its dissolution among people living together

[which] is neither attainable nor desirable, not in one's personal life – love and friendship – nor in the community," but rather the construction of "a social and legal space in which conflicts can manifest themselves and develop, without the opposition to the other leading to the suppression of the other, destroying it, reducing it to impotence or silencing it. Rosene Zaros and Steven J. Stewart, "Estanislao Zuleta" (ABSINTHE Minded, 2008). Organizations like CORECO are vitally important and act as alternatives given that nation-states have shown, more often than not, their capacity to inflame, rather than calm, disagreements.

60. Leela Gandhi, *Affective Communities: Anticolonial Thought, Fin-De-Siècle Radicalism, and the Politics of Friendship* (Durham, NC: Duke University Press, 2005); Taha Jabir Al'Alwani, *The Ethics of Disagreement in Islam* (Herndon: International Institute of Islamic Thought (IIIT), 2015); also see Giorgio Agamben, *The Coming Community*, vol. 1 (Minneapolis: University of Minnesota Press, 1993); Ronald Bogue, *Deleuze's Wake* (New York: SUNY Press, 2004); Jacques Derrida, *Of Hospitality: Anne Dufourmantelle Invites Jacques Derrida to Respond*, trans. R. Bowlby (Palo Alto: Stanford University Press, 2000); *Hospitality. Acts of Religion*, ed. G. Anidjar (London: Routledge, 2002).
61. Richard J.F. Day, *Gramsci Is Dead: Anarchist Currents in the Newest Social* Movements (London and Toronto: Pluto Press and Between the Lines, 2005), 18, 186–202.
62. Dalia Gebrial, Decolonising Desire: The Politics of Love (London: Verso, 2017).

Index

9/11 (11 September 2001) 6

Abbassid Caliphate 121
'Abd Allāh ibn al-Zubayr ibn al-'Awwām 221
Abduh, Muhammad 23
Abdullah, Yasser 73
Abou El Fadl, Khaled "The Epistemology of Truth in modern Islam" 50–1
Aboul-Enein, Youssef *Islamic Rulings on Warfare* 123
Abraham, Prophet 118
Abū 'Abdillāh Muḥammad ibn Idrīs al-Shāfi'ī104
Abū al-Wafā 'Alī Ibn 'Aqil 104–5
Abū Bakr al-Ṣiddiq 93, 94, 199
Abū Bakr Muḥammad ibn Zakariyyā' al-Rāzī 97
Abu Ghraib prison 232
Abul Alā Al-Mawdūdī 23, 24, 72, 118
Abyssinia 198, 200, 233
ACT for America (organization) 223
Ādam and Eve 112
Adams, Jason 19
  "Nonwestern Anarchisms" 73
Agamben, Giorgio 211
Ahmed, Sara 140–1, 222
  Queer Phenomenology 140
al-Abbas (uncle of Muhammad) 121–2
Al-Ansari, Mohammad 118
Al-Arian, Ali 33–4
Al-Azami, Usaama "The Question of Rebellion in the Islamic Tradition" 220–1
Al-Azhar University 51, 95, 96, 97, 126
Al-Azmeh, Aziz *Islam and Modernities* 22
al-Baghdadi, Abu Bakr 5, 18, 179
al-Bahnasi, Ahmad Fathi 106
al-Barghouti, Tamim 12, 18, 83, 113, 122, 195
  on colonialism 123
  on *Dawla* 15–16
  on *Īmāms* 101–2
  on nationalism 124–6
  on *Umma* 118
al-Fuwaṭī, Hishām 17
al-Ghazali, Muhammad 104
Al-Mawardi, Abu'l Hasan 103, 104
al-Naẓẓām 17
al-Qaeda viii, 24, 34, 231
Al-Raghib al-Isfahani 194
al-Sisi, Abdel-Fattah 228
Alain de Libera 107
Albright, Madeleine 2–3
Alexander, M. Jacqui 9
Ali, Kecia 100, 136–7
Ali, Muhammad 4
'Alī ibn Abī Ṭālib 93, 94, 147
Ali ibn Naṣr Al-Kātib *Encyclopedia of Pleasure* 7
Allāh 10, 23, 37, 110–11
Alston, Ashanti 76
Amadahy, Zainab 145, 146
Amazon Corporation 184
Americas: colonization of (1492) 12
Anarcha-Islām vii–x, 10–11, 16, 20–1, 33, 34, 37, 42–3, 52, 77, 81, 109–11
  anti-authoritarian culture of 36–7, 52, 72–3, 81, 101
  and *Siyāsa* 106–7

Anarchic Ijthād 11, 35–7, 47–52, 70, 73, 228
anarchism and anarchists 18–20, 73, 75–7, 79, 112, 170
ethics of disagreement ix, 31–2
see also Euro-American anarchists; Muslim anarchists
Anarchist Federation (UK) 77
Anas, Malik ibn 108
Andrews, Charles Freer 80
Arab nationalism 113–4, 115, 118
Arab Spring/Islamic Winter vii, 63, 220, 229, 232, 237
Arab supremacy 114–5, 128, 136
Arabic language: post-colonial alterations to 120
Armstrong, Jeannette 143, 144, 146, 173
Armstrong, Karen *Fields of Blood* 123
Arnold, Thomas *The Spread of Islam in the World* 123
"arrivants" 134, 140–1, 235
Artaud, Antonin 147
Asad, Talal 9, 82
Ataturk, Mustafa Kemal 107
atheism 8, 9, 11, 112
Atta, Muhammad 6, 168, 180, 181
Awan, Akhtar 15
Ayubi, Zahra *Gendered Morality* 100
Azad, Maulana Abdul Kalam 213

Badiou, Alain 174–5
Bahrain Islamic Bank 163
Bamyeh, Mohammed 174
Banu Abd-Shams clan 109
Banu Bakr clan 204
Banu Hashim clan 196
Barakat, General Hisham 183
Bauerkemper, Joseph 230
Bayat, Asef 22, 23, 47, 48
Bayt Al-Hikmah (House of Wisdom) 96
Bayyah, Abdullah bin 210
Beydoun, Khaled 136
Bin Hājj, Abu 'Abd al-Fattāḥ, 'Ali 106
Bin Laden, Osama 6, 179
Black Lives Matter 13, 47, 220
Black people 135–8, 218–9
Black/Indigenous peoples relationship 134–6
Blackwater Corporation 212
Blair, Tony 179
Blanchot, Maurice 80
Bohne, Luciana 231
Bourmeche, Ameer 232
Brain-Fear (blog) 77
Brandzel, Amy 133
Brathwaite, Kamau 134
Braudel, Fernand 62
"Burning-Man" 77
Bush, George W. 179
Byrd, Jodi 4–5, 129, 131, 134, 140, 143–4

Caliphate *see Khalīfah*
Canada
Indian Acts 130, 235
Indigenous peoples 32, 235
and slavery 135–6
Canton Commune (1927) 171
capitalism 68
and banking 164
and the nation-state 35, 62–3, 70
racial capitalism 147
caretakers (of God's property) 100, 147–8, 150–1, 153–5, 158–9
communal caretakers 148, 151–2
individual caretakers 148
sole caretakers 152–4
Césaire, Aimé 72
China 61
Christian churches 124, 223
Christian secularism 8, 13, 33, 70, 107, 108, 149, 223
Clinton, Hillary 69, 179
Coates, Ta-Nehisi 167

colonialism viii, 23, 29, 72, 106, 131–2
impact on *Dawla* 122–3
and race 129, 132, 133, 136, 146
see also decolonization; franchise colonialism; neo-colonialism; post-colonialism; settler-colonialism
Comrades from Cairo (organization) 182
Conflict Armament Research (CAR) 231
conflict resolution 31, 169, 189, 238
Cooper, Afua 135
Coulthard, Glen 131
Counter-Intelligence Program (COINTEL) 17
Crone, Patricia *Ninth-Century Muslim Anarchists* 17
Crusades 95, 192
culture: Western concepts of 25–6

Daniel, Mina 187
Davis, Angela 3
Dawla (state) 14, 15–16, 103, 120–2
Day, Richard J.F. viii, 60, 188–9, 190, 239
on social movements 30–1
on the state 42, 63
on power 66
decolonization x, 28, 35, 40, 43–6, 70, 128–9, 130, 131–3, 139
and liberation 43–6, 61–2, 238
reformist approach to 69
and reparations 167, 168
terminologies of 74–5
transnational decolonization 36, 168–9
Deleuze, Gilles 1, 36, 62, 183
Deleuze, Gilles and Félix Guattari 41, 63–4, 67
Anti-Oedipus 62
Deloria, Philip 131
Derrida, Jacques 80, 178
Desai, Gaurav 143–4
Dhamoon, Rita 130, 141, 142
Dhimmīs (protection) 210
Dokhanchi, Milad 48, 74–5
dot.com companies 68
Douglass, Frederick 223
Dream Defenders (organization) 168
Du Bois, W.E.B. 4
Dua, Enakshi 133, 134
Dubai Islamic Bank 163
Dutch tulip bulb bubble 68
dynasties 121–2

Eberhardt, Isabelle vii, 30
eco-anarchists 172
Egypt 65, 66, 116, 129, 176, 182–3, 228, 236
attitudes in 27, 57
attitudes to sex in 58
Black Bloc protest movement 73
invasion by Napoleon of 125–6
and piety movement 26
and racial identity 136
see also Tahrir Uprising
Ehrenreich, Barbara 180
El-Sisi, Abdel-Fattah 65
Elsayed, Ahmed 183
Eng, David 59
Esposito, John 99, 100, 123–4
Esteva, Gustavo 128, 169–70
Euro-America ix, 6–7, 8–9, 13, 26, 35, 179, 230
Euro-American anarchists 73, 79
Euro-American Christianity 8, 13, 33, 223, 236, 239
Euro-American Islam 107, 108
Euro-American Marxism 60
Ex-Muslims of North America and Britain (organization) 223
Ezzat, Heba Raouf 75

Fanon, Frantz 38, 174, 178–9, 225, 238

Farīd al-Din 'Aṭṭār *Conference of the Birds* 7
fascism ix, 41–2, 67–8
  micro-fascism 67, 89, 175–6
Fatwā (legal ruling) 97
Felix, Sergeant Joseph 232
feminism and feminists 26, 52, 100, 129, 180, 190
  Euro-American feminists 26
  Muslim feminists 52, 100
  post-colonial feminists 129
Ferguson, Roderick *Aberrations in Black* 58–9
Fidaí (sacrifice) 178–9
Fiqh al-lughah 55
Fisk, Robert "Isis Has Not Radicalized Young Muslims, It Has Infantilized them" 230
Fiṭra (state of purity at birth) 145, 146
Flood, Andrew "The Trouble with Islam" 78–9
Foucault, Michel 9, 62, 64, 65, 66, 126–7
  and counter-conduct 175
franchise colonialism 57–8, 132, 141, 224
friendship 80, 239

G4S Company 5
Gabriel, Brigitte *ACT for America* 223–4
Gandhi, Leela 239
  Affective Communities 80
Gandhi, Mahatma 80, 212, 213
Gelderloos, Peter 216–7
Ghose, Manmoham 80
Gilroy, Paul 59
God 37, 82, 109–10
  see also Allāh
Goldstein, Alyosha 133, 141
Goodman, Paul 170
Gopinath, Gayitri 59
Graeber, David 153, 163
  Debt: the First 5000 Years 164
Grande, Sandy 129
Green New Deals 11, 68
Grosz, Elizabeth 219
Guantanamo Bay prison 232
Guattari, Félix 36, 62, 72, 90, 183
Guattari, Félix and Antonio Negri 152

Hall, Stuart 59
Hallaq, Wael *The Impossible State* 11, 15, 116
Hamas 24
Hannah-Jones, Nikole 12
Harb, Ja'far ibn 17
Harsha Walia 190–1
Hartman, Saidiya V. 69, 135
Hārūn ar-Rašīd 96
Hassan, Budour 73
Hawez, Rekan 232
Heckert, Jamie 170
Henderson, James Youngblood 173–4
Herman, Edward S. and Noam Chomsky *Manufacturing Consent* 32
Hezbollah 24
Hijra (migration) 198, 233
Hodgson, Marshall *The Venture of Islam* 123
Holocaust, The 167, 236
"holy war" 192
  see also jihad
hooks, bell 40, 190
Hourani, Albert *A History of the Arab Peoples* 123
Howard, Greg *America is not for Black People* 218–9
humankind: origins of 112
Husayn, Sayyiduna 221
Hussein, Saddam 125
Hussein, Taha 125

Ibn al-Tiqtiqa 105
Ibn Hanbal, Ahmed 108

Ibn Khaldūn 121–2
Ibn Nujaym 105
Ibn Taymiyya, Ahmad 105
identity politics 26–7, 60, 80
Idle No More (protest movement) 47
Ijmā (community) 17, 36, 81, 84, 85, 89–90, 91
Ijtihād (reasoning) 18, 22, 35, 48–9, 90
Ikhtilāf (dissension) 90
Īmāms 11, 16, 101–2, 103
India 213–4
indigeneity 27, 143–6
Indigenous peoples 27–8, 109, 129–32, 141–2, 173, 191, 235
  dispossession of 29, 129
insurrections 171, 174–5, 176–7
International Financial Services (UK) 164
Iqbal, Muhammad 23, 24
Iran 75
Iranian Revolution (1979) 22
Ishaq, George 210
ISIS viii, 24, 120
Islāḥ al-nafs (betterment of the self) 86
Islām vii, 14, 21–2, 123–4
  anti-authoritarian tradition of 14–15, 16–17, 36–7, 83–4
  Arabization of 114, 120
  attitudes to mental health 96–7
  definition of 110–11
  epistemologies of 50–1
  ethics of 50
  ethics of disagreement in ix–x, 31–2, 90
  ethics of hospitality in 90–1, 112, 169, 189, 238–9
  financial systems in 154–60
  Golden Era of 16, 93
  identity crisis in 23–4, 181
  impact of Enlightenment on 12–13
  impact on conquered countries of 123–4
  inheritance laws 149, 166, 168
  Meccan period 195–6, 199
  Medinan period 195, 201
  negative perceptions of 77, 78–9, 81, 123
  no compulsion to believe in 21, 37, 110, 117, 229
  Oral Tradition of 14, 36, 48, 54, 87, 95, 228
  and politics 48, 92, 104–5, 109
  racialization of 12–13
  rise of authoritarianism 16–17, 93, 95
  for other topics related to Islam, *see* the topic, e.g. property; war
Islam, Yakub vii, 30
Islamic anarchism 19, 30, 42–3
Islamic banking 149, 159–60, 162–6
  profit and loss sharing (PLS) 166
Islamic Development Bank, Jeddah 163
Islamic heritage sites 168–9
Islamic scholarship 28, 96–7
Islamophobia 4, 8, 13, 71, 78, 138, 223, 226
Ismā'īl ibn 'Umar ibn Kathīr 212
Israel 34, 167, 226–7, 231
Israel/Palestine 65, 212, 231, 234, 236
  and Boycott Divestment and Sanctions campaign (BDS) 193, 227, 234, 236

Ja'far al-Ṣādiq 87
Jackson, George 213
Jackson, Sherman 4, 108
Jafri, Beenash 142
Japan: property bubble 68
Jerusalem: US recognition as capital of Israel 227, 231
Jewish tribes 116, 118–9

jihad (struggle) 72, 87, 192–7, 200, 209–10
jizyā (tribute) 210
Jossot, Gustave-Henri vii, 30

Ka'bah (House of Ibrahim) 168
Kazmi, Zahir *The Limits of Muslim Liberalism* 9–10
Kefaya movement 210
Kennedy, Hugh N. *The Great Arab Conquests* 123
Khalīfah viii, 15, 16, 17, 81–2, 95, 98–9, 100–1, 104
Khallaf, Abd al-Wahhab 106
Khan, Wahiduddin 206
Khārijites (rebels) 17, 18
Khilāfah (representation) 81–2, 98, 100
Khuri-Makdisi, Ilham 74
Kimmel, Michael 180–1
King, Martin Luther 212
When Peace Becomes Obnoxious 212–3
King, Tiffany Lethabo 135
Knight, Michael Muhammad vii, 30
Kozma, Liat 25
Kropotkin, Peter 170
Kuwait Finance House 113

Laguna Pueblo tribe 40–1
land
expropriation of 130–2
liberation of 71, 183
relationship to 28, 44, 170–1
Lapidus, Ira *A History of Islamic Societies* 123
Lawrence, Bonita 133, 134
Lee, Umar 137
Lewis, Adam 76
liberal multiculturalism 3, 28, 34–5, 69, 87, 108–9, 144, 145, 225
liberal-left x, 11, 28, 74
liberalism 10, 227, 231
impact on diasporic Muslims 3–4, 5–6, 226
see also neoliberalism
Lipsitz, George 60
Lisan al-Arab (dictionary) 118
Lorde, Audre 47
Lovelace, Robert 143, 144–6
Lowe, Lisa 7

Machiavelli, Niccolò *The Art of War* 212
Mahmood, Saba 123
Politics of Piety 26
Makhzum clan 196
Malik, Fazlur Rahman 23
Malik, Sylvia Chan 12
Malik ibn Anas 98
Marcos, Subcomandante 178
martyrdom 193–4, 196–7
Marxism 60–1
Marxist-Leninist movements 130
Maṣlaḥa (public interest) 17, 36, 81, 84, 85, 90–1, 105, 210
Massad, Joseph A. 1–2, 77–8, 123, 127
Masud, Muhammad Khalid 105, 106
The Doctrine of Siyasa in Islamic Law 103
Mateen, Omar Mir Seddique 5, 6
May, Todd 60
Mbembe, Achilles *Necropolitics* 131–2
McKittrick, Katherine 135
Mecca 169, 204
Medina Charter 11, 37, 83, 116–7, 118–9, 228, 229
Mexican-American War 167
Middle East and North Africa (MENA) 12
Mile-High Tower, Saudi Arabia 168
Mogahed, Dalia 4, 108
Mongol invasions 105
Montgomery, Nicholas 172–3
Morsi, Mohamed 65, 183
Mubarak, Hosni 65, 210–11
Muḍārabah/Mushārakah (financial system) 148, 154–60

Muftīs (Muslim jurists) 51
Muhammad, Prophet 11, 14, 15, 37, 86, 92, 98, 99–100
on Arab supremacy 115, 116, 118–9
on *jihad* 201
on martyrdom 193–4, 196, 197
as messenger 82, 109–10, 198
legend of spider and doves 199
successors to 93–5
on war 204–5, 220
Muḥammad Ibn al-Qayyim al-Jawziyya 105, 194–5
Muñoz, José, Esteban 25, 59
Muslim anarchists 17–18, 29–32, 77, 80–1, 171–2, 226, 227
Muslim Brotherhood 179, 183, 230
Muslim erotic literature 7
Muslim feminists 52, 100
Muslim governance 15–18
Muslim Jewish Advisory Council (MJAC) 226
Muslim Leadership Initiative (MLI) 226
Muslim men: sexuality of 5–6, 13, 180–1, 230–1
Muslim women 26, 179
Muslims
assimilation of viii–ix, 4–5, 235
attitudes to sex of 5–7
conservative Muslims 5–7
diasporic Muslims 3–4, 5–6, 29–30, 71, 219, 228, 229
ex-Muslims 8–9, 223
identity crisis of viii, 23, 181, 223, 229
infantilization of 5, 230–1
migrations of 198–9, 233–4
liberal progressive Muslims 5–7, 225, 226
perceptions of ix, 179
persecution of 196–7
self-shame of 8, 13, 225–6, 228–9

Naidu, Sarojini 213
Nair, Supriya 143
Nairn, Tom 56
Nancy, Jean-Luc 80
Napoleon 1, Emperor 125–6
Naṣīr al-Dīn al-Ṭūsī *The Sultan's Sex Potions* 7
Nasser, Gamal Abdul 107
nation-state, the 12, 56, 64
see also capitalism
nationalism 24, 56–7, 60, 124–5
Negus, King 198
Nelson, Melissa K. *Original Instructions* 173
neocolonialism 12, 136
neoliberalism 29, 62, 126–7, 167
nepotism 152–3
Newman, Saul 36, 37, 82, 112
Nietzsche, Friedrich 207
No One Is Illegal (network) 30
NoDAPL (protest movement) 47
non-violence 38, 184, 201, 211–3, 215–7, 237

Oaxaca Commune 171
Obama, Barack 2, 179, 231–2
Ocasio-Cortez, Alexandria 34
Occupy movement 61, 174 182
Oedipal triad 36, 62–3, 67–8
Omar, Ilhan 1, 2, 108
Orwell, George *1984* 183
Ottoman Empire 12

Palestine *see* Israel/Palestine
Paris Commune (1871) 171
Pêcheux, Michel 59
Pegues, Juliana Hu 133, 141
Pérez, Hiram 59
Pérez, Rolando 36
Phung, Melissa 142
Piketty, Thomas 167
Pilger, John 231–2
"On the Beach" 231
PJP (blog) 77

post-colonialism 35, 126, 128–30
power: and nation-state 64–6
Prado, Abdennur vii, 30
property 147, 149–50
prophets 15, 110–11
protest movements 171, 174, 176–7, 186–9
Protestant Ethic 86
Puar, Jasbir *Terrorist Assemblages* 180, 181
Pulse nightclub, Orlando 5

Qawm (a people) 112, 116
Qawmiyyah (Arab nationalism) 113–4, 115–6, 120, 124–5
Qitāl (battle) 192, 193, 205–9
Qu'rān 14, 16, 23, 102, 229
  Alif Lām Mīm 52–3
  critical exegesis of 48–50, 228
  definition of Islam 110–11
  on disbelievers 21–2, 117, 119
  on equality of all peoples 112, 114, 117, 229
  language of 52–5, 88
  for other topics related to Qu'ran, *see* the topic, e.g. martyrdom; war
queer theory 27–8, 58–9
Quraysh (clans) 196–7, 203
Qutb, Sayyd 23–4

Rafanelli, Leda Bruna vii, 30
Ramaḍān (fast) 149, 161–2
Ramadan, Tariq 107–8
Ramnath, Maia 73
Rand Corporation 212
Raphaeli, Nimrod 164
Razack, Sherene 131, 190
Reagan, Nancy 131
rebellions: failures of 186–9
Ribā (interest) 148–9, 154, 159–60, 166
Rifāʿah Rāfi aṭ-Ṭahṭāwī 106
Rodinson, Maxime 96
Rothberg, Michael 129, 143–4
Roy, Arundhati 215
Roy, Olivier 22–3, 47

Saadeh, Antoine 125
Ṣadaqat al-Fiṭr (alms) 149, 161–2
Saeed, Khaled 187
Šahada (martyrdom) 193
Said, Edward 12
  Covering Islam 123
  Culture and Imperialism 123
Sanders, Bernie x, 34, 69, 227, 231
Sarsour, Linda 4, 108, 227
Sartre, Jean-Paul 178, 214
Saudi Arabia 34, 168–9, 231, 236
Sayyid, Salman 12
Schmitt, Carl 211
  Political Theology 9
secularism 24, 107, 227
  see also Christian secularism
Sefer, Akin 74
Sehdev, Robinder 142
self-defense 186, 189, 192, 214, 217
settler privilege 142
settler-colonialism 5, 35, 40, 45, 57, 76, 129–30
  complicity of arrivants in 29, 34–5, 44, 134, 141–2
sexualities 7, 13, 58–9, 96–8
  and terrorism 180–1
Shakir, Zaid 4, 108
Sharīa law 50, 105
Sharma, Nandita 141, 142
Shi-ism 22
Shi-ite Islam 94
Shu'ūb 116
Shumayyil, Shibili vii, 30
Shūrā (consensus) 17, 36, 81, 84, 85–90, 105, 210
Silko, Leslie Marmon 40
Simpson, Audra 131
Simpson, Leanne 222
Siyāsa (politics) 103–6

slavery and slave trade 69, 135–8
"afterlife" slavery 69, 167
Middle Passage 12, 135, 136
modern slavery 69, 137
Slayman, Abbas ibn 17
Smith, Linda Tuhiwai 133
social movements viii, ix, 11, 30–1, 36, 42, 80–1, 226, 238
transnational social movements 32, 191, 223–4
socialism 79–80
Socialist Workers Party (UK) 78
Solidarity Across Borders (SAB) 30
South West Asia and North Africa (SWANA) 28, 35, 74
SWANA Muslims 35, 71, 170–1, 224, 226, 232–3, 235
spirituality 9, 107
and politics 105, 106–7, 109
Spivak, Gayatri 25–6, 73, 123
Stark, Heidi Kiiwetinepinesii 230
state, the 70, 174–5
and control societies 66–7
state violence 184, 211, 212–7
Stirner, Max 174
Suhayl ibn Amr 204
Suleiman, Omar 4, 108
Sun Tzu *The Art of War* 190
Sunnah (Prophetic practice) 14, 48–9
Sunni Islam 94
Hanafi Fiqh tradition 210
Sykes-Picot Agreement (1916) 95, 113
Syria 231

Tahrir Uprisings (2011-13) viii, 27, 32, 42, 174, 176, 211–2, 230, 237
collapse of 65, 176, 182–3
Taqī al-Dīn Ahmad Al-Maqrīzī 105–6
Taqut (idolatry) 75
Tawḥīd (allegiance to God) 10–11, 24, 81, 84–5, 92
terrorism 179–80, 216
Thatcher, Margaret 2
Tiger, Lionel 180
Tlaib, Rashida 4, 108
Tlili, Sarra *Animals in the Qu'ran* 100
totalitarianism 41, 42
tower buildings 168, 169
Treaty of Ḥudaybiyah 37, 117, 119, 203–4
Trump, Donald 42, 179, 220, 231, 236
Tuck, Eve and K. Wayne Yang 41, 61, 129–30, 131, 133, 141
Two Row Wampum Treaty (1613) 233

'Umar ibn al-Khaṭṭāb 93
'Umar ibn Muḥammad al-Nafzāwī *The Perfumed Garden* 7
Umma 11, 14, 15, 23, 86, 102, 127, 145
decolonized *Umma* 229–30
interpretations of 118–9
Ummayyad Caliphate 121
United Arab Emirates (UAE) 34
United States 68, 184, 231
and state violence 184, 217–9, 223
United States Africa Command (AFRICOM) 237
United States Army: Muslim conscripts in 232
Universal Islamic Declaration of Human Rights (1996) 101
'Uthmān ibn 'Affān 93
Uzelman, Scott 64–5, 66

Veracini, Lorenzo 57–8
Vía Campesina, La 47, 171
Vimalassery, Manu 1, 133, 141
violence 38, 211–19
see also non-violence; self-defense; state violence

Walcott, Rinaldo 135
Wall Street Crash (1929) 68
war and warfare 192–3, 201–3, 205–9, 220
"War on Terror" 29, 179, 223
Warren, Elizabeth 131
Waṭaniyyah (nation) 95, 124–5, 127
white supremacy 45, 56, 140, 176, 236
  and culture of whiteness 7–8, 11, 56, 179
  and "race to innocence" 131
Wilde, Oscar 80
Wilson, Peter Lamborn vii, 30, 54
Wolfe, Patrick 57, 130
Women's March x, 34
World Trade Organization Seattle conference (1999) 32, 171
Wright, Cynthia 141, 142

X, Malcolm 4, 214

Yusuf, Hamza 4, 34, 108, 220

Zakāt (alms) 148–9, 160–1
Zapatistas 32, 43, 47, 171, 189
Zaytuna Institute 34, 108
Zionism 236
  Muslim support for 226–7
Žižek, Slavoj 211